DRAGON in the Caribbean

DRAGON in the Caribbean

China's Global Re-Dimensioning - Challenges and Opportunities for the Caribbean

Revised Edition

Richard L. Bernal

IAN RANDLE PUBLISHERS
Kingston • Miami

Revised Edition, 2016
First published in Jamaica, 2014 by
Ian Randle Publishers
16 Herb McKenley Drive
Box 686
Kingston 6
www.ianrandlepublishers.com

National Library of Jamaica
Cataloguing-In-Publication Data

Bernal, Richard L.
Dragon in the Caribbean: China's global re-dimensioning: challenges and opportunities for the Caribbean / Richard L. Bernal

p. : ill. ; cm.
Bibliography: p.
ISBN 978-976-637-925-4 (pbk)

1. Economic assistance, Chinese – Caribbean Area
2. China – Foreign economic relations – Caribbean Area
3. Caribbean Area – Foreign economic relations – China
I. Title

338.91510729 - dc23

Cover and Book Design by Ian Randle Publishers
Printed and Bound in the United States of America

Contents

List of Figures and Tables
VI

Foreword by Sir Alister McIntyre
VII

Acknowledgements
IX

Introduction
XI

China's Global Re-Dimensioning
1

China's Expanded Relations with the Caribbean
65

Factors Explaining the Expanded China–Caribbean Relationship
115

Opportunities and Challenges
134

Epilogue
190

Appendix
203

Notes
245

Bibliography
299

Index
333

List of Figures and Tables

LIST OF FIGURES

Figure 2.1: Caribbean Imports from China and Exports to China /84

LIST OF TABLES

Table 1.1: Asia's Lead: Dates of Innovation in Asia and the West /18

Table 1.2: Major Foreign Holders of Treasury Securities 2015 ($ Billions) /53

Table 2.1: Caribbean Countries – Population, Area and Gross National Income /66

Table 2.2: Embassies of China and US and Overseas Offices of Taiwan in the Caribbean and Central America /72

Table 2.3: Imports from China 2003–14 ($ millions) /81

Table 2.4: Exports to China 2002–14 ($ millions) /82

Table 2.5: Caribbean Exports According to Main Destination, Percent of Total Exports 2000 and 2009 /83

Table 2.6: Caribbean-China Trade Deficits (2003–14) /84

Table 2.7: Net Trade Effect of China /88

Table 2.8: China's Development Assistance to Caribbean Countries (US$) /93

Table 2.9: Chinese FDI Stock in the Caribbean by Country 2005–13 (US$ millions) /99

Table 2.10: Chinese FDI in the Caribbean by Country, Company, Sector and US$ Value /102

Table 3.1: Caribbean Countries Recognizing China /116

APPENDIX

Economic, Trade and Technological Cooperation between CARICOM and China /203

Foreword by Sir Alister McIntyre

China has achieved and sustained economic growth of over ten per cent per annum. This growth experience is unprecedented in recorded economic history and has transformed China's place in the global economy. The emergence of China as a significant and rapidly growing part of the world economy and its concomitant rise as a superpower demands the attention of scholars and policymakers in the Caribbean. The rise of China is not a change in the weather but a change in the climate of global economic and political affairs. Richard Bernal characterizes this multi-faceted process as the global re-dimensioning of China and discusses this in chapter one.

History teaches us that whenever there is a change in climate, societies have to change their perceptions about their future development and find ways to adapt to the changing environment. The small highly open economies of the Caribbean will have to identify ways to engaging with the new international economic situation, an integral aspect of which will be relations with China. It will involve some adjustment to the traditional economic and diplomatic relations which have dominated the external relations of the Caribbean.

The interdependence and dynamism of the world economy have altered beyond recognition. China's economic relations with the Caribbean have changed rapidly in recent years. The dominant feature has been development aid and increased imports from China. These and other less prominent features are reviewed by Bernal in chapter two. The picture he reveals is one of underutilized opportunities in exports, investment and tourism. This indicates that the challenge for the Caribbean is how to design a proactive involvement with the new global circumstances in a way that can promote their economic development and enhance their political independence. Later in the text, Bernal points out that the vast Chinese market affords opportunities which portend a reorganization of Caribbean economic activities to produce internationally competitive goods and services for that market. In other words, international trade will be about integration into the global economy and positioning within niche markets and networks of companies to become part of chains of adding value to production and marketing processes stretched across the global economy.

China has raised the level of competitiveness across a wide range of products traded internationally. The essence of trade and related economic growth in the new and changing global economic configuration is transformation – broadening the base of production by developing new products or improving existing ones.

A country's economy must therefore become part of the momentum of world production and growth. If Caribbean economies do not change their trade and production patterns they will be characterized by slow growth and continued stagnation. The prospect of exporting to China raises fundamental questions for Caribbean countries: what new goods and services are we producing? What improvements have been effected in producing existing goods?

Relations with China will be more complicated than relations with Western countries because of China's unique, complicated and rapidly evolving economic and political systems. The fact of the matter is that to develop and consolidate a successful relationship with China, Caribbean governments have to get a firm grip on a number of technical and diplomatic issues. The maturation of China–Caribbean relations will take time and must be based on the essential elements of adaptability and resilience, so that the Caribbean can shift with comparative ease from aid dominated relations to a more diversified format. This requires the development of a strong diplomatic nexus and a cadre of highly trained and experienced officials, entrepreneurs and managers, who can identitify opportunities at home and abroad, and put together projects to take advantage of them. Countries should not delay in pursuing the build-up of a wide array of inter-governmental exchanges for educating and training a critical mass of entrepreneurs, managers and technologists. But this cannot be accomplished overnight.

China has become an important source of foreign capital for the Caribbean. This development aid (loans and grants) has been critical to infrastructure projects at a time when the global economic crisis has constrained economic growth of the open, undiversified economies of the region. There is unfortunately a tendency in some quarters, fortunately confined to a minority, to depict Caribbean governments as mendicants, always on the look-out for economic aid from China. This view overlooks the coincidence of interest between China and the Caribbean. Bernal explains the political and economic motives of both parties in chapter three. It is clear from what Bernal argues that the current character of the relationship should be seen as the opening phase of a relationship which holds a wide array of opportunities that Bernal discusses in chapter four. He emphasizes that while there are already masks, much more needs to be done on the emergent initiatives to penetrate the Chinese market and to encourage Chinese tourists to discover the Caribbean. For this to be accomplished, he argues that Caribbean governments individually and collectively as a whole, need to improve their understanding of a wide range of issues which, for better or worse, result from the rise of China and which will increasingly impact on their lives and economic livelihood.

Richard Bernal has brought to bear his economic training and his diplomatic and policy experience to analyse relations between China and the Caribbean. The current status and future possibilities of the Caribbean's relations with China is a subject of vital importance to the Caribbean. Bernal's study is timely and important for policymakers and scholars.

Acknowledgements

This book emerged from three intersecting factors. First, a recognition that the re-dimensioning of China in the global economy and international affairs meant that the world was not changing but had changed. This realization required no particular prescience; however, it prompted me to start thinking that this change meant that the future is not what it was a few years ago. I was not merely curious but concerned about the implications for the countries of the Caribbean. Second, I knew that to gain some understanding of this phenomenon and the issues that it posed, reading as much as possible on the subject would not be sufficient. A better comprehension of any subject requires going beyond gathering and assimilating information to write. The process of writing requires organization and clarification of one's thinking and precision in the expression of the conclusions. Third, the book is the culmination of a long standing interest in China which was evident even before graduating from high school. A short article I wrote in my first term at university was published in *Public Opinion*, a small Jamaican newspaper. The article entitled, 'Why China Fears Taiwan', was my first publication. It was very much concerned with Cold War politics. Beyond that context, my interest did not wane due to the enigma of the Cultural Revolution and the thought of Mao Zedong condensed in the *Little Red Book*, which was then on a list of books banned by the government of Jamaica. My copy was always carefully secreted.

The initial result of my extensive reading and research process was a paper on China–CARICOM economic relations. Having completed that exercise, there was a need to locate the discussion of these economic interactions in the context of China's rise and the consequences for the world as a whole. That led me to write on the global re-dimensioning of China and what this could mean for the world. The logical extension of this exercise was to analyze the challenges and implications for the Caribbean.

None of this would have been possible without the understanding and support of my wife, Margaret, whose reading and writing allowed me to do the same without feeling the guilt of depriving her of time. My work benefitted from the peace of mind which emanated from a life-long camaraderie with my sons, Brian and Darren. My determination to complete the years of reflection and research that have gone into this book was constantly energized by knowing that Nile and Elle will live and work in a much changed world and my desire to do whatever I can to make a better place. The audacity of publishing a book owes much to the example of my father, Franklin, who published three books. The publication of Margaret's first book further emboldened me to persevere and complete the manuscript.

Writing a long manuscript, even with the advice of readers and editors, is still a great undertaking for any author who has the sole responsibility of making the final judgments on content, organization and style. In the process there is rewriting and revisions. In this regard, I have benefited from the sage advice of Adlith Brown who encouraged putting aside my manuscript for a while and then revisiting it later to reveal where improvements can be made and where insights can be added to improve the writing.

Although not directly connected to this project, I acknowledge with gratitude that I learnt much from working with the late Professor Norman Girvan and from his encouragement when I was a young academic.

The research and writing has benefited from a small coterie of friends and mentors who have consistently encouraged me during the preparation of the manuscript. I have benefited from discussions with several persons who know far more about China than I ever will, in particular, R. Evan Ellis and Enrique Dussel Peters who were always willing to share their ideas and publications. Librarians, typists and proofreaders in Jamaica and the US too numerous to mention have helped by responding to my many requests. Kia Penso helped with editing and Sha-Shana Crichton gave valuable legal advice. Research assistance was provided by Kristina Sibblies whose work was supported by the Jamaica-China Friendship Association and Pepe Ge Zang. Doreen Burgess helped to edit the text and Lisandra Colley, recently returned from doctoral studies in China, helped to keep the narrative up to date. I thank Christine Randle for her constant faith in the project and the production team of Ian Randle Publishers for their patience and forbearance. I express my gratitude to all those who assisted in one way or another but who I have not explicitly mentioned.

The revised, updated and expanded second edition of this book could not have been published without the support of the Caribbean Development Bank. Dr Warren Smith, president of the CDB, recognized that the conduct of research and the publication of that research is an important input to the dialogue on policies to promote the economic development of the Caribbean.

The views expressed in this book are entirely those of the author and do not in any way reflect the views of the Inter-American Development Bank, its directors or any of the governments of the countries that are members of the Bank.

Introduction

INTRODUCTION

During the last decade in particular, China has been expanding its economic and political relations with developing countries as it expands its involvement in international affairs. In the case of the Caribbean, China's economic relationship with the countries of this region has grown significantly with a concomitant increase in political linkage between China and the Caribbean states. This growing presence by China in the Caribbean appears to be an anomaly because generally superpowers find little interest in relationships with small states. Indeed, relations with small states are usually a low priority for superpowers preoccupied with global perspectives. China's interest and increased presence in the small states of the Caribbean is unusual, especially for China which has not been active in the Western Hemisphere where the US has been the undisputed hegemon. The new presence of China is a subject that warrants investigation and discussion. The subject is also of interest because relations with China have assumed prominence in the international relations of several Caribbean states. This unique subject has prompted much journalistic debate, but there has been very limited output of scholarly research and analysis. While this study does not lay claim to scholarship, it has the advantage of being devoted in its entirety to the subject and is not confined to the conventional length of academic journal articles or policy papers[1] which of necessity has made the existing literature either partial in scope, e.g., economic relations[2] or constrained in the extent to which the discussion could be detailed.[3]

Prior to the publication of the first edition of this book, those interested in the subject of relations between China and Caribbean states have had to satisfy their curiosity by gleaning some information albeit limited from the burgeoning literature on China's relations with Latin America and the Caribbean, which in reality is largely a euphemism for China–Latin America relations. Several publications examine the growing economic presence of China in Latin America, but these studies give little or no data nor make comments specifically on the Caribbean.[4] In addition, even a cursory perusal of this literature reveals that China's economic presence in the Caribbean does not exhibit the same characteristics that it does in South America and in Central America. For example, exports of agricultural products from Latin America to China have grown dramatically in recent years, but exports of agricultural commodities are not significant for the Caribbean. Given this lacuna in the existing literature, it is necessary to isolate the Caribbean sub-region for closer examination.

The necessity for a separate treatment of the issue of China's economic presence in the Caribbean derives from the lack of the region's visibility in discussions on China–Latin America economic relations and implications. This lack of visibility causes three problems: first, the term 'Latin America' may or may not include the Caribbean, and when it does encompass the Caribbean the treatment is brief[5] or confined to a few rows in tables covering all of South America or South and Central America.[6] It is risky to draw inference from generalization about Latin America and the Caribbean as a whole. This danger is particularly pronounced when little or no data on the Caribbean are included in discussions that review the Americas south of the US. Secondly, can it be assumed that China's economic presence in South America and Central America is the same as it is in the Caribbean? The small developing economies of the Caribbean differ from those of Latin America in size or level of development – or both. Generalizations about Latin America have to be examined carefully; indeed, Daniel Lederman, Marcelo Olarreaga, and Guillerma E. Perry[7] point out 'there is significant heterogeneity across the LAC sub-regions.' Third, economic interaction with China cannot be fully understood without factoring in the geopolitics. There are important geopolitical differences that obtain between China and Brazil, and those that operate between China and St Kitts. Specifically, some important aspects of China's economic presence in the Caribbean are inseparable from the rivalry between China and Taiwan,[8] which is not a significant factor in South America. The nuances and specificities of China's relations with the Caribbean is glossed over or not differentiated in the literature on China's political and diplomatic relations with Latin America. In many of these studies, the title suggests that the nomenclature, 'Latin America', is inclusive of the Caribbean, but the coverage is confined to South America.[9] An exception in this regard is the work of R. Evan Ellis which includes a brief section on the Caribbean, including Cuba.[10]

This book provides a study devoted exclusively to the relationship between China and the Caribbean. The relationship merits in-depth examination and analysis because it has assumed considerable political and economic importance in the Caribbean. This study will fill a lacuna in the literature and will establish the specificity of the relationship. For the purposes of this study, the Caribbean is defined to include Antigua and Barbuda, The Bahamas, Barbados, Belize, Dominica, the Dominican Republic, Grenada, Guyana, Haiti, Jamaica, St Kitts and Nevis, St Lucia, St Vincent and the Grenadines, Suriname, and Trinidad and Tobago. Cuba is not included because as a socialist country its modalities of economic interaction with China are very different from that of the rest of the Caribbean. In addition, as a socialist country, there was never any question about recognizing the People's Republic of China as the rightful and actual government of China. The relationship between Beijing and Havana was affected by the period in which there were Sino–Soviet tensions. A further complication is the paucity of information as both China and Cuba release very little information on their economic and political interrelations.

Chapter 1 provides an overview of China's global re-dimensioning with a focus on the economic and political aspects of this process. The term global re-dimensioning is intended to convey the fact that China's presence and 'weight' have grown, especially in the world economy and this has been accompanied by a concomitant rise in influence in international affairs. The formulation and application of the concept of global re-dimensioning is not to intimate any inevitability of the continued rise of China nor is to declare China an inevitable dominant superpower as suggested by some authors such as Martin Jacques whose book is boldly entitled *When China Rules the World*[11] but dismissed by others, like David Shambaugh.[12] Whether or not China achieves a position of dominance similar to that attained by Britain and the US in their halcyon era is an ongoing debate. This opening chapter discusses the different perspectives suggesting that China's rise will continue for the foreseeable future and that China's relationship with the US, involving rivalry[13] and interdependence,[14] will be a critically important factor in international affairs. The discussion of China's global re-dimensioning does not provide an extensive analysis of internal economic and political developments[15] that have taken place in China but takes account of events and developments to the extent that they relate to the rise of China in world affairs, particularly as they have implications for the rest of the world. The objective is to provide an overview of China's global re-dimensioning as the context in which to examine China's relations with the countries of the Caribbean.

Having outlined the context in which China's growing economic and political presence in the Caribbean is taking place, chapter 2 examines and analyses the nature, extent and character of this development by reviewing development assistance, trade and foreign investment. The analysis is constrained by the limited statistical data particularly on development assistance and foreign direct investment. The publicly available data suffers from not being up to date and not being in a form which makes it comparable with the conventional definitions. This makes a comparative analysis of development aid flows from donor countries an exercise not directly rooted in unambiguous data. Relative movements can be imputed by looking at broad trends. The problem arises from the reticence of both China and the governments of the Caribbean to make full disclosure. Tracking foreign direct investment is problematic because official data is based on government-approved projects and does include many private investments some of which are channelled through tax havens. These difficulties plague all research of Chinese development assistance and its foreign economic relations.

Chapter 3 first explores the motivations of China, which explains its increased interaction with the countries of the Caribbean and secondly examines the reasons for the receptivity to China by the governments of the Caribbean to deepening their relationship with China.[16] The discussion covers the economic and political-diplomatic reasons for the enhanced engagement cognizant of the centrality of the rivalry between China and Taiwan for diplomatic recognition.

Chapter 4 discusses the challenges and opportunities for the Caribbean which the relationship with China presents in the immediate future. It also argues that if this relationship is to continue and be strengthened, it cannot be assumed that rivalry between China and Taiwan will be as intense. A secure future relationship capable of diversity will require a more multi-dimensional foreign policy approach by Caribbean governments. Essential to consolidating and diversifying the relationship must be a more informed and sophisticated approach by Caribbean governments to the relationship. This will require a deepened and more comprehensive knowledge and appreciation of China's history, culture, politics, economic development and changing global role. This approach is necessary because of the complexity of China, the rapid, far-reaching changes occurring in China and the fact that China is different from any other foreign policy relationship which Caribbean countries have had to date.

The Epilogue pulls together some of the salient points for emphasis primarily to comment on recent developments since the manuscript was completed. In the manuscript, changes were made to the first four chapters. Yet, additional material had to be included in the final chapter to keep what was already written as up to date as possible. To be absolutely current would require almost daily changes and additions. Therefore, as I continued to study, analyse new information and critically review my thinking, I gained more insight into the subject every day. However, at some point the author has to stop revising the proofs, traditionally at the behest of the publisher. This book was no exception to this tradition.

This book provides information and analysis on the relations between China and the Caribbean and points out opportunities and challenges that emanate from the relationship. Its ultimate objective is to inform the Caribbean public and interested readers in general and to assist those responsible for the policy of Caribbean countries towards China. This book is a second edition that has been revised, expanded and updated. This was made necessary by the developments which have taken place since the first edition was written. This revision keeps the book as current and relevant as possible, and responds to the strong public interest for more information by providing answers to questions raised by readers regarding the content, and incorporating readers' suggestions to explore certain topics more extensively.

CHAPTER 1

China's Global Re-Dimensioning

INTRODUCTION

The world is undergoing a tectonic reconfiguration in economic and political power and to a lesser extent military prowess. Asia which dominated the world until the dawn of the nineteenth century is rising economically and politically. China's rise, or more correctly, resurgence is at the centre of a tectonic shift in the world. China's global re-dimensioning is part of a complex dialectic involving the rise of China and the relative decline of the US, which has been the single superpower since the collapse of the Soviet Union. One dramatic indicator of the shift in global economic power is that China in the last decade has become the largest trading partner for several countries in Africa and Latin America. Another example is that China is the largest holder of US Treasury paper and is therefore a significant financier of the US Federal budget. An even more telling example is the exploration by various European countries to convince China to purchase a sufficient amount of European bonds to alleviate the European debt crisis.[1]

The global re-ordering is a multidimensional process encompassing several different aspects of power evolving and interacting at different speeds and modalities, simultaneously driven internally and externally. National power is amalgam of economic, military and soft power, and the relative weight of each component shifts continually within an overarching matrix. Mankind is on the cusp of a new era of multi-polarity, an environment which has not been experienced since Britain's dominance in the nineteenth century expired at the start of the twentieth century. In the absence of a dominant superpower the first half of the twentieth century, an era of instability emerged that witnessed two World Wars and the Great Depression. The inexorable rise of the US and the revolutionary birthing of the Soviet Union produced the bitter bi-polar conflict of the Cold War. The implosion of the Soviet Union and its empire ushered in a brief interlude of a single superpower which is being steadily eroded by the rise of China.

China's rise relative to the US has set in motion a redistribution which Robert R. Ross and Zhu Feng describe as a 'power transition' in international contemporary affairs involving a redistribution of power that does not predestine a uni-polar or multi-polar outcome, although there will be strategic competition and conflict.[2] The present conjuncture is one of transition in which neither a single superpower nor genuine multi-polarity will exist. While the dominant feature of the current conjuncture is the rise of China, the emergence of secondary and regional powers such as India and Brazil and the residual powers of the European Union, Russia and Japan accompany this rise. The dispersal of power in its various manifestations resurrects notions of balance of power, security pacts, regional economic blocs and strategic diplomatic alliances. This fluid reconfiguration enormously complicates foreign policy for the rest of the states. Gone are the days when policy was simply giving abeyance to the sole superpower and hope for the best, and no longer will it be possible to play off rival ideologically divided superpowers against each other. How to operate in this new international milieu is an enigmatic prospect for all countries, but it presents a particularly acute dilemma for small states that find it difficult to influence superpowers[3] and international affairs.

This chapter consists of three parts. Part I discusses the global re-dimensioning of China, Part II examines aspects of the emerging global configuration and Part III deals with the implications and reactions of the rest of the world to the global redimensioning of China and the aspects of the emerging global configuration.

PART I
GLOBAL RE-DIMENSIONING OF CHINA

THE RISE OF CHINA

Asia dominated the world for most of recorded history until the early nineteenth century when Europe emerged in a substantial way in economic, commercial and military terms. Angus Maddison calculates that in 1820 Asia accounted for 58 per cent of world GDP while Europe's share was 27 per cent. However, by 1890, Asia had plunged to 32 per cent and Europe commanded 40 per cent of the world's GDP. The Second World War radically reallocated shares so that, in 1952, Asia was a mere 17 per cent, Europe was down to 30 per cent and the US had jumped to 28 per cent. By the threshold of the twenty-first century, Asia's resurgence placed its share of world GDP at 33 per cent with Europe and the US dropping to 23 per cent and 21 per cent respectively.[4] The most dramatic change has been that of China which plummeted from 32 per cent in 1820 to five per cent in 1952 but surged to 11 per cent in 1998.[5]

Since 1979 when China began to increase its engagement in the global economy through trade and investment, economic growth in China averaged ten per cent per annum during the period 1980–2008.[6] China was able to maintain high rates of economic growth even during the global economic crisis with real GDP growth averaging 9.6 per cent during 2008–11 but slowed to 7.6 per cent in 2012–14.[7] Today, China is the world's second largest economy in the world having become the largest merchandise exporter, largest producer of manufactured goods and largest holder of foreign exchange reserves. It is second only to the US as an import market and a destination for foreign direct investment while becoming an important source of development aid and foreign direct investment.

Based on the assumption that China will continue its rapid economic growth, experts have suggested that China's economy could become larger than that of the US. In 2004, Jeffrey Sachs predicted that China could overtake the share of the US in world GDP by 2050.[8] The veracity of these projections depended on eight to ten per cent economic growth in China, which in turn was based on an annual average rate of growth in exports of 23 per cent. Some doubted whether the rapid export-oriented economic growth of China could be sustained due to a combination of internal and external factors. For example, Kai Guo and Papa N'Diaye of the International Monetary Fund (IMF) argue that this would be difficult to accomplish within existing profit margins or by productivity gains. Nor would shifting the composition of exports to move up the value-added chain suffice, hence the need to rely increasingly on domestic private consumption.[9] By 2013, the IMF, using purchasing power parity, estimated that the Chinese economy was valued at $18.98 trillion, higher than the $18.12 trillion estimated for the US.[10] China is now the largest economy in the world, a position the US has held since 1872 when it exceeded the United Kingdom (UK).

The prominence of Asia,[11] indeed the renaissance of Asia, in particular the emergence of China and India, will re-shape the prevailing global power structure,[12] ushering in a new phase of multi-polarity, a goal shared by China and India. The relationship will embody aspects of synergy or rivalry and even conflicts which in the past led to military confrontation. The nature of the relationship depends not only on their respective strategies but also on their relations with other world powers in particular the US. The coming configuration will see Asia's influence escalating dramatically. This is clearly a projection of the amazing economic growth achieved across Asian economies in the last 30 years. Along with a far more important role in the world economy, will come cultural and political influence as can be expected from a region that commands the largest share of the world's population and evincing the values, preferences and traditions of ancient cultures. Although some like Jeffrey Sachs regard China and India late-starting economic underachievers for squandering their chance of economic growth due to Chairman Mao's communism and Jawaharlal Nehru's socialism, Sachs and others still anticipate them overtaking the US by mid-century.[13] Many authors envisioned the future to be Asian dominated, e.g., Nikolas D. Kristof and Sheryl WuDunn, long before it became fashionable, and predicted that the centre of the world was shifting and would eventually settle in Asia.[14] Today, it is common to hear of the Asian Century,[15] but it should not be taken as inevitable and just a matter of time. After all, history's evolution is not a linear trajectory. Minxin Pei warns not to believe the hype about the dawn of a new Asian age as it will be many decades before China, India and the rest of Asia take over the world, if they ever do.[16] He challenges as fallacies much of the underlying reasoning of those who, like Kishore Mahbubani, speak of the 'irresistible shift of power to the East'.[17] Some might think it premature to move ahead to discuss as Jacques does the issue of 'when China rules the world'.[18]

One of the frequently glossed over complexities is that Asia is not a homogenous region although it has commonalities, however it is defined. Asia is a concept which comes from outside the region, from Europe. Definitions vary depending on whether the Middle East is included or not, whether Central Asia is considered to be a part or not and whether Australia and New Zealand are regarded as members. Bill Emmott explains that:

> Asia has been not so much a continent as an array of subcontinents, or sub-regions, dotted across thousands of miles of ocean and land, whether in the minds of military strategists, of economists, of international relations scholars or Asia's own politicians. That fragmentation owed a lot to geographic reality as to culture.[19]

Asia is a region of historical tensions, border disputes, economic rivalries and political jealousies. The relationship among the three most powerful countries, Japan, China and India, is riven with differences.[20] Some of the hostilities have a long history, for example, cultural; some are fresh in the memories of contemporaries. Japanese invasions and others have eased but left a legacy of ideological mistrust. The acceptance of China as a lead state in Asia requires overlooking long-standing suspicions that China was more committed to communist allies than to Asian neighbours.[21] Other examples, include India's border disputes with China and Pakistan over which it has clashed militarily, and disputes over water with Bangladesh.

Asia has limited institutional arrangements for promoting regional cooperation and economic integration reflecting political, ideological and cultural differences. Ironically, the level of intra-regional trade is approaching that of formal trade agreements such as the North American Free Trade Area. Although trade has been a catalytic component of the rapid economic growth for which the region is justifiably renown, its importance varies.

For example, in 2003, the trade/GDP ratio was 66 per cent in China but only 35 per cent in India.[22] Economic integration has not been paralleled by political cooperation. It was not until 2005 the East Asia Summit was established, replacing the Association of South East Asian Nations (ASEAN) and its various mutations. The lack of formal institutional arrangements to foster intra-regional trade may change in the near future as region-wide free trade agreements are being discussed, e.g., the East Asian Free Trade Agreement and the Comprehensive Partnership Agreement. The Transpacific Strategic Economic Partnership agreement, which could include the US, was signed on February 4, 2016.

China is now the epicentre of a rapidly growing Asian economic region which consists of concentric economic rings. The core ring involves of Hong Kong, Macau and Taiwan and a second ring involves economic relations with Japan, and the 'Asian Tigers', South Korea and Singapore. The third circle is the rest of Asia, Australia and New Zealand. This part of the world has been experiencing the very high rates of economic growth and intra-regional trade and investment. China is consolidating those economic ties by completing trade agreements with Japan, South Korea, India, Australia and New Zealand. The China–ASEAN Free Trade Agreement (2005) encompasses 1.9 billion people, making it the largest in the world.[23] Trade between China and the ASEAN countries has grown from $59.6 billion in 2003 to $192.5 billion in 2008.[24] New Zealand–China Free Trade Area entered into force in October 2008. And on January 1, 2010, the ASEAN-Australia-New Zealand Free Trade Agreement came into force.

While there are forces which impel Asia to overcome long-standing differences and come together, new issues will separate the region. One such issue, which is likely to become more of an irritant in the future, is that China's ascendance will create jealousy, especially in Japan and India. In Japan, there is concern that China will become the key interlocutor with the US, and that China will displace Japan in some economic sectors which have traditionally been the preserve of Japanese companies and brands. In India, feelings of being second best in economic progress arouse envy in both the public and governing circles. A senior member of India's ruling Congress party has stated that Indians, especially those living in border areas neighbouring China, are beginning to envy its fast-paced development to the point of regretting being Indian.[25] India is tired of being compared with China only to be consigned to the status of a regional power while China is hailed as a new superpower.[26] At the highest political levels in India, a mixture of nationalism and security concerns fuel intense China watching and careful comparative scrutiny of how other countries treat with China and India, in particular the US.[27] A calmer more sanguine perspective to the eponymous China on the rise is that of Manmohan Singh, former Prime Minister of India, who opines: 'there is enough space in the world to accommodate the ambitions of both India and China.'[28]

India has long aspired to the status of a major power and many felt that being an ancient civilization, and having one of the largest populations in the world it was natural to be a great power. Jawaharlal Nehru actively pursued this objective 'convinced that India was destined to be a key player'.[29] Stephen P. Cohen notes that 'Indian officials believe they are representing not just a state but a civilization...

Believing that India should be accorded deference and respect because of its intrinsic civilizational qualities.'[30] Which countries become superpowers or major powers is a matter of competition, in which some are rising and some declining. India has been conscious of China as a natural rival, and to the extent that China rises constrains India's prospects. There are those who believe that it is possible for India to catch up or actually overtake China.[31] Yet, India does not have and may not acquire the economic and military capabilities to be a superpower and will have to be content with the status of a regional power.[32] Nevertheless, the current debate in India is not whether it wants to be or should be a great power but will it be a great power or remain a regional power with a role in international affairs based on its traditional leadership in developing country and non-aligned alliances.

RELATIVE DECLINE OF THE UNITED STATES

Given the dominance of the US in the years immediately following the Second World war, it was inevitable that that the US would decline relative to other countries as they recovered from the ravages of the war. As this process evolved, it has encouraged a debate which has intensified as the relative positions of countries have changed. The development of nuclear weapons, control of Eastern European countries by the Soviet Union and the launch of Sputnik in 1957 set off the debate on the relative decline of the US. The preoccupation during the Cold War was competition over who was ahead in nuclear warheads and by how much. By the late 1960s and early 1970s, the economic recovery of Japan, the non-convertibility of the US$ into gold and the Vietnam War became emblematic of the ebb of US supremacy. The oil shock of 1973 and the Iranian hostage crisis were potent reminders of the limits of US power and galvanized the debate about the end of undisputed dominance.

By the late 1980s, it was evident that the US was not as dominant as it was in the three decades immediately after the Second World War, but the implosion of the Soviet Union left the US as the sole superpower. This diminution of US dominance set off a debate on whether the decline was relative or absolute and whether the decline was across all aspects of power, e.g., economic, military and cultural. Paul Kennedy argued that the relative decline of superpowers is inevitable and hence a natural and predictable decline for the US.[33] Henry R. Nau contested the proposition of the absolute decline of the US, positing the change as a relative decline that left US dominance intact.[34] Whether the decline is absolute or relative, the US was still sufficiently dominant to 'go it alone' according to Joseph S. Nye.[35] The US was seen by David P. Calleo as a 'hegemon in decay'[36] with Immanuel Wallerstein going further to describe the decline of the US as signalling the end of Pax Americana[37] and ushering in an era that Fareed Zakaria calls the 'Post-American World'.[38] Joseph Joffe[39] reviews what he calls the literature of 'declinism' which has propagated the 'myth of America's decline'. Indeed, several predications have been made to look ridiculous by the passage of time. For example, several of these so-called economic miracles of Japan were the first perceived economic threat. David P. Calleo and Benjamin M. Rowland, writing in 1973, speculated that Japan's GNP would equal that of the US by 1990, and that 2000 could see the start of a 'Japanese century.'[40] By 1979, Ezra Vogel was worrying about 'Japan as Number One'[41] as Japan was supposed to be the next superpower.[42]

Robert O. Keohane sees this literature of decline as the latest of several waves and suggests that this 'surge of pessimism has produced a counter surge of defensive optimism, with arguments put forward about the value and feasibility of U.S. global leadership.'[43] The decline in US preponderance is reflected in that while it was the country with the undisputed capability to globally deploy overwhelming military and naval power, it was deemed important to have international support for the use of that power. An example of this was the US-led coalitions of less powerful countries such as during 'Operation Desert Storm' in Kuwait. It was not that the US needed any military or naval support, but it felt the need for legitimacy for exercise of lethal power which an international coalition of countries provided. Some are of the view that the US provides indispensable 'public goods', notably security, and that the majority of the world values this and supports US suzerainty. This literature suffers from the assumption that the world accepts and even welcomes American leadership[44] because they subscribe to American goals and values. The myth is descended from the doctrine of 'manifest destiny' and the deeply ingrained belief in the US in 'American exceptionalism'.[45] Whether exceptionalism was an apt way to describe or justify the unique role of the US since the end of the Second World War is an issue for debate. For some like Andrew Bacevich[46] circumstances have already put an end to the period that might be so characterized.

The global configuration of power after the unipolar moment[47] of US suzerainty is one in which there is an inevitable emergence of new powers, e.g., China, or the assertion of already existing major powers, e.g., Europe. T.R. Reid[48] and Mark Lenard[49] variously envisioned the twenty-first century as one dominated by a politically united and economically integrated Europe in the form of an expanded European Union. This view discounts the possible rise of other non-Western powers such as China, and makes an expansive projection beyond the fact that the US–EU relationship will be a fundamental and problematic axis in international affairs for the foreseeable future.[50] Europe will not easily countenance a diminution in influence, but does not aspire to repeat its nineteenth-century role.

The decline of US power and influence is so widely accepted that popular magazines such as *Newsweek* take this decline as a premise for lead articles, exploring the inevitable cycle of all hegemons which is now manifesting itself in the US. The global financial crisis was the latest harbinger of decline. Niall Ferguson warns that there is a 'fatal arithmetic of imperial decline. Without radical fiscal reform, it could apply to America next.'[51] This echoes the accepted proposition that the hegemonic power eventually declines in power and influence because of imperial overstretch or the rise of other powers or exhaustion of imperial hubris. The 'imperial overstretch' thesis was given prominence by historian Paul Kennedy.[52] Niall Ferguson raises the intriguing and highly pertinent dynamic between countries specifically what he calls 'Chimerica', i.e., the interdependence between China and the US, and advances the idea that the Asian savings glut is integrally connected with the flood of cheap credit which spawned the sub-prime mortgage crisis.[53] If the US is no longer able or willing to shoulder the burden of hegemon and sheriff of the world, and Asia as a region and China in particular is willing to assume an expanded role in world affairs, then it may portend an era of multilateralism. This sharing of aspects of the dominant role is what Joseph Nye appositely describes as the 'Paradox of American Power'.[54] Zbigniew Brzezinski suggests that the world should be run by the 'Group of Two' (G2) of China and the US by deepening and widening geostrategic cooperation through regular informal meetings.[55]

David Gordon posed the intriguing question of whether it was necessary for the US to be number one.[56] A number one position has advantages such as the seigniorage of the US dollar as the leading international currency, but there are also costs such as being dominant in military capability and the use of it to a sufficient extent to make superiority credible. Being the dominant or sole superpower may still be a goal for some policymakers and politicians in the US, but the pursuit of such a status and concomitant role poses political problems at home and a threat to peace abroad not the least of which is 'imperial overstretch'. Ferguson worries that:

> If the United States retreats from its hegemonic role, who would supplant it? Not Europe, not China, not the Muslim world-and certainly not the United Nations. Unfortunately, the alternative to a single superpower is "not a multilateral utopia, but the anarchic nightmare of a new Dark Age."[57]

The diversification of power among several rising powers may leave a less dominant US still in the role of most powerful. In such a scenario, and even with the rise of China, Bruce Jones believes that it will be 'still ours (Americans) to lead,'[58] but lead does not mean dominance. American power will endure and the US will still be the most influential country with the support of allies and those rising powers that do not want more influence in the current order.

Many are worried that the US has fallen behind and that it should make a concerted effort to regain its superiority or at least competitiveness. Thomas Friedman and Michael Mandelbaum worry about a sense of resignation in the

US, that America's best days are behind it and China's are ahead of it,[59] and Fareed Zakaria discusses the future as the 'Post-American World'.[60] However, some are optimistic about a 'better, stronger, faster' US.[61] But when Standard and Poor downgrades US debt from AAA, an event few if any could have imagined, then Edward Luce is certainly correct when he says that 'it is time to start thinking' because America is in an 'age of descent'.[62] Mandelbaum suggests that as Americans think about the global role of the US, there may be a lack of will. For him, the dilemma is that: 'The great danger to the American role as global policeman comes not from an international consensus against it but from a lack of a domestic consensus in favour of it.'[63] Ian Bremmer suggests that turning inward would not be a viable option because engagement is vital to US security and prosperity.[64]

Since the Second World War, the US has felt that it belongs in and has a determining role in Asia. This perspective is a reflection of the inevitability of involvement of a superpower and resisting the spread of communism as the central plank in its international security policy, hence fighting wars in Korea and Vietnam. However, the rise of Asia, in particular China and India, will change the role and influence of the US, and this eventuality needs to be recognized in Washington, DC. Martin Sieff puts it bluntly when he states: 'The very idea that the United States can and should maintain itself in the long run as the dominant power in continental Asia is a chimera born of the distorting experience of the cold war.'[65]

EMERGENCE OF NEW SUPERPOWERS

When a superpower declines it is relative to its previous unchallenged dominance, and this diminution is invariable because other countries rise to the status of major power or superpower. During the epoch of American hegemony, there has been a number of contenders. During the Cold War era, the Soviet Union was the antagonistic rival until its implosion. During that period, the struggle was waged on the military, political, ideological and economic fronts. The end of the Cold War ushered in a moment of euphoria in which American dominance would be the centre of the permanence of democracy and capitalism. This triumphalism was expressed by Francis Fukuyama in his thesis on the 'End of History' because it was 'the end point of mankind's ideological evolution and the universalization of Western liberal democracy as the final form of human government'.[66] Robert Kagan's response argued that the reality was too complex to warrant such simplification and optimism.[67]

Japan's astonishing economic growth from the end of the Second World War into the 1980s prompted speculation that Japan was an emerging economic superpower, challenging the US in this arena in a way that it could not in military might. Emblematic of this expectation was a popular book of the 1980s entitled *Japan as No. 1: Lessons for America.* A critical passage for Vogel was: 'In gross national product per person, Japan passed the United States in 1977 or 1978.' [68] A new East Asian economic configuration[69] was emerging in which Japan held an important role in investment and trade. However, formal organization of an economic grouping had not taken place although intra-regional trade had grown rapidly. There was no effort by Japan to organize a trade bloc or a yen bloc.[70] The Japanese economic model, Japanese-style capitalism, Japanese management and Japanese corporate formations were in vogue and were widely admired and studied. Those in the US who habitually look over their shoulders at who might be coming were convinced that there was an ominous element to Japan's economic prowess which threatened the US economy.[71] Clyde V. Prestowitz raised the alarm of Japan usurping the economic future[72] and the operations of the Ministry of International Trade and Industry (MITI) were examined.[73] The relationship between the US and Japan was cast in terms of an 'economic conflict', e.g., by Fred Bergsten and Marcus Noland[74] and Ronald McKinnon and Kenichi Ohno.[75] A more nuanced view argues that Japan's economic success made its international involvement unavoidable albeit reluctantly.[76] Prospect for a more assertive Japan has dimmed because the halcyon days of high economic growth have given way to a period referred to as the 'lost decade of the 1990s' in which Japan's economy has experienced severe difficulties. This economic malaise, which has continued into the contemporary period, is compounded by a political sclerosis.[77] The din of Japan as an economic superpower has diminished to the point that Robert Barbera dismissively states: 'The Japanese economy, feared as a rival to the US in the late 1980s, receded into near obscurity over the next ten years'.[78] Two factors coincided to change the economic fortunes of Japan. First, the relative cost of Japanese labour rose significantly with the result that labour-intensive industries relocated elsewhere in Asia. Second, Japanese firms found it necessary to establish manufacturing and servicing facilities closer to their final markets, e.g., the relocation of some automobile manufacturing to the US.[79]

From its formation as a communist state until recently, the US has regarded China primarily as an enemy, but since the embrace of 'Market Leninism' the relationship has become far less antagonistic. By its preponderant demographic, military and economic size, China is a superpower. As a superpower, China wants to have a presence in all regions of the globe and, therefore, the Caribbean, despite its small size and remoteness from China, has a place in China's foreign policy. The size and modernization of China's military is a reflection of continuity from the Cold War era, a hangover from the role of the military in communist political economy, a natural aspect of an emerging superpower and the pride and desire to be accorded respect.

The term 'the Chinese Century' has become a common neologism. The supposition is widespread that the nineteenth century was a British-dominated century, the twentieth century was one of American suzerainty and this century will be the Chinese epoch.[80] The dominance of China in this century is widely accepted as inevitable. Indeed, former US Secretary of State, Madeleine Albright, in her 2008 book entitled, *Memo to the President Elect*, speaks of America's place in the Chinese century.[81] China's ascent as a starting supposition, while reasonable, needs to be more cognizant of its internal problems in shaping the speed and trajectory of China.[82] Jonathan Fenby is convinced that internal contradictions will prevent China's continued rise, and indeed these problems will at least slow down China and could even lead to its 'destruction'.[83] Similarly, Mel Gurtov is sceptical of China's continued rise because of social, internal, political and environmental problems.[84] These predictions are based on a projection of demographic, social, political, environmental and economic trends. Even if such a tectonic shift does not materialize in the next 20–30 years, there will be a progressive reordering of global affairs in which China, along with Asia as a whole, will be prominent, and this will translate into more assertive engagement and influence in all aspects of international affairs. The enormous growth of China has changed and will continue to change the pattern of trade and investment in the world economy. China is forecasted to become the world's largest economy in 30 years. The rise towards economic dominance, together with its enormous military prowess, ranging from nuclear weapons to the largest army in the world, will ensure that China's influence and power in international politics increases dramatically.

Another perspective on developments and trends makes the plausible proposition that this century will be the 'Asian Century' with China being prominent amid India, Japan and the 'Asian Tigers'. The simultaneous economic rise of Asia and the relative decline of the US and Europe will produce an increase in the global influence of Asia politically and perhaps culturally. The ascendancy of Asia will generate inevitable change and friction with the West, but there will also be tensions and rivalries within Asia, particularly among Japan, China and India. Some of the intra-Asian issues will embroil countries outside the region, especially the US which has had and continues to have a major role in Asian affairs. Japan has long been one of the most developed countries which has been coy in asserting itself in international and regional affairs, but whose pride and self-interest will not allow it to be taken for granted. India's sheer size and ancient civilization status must be reckoned with, and because of the contribution and psychological allure of its ancient civilization, the world has given India a prominence not yet matched by its economic development. India presents the enigma of mass poverty with a capability for nuclear weapons.

Whatever the relative economic weights of regions and countries, Asia would be the world's most populous region and the centre of the world economy would have shifted to Asia. China is now a larger economy than the US, and India will do likewise in 2043.[85] While this is a very crude indicator, it cannot be dismissed although one might be more cautious than Bill Emmott who is convinced that: 'The future does, however, belong to Asia.'[86] If this eventually materializes, it will occasion adjustment in the US and Europe although there are those who point out that Asia's rise does not necessarily imply a corresponding decline in US influence. Anne-Marie Slaughter sees the US edge as its superior 'connectedness'[87] and Nye makes the case that the means to success lie in the use by the US of its 'soft power', a point discarded by the neo-conservatives of the George W. Bush administration.[88]

If, as thought by some in the US, the reigning, lone superpower, is declining relatively, and there is a burgeoning of China then this portends a bi-polar or multi-polar world. Waning global powers are typically wary of rising powers, especially if they aspire to a more powerful role and the commensurate status.[89] How the relationship between the US and China evolves will be critical in determining the evolution of the global economy and the reconfiguration of power in international affairs. An important factor will be willingness of the US to modify its 'affinity for unipolar policy'.[90] Many American foreign policy cognoscenti feel that the bilateral relationship is fraught with 'mismatched interests, values and capabilities'.[91]A strong current of opinion sees China as set on global domination and is, therefore, a threat to and in conflict with the US.[92] The prescription which emanates from this perspective is to counter China's rising influence in every region, including the Caribbean.

In reality, China's rise is a rebalancing of world affairs to take account of a nuclear power with the largest population in the world. For China, it is destiny fulfilled by the inevitable and long-awaited turning of the 'wheel of fortune', returning it to a position held for centuries[93] before what Kenneth Pomeranz[94] calls the 'Great Divergence' and the usurpation by what the Chinese refer to disparagingly as 'barbarian' European powers. As recently as the early nineteenth century, China accounted for 36 per cent of the GDP of the world before beginning the 'Century of Humiliation' with the nadir at five per cent in 1950.[95]

By its sheer economic, demographic, military size and phenomenal growth, China's integration into the world economy will seriously affect the level, pattern and tempo of world trade and investment. As Tim Summers appositely puts it: developments in China have resulted in 'a major shift in the country's global weight'.[96] Whether or not China continues to rise; whether or not it becomes the dominant superpower; whether or not it becomes a superpower; and whether or not it turns out to be so dominant that it ushers in the so-called Chinese Century are not possibilities which require predictions in this study. For the purposes of this study, it is sufficient to recognize that the rise of China has already had positive and negative effects on a variety of countries and, indeed, on the world as a whole. An example of China's negative impact is that its exports have had a disruptive effect on the economies of some developing countries, particularly in labour-intensive manufactured goods, for example, the displacement of Mexican manufactured textiles and electronics in the US market.[97] China is increasingly 'out competing' Latin American manufactured exports in regional and global markets, and this is having and will have adverse effect on Latin American economies.[98] Chinese products have also had a negative impact on textile production in Africa.[99] It has even been suggested that Chinese competition affected Asian producers in a way that was a contributing factor to the Asian financial crisis of 1997–98.[100] However, an example of China's positive impact has been its massive development aid and investment in developing countries in Africa, Latin America and the Caribbean. Whatever the future holds for China, it will impact many countries worldwide, yet the nature of that impact depends both on internal and external factors, including how the rest of the world reacts to China.

BI-POLAR OR MULTI-POLAR WORLD

A multi-polar world is one in which there is less certainty, greater potential for conflict and conflict resolution requires cooperation among a group of the most powerful countries. The eighteenth century was one of conflict born of the rivalry among the British, French, Dutch, Spanish and Portuguese. Britain was the superpower of the nineteenth century, exercising an acknowledged suzerainty in world affairs. The first half of the twentieth century witnessed the decline of Britain as a superpower and the rise of the US, and the conflicts of two world wars and the economic rivalry and breakdown of cooperation which compounded factors already impelling the Great Depression. The Cold War rivalry of two superpowers, the US and the Soviet Union was intensified by differences, sometimes diametrically opposed, in philosophy, political systems and economic organization. This period lasted from the end of the Second World War until the implosion of the Soviet Union in the 1980s. However, while there was military, economic and political rivalry, the US carried out the role of hegemony in the world capitalist system.

During the last two decades, there has been a relative decline of the US which, in spite of this, remained economically and militarily dominant. At times Japan and the European Union both appeared to emerge, but it was not sustained. But more recently, China has increasingly become more of a rival to the US with India as an aspirant and distant possibility. As a measure of the change in world affairs, the president of Brazil in looking to the future opined: 'I believe Brazil and the U.S. have to play a role together in the world.'[101]

There has been a dispersal of power from the West, where it has been concentrated in the modern era, most recently in the US, to China in particular. However, this dispersal is being diluted by the continued role of Russia and the EU, and the rise of India and Brazil. In global situations such as the contemporary conjuncture, the stabilizing role in global affairs has to be shared, otherwise instability can arise and, as history has shown, such a state of affairs can generate or escalate into turmoil. It is clear that the US and China both want a peaceful political world and an orderly global economy, so there will have to be a certain predictable coordinating function in international economic affairs. The historical experience clearly demonstrates that the role of hegemon in the world economy is easier to exercise when it is not shared but managed by a single superpower. Considerable literature on the history of international monetary affairs conclude that there is greater stability when there is a single hegemon. The establishment of the Bretton Woods institutions was intended to share some of that role, with the US having the final say. The next 10–20 years will test whether such multilateral institutions can operate successfully if economic governance responsibilities are shared. Robert Kaplan, in speculating on this type of scenario, wonders what will happen when as he puts it: there is a 'world with no one in charge'.[102] Peter Temin and David Vines believe the world economy is already leaderless, and worry how the international cooperation necessary for recovery will occur. Former US national security advisor, Brezezinski, acknowledges the waning of American power but with the retention of residual capacities and if the US falters he foresees 'a protracted phase of rather inconclusive and somewhat chaotic alignments of both global and regional power, with no grand winners and many more losers, in a setting of international uncertainty and even of potentially fatal risks to global well-being.'[103] Some like Charles A. Kupchan[104] do not share this dystopian outlook and envision multilateral cooperation rather than conflict or competition.

CHINA'S ROLE IN THE WORLD

The term 'the Chinese Century' is now widely used in the media. It is assumed that China will take over from the US as the US once replaced Britain, and this century will be the Chinese era.[105] There are opposing schools of thought about whether China's dominance is inevitable. Martin Jacques is in no doubt that China will 'rule the world'[106] whereas David Shambaugh is equally emphatic stating that 'China has a long way to go before it becomes – if it ever becomes – a truly global power. And it will never rule the world.'[107] Jonathan Fenby[108] and Thomas J. Christensen[109] argue that China will not dominate the twenty-first century. Even if such a tectonic shift does not materialize for 20–30 years, there will be a progressive reordering of global affairs in which China, along with Asia as a whole, will be prominent.[110] This will translate into more assertive engagement and influence in all aspects of international affairs in what Fareed Zakaria calls the 'Post-American World'.[111] The enormous growth of China has and will continue to change the pattern of trade and investment in the world economy. Its economic weight and uniqueness poses challenges for the tenets and rules of conduct of the prevailing international regime.[112] China has become the world's largest economy much earlier than predicted. The spectacular economic progress, its sheer size (one-fifth of mankind) and its enormous military prowess ranging from nuclear weapons to the largest army in the world, will ensure that China's influence and power in international politics will increase.

China has grown at an average rate of ten per cent per year during the period 1990–2005. It is one of the engines of growth in the new global economy, accounting in recent years for 12 per cent of all growth in world trade[113] and has had a stimulating effect on economic growth in Latin America, Asia and Africa. Economic growth has continued but has slowed since 2012. Notwithstanding these circumstances, China's economy has continued its phenomenal economic growth rate. Even with decline in China's economic growth to single digit levels, the economy still represents a robust business opportunity for foreign investors and exporters particularly if they are provided with the support needed to navigate the bureaucratic obstacles to market penetration. In spite of its achievements, the question is still being asked: Can China continue and can it play a constructive leadership role in international affairs? Those who predict that China's economic growth will only continue if it changes its economic model to a Western-style capitalist economy, shrinking the role of the state and minimize if not eliminate the role of the Communist Party in favour of multi-party electoral democracy. Regina M. Abrami, William C. Kerby and F. Warren McFarlan speak of the need to change the economic and political factors which limit future economic progress but are pessimistic opining that China will neither rule nor lead the world.[114] Nicholas Eberstadt describes the dilemma as 'sclerosis from a trapped transition'.[115]

Those who argue for China to change to capitalism and democracy should be cautious as China is unique, and its recent economic growth has confounded existing models and achieved remarkable growth. The model may not be applicable in other countries but it has produced results which few if any could have predicted. In the case of China, past economic development experience has not been a guide nor should anyone say never. It is unhelpful to read the burgeoning literature which argue that economic growth in China cannot continue because of a litany of internal problems which will only be resolved by adopting Western capitalism and electoral democracy. It would be wise to recognize that all the most noteworthy economic successes were unique, e.g., Britain, the US, Germany, Japan, South Korea and Singapore. Interestingly, in all cases, democracy came long after the economic progress. In England, the 'Industrial Revolution' is agreed by historians to have started in the eighteenth century, but women did not have the right to vote until the early twentieth century. In the US, slavery was not abolished until the 1860s, and all African Americans could not vote until 1968, long after the US had become the dominant capitalist country in the world. Singapore's economic miracle was under the autocratic rule of Lee Kwan Yew which according to Kaplan 'implies that virtue is not altogether connected to democracy and that meritocratic quasi-autocracy can in a poor country achieve economic results quicker than can weak and chaotic parliamentary system'.[116]

Whether China assumes a global leader's role also depends on how China tackles defining and asserting its international role. This is not clear and is changing as the world evolves and Chinese thinking develops. Shambaugh finds China's efforts to be incompetent. He states that 'China is in the international community of nations but in many ways is not really part of the community' and found 'its diplomacy to be hesitant, risk-averse, and narrowly self-interested. China often makes known what it is against but not what it is for.'[117] This description certainly does not do justice to the style, modalities, complexity and sophistication of Chinese diplomacy as illustration by Henry Kissinger[118] and Margaret MacMillan.[119] Closer to the truth is Zheng Bijian when he states that change will 'transcend the traditional ways for great powers to emerge'[120]

The growth of China in the world economy has implications both negative and positive, for all countries, for example, China's demand for food has driven up prices and, demand for commodities. China's recent slowdown in economic growth caused a decline in commodity prices.[121] China's exports can be disruptive to the economies of developing countries particularly in labour-intensive manufactured goods as has happened with the displacement of Mexican manufactured textiles and electronics in the US market.[122] There is concern that the amount of foreign direct investment going to China could be crowding out other developing countries. Foreign investment in China has grown exponentially since 1979 when the first joint venture law was passed and, by 2002, when total FDI inflows reached US$53 billion, when it became the largest recipient of FDI, surpassing the US.[123] China's economic growth and its demand for energy and primary commodities is an enormous opportunity. The countries which have been able to supply the Chinese market have had their economic growth stimulated by these exports. This has been the experience of many countries in Latin America[124] and Africa[125] that export oil and primary products. Indeed, China has become the largest trading partner of several such countries.

There are numerous indicators that China has emerged as an economic power. This is evident in its massive foreign exchange reserves, and Chinese banks at the end of 2009 commanded four of the five highest spots of the most highly valued financial institutions as measured by share prices as a multiple of their book value. The highest US bank is at number 14. This is a reversal of figures from the year 2000 when US banks held four of the top five positions.[126] China has become the Mecca for governments and corporations looking for financing and investment.[127] At the same time, China has overtaken Germany to become the world's leading exporter and the world's largest market for automobiles.[128] More ominous for the US and other developed countries is that China is competitive not only in manufacturing, which these countries have resigned themselves to relinquishing, but in the high value activities which they intend to rely on in the future. The *Financial Times* reported that 'China far out performed every other nation, with a 64-fold increase in peer reviewed scientific papers since 1981' and is 'now the second-largest producer of scientific knowledge' and is 'on course to overtake the US by 2020'.[129]

As China assumes the role of a superpower, it must continually adjust its foreign policy and its approach to international issues. In this regard, perceptions and long-standing traditions and assumptions have to be updated by both China and the rest of the world. One very important factor is that China and some of the leading protagonists, in particular the US has to relinquish the mindset that their goals and policies are inevitably in opposition to each other and that economic competition must lead to conflict. Too many in the US believe that China's rises at the expense of the US and that it is China's goal to undermine the US. Similarly, China sees the US and the Western powers as resisting its rise as a global power, and accepts that the US will be dominant in the immediate future despite its relative decline.[130]

US RESPONSE TO THE RISE OF CHINA

The response of the US to the rise of Asia has to be understood against the background of how the 'Western World' has failed to see Asia in a realistic, and as far as possible, unbiased perspective. Perceptions of Asia or the East have underrepresented, undervalued and distorted its contribution to the history of the world. Edward Said[131] termed this 'Orientalism' which he explains as denigrating the East and positing the West in a contrasting and positive light. This type of world view had its beginnings in the nineteenth century when in addition to representing prejudice it was functional to imperialism as Victor G. Kiernan[132] has documented. The critique of what has more popularly been labelled 'Eurocentricism'[133] spread across the social science disciplines.[134] John M. Hobson has sought to correct the distortion of the teleology of the West as superior to the East by showing that the East was far more advanced than the West between 500 and 1800 and played a 'crucial role in enabling the rise of Western civilization' through what he calls 'oriental globalisation'.[135] Accepting that China was ahead of the West before 1800 does not gainsay that thereafter a 'great divergence' occurred.[136]

Table 1.1: Asia's Lead: Dates of Innovation in Asia and the West

Innovation	Asia	The West
Cotton Cloth or Clothing	3rd millennium BC (India)	16th century
Iron Casting	2nd century BC (China)	13th century
Planting with Automatic Seeder	1st century BC (China)	1700
Curved Iron Plows	1st century BC (China)	1700
Paper	2nd century BC (China)	1150
Rotary Fan for Ventilation	2nd century BC (China)	1556
Wheelbarrow	3rd century BC (China)	1200
Porcelain	3rd century BC (China)	1709
Watertight Compartments in Ships	5th century BC (China)	1790
Printing with Wood Blocks	8th century BC (China)	1400
Gunpowder	10th century BC (China)	13th century
Bombs	1000 (China)	16th century
Printing with Moveable Type	1045 (China)	1440
Iron-clad Warships	1592 (Korea)	1862

Source: Nicholas D. Kristol and Sheryl Wudunn, Thunder from the East: Portrait of a Rising Asia *(New York: Alfred A. Knopf, 2000), 29.*

The pre-eminence and contribution to the world of China should have been in no doubt after Joseph Needham's monumental *Science and Civilisation in China.*[137] Table 1.1 shows that Asia and China were ahead of the West in many important technologies.

As much as prejudicial historical approaches contribute to the failure to put Asia's rise in perspective, there is also another current of thinking which militates against frank analysis. This is the wilful reluctance to concede that part of the relative change is due to factors and policies which originate in the West. Stephen D. King elaborates this thesis and concludes that the West will be a shadow of its former self, both in terms of its falling share of the global economic pie and its rapidly diminishing share of the world's ever-increasing population.[138] Kagan draws comfort from what he perceives as an acceptance of American dominance and ventures that: 'American predominance is unlikely to fade anytime soon, largely because much of the world does not want it to do'.[139] The Chinese certainly do not accept American superiority, and the more China projects its multifaceted advances, the more that the rest of the world will notice this attitude and this reality. Simon Winchester explains the result of China's history:

> Within the framework of changelessness there is also, entirely discernible, something else that resists change – something that can only be described

> as an attitude. It is a Chinese state of mind...It is an attitude of ineluctable and self-knowing Chinese superiority, and it results from the antiquity and the longevity of the Chinese people's endeavors.[140]

In November 2009, US President Barack Obama visited China and did not attempt to wield a 'Big Stick'. Instead, he set a tone of cooperation, a diplomatic approach which The *Economist* dismissed as 'pussy footing'.[141] In the US, some are concerned about the rise of China in world affairs, and in some quarters this gives way to thinking which borders on paranoia.[142] Books with titles like *The Coming Conflict with China, China: Friend or Foe?, China's Master Plan to Destroy America, Showdown: Why China Wants War with the United States* and *America's Coming War with China* are characteristic of an attitude which is predisposed to viewing relations with China as one of conflict.[143] The growing preoccupation with China and Asia affairs goes back a century with US President Theodore Roosevelt opining in June 1905 that: 'Our Future will be more determined by our position on the Pacific facing China than by our position on the Atlantic facing Europe.'[144] *Newsweek* magazine's lead story in the first issue of 2008 was on China, arguing that China is a fierce and fragile superpower. 'Conflict and competition – particularly in the economic realm – between China and the United States is inevitable. But whether this turns ugly depends largely on policy choices that will be made in Washington and Beijing.'[145] Calmer voices recognized that genuine friendship may not exist, but the interests are so intertwined that cooperation is the best option.[146] John Ikenberry has suggested that China's rise will end the 'United States' unipolar moment', but the US can remain dominant in the international order while integrating China.[147] Several analysts believe that the rising powers, including China and India, have a vested interest in a stable world order and would avoid a frontal conflict with the US while asserting increased influence in world affairs.[148] The administration of George W. Bush developed a policy of engagement and dialogue with China, emphasizing interdependence and cooperation.[149] This approach has been continued by the Obama administration. Martin Wolf gets to the heart of the matter when he points out that the political and economic consequences of a breakdown between China and the West would be 'catastrophic'.[150] The degree of assertiveness in international affairs is still debated in Beijing, including the extent to which China would go to prevent Taiwan's independence.[151] There are a variety of currents of thinking in China and hence[152] Jiang Shixue states that in the conduct of foreign policy 'a consensus has never been reached on the balance between keeping a low profile and taking action.'[153] As China's profile and tangible presence increases it will have to work assiduously through its foreign policy to prevent resentment and ensure harmonious trading relationships.[154] It will avoid head-on confrontations with the US by careful diplomacy aimed at not clashing with the US nor aggressively contesting the global terrain. This mode of diplomacy with the US has been described by Zakaria as: 'China has always played the weak hand brilliantly.'[155] While not challenging US dominance, China's increased economic and diplomatic involvement in Latin America and the Caribbean, a region which the US regards as their exclusive preserve, has not gone unnoticed in Washington, DC.[156] The US was sanguine about China's deployment of 143 peacekeepers in Haiti in 2007, which constituted a precedent in the Western Hemisphere.[157] China has also added a new dimension to its foreign policy towards the US by lobbying Congress directly rather than engaging in merely arm's length diplomacy with the State Department and the White House.[158] The willingness to allow China's gradual assertion has aroused calls for action both in regard to Chinese economic encroachment and steadily growing diplomatic presence. 'China is just pushing through an open door across the globe – and in the U.S. backyard,' said China expert Nick Lardy of the Institute for International Economics in Washington, DC.[159]

Robert Kaplan has opined that China's challenge to the US is 'primarily geographic' and argues that 'China's emerging area of influence in Eurasia and Africa is growing, not in a nineteenth-century imperialistic sense but in a more subtle manner better suited to the era of globalization.'[160] In late 2011 and early 2012, the US elevated Asia to a priority place in its foreign policy, reflecting China's rise and the scaling down of US operations in Afghanistan and Iraq. President Obama signalled the change in his November 2011 trip to Asia and reconfirmed the new policy orientation in February 2012 when Hu Jintao, President of China, made an official visit to Washington, DC. The US has strengthened security alliances with Australia, Japan, the Philippines, South Korea and Thailand. It has given more attention to India, Indonesia, Malaysia and Vietnam.[161] Former US Secretary of State, Hillary Clinton,[162] announced the Asia-Pacific Strategic Engagement Initiative (APSEI) on July 12, 2012, which in the words of the State Department, 'is a new integrated assistance framework that engages on current pressing bilateral and transnational issues, and positions the United States and its partners to sustain regional stability and support an inclusive regional economy.'[163] Consistent with the new more assertive stance, Secretary Clinton characterized as 'confrontational'[164] China's approach to the territorial disputes in the South China Sea, an issue about which China feels very strongly.[165]

Despite the new approach to relations with China, the Obama administration is criticized for not being firm enough with China.[166] On the economic front, the US is determined to maintain its place in the rapidly growing Asian markets. In October 2011, the US Congress approved a free trade agreement between South Korea and the US. Originally negotiated in 2007 and re-negotiated in 2010, the Republic of Korea–United States Free Trade Agreement (KORUS FTA) is the most important trade deal for the US since the North American Free Trade Agreement

(NAFTA) in 1993. The KORUS FTA eliminates tariff, 95 per cent of tariffs on goods over a five-year period from March 2012 with most of the remaining tariffs to be eliminated within ten years.[167] It is envisioned that the bilateral initiatives are to be overtaking by the Trans-Pacific Partnership (TPP) the prospects of which received a boost in June 2015 when the Obama administration was guaranteed Trade Promotion Authority (TPA) the absence of which would have stymied the negotiations. The TPP is an expansion of the Trans-Pacific Strategic Economic Partnership Agreement (TPSEP) which was signed in 2005 by Brunei, Chile, Singapore, and New Zealand in 2006. Australia, Canada, Japan, Malaysia, Mexico, Peru, the US and Vietnam joined the negotiations in 2008. The TPP was signed by 12 countries on February 4, 2016.

The TPP project is impelled by both economic and security motives. The US regards the TPP as an essential bulwark against China's economic and political prominence in Asia and a mechanism for reinforcing its ties and status in Asia. How the US Congress will vote on the TPP is at beast uncertain particularly in the run up the presidential election in 2016. President Obama's administration will have to work hard and astutely to ensure support from the majority of Democrats in the House of Representatives. The TPP is a mix of potential trade boosting measure, e.g., lower tariffs on goods and uncertainty over topics such as intellectual property rights, which taken together could add up to a limited impact on growth and employment. Expanded membership through an accession clause could serve the economic and political interests of the current members especially given the stalemate in multilateral trade negotiations.

The rise of China relative to the US and its concomitant increase in influence is evident everywhere. At the Copenhagen Conference on Climate Change, the major outcomes were the result of decisions that were made jointly by the US and China. This type of influence will soon manifest itself in international fora in which China has been a marginal player. It is incumbent on both parties to change their thinking and relinquish antiquated ideas such as the notion of the inevitability that capitalism will prevail in China and that capitalism will lead to democracy. Yu Liu and Dingding Chen assert that a fundamental political transformation is already taking place in China and predict that 'China is moving closer to vindicating classical modernization theory, which states that economic development eventually leads to democratization.'[168] W. James Mann argues that this widely held view in the US is not likely to become reality partly because it is an ill-conceived concept, and partly because it misinterprets developments in China.[169] The political system of China, like its economy and economic development, will be unique and therefore application of concepts and models based on the experience of other countries is going to be of limited use in predicting the future of China. It is not useful to try to squeeze China into existing categories. For example, labelling

China as a developing country, even as Thomas J. Christensen posits it is 'by far the most influential developing country in world history',[170] China's economic and foreign policy and its role in the global economy and in international affairs as it becomes more engaged in world affairs will be uniquely Chinese. While it is true that China is becoming increasingly integrated into the world economy, its policies will not conform to the Western World's. US Treasury Secretary Robert Rubin's observations about China are instructive. After acknowledging the constructive role played by China in stabilizing the world economy, he stated: 'Its leaders were tough, independent-minded and unresponsive to pressure' and predicted that in 'the twenty-first century, China will be a formidable and staunchly independent force.'[171]

The rapid economic growth associated with the integration of China into the global economy has actually reduced the pressure for change in the autocratic rule of the Communist Party, and if it can continue to provide an improved standard of living it may cope with the forces which could either foment forces that could lead to an implosion, as was the case in the Soviet Union, or press for greater political freedom. As Stefan Halper has explained:

> China's economic miracle has saved the ruling party from extinction, but only because the nation replaced ideology with economic growth, a rekindled sense of nationalism, and a certain amount of pragmatic flexibility. Accordingly, the legitimacy of the Chinese Communist Party hinges on its ability to deliver economic growth.[172]

OBAMA'S CHINA POLICY

It is difficult for any US administration to maintain a non-confrontational policy of cooperation towards China because the foreign policy environment is one where many insist on conceiving of China as a protagonist motivated by nefarious goals of overtaking or undermining security. This portrayal is a continuation of the Cold War prism of competition as head-on confrontation. The state of mind is perpetuated and propagated by an embattled view of security of 'us versus them', heightened since the events of 9/11 and the subsequent US 'War on Terrorism'. Public receptivity of the view that China is an antagonistic rival is fostered by sensational media reporting which portrays China as a rival global power whose influence is almost at a zenith, but is destined not to last perhaps far beyond a decade as debilitating internal problems take their toll portending a dystopian future of uncertain character. Emblematic of such journalism is an article in *Time* magazine of August 31, 2015 which reports that 'many outsiders see China as a country where dark forces may one day ignite a sudden conflagration inflicting massive damage – for reasons that are murky.'[173] It goes on to opine that the world is already in what it calls the 'China Decade' because of 'a favourable geopolitical environment over the short term', but which ends when long-term internal demographic, environmental and economic problems inevitably take their toll. Given that a US policy of containment as practised toward the Soviet Union after the Second World War is not a feasible strategy, this type of narrative is both comforting and misleading. It purveys a scenario of a temporary threat which recedes in a decade with certain but unspecified inevitability lent plausibility by evoking a vague analogy to the implosion of the Soviet Union.

This type of media opinion may make for saleable copy, but it creates uncertainty and anxiety about China. To the credit of both the Bush and Obama administrations, they have managed to resist this type of thinking instead, opting for constructive engagement with China. The intention has been to induce China to be a compatible multilateral player with a vested interest in the stability of the current American-designed and managed international order. The policy has been a pragmatic blend of accommodating assertive but reasonable Chinese positions and resisting revision of the existing security parameters and geographic deployment. Where, how and when to yield and pushback has been a continuous recalibrated multidimensional mix within the overall spectrum of its global policy priorities and deployment. Among the most pressing objectives for the US have been to reassure Asian allies that it will be resolute in resisting and even blocking China's rapid escalation of assertiveness in the Pacific. Jeffrey Bader who served in the National Security Council of the Obama administration makes the profound observation that 'the problems in U.S. leadership in Asia was not the consequence of Asia-specific policy errors, but rather of the spill-over effect of misguided policies elsewhere in the world that had consequences everywhere.'[174]

PAX AMERICANA TO PRIMUS INTER PARES

A bi-polar or multi-polar world has two or more powers but without any one power being able to dominate all the others. Such a world is likely to be characterized by rivalry, conflict and instability which is not contained by cooperation. The circumstances which are most propitious for stability exist when there is a single hegemonic power. This observation was elevated to a 'theory of hegemonic stability' by Robert Keohane who explains that 'hegemonic structures of power, dominated by a single country, are most conducive to the development of strong international regimes whose rules are relatively precise and well obeyed.'[175] Robert Gilpin states that 'in the absence of a dominant liberal power, international economic cooperation has been difficult to attain or sustain and conflict has been the norm'.[176] After an empirical analysis, Michael C. Webb and Stephen D. Krasner conclude that 'a strong hegemon can exert a positive influence on stability in the international system'.[177] Some have even taken the extreme stance that a unipolar conjuncture is much more likely to be peaceful and that that likelihood increases with the greater the degree of concentration of power.[178] Without delving into the extensive literature on this topic, it is worth mentioning that the theory has been employed to explain different phases in the evolution of the international monetary system. This strand of the literature is pertinent because China could become a rival superpower to the US, and the rise of China could be reflected in its role in the international monetary system.

The question of the stability of the international monetary system is posed by the current global imbalances and by China's rise, which creates a situation in which it is not a unipolar world with the US as absolute hegemon but also not a bipolar situation, although China is now an important player. Peter Temin and David Vines believe that the global financial situation is one they describe as 'the leaderless economy' and that what is now urgently needed is a cooperative intervention, but worry if this will materialize because this 'type of cooperation will be encouraged if a hegemon emerges to stimulate and guide it'.[179] China has the largest international reserves and is the country with the largest holding of US Treasury paper. Not surprisingly, the IMF has included the Renminbi (RMB) in the special drawing rights (SDR) as one of five internationally accepted currencies. Some think it is only a matter of time.[180] Therefore, what are the implications for the US Dollar, the Euro and the stability of the international monetary system? Charles P. Kindleberger states that 'for the world economy to be stable, it needs a stabilizer',[181] and posited that the international monetary system during interwar years was unstable as the lack of leadership meant having no dominant economic power to perform the role of international lender of last resort.[182] Proponents of this approach argued that the international monetary system experiences stability when there is a hegemonic national economy, but exhibits instability in the absence of such a hegemon. This line of reasoning is supported by reference to Britain's dominance during the halcyon days of the gold standard 1890–1914 and the Bretton Woods System, 1945–71, a period in which the US was dominant. These periods of stability are contrasted with the instability of the interwar gold exchange standard and the international monetary system since 1971. Not everyone is convinced after scrutiny of the history. For example, Barry Eichengreen states: 'more than a dominant economic power was generally required to insure the provision and maintenance of international monetary stability.'[183] Robert J. Skidelsky also believes this view when he ventures that 'a system that depends on the exertions of a preponderant power is inherently unstable in the long run.'[184] Harold Van B. Cleveland suggests that a dominant economic power is only necessary if stability is synonymous with fixed exchange rates.[185]

The RMB has, in recent years, attained more prominence as an internationally accepted means of payment in international trade and financial transactions.

As China's share of world trade has grown, so too has the use of the RMB. The RMB has been severely criticized by the US, arguing that its exchange rate has for years been systematically and astutely manipulated to give China's exports an unfair advantage. This alleged exchange rate manipulation was supposed to be a principal factor explaining why China's exports have grown so rapidly in international markets and why the US has such a large and increasing trade deficit with China. This assertion has to be weighed against the fact that China's exports are very competitive in price and quality because of low wages, economies of scale and support from the state. Doubts were also expressed about whether the RMB would or could become an internationally accepted and used currency. Eswar Prasad, former chief economist of the IMF, declared as recently as 2014 that the RMB was unlikely to become a prominent reserve currency, and would not challenge the US dollar's dominance because the requirements for the RMB to be a global currency did not exist in China, in particular convertibility and full capital account liberalization.[186] Subsequent events have proven him wrong.

In December 2015, the IMF announced that the RMB, starting October 1, 2016, will be one of five currencies included basket of currencies in the SDR of the IMF. This is a signal that the RMB is now one of only five internationally accepted currencies. The RMB joins the elite club of the US dollar, the Euro, the Pound Sterling and the Yen. The signal came in when the IMF's managing director announced that the RMB would be included in a basket of currencies which comprise the IMF's Special Drawing Rights. The value of the SDR will be based on a weighted average of the values of the basket of currencies. These are the US dollar (41.73 per cent, the Pound Sterling (8.09 per cent), the Japanese Yen (8.33 per cent), the Chinese RMB (10.92 per cent) and the Euro (30.93 per cent).[187]

This designation of the RMB is recognition by the IMF as 'freely usable currency'. In recent years, the RMB has increasingly been used in international payments, reflecting China's importance in the world economy, and are a validation of the reforms made in the monetary and financial system.[188] The new status of the RMB is the realization of a strategy of internationalization which China has been avidly pursuing and will enhance China's role and influence in the international monetary system. The announcement will encourage central banks to hold RMB as part of their international reserves and will stimulate its wider use in international payments. In 2014, the RMB was used only in 38 countries in their international reserves, accounting for 1.1 per cent of total foreign reserves, while the US dollar was used by 127 countries, accounting for almost 64 per cent of global reserves. The Euro accounted for 21 per cent.[189] China has calmed lingering uncertainty by indicating that there would be no sudden changes in the value of the RMB.[190]

The US dollar has remained dominant although less so over time, reflecting three trends: decline in US dominance, the gradual emergence of the Euro and the expansion of international financial markets evident in the volume of foreign exchange traded daily ($5.3 trillion) which far exceeds individual national ($4 trillion by China) and collective official reserves of governments.[191] This has culminated in what Susan Strange describes as 'the diffusion of power in the world economy'.[192] Benjamin J. Cohen is correct in stressing that the stability of the international financial system is now a dialectic between national governments and international operating market agents.[193]

The question is: does a world in Keohane's phrase 'after hegemony'[194] have to suffer from interruptions of stability? Hyman P. Minsky's[195] financial instability hypothesis has argued that periodic financial crises emanating from speculative eruptions that are inherent in global capitalism or as Reinhart and Rogoff[196] cyclical bouts of excessive exuberance in which actors in the market are convinced that 'this time it is different'. Galbraith noticed these bouts of reckless euphoria.[197] There is also the human element in managing the international monetary system even when reputed to be based on a certain rules-based automaticity of the Gold Standard much less in more market-oriented systems. Certainly, the personalities and idiosyncrasies of leading central bankers responsible for international monetary policy cooperation is a factor, but cannot be the basis for a discussion of systemic behaviour.[198]

It took the Great Depression and the ravages of the Second World War to create the conditions in which the US could wrest the role of monetary hegemon from Britain. The US pursued a deliberate policy of undermining Britain's hegemonic role by systematically and relentlessly dismembering the British Empire by dismantling the mercantilist trade arrangements[199] and thereby diminishing the role of Sterling as both a store of value and as a means of international payment.[200] The formalization of the transfer of the former British role to the US was the decisions taken at the Bretton Woods Conference, which established the International Monetary Fund on the American design embodied in the White Plan instead of the Keynes Plan advocated by the British.[201] The lesson to be learnt from this experience is that the hegemonic role has to be seized by a global power superior in strength from the existing hegemon, and that there will be resistance to changes in the status quo.

To date, international monetary orders have reflected the dominance of a hegemon or the respective strengths of the most powerful capitalist countries,[202] but the rise of China signals the possibility that one of the influential countries in a future international monetary system may not be a capitalist country in the traditional sense of the word. China is gaining daily in global economic importance and as a nuclear-armed military power. However, it is not yet in a position to challenge the US. While China is important to the international financial system and to the US financial system in particular, none of China's financial centres is on par with those in the US, for example, the international financial centre, New York. Therefore, China is not in a position, comparable to the US which has been able to influence directly international credit, which is one of the functions that a monetary hegemon has to perform[203] for the global economy. Some believe that this may never happen although the extent of predominance will decline in a process of transition from Pax Americana to Primus Inter Pares.

PART II
ASPECTS OF AN EMERGING GLOBAL CONFUGURATION

The interactions between the waning superpower, the US, and the rising superpower, China, will dominate international affairs. Among the major areas of possible conflict between the US and China are the psychological transition to Chinese dominance, the shifting balance of economic interdependence, China's place in and responsibilities in global governance, China's role in development finance, cyber-security and mega trans-regional trade agreements.

1. Psychological Transition to Chinese Prominence

The world will have to become accustomed to the prominence of China not only in economic matters but in political affairs and culture. This psychological transformation and the transition to a knowledge of and comfort with Chinese dominance will not be easy. The difficulties arise from the fact that for the last 400–500 years the world in all aspects has been dominated by Western power and thinking. The very concepts being used to understand the rise of China and to foresee its future behaviour, goals and policies are essentially Western, and to varying degrees will not be adequate conceptual tools to interrogate the subject of China's rise and dominance. The task of comprehension and more so adjustment is complicated by a rapid and historic rise of change. China, like Rome, was not built in a day, but its dominance in world affairs may be only 10 or 20 years away.

The world has been habituated to Western political models, Western notions of economic policy, Western views of science, Western cultural patterns, Western media and entertainment and the psychology of Western centrality in daily life. The world will have to get to know China's history and its culture and how to conduct diplomatic relations and business transactions with China. This necessitates both learning and, as important, unlearning Western thought processes and conceptual frameworks. The content of university education will have to incorporate things Chinese, which at present make no reference to Chinese thought such as philosophy, politics, economics and sociology. Western ideas will no longer be the foundation and arbiter of what is and what should be in basic concepts in Western ideation systems. The basic concepts in Western Ideation Systems will be challenged, for example, the notions of what is democracy, what is economic development, what is the nation state, what is the role of the state, etc. The world will have to re-examine and even re-write the corpus of many subjects such as history.[204] It will also have to include disputes over events the Western world regards as facts such as who first had contact with North America. For Westerners, the Europeans came first; the Chinese asserts they first had contact with North America.

Thought will have to be accompanied by rearrangements and redeployment. If the largest source of bi-lateral development assistance is China, then there will have to be a redeployment of the infrastructure of international relations by developing countries. The capitals of the world are no longer only Washington, DC, Moscow and Paris, and the economic news that matters is not confined to London, Tokyo and Bonn. Everyone needs to pay attention to what emanates from Beijing, Hong Kong and Shanghai.

There are several unique features of the rise and coming prominence of China that pose unprecedented challenges with which the world will have to grapple. First, if the now ubiquitously cited Goldman-Sachs forecast that China will surpass the US as the world's largest economy as early as 2020 is correct, then for the first time the world economy will be dominated by a country which, in many respects, will still be a developing country. China may not be the typical developing country, but it will certainly not be a developed country. Second, it will be the first time that the world's largest economy will not be a capitalist economy but a hybrid mixed economy with a very large state-controlled sector. Third, the concept of development and modernity will no longer be dominated by Western values and ideology, and the notions of economic development and economic progress will have to take account of Chinese and, by extension, the legitimacy of non-Western perspectives. Martin Jacques speaks of contested modernity: 'instead of there being one dominant Western modernity (itself, of course, a pluralistic phenomenon) there will be many distinct modernities. It is clear that we have already entered this era of multiple modernities.'[205] The orthodoxies and prevailing paradigms in all fields will be challenged, and will meet resistance because the long-standing dominance of the Western world has never had to recognize and understand sufficiently non-Western cultures and ideas.

2. Shifting Balance of Economic Interdependence

Economic interdependence between the US and China has grown rapidly and profoundly in all aspects of economic and financial interaction. Trade between the two countries has grown from $5 billion in 1980 to $536 billion in 2012, making China the second-largest trading partner of the US, its third most important export market, and its largest source of imports.[206] China is the largest holder of US Treasury paper and, therefore, is integral to financing the Budget of the US federal government. China is the destination of a considerable stock of US foreign direct investment, reflecting the extensive operations of US companies in the country aimed at taking advantage of lower-cost labour for export production when selling their products.

Ferguson has coined the term 'Chimerica'[207] to describe this new reality, and Zachary Karabell speaks of a 'superfusion' which has made China and America not only interrelated but interdependent and together constitute the axis of the world economy.[208] In trade, China's dependence on the US as an export market is matched by US dependence on imports from China. Indeed, normal life in the US might not be possible without imports from China.[209] Many in the US are deeply concerned that many products and whole high value aspects of the supply chain, even in services, have been off-shored and outsourced to China. Trade with China is blamed for job losses and unemployment, and there are calls for nationalist and protectionist responses. Where China's expansion causes trade diversion and dislocation, it has prompted a backlash such as the attempts in the US to use phyto-sanitary and safety concerns to block Chinese exports, especially food items. Alongside this angst, there is an umbilical corporate strategic connection in which the global viability and profitability of many of the Fortune 500 companies depend on operating in China. In fact, Wal-Mart,[210] the largest retailer in the US, is the largest importer of products from China and responsible for exporting US jobs to China and perpetuating low wages by requiring lower prices from Chinese suppliers. Many US firms have invested in China because it has offered salvation from international competition especially imports from Chinese and non US firms in production in China. US companies have also salivated at the prospect of supplying the enormous Chinese markets, and this is most feasible by investing and operating in China. Numerous US firms have established and are doing business in China although this entails new challenges and unaccustomed difficulties.[211]

The US–China relationship is fraught with problems, the resolution of which will affect global events and all other relations. China is viewed by many in the US as an economic and military rival. In this respect, China is thought of in the same way as the Soviet Union during the Cold War. China is suspected of being responsible for breeches in the White House computer network.[212] The distrust was not dispelled by news that the Chinese government was involved in intrusions into the Google system.[213] Lingering prejudice and a hangover of distrust could limit Chinese economic relations. Security concerns can be used to limit Chinese investment in the US and the export of certain types of products to China. Chinese investment in key sectors could be prohibited in the same way that Dubai Ports were blocked from getting management contracts for port operations on the east coast of the US. The security anxiety is paralleled by the worry that China is taking over markets and buying up economic assets. The purchase of IBM's personal computer business by Lenovo did not arouse the ire of the US because most laptops are assembled overseas.

While some believe this event is 'creating a global enterprise with Chinese and American roots which is exactly the kind of experiment that Washington ought to be encouraging',[214] the more pervasive sentiment is a fear that China 'is buying the world'. Japanese investment originally faced this nationalistic hubris. Only the superiority of Japanese products, notably in automobiles, led to the gradual acceptance of Japanese products. It also helped that the acquisitions of the Empire State Building and Universal Pictures by Japanese interests was not viewed as inimical to US security because the long-time enemy was now an economic rival and a security ally. As Peter Nolan points out, the fear of Chinese investment is really overblown given the small share of Chinese FDI as a share of global FDI flows, the small share of the world's stock of FDI and the negligible presence of Chinese firms in global markets.[215] In the same way that the US reconciled to the economic rise of Japan, it needs to accept the arrival of China. The US needs to start thinking about China as a source of private direct foreign investment in the same way that it has accepted Japanese investment in automobile manufacturing.

There is concern about the unavoidable adjustment to China's exports and competition for raw materials, energy and food as well as rivalry in third markets. Apprehension in the US is being spurred by speculation on how 'cheap' products will gut whole sectors of the US economy and warning that internal social, environmental and political problems could lead to instability.[216] Some salivate at the prospects of what a fraction of the Chinese market can mean to the exports of a company or country despite the difficulties of doing business in China.[217] Others bemoan the difficulty of competing with Chinese-made goods because of low wages and unfair practices in particular counterfeiting.[218] These apprehensions are not assuaged by the commitments made on intellectual property rights on accession to the World Trade Organization.[219] Less attention is given to the important emergence of China as a source of advanced technology research and high technology products. By 2005, so-called 'high tech' exports[220] amounted to US$220 billion 'a stunning more than 100-fold increase compared to 1989' and accounted for one-third of total exports. In this regard, China is forging ahead in science education and research. *US News and World Report*, in its October 2015 release of the top universities in the world in engineering, ranked Tsinghua University in Beijing, China as number one in the world ahead of MIT at number two. In the top ten universities, there are four universities from China, four from the US and two from Singapore.[221]

3. China's Role in Global Governance

The economic rise of China and its military prowess have elevated its political power, and there has been a concomitant increase in influence on world affairs. China has been content to gradually employ its increased influence without demanding its formal recognition such as a percentage of the votes in the International Monetary Fund. This approach avoids the aggressive resistance of countries whose influence has declined and who vigorous resist adjustments which give recognition to the new power realities. The global community anticipates an expanded role for China in global governance, and some have welcomed China in the hope that it will assume a greater financial burden in international organizations. This notion of burden sharing extends to the view that China's economic success makes it incumbent on China to help resuscitate the world economy. Recovery from the global economic crisis which erupted in late 2008 has been sluggish and uneven and compounded by the recent deceleration in growth in China. There has been a call for China to play a greater role in stimulating a return to growth in the global economy. The impetus for China to shoulder more of the responsibility for the global economy is also an indication of the internal problems of the EU and the US. The suggestion has been mooted that the EU could look to China to assist it in coping with its debt crisis by buying EU bonds. The US, e.g., Treasury Secretary Geithner, has repeatedly called for China to effect a rebalancing of global demand by reducing its trade surplus with the US. This, it is argued, could be achieved by allowing the exchange rate between the RMB and the US dollar to sharply appreciate. Paul Krugman as an exemplar of this view stating 'China's policy of keeping its currency, the renminbi, undervalued has become a significant drag on global economic recovery.[222] The implicit assumption underpinning this perspective is that China has undervalued its currency in a deliberate and persistent practice of exchange rate manipulation to gain an advantage in trade. This view is almost pandemic in the US.[223] Exchange rate misalignments can affect economic growth among countries, so the issue here is not whether countries are doing this and which countries.[224] Fred Bergsten and Joseph Gagnon comment that 'China is the largest currency aggressor but has not been the major perpetuator of late.'[225]

China is one of the countries with a veto in the United Nations Security Council, and has used it to exert influence in the UN. China has the unique advantage among the countries with a veto in the Security Council of not being a purely capitalist country, and so it can claim empathy with developing countries since it is still in many ways a poor country and a member in a variety of international groups, which exclude the veto-empowered countries such as the Group of 77 and the Non-Aligned Movement. Its role in international affairs has changed rapidly so that it is now a major participant in all global forums. Its influence in the World Trade Organization (WTO) has increased to the point where the core power group in the negotiations comprises the US, the EU, Brazil, India and China. Before China joined the WTO, the inner core of decision-making was the so called 'quad' consisting of the US, EU, Canada and Japan.

China's impact on global governance is likely to be most evident in international financial institutions and, given the resistance to allowing China to exercise more influence in existing institutions, China will lead in the establishment of new multilateral institutions. This is clearly evident in China's reaction to the lack of reform in the International Monetary Fund and World Bank. Global powers always have at their disposal substantial financial resources and, indeed, the dominant superpower has in the past also been the dominant financial power, playing a hegemonic role in the international financial system. This central role in global finance has been termed the role of the 'monetary hegemon'. The country that has the role of monetary hegemon is usually the dominant superpower. Britain executed this role between 1890 and the beginning of the First World War, and the US after 1945 performed this role until the present. As China rises as a global economic power and superpower, it will inevitably have a growing and central role in global finance. The dominance of the monetary hegemon has been central to ensuring the stability and management of the international monetary system. However, in periods when the role is contested and shared, there has been instability such as the gold standard during the inter-war years. This view of the operation of the international monetary system is an extension to international economics the theory of hegemonic stability which is well known in the literature on international relations.

4. China's Role in Development Finance

In September 2015, China lent $5 billion to the financially strapped government of Venezuela,[226] hit by the sharp drop in the price of oil. This is emblematic of the amount and type of bilateral development finance which China is capable and willing to provide. China, in the last decade, has emerged as a major source of development finance through bilateral loans and is likely to continue to do so. However, China is frustrated with not having what it considers an adequate say in the governance of development finance institutions. China has also taken steps to increase its development financing through new regional and multinational development finance institutions and to dispense aid bilaterally rather than through international organizations. The rest of this section discusses the former channel of development finance; the latter is not addressed directly, but it suffices to cite that China has committed $3.1 billion in funding to help developing countries mitigate and adapt to climate change but not through existing United Nations bodies such as the Green Climate Fund.[227]

a. Frustration with International Financial Institutions

Developing countries, especially the more advanced and the BRICS (Brazil, Russia, India, China and South Africa)[228] countries, have never exercised the influence they regard as a just entitlement and a fair representation in decision-making in the Bretton Woods institutions. Their representation in the IMF and World Bank has never been commensurate to their share in the world's population, trade and GDP. Their voting representation on the boards of the IMF and World Bank has never matched their economic standing or their aspirations. China's share of global GDP is 16.1 per cent, yet its share of IMF voting rights is only 6.19 per cent. The fact that a citizen of China and the developing countries has never held the top post in these institutions adds to the sense of exclusion. Since their inception in 1944, the President of the World Bank has always been an American and the Managing Director of the IMF has always been a European, usually French. Christine Lagarde of France was appointed the Managing Director of the IMF. She was the eleventh consecutive European and the fifth citizen of France who collectively have held the post for over 40 years. The US has maintained the unbroken tradition of appointing the President of the World Bank. This is in contrast to the United Nations and the World Trade Organization which have had several non-European heads and no Americans.

This ossified governance structure has progressively reduced the legitimacy of the IMF and World Bank in the developing countries which constitute the overwhelming majority of members. The failure of governance reform is the fundamental cause of all the other problems of the World Bank. Former Inter-American Development Bank (IDB) Executive Vice-president, Nancy Birdsall, concurs with this view when she opines:

> The problems of legitimacy, effectiveness, and relevance at the World Bank is all rooted in the failure of its members to adjust its governance structure to the economic, social and normative changes in the global system over the last fifty years and to globalization itself.[229]

Similarly, Peter B. Kenen argues that a transparent selection process for Managing Director in the IMF would enhance the legitimacy of the institution widely criticized as run by a small group of rich countries.[230]

The expressed commitments made by the G-20 to move to genuinely representative allocation of votes in the governance structure of these institutions and a merit based selection for the leadership positions of has not been implemented. As recently as the 2010 G-20 summit the BRICS were party to the statement: 'We reiterate our commitment to completing an ambitious replenishment for the concessional lending facilities of the MDBs' and 'We reiterate the urgency of promptly concluding the 2008 IMF Quota and Voice Reforms.' The

G-20 declaration continues: 'The reforms are an important step toward a more legitimate, credible and effective IMF, by ensuring that quotas and Executive Board composition are more reflective of new global economic realities and specifically:

> Continuing the dynamic process aimed at enhancing the voice and representation of emerging market and developing countries, including the poorest, through a comprehensive review of the quota formula by January 2013 to better reflect the economic weights; and through completion of the next general review of quotas by January 2014.

The 14th review of the IMF quotas approved in 2010 came into effect in January 2016. Even this reallocation of voting power in the IMF and World Bank will not significantly increase the voice of the vast majority of developing countries.

China and the developing countries have sought to influence the IMF and World Bank through other tangential bodies such as the G-24. The mandate of the Group of 24 (G-24), which was established in 1971, is to coordinate the positions of developing countries on international monetary and development finance issues and to ensure that their interests are adequately represented in negotiations on international monetary matters. Coordination relates particularly to monetary and development issues on the agendas of the International Monetary and Financial Committee (IMFC) and the Development Committee (DC). The objective is to ensure increased participation and more effective representation of the interests and views of developing countries in negotiations on the reform of the international monetary system. In spite of such fora as the G-24 developing countries have resigned themselves to the political underrepresentation in the governance structure of the so-called 'Bretton Woods' institutions. This is particularly irksome to China and the emerging market economies of the Asia although as the authors of a IMF working paper concede the 'pace of change since 2000 has, however, accelerated with the fulcrum of economic weight shifting from the North Atlantic to Asia.'[231] China suffered the indignity of Taiwan having a seat of the IMF broad until 1972 and the PRC was not recognized by the Fund until 1980.

The refusal of the US Congress to approve, much less, countenance reforms, which would give China and developing countries more say at the IMF and World Bank, contributed to China's decision to form the BRICS Development Bank (BDB) and the Asian Infrastructure Investment Bank (AIIB). Nor is this attitude in Congress likely to change in the near future in a way that would countenance a reduction in US influence. Congress has from the inception insisted on US control of the World Bank in the form of a veto. Those calling for reform of the World Bank have had to be mindful of the repeated calls in Congress from conservatives to scale-down US involvement.[232] This has ensured that World Bank policies have been consistent with what the US wanted. Prospects for a change in disposition by Congress are not propitious. As Sarah Babb observes: 'The political dynamics of the Banks' most demanding shareholder are particularly uncongenial to major changes.'[233]

China's role in regional financial institutions has been limited to date, and it is not clear whether China is content with the status quo or intends to increase its role in existing institutions or invest in new institutions. One such case is the IDB. China became the 48th member country of the IDB in October 2008 when it purchased 184 shares, the equivalent of 0.004 per cent of the IDB's ordinary capital, which became available after the breakup of Yugoslavia. On joining, China contributed $350 million to the IDB Group and, in March 2013, The IDB and the People's Bank of China (PBC) established the China Co-financing Fund for Latin America and the Caribbean, the objective of which is to finance public and private sector projects that promote sustainable economic growth. The Fund, the first of its kind established by China and a multilateral development bank is designed to co-finance $500 million public sector loans and $1.5 billion to private sector entities. China's membership in 2008 came after many years of negotiation and provides China its own seat on the Board. With 0.004 per cent of the votes, China along with Korea, has the smallest percentage of total votes of the 48 member countries of the IDB. China has less votes than any of the Caribbean countries while the US the largest shareholder has 30.006 per cent of total votes. It is not clear if China is satisfied with the status quo or whether it wants to increase its share-holding and, if so, how this could be done.

b. A Developing Country Bank

After years of marginal or token change in making the governance of current institutions more representative and transparent, the BRICS have become exasperated and justifiably impatient. Frustration has escalated and the BRICS have shifted from reforming the existing institutions to establishing their own banks. However, the demand for a new type of development bank emanates not only from the immutable governance structure but also originates with concerns among developing countries about the nature of the policies of the IMF and World Bank.[234] Many developing countries have consistently expressed concerns about the approach to economic development which informs the policy recommendations of these institutions. Indeed, it is paradigm which would not have accommodated the economic strategies pursued in China and India. The most prominent criticisms have been of the efficacy of World Bank's structural adjustment policies,[235] the stabilization programmes of the IMF[236] and the Washington Consensus.[237] The critique, including from former members of staff,[238] has prompted calls for change ranging from reform[239] to abandonment of these types of lending[240] to a new Bretton Woods, e.g., Stuart Holland.[241] Attempts at internal reform of the World Bank's mission, approach to economic development and the modalities of its operations have led Johnathan R. Pincus and Jeffrey A. Winters[242] to conclude that the World Bank cannot reform itself by an internal driven process and must be reinvented by an external process of transformation of its mission, concepts of development, operations and governance. Phillips is equally discouraging about the likely efficacy of internal reform after examining the many attempts between 1987 and 2007, concluding that it was 'flawed organizational reform'.[243] Issues of governance, reform and policies of the IMF and World Bank led to ideas of alternative financial institutions.

The idea of a bank for developing countries dates back to the time of the first oil crisis when there was talk of the countries of the Organization of Petroleum Exporting Countries (OPEC) establishing such a bank. The 'South Bank' was an integral aspect of the discussions on south-south financial cooperation which were being given specificity in the early 1980s.[244] The objectives of a South Bank were: (1) lend for development projects, (2) balance of payments financing, (3) provide export credit and (4) finance commodity stabilization mechanisms. The institution would also provide technical advice and financial management. The concept of a South Bank and its feasibility received serious consideration at two meetings of the Group of 77, in March 1982, in Kingston, Jamaica and Ljubljana, Yugoslavia in August 1983. Developing countries looked to the OPEC countries to use such a bank to recycle some of the windfall of Petro-dollars. Algeria, Libya and Venezuela expressed support for such an institution while Kuwait, Qatar, Nigeria, Saudi Arabia, the United Arab Emirates stated that they could not take on any additional financial responsibilities. At the Group of 77's meeting in April 1984, the concept of a South Bank was endorsed but never materialized because 'mobilizing the political support and securing financial commitments from a sufficient large number of developing countries to make this a commercially viable project'[245] was not achieved. The South Commission Report of 1990 recognized this difficulty and while reiterating the need for such an institution called for:

> The scope of the operations of the proposed South Bank needs to be re-examined in the light of a realistic assessment of the volumes and sources of finance available in the South and of the terms on which they could be mobilized.[246]

c. China and the Future of Development Banking

The failure of timely reform of the IMF and the World Bank has motivated the BRICS and China in particular to move towards establishing alternative multilateral financial and development institutions. In tandem with the BRICS, China has pushed for change in global governance institutions. The declaration of the 2014 BRICS summit makes this clear:

> International governance structures designed within a different power configuration show increasingly evident signs of losing legitimacy and effectiveness, as transitional and ad hoc arrangements become increasingly prevalent, often at the expense of multilateralism. We believe the BRICS are an important force for incremental change and reform of current institutions towards more representative and realistic equitable governance, capable of generating more inclusive global growth and fostering a stable, peaceful and prosperous world.[247]

This perspective is evident in the efforts to attain more influence in global development finance institutions through the auspices of the G-20, the discussion to increase the shareholding and votes of the emerging economies of the BRICS and in the initiatives to establish a BRICS Development Bank and an Asian Infrastructure Investment Bank. In contrast to the lack of progress on the reform of existing institutions, the establishment of new institutions such as the BRICS Development Bank which started in December 2015 and the Asian Infrastructure Investment Bank due to start in 2016. The design of the governance arrangements in the new institutions seems to address some of the frustrations over representation.

d. New Development Bank

The BRICS have significantly increased their share of the world economy in the last 20 years. The BRICS countries now have a combined share of world GDP (PPP basis) from 17 per cent in 1992 to 31 per cent. According to the IMF estimates (IMF 2015a), by 2017 the share of the BRICS will exceed that of the G7. At market exchange rates, the share of BRICS in global GDP is about 21 per cent, almost the equivalent of the US with 22 per cent and the European Union with 24 per cent.[248] The share of global GDP of the US, EU and the BRICS are roughly the same, yet their quota shares differ considerably. The quota shares as of the last review in 2008 is the EU with 32.0, the US with 17.7, the BRICS with 11.5 and the rest of the world with 38.8.[249] It is projected that the share of G7 countries in global GDP (PPP) will fall from about 44 per cent in 2000 to an estimated 30 per cent by 2020 while the share of BRICS is forecasted to increase from 19 per cent in 2000 to 33 per cent in 2020.[250]

The BRICS announced the establishment of a new global development bank in July 2015 at the BRICS summit in Russia. The New Development Bank (NDB), formerly referred to as the BRICS Development Bank, will start with $50 billion in capital and $100 billion as a currency reserve fund for liquidity crises. Of the total subscribed capital, $40 billion is callable and $10 billion of paid-in shares will be made over seven years. The group is considering offering a stake of 40–45 per cent to non-Brics countries.[251] The objectives are both to promote economic development and to increase political influence. The BRICS want to free development lending from the approach of Western-dominated institutions, in particular the World Bank and the International Monetary Fund. In reducing the reliance on financial sources subject to the influence of the US and Europe, they increase their degrees of freedom in economic policy. When the new bank lends to developing countries it enhances the international political influence of the BRICS, in particular that of China.

China is the dominant driver in this process for the New Development Bank, and this reflects the fact that China's GDP is larger than the combined GDP of the other four BRICS. China will have to proceed carefully as the economically largest among political equals with a variety of motives lest it be viewed as just another hegemon.[252] In this regard, it is worth recalling that the BRICS met at the initiative of Russia and the first meeting was held in Yekaterinburg, Russia on June 16, 2009 with the impetus coming from the global economic crisis. Subsequently, summits at the level of heads of state have been convened annually in Brasília in 2010; Sanya in 2011 when South Africa joined the group; New Delhi in 2012; Durban in 2013; and Fortaleza in 2014.

The New Development Bank intends to 'mobiliz[e] resources for infrastructure and sustainable development projects in BRICS and other emerging economies and developing countries'.[253] The unmet financing needs for developing countries has been estimated to be between US$1.0 and 1.4 trillion.[254] One of the ongoing needs of emerging and developing countries has been balance of payments financing. The BRICS plan to establish a Contingent Reserve Arrangement (CRA) which will be a central bank coordinated stabilization fund of $100 billion. The objectives of the CRA are to 'forestall short-term liquidity pressures, provide mutual support and further strengthen financial stability'.[255]

e. Asian Infrastructure Investment Bank

In addition to the proposal by the BRICS to establish their own multilateral development bank, China led the creation of an Asian Infrastructure Investment Bank (AIIB), although there is an Asian Development Bank (ADB). Representatives from 31 Asian nations signed an agreement to establish the AIIB. Britain has agreed to be a founding member in spite of discouragement by the US since the idea was broached in 2013. Subsequently, 13 other European countries, including Germany, France and Italy decided to do likewise. Britain's decision was made in spite of the known discomfort it would cause in Japan and the US. British Chancellor of the Exchequer, Geoffrey Osborne, prevailed against the warnings from the Foreign and Commonwealth Office that this action would incur the expressed displeasure of the US.[256] The anticipated economic benefits outweighed the political fallout with Britain's closest ally.[257]Among the consideration is that China has not decided where to locate the European office of the AIIB amid competition among London, Paris, Frankfurt and Luxembourg.[258]

The Beijing led initiative is in part a reaction to the lack of change in global economic governance arrangements. The initiative has been unfairly criticized even before beginning operations for a laxity of prudential standards and a willingness to ignore best practices on environment and labour. The US has decided not to join the AIIB but claims that it welcomes the concept of the AIIB and has denied that it sought to persuade its allies not to join the new institution. However, it simultaneously 'strongly urges it to meet international standards of governance and transparency'.[259] Robert Zoellick, former president of the World Bank, said that shunning China's new infrastructure bank was a mistake by the US.[260] Ben Bernanke, former chairman of the Federal Reserve, blamed Congress for pushing China to form new banks because of its refusal to approved reform of the IMF and World Bank.[261] Ironically, the US should find comfort in knowing that its Western allies who have joined the bank will be insisting on those very standards. There does not seem to be any *prima facie* reason to assume a lack of prudence. Stephanie Griffith-Jones suggest several measures to prevent any question of prudential laxity, including an emphasis on quality of projects; a balance in the loan portfolio between loans to BRICS, emerging, developing and less developed countries; simplicity of financial instruments; having the largest possible paid-in capital; and that founding members should have the highest credit rating and co-financing with reputable lenders.[262]

Japan has declined to join the AIIB, but 46 other countries have joined and 29 will be founding members.[263] Interestingly, Taiwan has decided to participate in the AIIB.[264] The absence of the US and Japan does not deprive the AIIB of irreplaceable funding because China and the emerging market economies have savings and large foreign exchange reserves most of which is invested in developed countries at relatively low interest rates and, hence, could be reallocated to the new institution.

Since their inception, the traditional development banks, in particular the World Bank established in 1944, have been criticized for the conditionality which they require when providing loans to governments of developing countries. Many governments have felt that the World Bank and other development banks have imposed a development model which required abandonment of their own economic development strategy and thereby subverted their national sovereignty. Among the most criticized policies were the structural adjustment programmes which were said to have not achieved their goals[265] and had a strong propensity for recidivism and often led to undermining the political support for the implementing government.[266] Woods concludes that the IMF and World Bank 'have integrated a large number of developing countries into the global economy by requiring governments to open to global trade, investments and capital' at the behest of their most powerful member countries.[267] These criticisms have not been assuaged by the World Bank's claim to comparative knowledge, a pool of high-level experts on development economics and that their policy recommendations are merely pragmatic based on comparative international experience. The World Bank was so sure of its policy that it 'often succumbed to the temptation to prescribe policy reform even in markets where its own analysis had revealed no significant distortion and rode into battle, like Don Quixote with his lance tilted, even in fields where there were no noble deeds to be done.'[268]

Traditional development banks are no longer the largest sovereign lenders to sovereign borrowers. China's bilateral development aid exceeds the total lending of the World Bank. The Brazilian Development Bank, also known as National Bank for Economic and Social Development, has total assets of US$350 billion and dwarfs the US$100 billion held by the IDB. The World Bank and the ADB cannot meet Asia's estimated need for US$8 trillion to fund infrastructure between now and 2020. In addition, private lenders and international financial markets are increasingly providing finance in areas which previously were the exclusive domain of development banks and, although they charge higher interest rates, their terms are more flexible and are not accompanied by any particular development philosophy. Governments in developing countries relish the freedom to chart their own course even when this leads to or contributes to economic debacles.

The political control of decision-making in the World Bank and a US monopoly on the presidency of the World Bank since 1944 is no longer merely irksome; it is not reflective of the state of the world. The board of the World Bank has been dominated by the US and the European countries which are over-represented in the share of voting power. The unwillingness of the existing powers to reallocate voting rights in a more balanced and representative way has continued to stoke the discontentment of developing countries especially China, Brazil and India. Between 1980 and 2015, the G-7's share of world GDP declined from roughly 55 per cent to 35 per cent, meanwhile the share of the BRIC's increased from approximately ten per cent to 30 per cent.[269] More than five years ago, the Group of 20 agreed on new allocation of quotas and voting rights that would reduce US and European dominance at the International Monetary Fund. However, nothing has been implemented because the US Congress has not passed legislation ratifying the proposed changes. This situation is politically untenable and some modification cannot be postponed much longer because the BRICs account for 40 per cent of the world's population; two are permanent members of the UN Security Council and three of them have nuclear weapons. It could be argued the best people to run a 'development bank' would be people from developing countries, in particular China. Although China is not a typical developing country, its economic growth record uniquely positions it to assume this role. Both the BDB and the AIIB have development governance structures in which voting rights are more equitably distributed and the top positions are shared and rotated. For example, for the BDB, the president will be an Indian for the first six years (K.V. Kamath, former chief executive of ICICI Bank, has been appointed president); a Russian will be Chair of Board of Governors; a Brazilian will be Chair of the Board of Directors; and a headquarters will be in Shanghai.[270] No member country will have a veto. The first regional office of the BDB was opened in South Africa.

f. Silk Road Fund

To expand and consolidate international economic links, China has launched a major new financing initiative. In November 2014, Chinese President, Xi Jinping, as part of China's 'One Belt, One Road' strategy, announced the Silk Road Fund (SRF) capitalized at $40 billion. This strategy involves two avenues, the 'Silk Road Economic Belt' and the 'Twenty First Century Maritime Silk Road'. The initiative will aim to promote economic cooperation by providing financing for infrastructure in the countries that were on the original pristine Silk Road route through Asia, the Middle East and Europe. In addition to the AIIB, financing will be available through the SRF which was established in December 2015. The SRF will be capitalized by the State Administration of Foreign Exchange (65 per cent), the China Investment Corporation (15 per cent), China Export Import Bank (15 per cent) and the China Development Bank (five per cent). The 'Twenty First Century Maritime Silk Road' embraces the Asian countries of the Pacific and Indian oceans. In April 2015, the SRF announced its first project, the US$1.65B Karot hydropower project in Pakistan.[271]

g. Will the New Development Banks make a Difference?

The tectonic shifts in the distribution of global economic activity and the consequential reallocation of geopolitical power requires technical, managerial and political change in traditional development banks, starting with the World Bank. If these changes are not forthcoming the traditional development banks will be marginalized and their role diminished. Institutions that do not adapt when the environment in which they operate changes eventually wither away. The new institutions will certainly increase the amount of resources for development finance but will diminish the relative importance of the World Bank. Will developing countries have more influence in a New Development Bank or the Asian Infrastructure Investment Bank (AIIB) dominated by China? Whether there will be a dramatic change in political representation for the majority of developing countries is a question yet to be answered and will depend on the extent to which the BRICS learn from the experience of the existing development banks. If developing countries, i.e., the borrowing member countries do not gain a meaningful influence over decision-making in AIIB and BRICS Development Bank, these new institutions could become the subject of many of the criticisms made about the traditional institutions. Primary among the errors to be corrected is the underrepresented in voting rights vis-à-vis those of non-borrowing countries or those that can both contribute and borrow. The power sharing formulae must remain sufficiently flexible to allow periodic adjustments.

Another egregious problem is the abandonment of meritocracy in staffing with no country being allowed to monopolize the top post. Transparency in recruitment is necessary to ensure that the staff, especially the top positions, are selected on merit and not as spoils to be divided up by political allocation. Staffing should be based on non-discrimination, inclusiveness and diversity among people from member countries as regards ethnicity, gender and university attended. Conditionality must reflect a pragmatic balance of fiduciary probity and goals and policy measures which are client-driven.

5. Cyber-Security

A particularly contentious security issue which has aroused strong feelings in the US is cyber-security with the US accusing China of operating a massive and systemic programme of cyber-espionage encompassing government and private computer and information systems. The US government specifically accuses the Chinese of targeting private economic data and sensitive national security information, including defence contractors. 'Both the U.S. Department of Defense and the Chinese People's Liberation Army (PLA) view cyberspace as a new domain of conflict, and they eye each other warily.'[272] Industrial espionage to acquire illegally leading-edge technology is not new. Indeed, those countries that complain about the theft of technology may very well have been guilty of the same crime at some stage. Industrial espionage is motivated by the desire of firms and governments to acquire the latest technology. Hajoon Chang has argued that illegal acquisition of the latest technology has always been practised by countries that find themselves at a competitive disadvantage, including some now developed countries at an earlier stage of their development.[273] Interestingly, when China was ahead in technology they encountered technological predators, including campaigns designed and executed by foreign governments. For example, the acquisition of tea plants from China by the British to start the tea industry in India was by government-backed subterfuge.[274]

China is regarded as the single greatest risk to the security of American military and commercial technologies. The preoccupation with China as an enemy should not divert attention from the fact cyber-security is a pandemic in which hackers have broken into the computer systems of the US Army, Pentagon, Federal Reserve, NASA and the US Missile Defense Agency.[275] The Obama administration has repeatedly and explicitly accused China's military of mounting cyber-attacks on American government computer systems and defence contractors.[276] The US is concerned about China's cyberwarfare capabilities which involve collecting intelligence and penetrating national security computer networks. These intrusions are aimed at 'exfiltrating' information that could be used to disrupt network-based logistics, communications, and commercial activities.[277] China has emphatically denied these allegations. The US and China have agreed to hold regular talks on cyber-security issues as part of the Strategic and Economic Dialogue in the quest for what has been aptly called 'cyber détente'.[278] The seventh joint meeting of the US–China Strategic and Economic Dialogue was held in Washington, DC, June 23–24, 2015. China–US cooperation on cyber security would be an international public good. All nations want to protect their networks from cyber-attack but many are finding it difficult to do so effectively because the global cyber landscape is changing rapidly and is increasingly more sophisticated and complex. All of this is made more difficult by the number and sophistication of individual hackers disrupting both private and government computer systems as was revealed when private hackers forced Fiat Chrysler to recall 1.4 million vehicles.[279] The US is in the process of preparing sanctions against individual Chinese hackers to try to reduce cyber theft of technology and commercial information.[280] The prospects of meaningful cooperation are slim because as Lieberthal and Singer point out:

> There is no issue that has risen so quickly and generated so much friction as cybersecurity. Distrust of each other's actions in the cyber realm is growing and starting to generate deeply negative assessments of each country's long term strategic intentions.[281]

Cyber-security is new, and its complexity is not adequately appreciated by many poorer countries that do not have the technical and human capacity to protect themselves. Among those countries struggling with pervasiveness and complexity of cyber security are those in the Caribbean.[282]

6. Mega-Trans-Regional Trade Agreements

The Transatlantic Trade and Investment Partnership (TTIP), which is being negotiated between the EU and the US, is intended to maintain and expand trade between the two already highly integrated economic blocs. A study by the Centre for Economic Policy Research (CEPR) projects substantial economic gains from such an agreement.[283] These estimates have been criticized in the US by those claiming the very opposite.[284] If the latter commentary is correct about minimal economic gains to be derived then it suggests that there are geopolitical motives and considerations, and these could include China's growing share of world trade and initiatives to form trade groups in Asia which exclude the US. China has been pressing vigorously to accelerate the formation of the Free Trade Area of the Asia-Pacific (FTAAP) between itself and Asian countries but not including the US. In February 2016, the US signed the Trans-Pacific Partnership (TPP) between itself, Canada, Mexico, Chile, Peru, Japan, Singapore, Brunei, Vietnam, Malaysia, Australia and New Zealand. Together, the member countries have a combined annual GDP of $28 trillion which represents roughly 40 per cent of global GDP and one-third of world trade. These mega trans-regional trade agreements could affect the current pattern of multilateral trade and could divide Latin America into a Pacific side and an Atlantic side and marginalize some countries and regions, including the Caribbean. This mega-trans-regional agreements may not seriously affect the Caribbean countries which have specialized trade arrangements such as Caribbean Basin Economic Recovery Act provided by the US, the Caribbean–Canada Trade Agreement with Canada and the CARIFORUM–EU Economic Partnership Agreement with the European Union.[285]

PART III
INTERNATIONAL REACTIONS AND IMPLICATIONS

The global re-dimensioning of China and the emerging global configuration, while primarily affected by China and the US, is influenced by the reactions of the rest of the world, and all of this has implications for the entire world. The following discussion is conducted in the context of regions starting with Asia.

ASIA

China will have a multidimensional role in Asia, and some aspects of this relationship are likely to impact intra-Asian tensions. In economic terms, China will be the core, both in size and dynamism of Asia, the region that is likely to be the centre of gravity of the world economy in the immediate future. China which has been a magnet for foreign direct investment will become an important source of direct foreign investment for the region, particularly as it moves up the manufacturing value chain as a consequence of rising wages, increased technological capacity and industrial sophistication. Concomitantly, China will become more of an import market for goods from less expensive Asian countries. The tensions on the political and diplomatic fronts may be more problematic to handle as China's military and naval power will be a source of concern to many countries. These concerns arouse fears of China's control of sea lanes and resentment of Chinese dominance which have their roots in a reservoir of conflict and pain which in some cases is centuries old. China also has lingering feelings of hurt particularly towards the Japanese. The tensions are epitomized by the clash over the Senkaku Islands in the East China Sea. This group of minute, uninhabited islands are of little strategic value and without any known resources, although there is always the possibility of there being oil or gas in the offshore waters. Protests have erupted or been organized in

China, ignited by the recent purchase by the government of Japan of the islands from their private owners. China has also been building or enlarging an island in the South China Sea by enlarging submerged reefs. The Philippines has protested this action as a provocative, unilateral action of a disputed area. The US has called for an immediate and lasting halt to reclamation works by all claimants in disputed waters in the South China Sea.

a. Taiwan

It is enigmatic, and some might say irrational that two nuclear superpowers would quarrel for over half of a century over an island as small as Taiwan.[286] For China, the reincorporation of Taiwan represents the century's-old preoccupation with 'unity' and the final aspect of overcoming the Century of Humiliation. The Chinese people, it is reported, feel even more strongly than the Chinese state[287] that the reincorporation of Taiwan is non-negotiable. China has stated repeatedly that it is prepared to go to war to prevent Taiwan's political independence, and so the island exists in a sort of juridical limbo. For the US, the island of Taiwan has lost significance as a strategic military location, and it seems to be an anachronism from which the US feels it cannot resile without losing credibility as a defence partner. The US became seriously engaged with Taiwan when the Korean War started, and China's support for North Korea caused the US elevated the status of China as a Cold War enemy. Taiwan remained an obstacle to US–China relations and the tension only began to ease when Richard Nixon made his historic visit to China. Macmillan suggests that the Americans were prepared to make concessions on Taiwan and 'cut back their support for it' in exchange for Chinese pressure on North Korea to negotiate 'in good faith'.[288]

The growth of economic ties between Taiwan and China, less virulent nationalism in Taiwan and a long-term perspective in Beijing have ameliorated the tensions that could ignite a military conflict with serious implications for US–China relations.[289] As Richard C. Bush and Michael E. O'Hanlon point out US–China military conflict is neither impossible nor inevitable.[290] Because of areas of conflict and different points of view on how to handle such issues, US policy towards China has been marked by ambiguities. David E. Sanger explains that this dilemma continues because 'Washington has been engaged in a circular debate over whether Beijing is strategic partner or strategic competitor, and has been struggling to develop a strategy that recognizes the obvious fact that it is both.'[291] While the US–China relationship can withstand differences, Taiwan is a particular sensitivity. Former US Secretary of State, Hillary Clinton, explained the decision as: 'Everyone is aware of China as a rising power in the 21st century. But people want to see the United States as fully engaged in Asia, so that as China rises the United States is there as a force for peace.'[292] The decision of the US to sell $5.9 billion worth of arms to Taiwan has irked China, which has expressed its displeasure.[293] The Obama administration has subtly softened its stance on this issue in September 2011 when it opted not to sell Taiwan 66 F-16 fighter jets.[294]

The relationship between China and Taiwan is an extremely complex dialectic which is increasingly being influenced by their increasing economic ties. Daniel H. Rosen and Zhi Wang explain:

> In terms of trade flows, direct investment and portfolio investment and flows of people, cross-strait economic fundamentals are changing profoundly every day. In terms of Taiwan's export dependence on China, and final consumption in China as a share of these exports, the fundamentals are changing as well. The gap in technological capabilities between Taiwan and China is narrowing rapidly. Public sentiment regarding the importance of economic interests and the importance of transcending the past tensions also demonstrate significant changes.[295]

Relations between China and Taiwan have become less antagonistic consequent on their increasing economic integration, which has been driven by market forces and facilitated by policy changes in China.[296] During the period 1991–2008, there were 37,000 investment projects worth an estimated $75.6 billion.[297] The importance of the economic ties has been a consideration influencing less combative approaches by their respective leaderships. An unwritten informal truce has existed between Beijing and Taipei since 2008 when Ma Ying-Jeou was elected president of Taiwan. Both governments now refrain from inducing countries to switch their diplomatic allegiances. China and Taiwan have signed 18 cooperation agreements on economic, cultural and functional issues. These developments may reduce the potential for conflict. There will be repercussions for the US, the rest of Asia, and indeed the world, in military, economic and diplomatic terms.

If politics is the art of the possible then so is international diplomacy. A diplomatic solution to the Taiwan problem should not be ruled out. So many examples suggest that anything is possible. For example, all the European combatants from the Second World War are all in the EU; the US and Vietnam have trade and diplomatic relations. The issue of Taiwan which is flashpoint that Chinese distrust and tension with the US could be resolved if as Glaser[298] proposes a 'Grand Bargain' on security in Asia could be struck between Washington and Beijing. This would involve the US giving up its commitment to defend Taiwan on the assurance that China would not challenge the US security role in Asia, and that it would desist from expansionism in the South China Sea, perhaps accepting international control of the disputed territories. This has the downside of raising the question of the credibility of the US defence shield for allies in Asia, many of whom have genuine apprehensions about China's intentions.

b. India

The rise of India in the world economy and world affairs will bring it into a global scene in which China is a superpower. The relationship between these two Asian economic powers which have experienced military and political flashpoints[299] will impact the global economy and the process of globalization[300] with profound implications for Asia and the US.[301] In regard to economic competition, Anil K. Gupta and Haiyan Wang suggest that it is more useful to think of China and India not as China or India.[302] One projection sees China and India together accounting for 45 per cent of world GDP by 2050, up from six per cent in 2004. Meanwhile the US and Europe will decline from 62 per cent to 41 per cent.[303] Both are ancient civilizations with a strong awareness of their greatness, and this gives them what Frankel calls 'overlapping claims to greatness' and 'a historic destiny of their own nations to achieve great-power status'.[304] India acquired nuclear weapons capabilities because of security concerns, and its enduring aspiration to be a major power for which nuclear capability is regarded as an essential prerequisite.[305]

India is so large and integrating with the world at such a rapid rate that some observers sense a new confidence and a growing awareness that developments in India will have a global impact.[306] Many in India are convinced that it is India's destiny to become a superpower, and this arises from its size, but also because it is one of the world's ancient civilizations of importance to mankind's history akin to China, Egypt and Greece. India's rise to the status of a superpower would be a restoration of a position previously held. Sanjeev Sanyal explains this current thinking regarding India as being in the 'position of pre-eminent economic and cultural world power till around the eleventh century. After this, its relative position steadily declined'. India's share of world GDP fell from 33 per cent in AD1 to 29 per cent in AD 1000 to 16 per cent in 1820 to four per cent in 1947, and to three per cent in 1991.[307] Meanwhile, the share accounted for by China, Europe and later the US surpassed that of India. From its nadir in the 1990s, India's relative position has improved, but its progress has been overshadowed by the spectacular rise of China.

The rise of China as a global power is already a reality, but India is seen as rising with the size and potential to be a significant power but on the slow track with no certainty of fulfilling the promise. From the early 1990s, a growing number of observers have been touting India as one of the major powers in what they anticipate will be a multi-polar world in the twenty-first century. Henry Kissinger[308] saw India as one of six powers and Samuel P. Huntington[309] declares them to be one of eight core civilizations. Despite the possibility of major power status, its attainment is not automatic because several problems plague India. For many observers, India is encumbered with numerous social, ethnic and demographic impediments of indigenous origin, mass poverty and mired in stifling tradition.[310]

Parang Khanna states definitively that India will not become a superpower because a myriad of problems outweigh its large size.[311] Much has changed in India in recent decades, including India's perception of itself especially of its potential and future, a future unfettered by the fatalism of the past. V.S. Naipaul examined the perplexing complexity of India and dismissed the possibility of progress. In the 1960s, he referred to India as 'an area of dark',[312] in the 1970s he dismissed Indian society as a 'wounded civilization'[313] and in the 1990s he worried that it was doomed by 'a million mutinies'.[314] For many, India remains an enigma but so important that engagement is unavoidable. Part of the difficulty with formulating an appropriate policy towards India is its enormous size, economic inequity, cultural diversity, geographic variety, ethnic hostilities, caste rigidities and religious tensions.

Cognizant of its size and potential some have gone as far as predicting that India will be the next economic superpower.[315] At the other extreme, India's former Trade Minister, Kamal Nath,[316] trumpets an encouraging vision for the world's largest democracy as a society of people whose unifying commonalty is their innate industrious, innovation character. He is keenly aware of the comparative progress and prospects of China and India and believes that India's democracy (the world's largest) will help to differentiate the two giants. Some like Yasheng Huang[317]and Daniel Lak[318] go even further to argue that India's democratic institutions will in the long-term provide an advantage over China in economic growth. Such a judgment seems more hortatory than realistic. Indeed, George Perkovich is closer to the reality when he states: 'India's representative institutions often preserve rough order by cancelling out compensating factional interests, resulting in lowest common denominator policies that deprive the nation of clear direction.'[319]

Without denying the immense complexity of India, the co-founder of Infosys, Nandan Nilekani, poses an insightful and positive outlook centred on the dynamic of information technology and education in a practising democracy.[320] India accounts for 65 per cent of the global market in offshore information technology and 45 per cent of the world market in information-technology-enabled services.[321] Indian multinational corporations are now global players in information technology,[322] pharmaceuticals and steel. Mittal is the largest steel producer in the world, operating in over 60 companies. The Reliance Group is one of the world's largest manufacturers of textiles. These were large producers in a gigantic domestic market which was a platform from which to go global. More recently, Indian companies have started to acquire global brands such as Jaguar and Land Rover by the TATA Group. Tetley Tea which is emblematic of the British way of life is now Indian owned, ironic since the product has been based on tea leaves from India and other Asian countries.

India's most promising growth prospects may be in services rather than agriculture or manufacturing. The Bangalore hub of IT demonstrates India's large pool of inexpensive semi-skilled and highly skilled workers, technicians and managers. Infosys has been emblematic of the rapid success of Indian firms in an industry that employs 1.3 million and contributes almost five per cent of GDP.[323] Research and development have a bright future in India where 63 of the Fortune 500 companies already have R&D facilities in India.[324] There are enormous opportunities for the export of health services, for example, the cost of coronary by-pass surgery in India is five per cent of the cost in developed countries and a liver transplant in India costs one-tenth of that in the US.[325] A magnetic resonance imaging (MRI) is US$60 in India compared to US$700 in New York.[326] Indian culture has always had a presence in the culture of mankind, and its philosophies and spiritual mystique continue to intrigue people all over the world. Cultural industries have a bright future, especially film, which is beginning to spread outside of India and Indians overseas to general audiences as is evident when Bollywood gained new respectability when 'Slum Dog Millionaire' won an Oscar for best picture.

Despite having global corporations, much of the private sector is characterized by low productivity, low skill, and low-wage labour and rudimentary technology. The need to improve international competitiveness is reflected in the fact that India's share of world trade in goods is one per cent and services is 1.5 per cent. Comparatively, inexpensive labour will sustain some exports, but international competitiveness has to be raised by investments in infrastructure, health and education (35 per cent illiteracy). Ironically, despite its minute percentage of world trade, India has been able, along with Brazil, to establish themselves as developing country lead representatives in the negotiations in the World Trade Organization.

India's emergence as an economic giant albeit with mass poverty holds gigantic economic potential some of which is evident in the economic growth following the replacement of dirigiste planning by a progressive liberalization of the market. It has gradually but finally developed nuclear weapons and is now seen as a nuclear power. It is the world's second most populous country and boasts of being the world's largest democracy, yet it is not accorded the status of a world power by the global community. It feels a keen sense of rivalry with China, a state of mind shaped by the perpetual comparison with China. This keen sense of rivalry is not shared by China even after India achieved nuclear weapons capability.[327] India is caught up in the ongoing and escalating discourse of China as a measuring stick, political rival and an unavoidable competitor, according to Meredith in the simultaneous rise of *The Elephant and the Dragon: India is Frantically Racing to Catch up to China.*[328] In this regard, India is encouraged by South Korea, Japan and Taiwan looking for a counterweight to China in the Asian sphere. The *Economist* dismisses such a role because of India's integration with Asia is so limited that its place in Asia is 'primarily cartographic'.[329]

There is a common practice in the West of comparing China and India because they are ancient civilizations and are the two most populous countries in the world. This habit of comparing the two countries has also taken hold of the imagination of some in both countries but much more so in India, which is tired of hearing how far ahead China is in economic size and rate of economic growth. It has become irksome, and generated a sense of rivalry in which Indians measure their progress by comparison with China. The notion of rivalry is constantly fed by sources in the West, in particular it makes good copy in the Western press.[330] Third World countries have to be sensitive to this jealousy,[331] for example, President Obama's visit to China in late 2009 was followed within ten days by receiving the Prime Minister of India at the first state visit of the Obama administration. China-watching is becoming a national preoccupation, and the second place feeling is fed by what China has that India lacks. Envy flows from China's seat on the UN Security Council, hosting the Olympics, being ahead in space exploration and a myriad of other yardsticks.

The US has never regarded India as a military or economic threat in the way that it has viewed China during the Cold War era and even into the present period.[332] How the US treats India is integrally related to an overall Asian policy which was articulated by Henry Kissinger as:

> America's national interests in Asia is to prevent the domination of the continent by a single power, especially an adversarial one; to enlist the contribution of Asian nations to overall global prosperity; and to mitigate intra-Asian conflicts.[333]

The US focused its attention on India because of its border disputes with China and Pakistan[334] which has resulted in military clashes. Concern increased when India developed nuclear weapons, raising the spectre of a nuclear conflagration with Pakistan and China. Bill Emmott makes the point that 'India has long been hypersensitive about Chinese support for their archenemy, Pakistan, which included the supply of conventional arms and nuclear technical assistance.'[335]

US policy towards both China and India has attempted to use India to counterbalance in Asia since Japan has not resumed its aspirations of playing the role of major power. Edward Luce has pointed to Washington's tangible support for India to argue that this is designed to 'accelerate its nuclear program and counterbalance that of China.[336] While this may be the thrust of US policy, the relationship is much more complex and increasingly involves other considerations, both economic and political.[337]

India is not seen in the US as an economic menace notwithstanding the outsourcing[338] of information technology, research and services jobs. The loss of jobs in manufacturing due to imports from China instigates worry and resentment which is whipped into hysteria by alarmist predictions of a Chinese wipe-out of employment in the US economy. Typical of this palpable fear is Lou Dobbs who rattles off statements like: 'Employment in the U.S. auto industry has dropped by 200,000 jobs over the past four years. During that same time imports of Chinese auto parts have doubled.'[339]

President Obama visited India in November, 2010 and while there he announced US support for India's ambition for a seat on the Security Council of the United Nations.[340] This was motivated by the prospects of exports to the vast and growing Indian market and shoring up a counterweight to China in Asian and world affairs. There is also a growing awareness of the emergence of India but some have overreacted, for example, Robert Kaplan who now sees the Indian Ocean as the crucial arena for the future of US security.[341]

c. Japan

While longing for the respect, especially in Asia, which it had before the Second World War, Japan has not asserted itself in a prominent international role, and has not exerted a decisive influence in Asia, leaving the security role to the US. In spite of this ceding of the security responsibility, Japan is far less subject to US influence than it was immediately after its defeat in 1945 as was appositely expressed in the popular phrase 'the Japan that can say no'.[342] By the 1980s, Japan's economic growth and industrialization seemed destined to make Japan an economic superpower even if not a political and military global power. The decade of the 1980s marked a qualitative change in Japan–US relations with growing concern that Japan's economic prowess was a threat to US dominance with the large trade deficit and the increasing Japanese direct foreign investment in the US being cited. There was much discussion of what Japan's new global role would be.[343] However, the Japanese 'economic miracle' ground to a virtual standstill afflicted by problems in the financial and banking sectors. An aging and increasingly vulnerable Japan[344] has preferred to concentrate instead on its economic well-being by addressing several persistent policy issues.[345] Its political influence, even in Asia, has declined as a consequence of the waning of its economic supremacy in Asia,[346] although its relations with China and India will influence the development of Asia.[347]

Japan has reacted cautiously to the rise of China, concerned more about its economic implications than the political and security aspects of China's new ascendancy. China is now Japan's largest trading partner and this has helped to ameliorate a long history of Japanese colonialism and military intervention dating back to the sixteenth century. The Japanese military invasions of 1894–95, 1931 and 1937 and the Nanjing Massacre have not disappeared entirely from memory. Japan extracted reparations from China after the First Sino–Japanese War of 1894–95. While this history is a factor, pride more than the possibility of undersea oil deposits fuels the dispute with China over the Senkaku Islands, a group of tiny uninhabited islands of little strategic value in the East China Sea.[348] The sentiments of hostility have a long history between these two intensively proud ancient civilizations, and hence the demonstrations in both countries emanate from a reservoir of pain and resentment. Chalmers Johnson suggests that during the Second World War the Japanese were responsible for the death of approximately 23 million Chinese throughout East Asia.[349] The feelings of hostility continue in China because some feel Japan has not sufficiently acknowledged the 1937 Nanjing massacre and the atrocities committed during the Second World War. These feelings were not assuaged by an apology from Japan's prime minister 50 years after the end of the war. Chinese protesters were allowed to attack Japanese businesses and vandalize Japanese-made cars by a government not known for its tolerance of civil unrest. In addition, to the history, Beijing has never been comfortable with the Treaty of Mutual Cooperation and Security between the US and Japan signed in 1960 because it legitimizes US involvement in Asia.

Apart from the historical animosities, some intensifying tensions have arisen with China and various claimants throughout East Asia and Southeast Asia over its approach to maritime issues and claims. While it is primarily an intra-Asian conflict, Japan is looking to keep the US engaged in maintaining the status quo in security in the region on the basis that 30 per cent of world trade passes through Asian sea lanes. Prime Minister Abe of Japan, speaking in Washington, DC after meeting President Obama in October 2015, spelt this out:

> We (U.S. and Japan) are united in our resoluteness in opposing unilateral attempts to change the status quo in whatever form. Any dispute should be resolved peacefully based on international law and not through coercion or intimidation. Japan welcomes the United States policy of global rebalancing, which emphasizes the Asia Pacific.[350]

The relationship of the US with China, Japan and indeed Asia is one of ambiguity. The US values Asian allies in an alliance against China, but tempers these relationships with a wariness of Asian companies penetrating the US market. A virulent strain of nationalist xenophobia is evident in the actions of the US government to prevent a Chinese firm's investment in a controlling interest in a US firm on the specious basis of national security. This is similar to the hostility in the US to the purchase of the Empire State building by Japanese investors. An important financial nexus exists between China, Japan and Asia and the US. These countries are vital in funding the fiscal deficit of the US government. The facts are startling given that in 2009 the US fiscal deficit climbed to 11.2 per cent of GDP,[351] an all-time high for peacetime, and China is the largest creditor holding almost 25 per cent of US Treasury securities.[352] By June 2015, China held $1271.2 billion followed by Japan's holdings of $1,197.1 billion, but more interesting is that Hong

Table 1.2: Major Foreign Holders of Treasury Securities 2015 ($ Billions)

COUNTRY	AMOUNT	ASIA'S AMOUNT
All Countries	6175.2	
China	1,271.2	1,271.2
Japan	1197.1	2.468.3
Hong Kong	181.3	2.649.6
Taiwan	175.6	2.825.2
India	117.0	2.932.2
Singapore	113.7	3.045.9
Korea	76.7	3,122.6
Thailand	31.4	3154.0
Vietnam	13.6	3167.6

Source: Department of the Treasury/Federal Reserve Board, August 17, 2015.

Major Foreign Holders of Treasury Securities – United States Department of the Treasury www.treasury.gov/.../mfh.txt Accessed 10 September 2015.

Kong and Taiwan are the next largest holders with $181.3 billion and $175.6 billion respectively. Asia as a whole has a total of over 50 per cent of foreign holdings of US Treasury securities, see table 1.2. Some view this situation as the interdependence to be expected in a globalized financial system. However, at the other end of the opinion spectrum, some see a crippling dependence, which emasculates US economic, diplomatic and security policies. It is believed that China could destabilize the US dollar if it chose to reduce its investment in US government securities whereas Japanese holdings are seen as stabilizing and do not prompt anxiety. A more realistic perspective is one that recognizes that a stable US dollar and the store of value function of US government paper are in the interest of all parties, including China.

It is not always possible to discern a consistent Japanese policy regarding China as contending views in Japan abound about policy towards China. Still, all approach to this issue start with balancing relations with China and the US, taking careful cognizance of the complex ever-evolving dialectics between China and the US. This template is best understood as a triangle of China–Japan, China–US and US–Japan. Which of the different views on how to harmonize these three relationships informs Japan's policy depends on preferences of those in political power. This task is made difficult if we accept Narushige Michshita and Richard J. Samuels[353] typology of four distinct schools of thought.

d. North Korea–South Korea

The US regards South Korea as the frontline of defence against the spread of communism in Asia and the first line of defence against Soviet and Chinese expansion communism. In the immediate aftermath of the Second World War, following the takeover of Eastern Europe by the Soviet Union and at the height of the Cold War, the US deployed its military, air force and navy to defend South Korea in 1950 from an invasion by the communist North Korea. Subsequent to the conclusion of the Korean War in 1953, the Republic of Korea and the US formed a military alliance and, up to the present, the US maintained a substantial military presence. Cross-border skirmishes at the 38th Parallel and in the adjacent coastal waters are frequently recurring events. South Korea, through a process of industrialization,[354] had by the 1970s become one of the so called four 'Asian Tigers' and one of the 'Newly Industrialized Countries', and the US is its most important trading partner. South Korea is no longer a developing country, but is a high-income country in sharp contrast to the reclusive communist North Korea.

South Korea's economic transformation long preceded the beginning of China's economic progress, and its brands are able to compete in the global marketplace with products from China. The economic coexistence and competition is enmeshed in a tense diplomatic and political stand-off because of a long history riven by wars, atrocities and invasions. The relationship for the foreseeable future will only be cordial. The more important relationship for South Korea is with the US because it relies on the US as a guarantor of its security and a bastion against the unabashed assertiveness of China across the Pacific region.

Countries that have produced and can deliver a nuclear bomb or have the capacity to do so are members of the world's most exclusive club. The governments who constitute extant membership of the 'Club' agree on two principles. First, there must be no more members. Second, no member should use the nuclear bombs it possesses, but confine themselves to threatening to use them against non-members, i.e., those who cannot retaliate in kind. For the most part, use of nuclear weapons is an empty threat because whether or not there is retaliation we could all be dead either immediately or slowly. Detonating a nuclear device anywhere in the world would be catastrophic for mankind, and it does not matter who strikes first. We are all dead in the end. Therefore, nuclear states have no means of preventing those countries without the bomb from doing anything they want, including developing the capacity to construct and deploy nuclear weapons. It is no fear of opprobrium by the international community which inhibits the use of nuclear weapons but the certainty of self-inflicted wounds. Not even the largest and most populous countries could be assured of survival. Mao's old dictum that no matter what, some Chinese will survive is no comfort.

The exclusive club started in 1945 when the US dropped nuclear bombs on Hiroshima and Nagasaki. Thereafter, the sole nuclear power, the US with the enigmatic conflation of unabashed arrogance and naïveté appointed itself to the role of maintaining world peace. First the Soviet Union, then China and then some European countries that were former world powers refused this assurance. Possession of nuclear weapons was the tangible and emblematic basis for the status of world power. Proliferation set in because if your enemy has nuclear power, then so should you to deter aggression as in the case of India and Pakistan. Others sought protection by allowing their countries to be used as a base for nuclear weapons from one of the world powers.

The benefits of having nuclear weapons go beyond improved security and national hubris. When a government can make a credible threat to use its deadly capacity, it can induce other governments or the international community to provide food aid, embargoed technology and development assistance. North Korea, one of the poorest countries in the world, embarrassed by the economic development of ethnic and geographic neighbour, South Korea, has demonstrated the diabolical calculus of a rogue state intent on extortion.

North Korea's strategy at first glance is an enigma, but it cannot be discounted that the ruling regime may, in fact, feel genuine fear of a US attack, being overthrown by a popular upheaval by an impoverished and discontented populace or military coup from an oversized military. The regime has consistently expressed its apprehension about US hostility, and US covert support for regime change. This is an important driver of North Korea's foreign policy. There is an urgent need to garner economic assistance, including food aid. The failed, embattled and isolated cabal has demonstrated that it is prepared to resort to 'nuclear extortion'. Both the US and China will want to devise some means of limiting the proliferation of nuclear weapons and weapons technology, especially to irresponsible governments such as North Korea's. However, this cannot be done by telling countries that aspire to own nuclear weapons that they are forbidden. Several economically deprived countries that hope to own nuclear weapons, pose a danger to the international community; therefore, the wiser course of action is for global powers to engage them through trade and development aid. This would best be accomplished through a common approach by the US and China rather than the current divergence. North Korea's dependence on trade with China and the latter's investment in that country could lead to a policy of engagement which is in contrast to the US policy of imposition and enforcement of sanctions.

EUROPE

The leading countries of Western Europe were world powers with empires spread across the globe throughout the eighteenth and nineteenth centuries, and the first half of the twentieth century. Two World Wars in the first 50 years of the twentieth century weakened these countries, and they were overtaken as global hegemons by the US following the devastation of the Second World War. Their global influence has gradually but steadily declined in the last half of the last century and today the EU is mired in existential crisis. The crisis is both real and ideational, with the former aspect being evident in internal problems due to the limitations in the design of the political arrangements for integration, the resurgence of nationalism and the expansion of the membership. The crisis has been intensified by exogenous events most notably the massive migration of people fleeing across the Mediterranean Sea from the abject poverty of Northern Africa and those fleeing the civil war in Syria. The global economic crisis has taken its toll on the economies of the EU collectively and individually. The EU's formal integration and economic interdependence has been both an asset and a disadvantage. The struggle to prevent financial implosion and political instability in the throes of an ever deepening quagmire of debt and the associated efforts to preserve the Euro from disintegration outline the problem.[355] The EU is beset by a raft of internal problems which predated but have not been resolved by the integration process and its implementation problems such as immigration, the attachment to the nation state and different levels of economic development. The state of the EU prompted Walter Laqueur to speak of the end of the European dream and to contemplate the decline of a continent.[356] The notion of Europe as a community and a cultural sphere is threatened by divided ethnic, religious and cultural loyalties. Christopher Caldwell points to the projection that by the middle of the century, 30 per cent of the population of most European countries will be foreign-born, and with a large share being Muslim.[357] This outlook is in sharp contrast to a decade earlier when there were those who predicted Europe to be the next superpower and a rival to the US.[358]

In this context, the EU and the leading countries of Britain, France and Germany aspire to continue a traditional role which is now disproportionate to their economic and military weight in the world. The aspiration is both for reasons of pride and to maintain a strategic presence in the world, so the EU and Britain will resist the diminution of their global influence as long as possible. Europeans realize the rise of China and the potential value of cooperation. The willingness of Britain, France and Germany to participate in the Asian Infrastructure Investment Bank, in spite of strenuous US efforts to dissuade them, is emblematic of their approach to relations with China.

The rise of China does not seem to be a major preoccupation of the foreign policy agenda of the EU member states and certainly not to the extent to which it is a magnate for US apprehensions about its own global role and economic competitiveness. This perhaps reflects the fact that the EU's economic problems are more of an internal origin than related to trade with China, the fact that Europe long ago relinquished ambitions for a role in Asia and the Pacific. China and the EU have been engaged in a well-established series of meetings at a variety of technical and political levels. The EU–China Strategic 2020 Agenda for Cooperation agreed on at the EU–China Summit in 2013, is the arching document guiding the goals and modalities of the interactions. For example, the 17th annual EU–China summit was held on June 29, 2015.

The debt crisis in Greece and the Greek government's approach to economic management could have a harmful effect on the Euro and has placed internal economic issues at the top of the agenda of the EU. However, the issues raised go far beyond economics of adjustment to an existential crisis. A default and exit from the Euro Currency Union aka 'Grexit' was not likely to trigger a contagion that would destroy the Euro or cripple the banks in the way that it would less than five years ago when the magnitude of Greece's debt crisis became known. The banks have been making provisions, and the European Central Bank and national governments have taken action to protect the European banking system. The Euro would probably have withstood the exit of Greece if that eventuality had materialized, but would the unity of EU have remained intact? Could the belief in the validity of the vision of the EU survive a Greek meltdown? By agreeing to several bailout packages for Greece, a small country of no particular strategic importance, the EU salvaged not only that country but the very credibility of the EU. Without the rescue package albeit with its draconian conditionality and continued austerity, Greece could have experienced escalation of capital flight, the haemorrhage of technical and managerial expertise, a thriving foreign exchange 'black market' and the curtailment of international trade credit. A Greek default would create a temporary hiatus in lending to emerging markets and driven up rates of interest for borrowing in international capital markets. If Greece successfully meets the conditions, it will be a test case raising questions about the nature, extent and pace of austerity as a template for economic adjustment, fuelling a debate which has already begun.[359]

LATIN AMERICA

China–Latin America trade has grown rapidly in the last decade.[360] The value of merchandise trade between China and Latin America grew at an average rate of 27 per cent per annum during 2000–13,[361] leading to a 22-fold increase.[362] In that period, the value of trade increased from $10 billion to $257 billion, an increase of almost 2,500 per cent.[363] By 2014, China became the third largest export market for Latin America behind the US and the EU. China is the region's second largest source of imports following the US.[364] The pattern of trade in Latin America is to export primary products, mainly agricultural products and energy, while importing manufactured goods. In 2013, commodities accounted for 73 per cent of exports to China.[365] Imports from China have outstripped exports and hence most Latin American countries have a growing trade deficit with China except Brazil, Chile and Venezuela.[366] China has become the biggest export destination for Brazil, Chile and Peru and the second largest for Argentina, Uruguay and Venezuela. China is the largest source of imports for Panama and Paraguay and the second biggest supplier for nine other Latin American countries.[367] In spite of the growth of trade with China, the US is still the largest export market for Latin America, absorbing one-third to three-fourths of exports from Colombia (37 per cent), Costa Rica (38 per cent), Venezuela (41 per cent), Guatemala (41 per cent), Ecuador (45 per cent), El Salvador (47 per cent), Dominican Republic (56 per cent) and Mexico (77 per cent). The US dwarfs China as a supplier to Latin America although China has overtaken the US in Argentina, Bolivia, Brazil, Panama, Paraguay and Uruguay.[368] Exports to China have provided a significant boost to economic growth in Latin America[369] at a time when the world economy has been in recession and when the US, traditionally the main export market, has been experiencing anaemic economic growth rates. China has been providing investment funds in the energy, mining and agriculture sectors[370] to reinforce production for trade.

The growth of trade with China has had a positive impact on growth in several countries in Latin America, but the trade with China has shifted trade towards exporting commodities and importing manufactured goods. This pattern of trade has aroused a growing concern that there has been a de-industrialization[371] of Latin America and that the region is reverting inadvertently to a pattern of trade it has tried to change with varying degrees of success. Kevin Gallagher and Roberto Porzecanski warn this could get worse 'if LAC does not increase competitiveness across the globe, and home'.[372] Apparel and textiles[373] are among those industries whose exports could be adversely affected. It is estimated that during the period 1996/97–2007/08, Latin America market share lost to China in the US market for manufactured goods was eight per cent or $2.7 billion, and in low technology manufactures the loss was 18 per cent.[374]

The perception[375] of the persistence and progressive entrenchment of this pattern of trade touches a sensitive nerve in the Latin American psyche. As early as 1950, Paul Prebisch[376] diagnosed the problem of Latin American economic development as inherent in the structure of the international division of labour in which developing countries that constituted the 'periphery' exported primary products and imported manufactured goods from developed/industrialized countries that form the 'core'. The result was that a disproportionate share of the gains from international trade accrued to the industrialized/core countries because of the deteriorating terms of trade between manufactured goods and primary products. The manufactured goods/primary product, core-periphery model has a long, deeply-rooted history in Latin American thinking from the 'structuralist' like Prebisch to 'dependency school', for example, Celso Furtado,[377] Theotonio Dos Santos,[378] Fernando Henrique Cardoso[379] and Osvaldo Sunkel.[380] The principal policy recommendation which emanated from this perspective was state-led industrialization,[381] initially as import substitution industrialization[382] and later as export of manufactured goods so as to relocate within the international division of labour and escape the treadmill of deteriorating terms of trade. The pattern of trade with China described as 'primarization'[383] of the region's exports is reminiscent of one which has its origins in the colonial period. This has resurrected the fears of reverting to the old pattern of international trade as a 'new dependency'[384] or 'colonialism with Chinese characteristics',[385] which the continent has sought to change and could become a discordant aspect of the relationship with China.

Commerce has brought China and Latin America and the Caribbean into closer contact, and all have sought to reinforce diplomatic relations. The leaders of China and Latin America and the Caribbean met, in Brasilia, in July 2014. This meeting was followed by the establishment of the China and the Community of Latin American and Caribbean States (CELAC), which held its first forum in January 2015 in Beijing. At the Asia-Pacific Economic Cooperation (APEC) summit in November 2014, Chinese President, Xi Jinping, convinced the APEC countries to endorse the creation of a the Free Trade Area of the Asia-Pacific (FTAAP). The 21 member countries of APEC account for more than 50 per cent of world trade and 50 per cent of global GDP.[386] It appears that China has managed to inject some momentum into the FTAAP while President Obama did not get Trade Promotion Authority until June 2015. In Washington policy circles, many feel the US is too complacent about the economic penetration in Latin America. Eric Farnsworth suggests that: 'One way for the U.S. to improve its regional standing would be to again promote the idea of a hemispheric trade area among willing partners. Given China's growing regional footprint, now is the time to promote such an initiative.'[387] This might very well be the template for a new US foreign policy in Latin America for which many have called.[388]

AFRICA

China's relations with African countries have evolved rapidly, and have involved a profound change in the volume and intensity of trade. Driven by its escalating demand for oil,[389] natural gas and raw materials, China has aggressively pursued long-term contracts for oil by providing financing to governments in oil-rich countries. China is Africa's largest trading partner and its largest bilateral source of development aid. It is estimated that since 1956 there have been almost 900 Chinese-aid projects in Africa.[390] African governments have been very receptive to Chinese development aid because it has had less conditionality compared to bilateral aid from Western governments and international financial institutions.[391] China has provided loans and grants to 30 African countries that did not attain the standards of democracy as defined by Freedom House.[392] Apart from economic support, African countries are receptive to China because it has no history of colonialism in the continent and because the Chinese do not 'lecture' African rulers about human rights, electoral democracy, transparency and corruption. Since the 1950s, the People's Republic of China (PRC) has armed and politically supported anti-colonial struggles, and it was no surprise that African countries strongly supported the PRC joining the United Nations and having a seat on the Security Council. China's engagement of Africa was extended beyond the usual trade, investment and economic assistance to education, training and human resource development.[393] This started in Africa and in China in 2006 with the promulgation of 'China's Africa Policy' and this has served to consolidate goodwill.

There are aspects of China's engagement with Africa which have caused concern and even alarm. During the period 1997–2008, the area of arable farmland in China declined by 12.3 million hectares[394] and, in 2010, China became a net importer of food for the first time. China is conscious of the need to feed the world's largest population with a dwindling amount of arable land. Some Chinese enterprises have acquired land in Africa, and this has, in some cases, resulted in friction between Chinese and displaced African workers who traditionally used the land for subsistence farming. This is a general problem involving Western private investors. Oxfam claims that in one incident, 20,000 Ugandans were driven off their ancestral land to make way for a tree plantation managed by a British company.[395] There is some hysteria about Chinese acquisition of land, but there is much 'misinformation and rumour.'[396] The issue of foreigners acquiring large tracts of land in Africa is likely to be an ongoing one. Arable land, along with other increasingly scarce resources such as potable water and oil, could be the basis of fierce competition which could escalate into conflict and even war[397] in what Michael T. Klare calls the 'New Geography of Conflict.'[398] The availability of the scarce resources of oil and water (the Tigris and the Euphrates rivers) explains the strategic importance of Iraq in a water-stressed region and where the territory claimed by the Kurds straddles the headwaters of both rivers. Alex Prud'homme has attributed China's invasion of Tibet in 1950 'in part to control the water stored in the Himalayan glaciers.'[399]

BRICS

The acronym BRICS stands for Brazil, Russia, India, China and South Africa. They are an odd mix of a Russia, the core of a former superpower, the Soviet Union, China, a rising superpower and Brazil, India and South Africa, three regional powers who aspire to more international influence. They appear to have little in common except not being superpowers but being sufficiently large not to be ignored in global affairs. The five BRICS countries represent almost three billion people or 40 per cent of the world population, 30 per cent of the earth's land area and a combined GDP which amounts to 25 per cent of the world product.[400] Three of them have nuclear weapons, and two of them have permanent seats on the UN Security Council. Since 2010, the BRICS have met annually at formal summits the most recent the seventh summit was held, in Russia, in July 2015.

In the past, BRICS have been dismissed as too different in interests to achieve anything tangible, but this no longer holds because they have conceived and brought to fruition the new BRICS Development Bank, which was launched in July 2015. Their cohesion and capacity to act decisively and in a planned strategic manner cannot be dismissed, although there are obviously differences on many issues. Within the group, China has an influential role. However, it is by no means the undisputed and dominant country, and China does not need to be for the BRICS to operate. In fact, if any one country was to become dominant, it would be the antithesis of what the BRICS share as a modus operandi.

SMALL ISLAND DEVELOPING STATES[401]

China's expanded global reach has encompassed relations with small island developing states (SIDS), which some find to be an enigma given their apparently marginal, if not irrelevant significance to a global superpower. The United Nations recognizes 51 countries as Small Island Developing States (SIDS).[402] The driving force behind China's engagement is its rivalry with Taiwan for diplomatic recognition and that 38 are members of the United Nations and of the 23 countries that still recognize Taiwan, 19 of them are SIDS. Allegiance to either China or Taiwan impacts development aid. Some SIDS governments, for example, St Lucia, Grenada and Nauru, have switched allegiance. In July 2002, Nauru switched its diplomatic recognition from Taiwan to China after a relationship of 22 years. In doing so, China agreed to provide $150 million in aid to St Lucia, and Taiwan severed economic ties to the nation as a result. In February 2005, Nauru restored diplomatic relations with Taiwan, and China shortly thereafter broke off relations.[403]

Global Visibility of the Chinese

What happens in China affects what happens in the rest of the world as is the case with the US. This status is proven as whatever happens in China and what China does is reported in the international news media and followed by people across the world. Whatever happens in the future, whether China becomes a superpower, the dominant superpower, or there is a bipolar or multipolar world and regardless of the impact of China on other countries and regions and their impact on China, one thing is certain: the world will have to get accustomed to encountering more Chinese people, Chinese products and Chinese culture everywhere.

Until China joined the World Trade Organization, encouraged foreign investment and increased engagement in the international economy, China's exports were limited to that sanctioned by the state and focused on internal production. Today, China is the world's leading producer of manufactured goods. Richard Dowden observes:

> At one time Coca-Cola was the only foreign product that reached everywhere on the continent. Time and again traveling in Africa I found myself in a remote village where I wondered if I was the first foreigner to reach it. Then I would be offered Coca-Cola. Now it is the Chinese and their products who reach everywhere.[404]

It is not only Chinese products that are everywhere but Chinese people as they migrate and travel. In the next ten years, China will be the largest source of tourists in the world. Chinese people have historically been frequent travellers, but they have been largely confined to China after the Communist Revolution in 1949. Until recently, few people from the People's Republic had the privilege of migrating or travelling outside the country. This has changed dramatically.

China is the country of origin of the largest number of immigrants to the US in 2013. The Census Bureau recorded 147,000 from China, 129,000 from India and 125,000 from Mexico.[405] These migrants will reinforce the economic role of the diaspora of 50 million Chinese. Chinese émigrés have played and will continue to play a significant role in the economic modernization and transformation of China. Nicholas D. Kristop and Sheryl Wudunn estimate that some:

> Three-fourths of foreign investment in China has come from ethnic Chinese abroad, mostly in Hong Kong and Taiwan, indeed, as labor costs soared in Southeast Asia, many overseas Chinese businessmen moved their entire assembly lines or their back offices into their ancestral hometowns in China.[406]

It is not only Chinese migrants that are exerting a presence but the temporary movement of people from China. Chinese tourists are to be found all over the world, and their numbers are going to increase significantly and rapidly. Cardenal and Araujo may overstate the extent of this influence when they speak of China's 'silent army' of traders, pioneers and workers 'remaking the world in Beijing's image', but they have identified a global phenomenon. They argue that this is particularly pronounced in the developing countries of Africa, Asia and Latin America, which are absorbing Chinese loans and 'umbilically' linked workers. This view of a rising Chinese influence differs from the conventional discussion of China's ascendancy posed in terms of GDP and military might. Importantly, this type of people-based influence will not be checked by the forces which are supposed to restrain China's rise and eclipse its possible global dominance.

Concomitant with its global spread will be the increased visibility of Chinese culture. This will be reinforced as China steps up its soft power strategy.[407] Xi Jinping has stated publicly that:

> To strengthen our cultural soft power, we should intensify our international right of speech, enhance our capability for international communication and spare no efforts in establishing a system for international speech to tell, in the right way, the true story of our country and make out voices heard though giving full play to the emerging media.[408]

China Central Television (CCTV) reaches a global audience in several languages with news and documentaries. It has launched a major expansion involving a tenfold increase in its overseas-based staff by 2016 to reach 500 staff in 80 bureaus.[409] This is complemented by the distribution of 2.5 million copies of the *China Watch* supplement in the *New York Times, Wall Street Journal, Washington Post, International Herald Tribune* and *Daily Telegraph.*[410]

OUTLOOK

China is a global power within the context of the growing importance of Asia as a prominent region in global affairs. China's rise to being a global superpower inevitably affects its relations with the US and tensions with its Asian neighbours, in particular Japan and India. How these relations develop and are managed have implications for China and international affairs in general, and therefore can impact Caribbean states. The increased prominence of China has had an impact on the world, in particular Asia and the many developing countries in Africa, Latin America and the Caribbean. Of paramount importance to the Caribbean is the direct relationship with China and the dynamics and contradictions of China–US relations especially the reaction of the US to the increasing presence across the globe and, in particular, the Western Hemisphere where US dominance has been unchallenged since the Second World War.

China's inexorable global re-dimensioning has implications for the Caribbean which must be addressed. First, China's economic rise has brought about profound and perhaps irreversible changes in the world economy. Indeed, the centre of gravity of the world economy has shifted to Asia, and China's economy is at the core of an Asian region that is the most successful and consistent engine of growth in the world economy in the last 20–25 years. This is likely to cause a diversification of trade and investment from the US and Europe towards China and to a lesser extent the rest of Asia. Second, international politics is now going to operate in a bi-polar world in which China and the emerging powers such as India and Brazil will have more influence in international organizations and fora. This will induce the Caribbean to diversify or re-balance its strategic alliances, a trend which will be accelerated if the traditional developed country partners continue to demonstrate a waning of interest in the region, evidenced by reduced development assistance. Third, as China expands its reach and influence globally, it is likely to have a growing presence in the Caribbean, and how the US reacts to China globally and regionally will have an impact on Caribbean countries. Fourth, China's re-dimensioning on a global scale will open a wide variety of relations which did not exist previously, for example, collaboration between the security forces in the region and their Chinese counterparts; China as a supplier of arms to the governments in the region and voting in support of Chinese positions in the United Nations instead of supporting the US or UK.

To be in a more informed position to discuss these and other possibilities, it is necessary to have a full appreciation of the growth of China's presence and involvement in the Caribbean, and this is what the next chapter sets out to accomplish.

CHAPTER 2

China's Expanded Relations with the Caribbean

1. OBJECTIVE

This chapter documents and analyses the growing presence of the People's Republic of China (China) in the Caribbean. Increased diplomatic and political interaction is reflected primarily in the expansion of the economic relationship between China and the Caribbean. The increased importance of the economic interaction is naturally associated with a growth in the potential for political influence. The following chapter discusses the challenges, opportunities and prospects which emanate from the relationship. Then, the motivations of China and the Caribbean states for an enhancement of their economic and political relations are examined.

The increase in Chinese engagement with the Caribbean is directly related to the rivalry between China and Taiwan for diplomatic recognition from Caribbean governments. Specifically, understanding the extent and form of most aspects of China's economic presence in the Caribbean is inseparable from the rivalry between China and Taiwan, which is not a significant factor in South America. This geopolitical rivalry for diplomatic recognition is global in scope, and the competition to retain or gain recognition is most fiercely contested among the small states of Central America,[1] the Caribbean and Oceana. Of the 26 countries that recognize Taiwan, four are in Central America, six are in the Caribbean and the rest are in Oceana.[2]

2. THE CARIBBEAN

In this study, the Caribbean is defined to include Antigua and Barbuda, The Bahamas, Barbados, Belize, Dominica, the Dominican Republic, Grenada, Guyana, Haiti, Jamaica, St Kitts and Nevis, St Lucia, St Vincent and the Grenadines, Suriname and Trinidad and Tobago. Cuba is not included because its economic and political systems are different from those in the rest of the Caribbean, and there is a paucity of published information. Table 2.1 shows the population, land area and gross national income for Caribbean countries. The most important distinguishing feature of these countries is that they are very small. There is no single definition of a small country, a small state, or a small economy. Indeed, any definition in quantitative terms would be open to debate because size is a relative concept. The question of how to define a small economy is not a new one, and historically, definitions have varied widely. The definition of 'small' is usually based on one or more of the following criteria: population, land area and GDP, or it is based on some combination of these criteria.[3]

Definitions based on quantitative criteria vary considerably because they employ different criteria and exhibit significant arbitrariness in the selection of cut-off points. Simon Kuznets and Paul Streeten used population as the criterion, selecting an upper limit of ten million,[4] while Hollis B. Chenery and M. Syrquin used five million.[5] A study by the UN Economic Commission for Latin America and the Caribbean (ECLAC) chose gross national product (GNP) of less than $15 billion.[6] William Demas opted for a population of five million or less, and less than 20,000 square miles of usable land.[7] The extent of the arbitrariness can be reduced by examining a distribution of economies based on a particular quantitative measure and identifying a cluster at the 'small' end of the spectrum.[8] Another problem is that the definition of a small economy or state may have to be revised over time if GNP or population is employed as the measure.

Table 2.1: Caribbean Countries – Population, Area and Gross National Income

Countries	Population	Surface Area	Population Density	Gross National Income per capita
	Thousands	Thousand sq. km	People per sq. km	$
	2014	2014	2014	2014
Antigua and Barbuda	89	0.4	207	13,360
The Bahamas	346	13.9	38	20,980
Barbados	257	0.4	659	14,960
Belize	345	23.0	15	4,350
Dominica	74	0.8	96	7,070
Dominican Republic	10,400	48.7	215	6,030
Grenada	104	0.3	313	7,850
Guyana	761	215.0	4	4,170
Jamaica	2,712	11.0	251	5,220
St Kitts and Nevis	50	0.3	211	14,490
St Lucia	174	0.6	301	7,080
St Vincent and Grenadines	109	0.4	280	6,560
Suriname	524	163.8	3	9,470
Trinidad and Tobago	1,344	5.1	264	15,550

Source: World Bank, World Development Indicators

For example, in 1985, the Commonwealth Secretariat used a population cut-off point of one million,[9] but by 1997 it had revised the upper limit to 1.5 million.[10] The United Nations recognizes 51 countries as small island developing states using the World Bank/Commonwealth Secretariat definition of 1.5 million, but includes larger countries such as Jamaica because they share many of the characteristics of smallness. The nomenclature of small island developing state encompasses countries that are not islands such as Belize and even some like Guyana which have relatively large land areas. By whatever measure or criteria, Caribbean countries are small.

3. CHINESE COMMUNITY IN THE CARIBBEAN

Contact between China and the Caribbean dates back centuries. Goods made in China such as tea and porcelain were known in the Caribbean from the seventeenth century, and there has been a small Chinese community in the Caribbean since the early nineteenth century.[11] The introduction into Guyana, Jamaica and Trinidad of Chinese as indentured labourers[12] began in the nineteenth century, motivated by the hope that they would be a cost-effective replacement for African slaves. They and their descendants, not unexpectedly, avoided paid employment on sugar plantations except in circumstances of absolute desperation. A second migration of free persons looking for a better life came to the Caribbean between the 1890s and the 1940s in spite of some restrictive requirements. The current Chinese community is descended from this second group of migrants.[13] Many Chinese immigrants established themselves in the retail trade, in particular in small grocery stores during the twentieth century.[14] These establishments were financed by personal savings, family loans and credit from the Chinese social network.[15] They mixed freely with the poorer classes, but were excluded from the élite social circle by the rigid, race-reinforced social stratification of British colonial society. They established institutions to serve their community and protect their business interests, for example, the Chinese Benevolent Society in Jamaica was founded in 1891 by Chin Tung-Kao and established at premises in downtown Kingston. Its aims were to offer assistance to the Chinese community, preserve Chinese culture, customs and identity, as well as make Chinese culture known to the wider society. In the modern era, these institutions declined as the Chinese became more integrated into Caribbean society.

In more recent years, since the attainment of political independence, their social mobility has increased, and persons of Chinese descent or origin are found in every profession and have accomplished a disproportionate presence and influence in business and commerce. Indeed, citizens of Chinese descent have held the post of president in Guyana and Trinidad and Tobago, and served in the House of Representatives and the Senate in Jamaica.

4. INTENSIFICATION OF THE RELATIONSHIP

After 30 years of routine engagement and limited activity, China during the last decade has made a concerted effort to consolidate and expand its relationship with Caribbean states. The enhanced interaction by China involved a strengthening of relations with countries with which diplomatic relations exist and an intensification of efforts to get countries that recognize Taiwan to switch their allegiance. The escalation of diplomatic activity in the Caribbean has coincided with a deliberate policy of greater involvement in global affairs and an assertive attitude to pursue relations with developing countries. A significant milestone in the build-up of the relationship was the First China–Caribbean Economic and Trade Cooperation Forum hosted by Jamaica, in Kingston, in February 2005. Previous to that year the relationship was limited as is evident by the fact that 'CARICOM: Our Caribbean Community' prepared by the CARICOM Secretariat and published in 2005 made no mention of China in the three chapters on foreign policy covering almost 100 pages.[16]

a. Long, Slow Build-up

The long patient build-up of confidence since 1973 is illustrative of the Chinese culture and concept of time. Diplomatic relations between the People's Republic of China and Jamaica were established on November 21, 1972 when the Michael Manley-led government subscribed to the One China Policy. The Chinese government established an embassy, in Kingston, in 1973. Diplomatic relations between the People's Republic of China and the Republic of Trinidad and Tobago were established on June 20, 1974. The Chinese government established an embassy in Port of Spain in April 1975, but it was 40 years later that Trinidad and Tobago established an embassy in Beijing in February 2014. Prime Minister Eric Williams of Trinidad and Tobago was the first Caribbean head of government to visit China in 1974 where he was received by Chairman Mao.

Starting in 1974, a number of commodity loan agreements and technical assistance agreements were signed with Jamaica, the most important of which related to the construction of a cotton polyester spinning and weaving mill.[17] Diplomatic relations between Guyana and China were established in June 1972. In 1975, China agreed to provide interest-free loans and to import Guyanese bauxite and sugar. The President of Guyana, Forbes Burnham, made an official state visit to China in 1983 to seek increased economic aid.[18] During the 1980s, the relationship with Jamaica languished, but in June 1985, a Jamaican government delegation headed by Hugh Shearer, then Deputy Prime Minister and Minister of Foreign Affairs and Foreign Trade, made an official visit to China. This was the first senior delegation to visit China. Prime Minister Michael Manley, who was an ardent advocate of non-alignment and south-south cooperation visited

China during June 2–6, 1991 in pursuance of a diversification of Jamaica's foreign relations. During the visit, the two governments signed several agreements.[19]

This was a bold move because it was done at the height of the Cold War and preceded by seven years of the formal re-establishment of diplomatic relations between the US and China. Formal diplomatic representation from Jamaica to China did not begin until 1992, when the Jamaican ambassador to Japan was accredited as a non-resident ambassador to China. Especially important in elevating the relationship was Prime Minister P.J. Patterson's June 2005 visit to Hong Kong and Beijing, accompanied by government officials and private sector representatives.[20] At the time, it was not lost on China's leaders that Patterson was the chairman of the Group of 77 of 132 countries. They would also have been aware of his considerable influence in CARICOM where he was undoubtedly the 'elder statesman'. The importance of the visit is evidenced by the fact that Patterson met with Premier, Wen Jiabao, President Hu Jintao and Chairman Wu Bangguo. The visit served to elevate the relationship which was followed by the appointment of a resident ambassador in July 2005. Prime Minister Patterson in his remarks at the opening of the China/Jamaica Business Seminar in Shanghai said:

> Jamaica/China relations have entered a new era, and I look forward to an exciting relationship. The Chinese delegation that visited Jamaica in February signaled a new beginning in the diplomatic and economic relations between the two countries. My visit here serves to confirm our intention and commitment to enter this new phase in the relationship.[21]

In 2008, China published a policy statement on relations with Latin America and the Caribbean which started from the premise that 'The move toward multi-polarity is irreversible and economic globalization is gaining momentum'. China characterized itself as 'the largest developing country in the world' and stated that it is 'committed to the path of peaceful development and the win-win strategy of opening-up' based on 'the Five Principles of Peaceful Coexistence' and the One China Principle. The paper sought to establish commonalities by pointing out that the 'two sides are at a similar stage of development and face the common task of achieving development'. The overall goal: 'Deepen cooperation and achieve win-win results. The two sides will leverage their respective strengths, tap the potential of cooperation, and seek to become each other's partner in economic cooperation and trade for mutual benefit and common development.'[22] In June 2012, Wen Jiabao, Premier of China, in speaking to the United Nations Economic Commission for Latin America and the Caribbean, highlighted deepening strategic economic cooperation, particularly in trade recognizing their shared status as developing countries. He announced:

> The China Development Bank will coordinate the efforts in setting up a special loan of US$10 billion to facilitate our cooperation in infrastructure development, including railways, roads, ports, power plants, power grids and telecommunication facilities that are closely linked to production and people's livelihood. We will continue to encourage competitive and reputable Chinese companies to invest in this region.[23]

In June 2013, China's President Xi Jinping met with ten Caribbean countries in Port of Spain and announced that China would make available $3 billion in loans.[24]

China has increased its diplomatic links with Caribbean governments through official visits of high level Chinese leaders, e.g., former Chinese Vice President, Xi Jinping, visited Jamaica in 2009 and broke ground for the Montego Bay Convention Centre, to be constructed and financed by the Chinese at a cost of $52 million.[25] Almost without exception, the heads of governments in the Caribbean have been on official visits to Beijing where they have been treated 'royally'. Three Jamaican prime ministers have visited Beijing in the last decade: P.J. Patterson in 2005; Bruce Golding in 2010 and Portia Simpson-Miller in 2013. Kamla Persad-Bissessar of Trinidad and Tobago made the 'pilgrimage' in 2014; Gaston Browne of Antigua and Barbuda in 2014; Tillman Thomas of Grenada in 2009; Roosevelt Skerrit of Dominica in 2015; Perry Christie of The Bahamas in 2015; Freundel Stuart of Barbados in 2011; and Desi Bouterse of Suriname in 2013. In nearly all cases, they were received by the president of China. President Donald Ramotar met with China's President, Xi Jinping, in Port of Spain, in 2013. Few could claim to have had a one-on-one audience with the president of the US.

b. Jamaica's Diplomatic Role in Sino–Caribbean Relations

China had taken a decision that Jamaica would be the entry point and launching pad for upgrading its involvement in the Caribbean. The decision was based (1) on a long relationship with Jamaica during which time confidence had been built, (2) Jamaica had proven itself to be willing to stand up for what it believed in and to express it in its foreign policy in spite of pressure, for example, from the US over its relationship with and support for Cuba, (3) Jamaica was the largest country in CARICOM, (4) the role that Jamaica has played in strengthening relations between China and the Caribbean and, (5) the comfort level because of the existence of a Chinese-Jamaican community.

Jamaica has had a special role in the development of relations between China and the Caribbean. The relationship was built on Jamaica's resolute stance on the One China Policy and support for China having a seat on the Security Council of the UN in spite of the expressed displeasure of the US. Jamaica, under the leadership of Michael Manley, revamped Jamaica's foreign policy to one built around Caribbean regionalism, non-alignment and south-south cooperation among developing countries. Jamaica made some bold decisions such as when it, along with Barbados, Guyana and Trinidad and Tobago, breached the US diplomatic embargo of Cuba when they established diplomatic ties with Cuba in 1973. This occasioned adverse reaction from the US throughout the 1970s. Jamaica sought to shape the international agenda. In the course of which, it assumed leadership roles in the African, Caribbean and Pacific group (ACP), the Non-Aligned Movement, the Group of 77 and Socialist International.[26]

The leadership of P.J. Patterson was particularly influential in the development of the relationship between China and the Caribbean. He was involved from the start of Jamaica's relations with China, being politically active from 1972. The People's National Party (PNP) formed the government from 1971 to 1980, from 1989 to 2007 and from 2012 to 2016, a total of 30 years of the 42-year relationship. P.J. Patterson was a Minister for 13 years during which he was Minister of Foreign Affairs for several of those and Prime Minister for 14 years (1992–2006). More than this, the length of his involvement is that he was instrumental in persuading several Caribbean governments of the correctness and advantages of adhering to or switching to the One China Policy. He was a decisive influence in the decisions made by Antigua, Dominica, Grenada and St Lucia (which later reverted to diplomatic relations with Taiwan). He was also able to mollify China's position on assistance to Haiti, a country that continues to grant diplomatic recognition to Taiwan.

The goodwill built up over a long time between Jamaica and China through people-to-people relationships is an intangible asset. The help given to the Chinese by Jamaicans during the Japanese invasion of China during the period 1937–45 was still remembered as late as 1992 when the survivors of the city of Chongqing confirmed this.

c. China's Flattering Diplomatic Demarche

The government and political leaders of tiny countries such as those in the Caribbean always feel they are overlooked or taken for granted. They particularly feel neglected by the US[27] which is the dominant superpower in that region of the world and has traditionally been the main economic partner of the Caribbean. This perception of inadequate attention is a measure in access to the US President and in the amount of development aid given. Several countries have middle-income developing country status because of their per capita incomes, and their well-established democracies have prompted the US to focus its aid on security issues. President Obama has visited the region twice: first at the Summit of the Americas in Port of Spain and then Jamaica in April 2015. Meanwhile, Chinese President, Xi Jinping, has visited the region twice. Nearly every Caribbean prime minister/president has been received in Beijing with full pomp and ceremony and promises of development assistance.

Table 2.2: Embassies of China and US and Overseas Offices of Taiwan in the Caribbean and Central America

Country	Embassy of China	Overseas Office of Taiwan	Embassy of the US
Antigua and Barbuda	X		
The Bahamas	X		X
Barbados	X		X
Belize		X	X
Cuba	X		
Dominica	X		
Dominican Republic		X	X
Guyana	X		X
Grenada	X		
Haiti		X	X
Jamaica	X		X
St Kitts and Nevis		X	
St Lucia		X	
St Vincent		X	
Suriname	X		X
Trinidad and Tobago	X		X

China exhibits sensitivity to the small Caribbean countries, for example, the Caribbean was specifically mentioned in the Beijing Declaration of the CELAC. 'We consider that a special treatment should be given to Caribbean countries regarding the strategies and cooperation projects in the Forum.'[28] There have been literally 'countless' Chinese delegations to the Caribbean countries with no country being overlooked no matter how small. China has established embassies in all Caribbean countries that adhere to the One China Policy even being present where there is no resident diplomat from the US. Table 2.2 shows China's diplomatic deployment in the Caribbean. Ironically, the US and China are almost matched in formal diplomatic representation in the region.

d. Style of Diplomacy

Chinese-style diplomacy has been well received in the Caribbean perhaps more so because it is in sharp contrast to American-style diplomacy which, while well-meaning on occasions, has not been as sensitive as it could have been. Small developing countries where sovereignty is more of an aspiration than a reality are extremely sensitive about the sovereignty which they do not possess. Therefore, the appearance and, even more so, the actuality of being treated with the respect accorded to other countries is critically important. The appearance of care and the formalities indicative of respect are important to the political leadership of the Caribbean, seeking out aid while fully aware of the real limitations on their economic and political self-determination. Callous diplomacy is particularly irksome to the Caribbean people having transcended the limitations of small economies to achieve world leadership in numerous fields of human endeavour. Top of world is evident in Sir Arthur Lewis, Marcus Garvey, Bob Marley, Brian, Lara, Garfield Sobers and Usain Bolt and in the genres of Reggae and the steel pan to name a few.

China and the US pursue different styles of diplomacy in the Caribbean, and the Chinese style has been more subtle and hence more palatable to Caribbean governments and people. Two examples suffice to make the point. First, when the prime minister or president of a Caribbean country goes to Beijing they are allowed for a fleeting moment to live the illusion of respect. The Chinese literally 'roll out the red carpet' with guards of honour, elaborate ceremonies in ornate surroundings and a meeting with the President of China. An appointment with the President of the US in the White House can be difficult to obtain because the US opts instead for meetings with groups of five to 15 or more at a time. Many of these meetings are confined to events such as the United Nations General Assembly or the Summit of the Americas. The US has a long tradition of telling countries what they should and should not do. This arrogance is offensive to almost every country, and those in a position to ignore US recommendations do what they choose as an expression of their sovereignty. Being 'lectured' is particularly irksome to those countries that cannot risk 'pushback' against the US. This is particularly the case of small states, including those in the Caribbean whose tourist arrivals and remittances depend on the US economy. Caribbean governments feel strongly that it is inappropriate conduct for representatives of the US to state publicly criticisms of their policies.

It is inconceivable that a spokesperson for a foreign government could publicly criticize the US about same sex marriage or comment on the number of African Americans killed by the police. Yet, President Obama on his visit to Kenya (homeland of his father) in July 2015 criticized and admonished the government for: a 'politics based solely on tribe and ethnicity is a politics that's doomed to tear a country apart. It is a failure.' He pointed out that the 'cancer of corruption' was costing the country 250,000 jobs per year and said 'Tough laws need to be on the books…people need to be prosecuted.' In addition, he described as 'bad traditions': early marriage, female genital mutilation, domestic abuse and lack of access to education.[29] The *Washington Post* commented: 'the heart of the speech was more a lecture than reminiscence' and that: 'Under different circumstances, or delivered by someone else, the speech could have sounded like intrusive moralizing by a foreign president.'[30]

The Chinese are always circumspect, and whether it is genuine sensitivity or disingenuous posturing, they speak in a non-judgmental tone and offer to help the governments of developing countries to achieve whatever those governments want with no comment on democracy or human rights and tendering no advice on how other countries should conduct their internal and external affairs. Communiqués, policy statements and speeches emanating from China and its leaders, e.g., those of Xi Jinping[31] are couched in terms such as friendship, sincerity, reciprocity, inclusiveness, partnership and cooperation. Nobody is naïve enough to believe that China is not pursuing its national interest. Surely, they are, but their words should not be dismissed as mere platitudes. The stance is not instructive or prescriptive or that of a martinet. China has the advantage of posing itself as a 'developing country' and to allude to both parties being: 'at a similar stage of development and face the common task of achieving development' and cooperating 'to make the international political and economic order more fair and equitable, promote democracy in international relations and uphold the legitimate rights and interests of developing countries'. A major point is that Chinese aid does not include certain types of non-economic conditionality common to Western development assistance. China's Policy Paper on Latin America and the Caribbean states: 'The Chinese Government will, according to its financial capability and level of economic and social development, continue to provide economic and technical assistance to relevant Latin American and Caribbean countries without attaching any political conditions.'[32]

e. Soft Power

The Chinese understand the importance of 'soft power' in the execution of foreign policy.[33] This is not new or recent as Sun Tzu in the *Art of War* advised that 'the supreme art of war is to subdue the enemy without fighting.' China has developed an increasingly sophisticated approach to the use of soft power in international relations since the mid-2000s,[34] and is spending significant sums on propagation of its history and culture. Shen Ding regards this 'cultural proselytization' as the core of China's use of 'cultural soft power'.[35] Joshua Kurlantzick speaks of China mounting 'a systematic, coherent soft power strategy' which he describes as a 'charm offensive'.[36] China has established Confucius Institutes since 2004 in 64 countries[37] to teach its language and expose its history and culture. China has also increased significantly the number of scholarships to allow foreign students to study in China. As a direct result, enrollment of foreign students in China numbered 240,000 in 2011 compared to just 36,000 a decade earlier. The soft power outreach has been effectively extended into the Caribbean and symbolized in Jamaica with the establishment of 600,000 square foot, 'feng shui'-based Chinese garden in the Hope Botanical Gardens in Kingston, Jamaica, in August 2015.[38]

By the end of 2015, there were 27 Jamaicans studying in China under full Chinese government scholarship, bringing the total to date to 70. Six Chinese coaches have received training in Jamaica, and four students are currently studying sports management at the G.C. Foster College.[39] By 2014, over 50 Barbadians have studied in China.[40] There were six Grenadian students in China in 2005 and that number has increase to 35 by 2015.[41] Over the ten years since Grenada established diplomatic ties with the PRC, 96 Grenadians have studied in China and 424 received short-term training courses in various fields. There are five Chinese lecturers based in Grenada and 650 students have taken the basic Chinese course. In addition, 11 cultural groups and 28 business delegations visited China.[42] Starting in 1993, the Chinese government sent more than 100 Chinese doctors and experts to assist Guyana's health sector, and 20 Guyanese are currently studying medicine in China.[43]

China also provides training in the Caribbean. In February 2009, during the Official Visit of then Vice President Xi Jinping to Jamaica, he inaugurated the Confucius Institute at the Mona Campus of the University of the West Indies, the first of its kind in the English-speaking Caribbean. The Confucius Institute began operating on July 19, 2010 with the objectives of teaching Mandarin and promoting Chinese culture. It currently offers courses in Mandarin, Chinese calligraphy, Tai Chi and Film Series on China.[44] Also in 2009, a Confucius Institute was opened in Cuba and has trained 2,000 students to date. It has since been refurbished and expanded to accommodate double the number of students.[45]A Confucius Institute was established at the College of The Bahamas in November 2013.[46] The Confucius Institute co-founded by the University of Guyana (UG) and Dalian University of Foreign Languages (DUFL) was officially inaugurated on May 19, 2014.[47] A Confucius Institute was officially launched at the Cave Hill Campus of the University of the West Indies, in Barbados, in April 2015.[48]

The people-to-people exchange has occurred in a number of ways. There are the ubiquitous friendship associations in Antigua, The Bahamas, Barbados, Guyana, Jamaica, Suriname and St Lucia which now has diplomatic ties with Taiwan. These associations are open to both citizens of Chinese descent and newly arrived migrants. The friendship association is illustrative of the activities of these associations in the Caribbean. Established in August 1976, the Jamaica China Friendship Association (JCFA) was an expression of civil society support of the One China Policy being pursued by the PRC. At that time, the One China Policy was controversial. Jamaica was an early supporter of the One China Policy and the application by the People's Republic of China (PRC) for admission to the United Nations. The PRC officially established diplomatic relations between Jamaica and China in 1972, and China opened its Embassy in Kingston the following year. JCFA was immediately embraced by the Chinese People's Association for Friendship with Foreign Countries (CPAFFC) whose mission is to promote relations between China's people-to-people outreach to those of Chinese origin across the world. The goal of JCFA is the deepening of friendship between Jamaica and China through people-to-people contact, the facilitation of cultural exchange and increasing understanding of Chinese history and achievements. Activities in furtherance of these objectives have included organizing visits to China in collaboration with CPAFFC, disseminating information about China's history, culture, etiquette and topical issues through lectures, newspaper articles and films, celebrating the Chinese New Year and hosting the annual gala banquet celebrating the National Day of China attended by the Governor General, the Minister of Foreign Affairs and the Ambassador of China. Its most notable achievement was organizing and hosting the first regional conference of the Friendship Associations in the Caribbean, Central and South America in 1998. This event marked the first time that a Friendship Association had established regional and international linkages between related Friendship Associations. In 2012, the JCFA held a successful forum on 'Doing Business with China' attended by over 400 persons.[49]

The role of friendship associations in keeping alive the Chinese culture and traditions is a task which has been made easier by the increasingly available Chinese news channel in English which is in the cable television packages in several Caribbean countries. In 2009–10, Beijing invested $8.9 billion in external publicity, including CCTV, a 24-hour news channel, and it ensures that China Radio International broadcasts in English (the most widely spoken language in the world) 24 hours a day.[50] This is at the same time that the US has downscaled resources in this area, continuing a trend started after the end of the Cold War.[51] News from China is available in many cable television packages throughout the Caribbean as it is in the US. In addition to its availability, China's news sources are becoming increasingly credible, and its coverage is much more global than US networks which focus on issues that are the priorities for the US. The expanding global coverage is attracting an increase share of global audiences to CCTV and Aljazeera in the way that BBC is seen as a credible global source.

f. China's Financial Outreach

The number of Chinese-owned enterprises operating overseas has been growing rapidly. In 2010, there were 13,000 Chinese-owned overseas enterprises in 177 countries,[52] and by 2012, there were 16,000 in 179 countries.[53] Most of the Chinese firms operating in the Caribbean have been service providers and not investors. These firms have been almost involved exclusively in the provision of construction services to governments in the Caribbean. The funding for the construction projects in which Chinese firms have been involved has come from agencies and financial institutions of the Chinese government. Investment, aid, and provision of construction services have been a nexus and a mechanism for the introduction of Chinese firms into Caribbean countries. Most of China's projects have been funded by preferential loans from state-owned Chinese banks, with the Chinese Development Bank being the most important.[54] For example, in Suriname, where the government has agreed on several infrastructure projects with two Chinese enterprises, Cheng Don International and China Harbour Engineering Company, involving the financing and execution of projects, Cheng Don International will construct 8,000 public housing units, and China Harbour will be engaged in road and railroad links between Suriname and Brazil, a deep-sea harbour, a sea dam from Albina to Nickerie, and a high-way to Zanderij.

China is interested in promoting, or at least facilitating and supporting, OFDI because it sees the obvious benefits of this type of development in terms of expansion of exports, outsourcing production, and control of raw material supplies. In September 2007, China announced that it would provide $530 million in concessional loans over three years to Chinese companies investing in the Caribbean. These funds from state-owned financial institutions have been used to finance projects in which Chinese firms have been awarded the contract for construction, financed by loans to governments in the Caribbean. In June 2013, President Xi Jinping announced that China would make available $3 billion for infrastructure projects in Caribbean countries that have diplomatic relations with China.[55] While undoubtedly the projects will be executed by Chinese companies, it could result in these firms becoming investors. The Inter-American Development Bank (IDB) has approved as much as $153 million in loans for the establishment of a new equity investment programme for Latin America and the Caribbean in partnership with the Export-Import Bank of China (China Exim). The new platform is expected to mobilize as much as $1.8 billion from a diversified pool of investors, including Chinese investors, to fund equity investments that will support economic and financial integration between Latin America and the Caribbean (LAC) and China. The platform is made up of three regional investment funds that will deploy risk capital in infrastructure, mid-size companies and natural resource projects, including agribusiness, energy and mining.

There is a learning experience which Chinese firms inevitably have to undergo, especially because of their limited experience with FDI in the Caribbean. The learning is not confined to the Caribbean as it is also taking place in Latin America,[56] but is complicated in the Caribbean because of the differences in the investment environments among the countries. The necessity for learning to establish and operate foreign direct investment is a national phenomenon in China[57] because in recent years the state has intensified its encouragement and facilitation of Chinese enterprises to invest abroad.

5. CHINA'S PRESENCE

The economic growth accomplished by China over the last 20 years is unprecedented and has resulted in one of the most rapid economic transformations achieved by any country. The concomitant rise of China as an economic superpower over the last decade is the most significant change in the international system since the end of the Cold War. China, in the course of its recent development, has become more integrated into the global economy and it is now an important engine of global economic growth. Engagement with such a large, powerful and rapidly expanding economy as that of China can have a transformative effect especially on developing country partners, and it also poses challenges.

China has expanded its economic presence in the Caribbean during the past decade, intensifying its efforts to expand economic interaction and consolidate diplomatic and political ties in the region. China's deepening involvement in the Caribbean, an expression of political and economic motivations, is reflected in its increased development assistance, technical assistance, continued expansion of trade, emerging foreign investment, and involvement in construction projects. The pursuit of both motives is taking place against the background of a re-dimensioning of China's involvement in world affairs commensurate with the role and status of a superpower.

Economic contact between China and the Caribbean dates back centuries and began with the importation of exotic Chinese goods such as tea and porcelain. Trade was relatively insignificant because of British colonial restrictions and China's isolation from the global economy after 1949. Over the last 20 years, China has become increasingly integrated into the world economy and is now the largest economy in the world. It has grown at an average rate of ten per cent per year during the period 1990–2005, the highest growth rate in the world. Indeed, growth has been at a pace and of a scope that the World Bank calls 'without historical precedent'.[58] China is now one of the engines of growth in the new global economy, accounting in recent years for 12 per cent of all growth in world trade.[59] China has continued to grow in spite of the global economic crisis that erupted in late 2008.

During the last decade, China's economic presence in Caribbean countries has increased, but has varied from country to country. The differentiation in the pattern of economic interaction reflects the fact that some countries recognize the People's Republic of China (China) and others have chosen to maintain diplomatic relations with the Republic of China (Taiwan). Some countries, such as St Lucia and Dominica, have switched diplomatic allegiance. At present, China is recognized by Antigua and Barbuda, The Bahamas, Barbados, Dominica, Grenada, Guyana, Jamaica, Suriname, and Trinidad and Tobago.[60] Belize, the Dominican Republic, Haiti, St Kitts and Nevis, St Lucia, and St Vincent and the Grenadines have relations with Taiwan. While there has been a steady expansion of exports from China to the

Caribbean encompassing a widening range of goods and services, exports from the Caribbean have not grown appreciably. Imports from China expanded rapidly during the last decade as China became more integrated into the world economy. Imports of Chinese goods have grown in all Caribbean countries although some countries have chosen to maintain diplomatic relations with Taiwan. Development assistance from China has increased significantly in those countries that maintain diplomatic relations with China or have changed their diplomatic allegiance.

The economic interaction between China and the Caribbean cannot be explained entirely by economic factors, but is best understood as an economic relationship which is embedded within a political and diplomatic relationship. Formal diplomatic relations between the People's Republic of China and Caribbean states began with the establishment of diplomatic ties with Guyana and Jamaica in the latter half of 1972, and shortly afterwards with Barbados and Trinidad and Tobago. These longstanding political relationships provided a platform for the expansion of trade when China emerged in the global economy. As China became a significant participant in international trade and international affairs, it set about expanding its engagement with the Caribbean. In this process, China has been cognizant of its diplomatic rivalry with Taiwan.

China and those Caribbean countries that practice a 'One China' policy have signed a variety of agreements aimed at enhancing economic cooperation, and they have established institutionalized arrangements to expand trade and investment. Institutional arrangements have been established to convene a regular schedule of meetings between China and Caribbean governments as a group. These include the China–Caribbean Economic and Trade Cooperation Forum, which met in February 2005, July 2007 and September 2011. The institutional vehicle for fostering business cooperation is the China–Caribbean Joint Business Council; it includes Antigua and Barbuda, The Bahamas, Barbados, Dominica, the Dominican Republic, Cuba, Grenada, Guyana, Haiti, Jamaica, Suriname, and Trinidad and Tobago. These institutional arrangements are supplemented and complemented by high-level visits to the region and the reception of Caribbean Heads of Government in Beijing.

6. TRADE

Although diplomatic relations between the Caribbean and China date back to the early 1970s, activity beyond diplomatic exchanges such as aid and trade has been limited until recently. The extent of trade with socialist countries was limited, including trade with the Soviet Union and Cuba in particular, and to a lesser extent Jamaica[61] and Guyana that were consciously attempting to expand economic relations with socialist countries. Trade between China and the Caribbean has expanded in recent years because of the increase in exports to the Caribbean, but the Caribbean has been slow to export to the Chinese market. Consequently, the trade deficit with China has grown. The prospects of exporting to China will improve as China's economy grows, the liberalization process[62] continues, and World Trade Organization (WTO) commitments are implemented.[63] The vast and rapidly expanding market of China presents a robust export opportunity for the Caribbean, particularly if firms in the region are provided with the support needed to navigate the bureaucratic obstacles to market penetration.[64]

a. Imports from China

Imports from China have grown substantially and rapidly as shown in table 2.3. Imports have increased from $577.8 million in 2003 to $4.2 billion in 2014. This is a reflection of the competitive prices and improved quality of Chinese goods. Demand has increased even where durability is questionable because for lower-income consumers affordability is more important than durability. The largest imports from China in recent years have been cargo vessels, tankers, floating docks, footwear, tires, T-shirts, electronics and television sets. Vessels imported from China are re-exported by some Caribbean countries. Most Chinese exports to the Caribbean do not compete with local production, but there are some significant areas where Chinese exports could displace local production, for example, in some manufactured goods and some foods. These include a range of processed food, tilapia fillets, Portland cement, apparel, furniture, paper products and plastic goods. In several consumer products, such as footwear, electronics, and T-shirts, the region has come to depend predominantly on imports from China. Despite the steady growth in imports,[65] there are some Chinese products that have not yet appeared in Caribbean markets, such as motor vehicles and medicines.

b. Exports to China

While China is an enormous and rapidly growing market, exports from Caribbean countries have not grown significantly. Exports increased from $120.6 million in 2003 to $661.7 million in 2014 as shown in table 2.4. During the period 2003–14, most countries exported less than US$10 million per annum and exports averaged less than $1 million for Antigua and Barbuda, St Kitts and Nevis, St Lucia and St Vincent and the Grenadines. Guyana, Jamaica, Haiti, Suriname, and Trinidad and Tobago have slowly increased their exports. The Dominican Republic has steadily increased its exports to China. The entire Caribbean represents less than 0.001 per cent of China's total imports. In recent years, bauxite and alumina exports have shown growth, reflecting that the production of aluminum in China doubled between 2004 and 2008.[66] China produces 25 per cent of the world's aluminum and is a net exporter, and therefore is vitally interested in supplies of bauxite and alumina.[67] China's demand for bauxite and alumina is likely to grow significantly once the global economic crisis abates. Other major export products from the Caribbean include lumber, asphalt, and scrap metal.

Table 2.3: Imports from China 2003–14 ($ millions)

Country	2003	2005	2007	2009	2010	2011	2012	2013	2014
Antigua and Barbuda	3.116	146.899	395.238	493.689	806.144	657.698	758.277		
Bahamas, The	133.896	170.993	178.928	459.568	690.419	605.011	656.571	369.995	818.878
Barbados	31.237	46.615	38.41[illegible]	100.703	78.484	158.247	105.712	77.238	78.795
Belize	11.185	35.281	28.438	36.266	44.314	55.080	57.684	134.350	105.434
Dominica	36.953	54.187	80.78[illegible]	24.552	45.022	29.296	28.138	25.309	41.087
Dominican Republic	163.896	243.924	466.77[illegible]	50.698	785.959	1,774.114	1,877.036	1,981.519	1,401.028
Grenada	0.426	2.998	3.29[illegible]	4.347	5.622	6.503	21.851	8.536	16.623
Guyana	21.245	29.930	72.02[illegible]	65.006	92.112	155.874	219.461	165.350	183.746
Haiti	15.735	33.243	8[illegible].75[illegible]	162.351	279.945	334.021	311.733	355.979	430.521
Jamaica	83.201	162.467	227.5[illegible]4	236.332	259.344	281.409	308.126	332.892	394.115
St Kitts and Nevis	0.168	0.660	2.8[illegible]4	1.327	2.936	4.819	2.955	17.151	29.329
St Lucia	1.687	2.729	7.5[illegible]4	7.466	8.920	11.167	31.664	21.812	32.893
St Vincent and the Grenadines	1.785	6.560	23.1[illegible]4	81.226	80.990	86.007	32.009	27.813	41.147
Suriname	8.919	19.310	23.[illegible]3	31.827	32.630	32.630	34.420	34.780	194.596
Trinidad and Tobago	64.380	104.265	289.[illegible]5	267.916	320.068	314.761	343.758	352.801	470.339
Caribbean	577.830	1,060.062	1,934.[illegible]32	2,023.290	3,503.064	4,506.637	4,789.395	3,905.525	4,238.437

Source: Direction of Trade, International Monetary Fund

Table 2.4: Exports to China 2002–14 ($ millions)

Country	2003	2005	2007	2008	2010	2011	2012	2013	2014
Antigua and Barbuda	-	-	-	0.076	0.053	0.051	0.071	0.000	0.000
Bahamas, The	0.710	0.172	16.473	0.552	0.139	57.183	106.259	69.566	170.975
Barbados	0.485	0.854	1.029	1.288	3.462	6.098	9.394	11.535	13.456
Belize	0.898	0.186	-	0.025	0.234	2.592	6.961	7.623	6.596
Dominica	0.691	0.860	27.825	34.684	2.299	0.357	1.042	0.099	0.514
Dominican Republic	7.290	43.516	191.257	109.541	117.107	288.365	354.289	248.555	254.876
Grenada	0.278	0.002	0.040	0.037	0.008	0.000	0.002	0.029	0.005
Guyana	0.273	6.815	16.504	15.707	15.727	13.218	23.687	7.282	36.576
Haiti	0.018	0.246	5.755	6.793	5.409	6.698	9.067	13.802	13.947
Jamaica	96.584	107.549	69.605	1.550	3.398	21.340	11.628	14.828	38.120
St Kitts and Nevis	-	-	0.008	0.130	0.276	0.432	0.122	0.251	0.385
St Lucia	0.006	29.734	0.105	0.045	0.112	0.262	0.109	0.024	0.030
St Vincent and the Grenadines	-	0.041	-	23.816	0.020	0.022	0.002	0.000	0.000
Suriname	4.073	1.690	2.319	5.433	5.340	3.252	2.589	3.888	47.779
Trinidad and Tobago	9.311	16.575	18.665	21.933	98.242	308.513	125.743	113.853	98.405
Caribbean	120.617	208.239	349.586	221.611	251.826	708.403	650.965	491.335	681.664

Source: Direction of Trade, International Monetary Fund

China's need for food, primary products, raw materials and capital goods constitutes demand, much of which can be purveyed by developing countries. The capacity to supply the Chinese market can encourage investment, development assistance, and technical assistance from China. China has pursued securing critical supplies and urgently needed raw materials by providing loans and development assistance to developing country and suppliers such as those in Africa.[68] Africa's exports to China grew by 48 per cent during the period 1999–2004, and this surge in exports was accompanied by the rapid expansion of Chinese investment, largely in extractive industries[69] such as oil refineries in Nigeria.[70] China has invested heavily in the energy sector in Argentina, Brazil, Colombia, Costa Rica, Cuba, Ecuador, Peru and Venezuela,[71] and the demand for sources of supply is likely to continue because China is experiencing electricity shortages in some provinces.[72]

The experience of the Caribbean has been different because of the paucity of energy resources and raw materials. Despite China being such a large and rapidly expanding market, Caribbean-based firms have achieved limited penetration there. China's importance as an export market for the Caribbean has not significantly increased. The US and the European Union continue to be more important than China (see table 2.5). This pattern is in contrast to the experience of Latin America, where China's importance as an export market has grown significantly in the last decade.[73] Exports to China as a share of total exports amount to 5.2 per cent for the Western Hemisphere, 10.5 per cent for Africa and 11.5 per cent for developing Asia.[74] By 2008, China was the largest export market for Brazil (seven per cent), and Chile (13 per cent) and the second largest export destination for Argentina, Costa Rica, Cuba and Peru.[75]

Table 2.5: Caribbean Exports According to Main Destination, Percent of Total Exports 2002–2009

Country	China		United States		EU-27	
	2002–09		2002 –09		2002–09	
Bahamas	0.0	0.0	48.3	33.7	29.8	24.7
Barbados	0.0	0.4	13.5	7.5	18.5	12.4
Belize	0.0	0.0	45.0	30.0	27.8	37.3
Dominican Republic	0.0	2.0	91.1	61.9	6.3	10.4
Dominica	0.0	0.7	10.9	1.8	56.9	26.3
Grenada	0.0	0.0	7.4	12.9	56.2	7.8
Guyana	0.0	1.0	20.5	15.6	48.5	25.1
Haiti	0.0	0.7	83.0	78.7	12.5	3.7
Jamaica	0.0	1.1	28.4	38.2	31.8	21.1
St Kitts and Nevis	0.0	0.0	61.3	62.7	34.2	4.5
St Lucia	0.0	0.0	16.6	9.3	68.9	46.0
St Vincent and the Grenadines	0.0	0.4	10.6	0.5	54.6	74.9
Suriname	0.0	0.5	11.8	9.5	38.3	24.2
Trinidad and Tobago	0.1	0.7	53.9	36.3	9.0	18.2

Source: The People's Republic of China and Latin America and the Caribbean: Towards a Strategic Relationship *(Santiago, Chile: Economic Commission for Latin America and the Caribbean, May, 2010).*

c. Trade Deficit

The trade deficit between China and the Caribbean increased substantially from $437.2 million in 2001 to $3.56 billion in 2014. See table 2.6 and fig. 2.1 in contrast to Latin America where China has a large deficit.[76] The increase in the trade deficit occurred because the growth of imports from China has far outpaced the expansion of exports from the region. This trend is indicative of the international competitiveness and improved quality of goods from China, and of the limited extent to which Caribbean goods have penetrated the vast market of China. Goods from China have proven attractive to Caribbean importers because of their prices; and consequently, they have increasingly substituted Chinese goods for those from traditional trading partners such as the US. The trend is likely to continue because China has now overtaken the US as the leading producer of manufactured goods. In 2010, China accounted for 19.8 per cent of world's manufactured goods output, exceeding the US share of 19.4 per cent (Marsh 2011).

Table 2.6: Caribbean-China Trade Deficits (2003–14)

US Dollar Millions

2003	2004	2005	2006	2007	2008
437.210	560.921	851.823	1,159.452	1,484.646	2,318.887
2009	**2010**	**2011**	**2012**	**2013**	**2014**
1,795.527	3,251.938	3,359.845	4,069.529	3,414.190	3,556.336

Source: Direction of Trade, International Monetary Fund

Figure 2.1: Caribbean Imports from China and Exports to China

US Dollar Millions

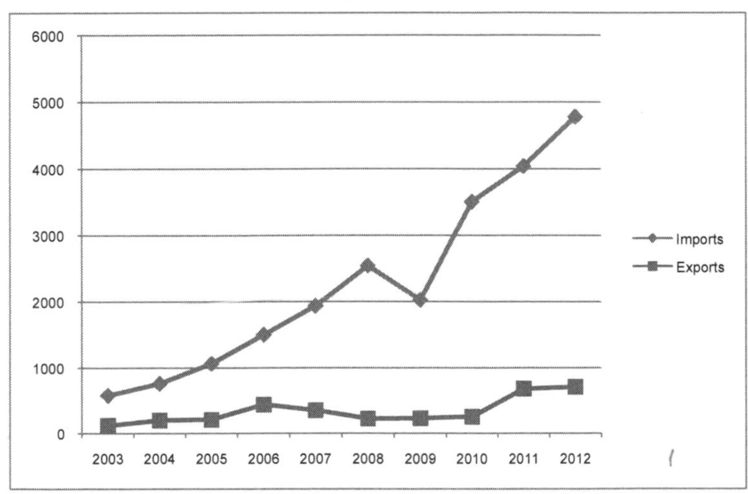

Source: Calculated from Direction of Trade, International Monetary Fund

The market penetration of Chinese goods is occurring across all product categories. Indeed, many of the souvenirs purchased by tourists visiting the region originate in China. So rapid and pervasive has been the increased consumption of Chinese products in Caribbean markets that in some areas this reliance has reached the point where normal life cannot be conducted without products from this source, as is the case in the US.[77] The Caribbean is likely to increasingly import capital goods from China, including automobiles traditionally sourced from Japan, Europe and the US. This trend is likely to be experienced across a range of products that includes machinery and equipment as China increases its capacity to produce high-tech exports which already account for 30 per cent of total exports.[78]

Prior to the global economic crisis, the Caribbean's leading exports were experiencing significant growth, and prospects were encouraging. This outlook has to be tempered in the current economic circumstances, but China remains a vibrant export market because the Chinese economy has maintained the momentum of its economic growth.[79] In the short term, the most promising prospects for export are raw materials and food products, e.g., bauxite, aluminum, asphalt, sugar. Trinidad and Tobago has been exporting ashalt to China since 2003.[80] Caribbean-based producers are not adequately exploiting opportunities for exporting high-value products such as coffee[81] and rum, and mass-market consumer items such as sugar, fish (dried, smoked, or frozen), lobster and shrimp. There are also several market niches that are new to the Caribbean but which can be exploited. For example, the export of scrap metal has become a sizeable industry in Jamaica. Caribbean Community (CARICOM) exporters have not exploited franchise opportunities for products with strong brands, such as the various rums that command a premium. The missed opportunity is evident in the decline of rum exports to China between 2001 and 2005, while China's expenditure on this product increased.

Exporting to China involves a learning process of how to do business in China, understanding government regulations and identifying strategic business partners. The effort to export Jamaica Blue Mountain coffee illustrates the difficulties confronting Caribbean exporters even when the product is a globally known high-value product. Chinese companies were contracted to import and sell the product, to design a marketing campaign to introduce Chinese consumers to the product and to arrange for its distribution. In April 2011, the first export of Jamaica Blue Mountain coffee was shipped to China as part of a two-year deal to export 70 tons per annum through Hangzhou City Coffee and Western Cuisine Association, who acted as Blue Mountain brand representatives in China.[82] One possibility for making exports to China easier would be to negotiate a Free Trade Agreement (FTA) with China as Costa Rica has done. The Free Trade Agreement between China and Costa Rica, which came into effect in August 2011, provides for 60 per cent of the two countries' products to immediately enter each other's duty-free market. Another 30 per cent of products will be liberalized over periods, varying between five and 15 years. The FTA is anticipated to boost trade in which China is already engaged as Costa Rica's second largest export market.[83]

Imports from China are likely to increase as both the merchant community and consumers in the Caribbean become more familiar with products from China. Undoubtedly, importers habituated to purchasing from the US, Japan, Great Britain, and the European Union will take time to learn the intricacies of trading with Chinese entities. Mandarin-speaking nationals of Chinese descent in commercial activities in some Caribbean countries are natural interlocutors for trade with China. Globally dispersed transnational Chinese business networks are active in trade and investment with China.[84] The ease of communication provided by language capacity could be enhanced by language training in Mandarin in the Caribbean. To foster greater language capability, the government of China established the Chinese Multimedia Language Laboratory at the University of the West Indies, Mona Campus, in Jamaica, in June 2004, staffed by two Chinese language instructors. Attendance has been less than ten in any year, but a new development has been the first batch of Jamaican students going to study, in China, in September 2010 to gain exposure to language and culture.[85] Previously, a few students from Guyana and Grenada availed themselves of the opportunity to study in China.

The export of services, which to date has been almost entirely in the construction sector, could expand into technical and scientific sectors in association with development assistance and direct foreign investment. It is likely that Chinese firms will expand from construction into various architectural and engineering services. China will also increasingly be a source of technology and technical services. The *Financial Times* reports that 'China far out-performed every other nation, with a 64-fold increase in peer-reviewed scientific papers since 1981,' and is 'now the second-largest producer of scientific knowledge', 'on course to overtake the US by 2020.'[86] According to US News and World Report, four of the top ten universities in engineering are in China, two are in Singapore and four are in the US.[87]

China's exports to the Caribbean are likely to continue to grow, given their competitive price and quality. They will also be driven by the connection to the increase in development assistance. Lines of credit and development loans and grants requiring use of Chinese funds, equipment and workers will boost these exports. In February 2010, a cooperation agreement between the Export-Import Banks of China and Jamaica established a US$100 million line of credit for trade financing, a US$10 million agreement for concessional financing between the Development Bank of Jamaica (DBJ) and the Chinese National Development Bank, a US$7.3 million provision for technical and economic support and a US$1.1 million agreement for the provision of agricultural equipment and machinery.[88]

d. Net Trade Effect

China's impact on Caribbean Trade are twofold: (1) the primary impact which is demand-driven operates through the effect of the growth in the value and volume of the Caribbean's exports to and imports from China; and (2) the secondary impact which is price driven operates through the effect that China's imports and exports have on prices in global markets. The substantial growth in China's demand for commodities has driven up prices, and this can either lead to an increase in the import bill of Caribbean countries or increased export earnings. A boost in export earnings can occur because the rise in commodity prices propelled by China's expanded demand can have a beneficial effect on countries exporting those commodities which have experienced price increases. The replacement of traditional supplies by less expensive goods from China can reduce the total import bill of Caribbean countries and lower or keep down the cost of living and inflation.[89]

The net trade effect of China differs significantly between Latin America and the Caribbean. China's trade with Latin America has expanded substantially during the last decade. Indeed, China has become the largest trading partner of Brazil, Chile and Peru and even when not in that position, China accounts for almost 20 per cent of trade in Paraguay.[90] Trade with China has resulted in economic growth in Latin America being increasingly synchronized with developments in China.[91] The net trade effect has been relatively insignificant because imports from China into the Caribbean have increased steadily but not on a sufficiently large scale to make China one of the top three trading partners of the region. Exports from the Caribbean to China have not grown substantially, reflecting the limited manufacturing sector outside of the Dominican Republic and Trinidad and Tobago and the predominance of services in the rest of the Caribbean. The net trade effect of China on the Caribbean is summarized in table 2.7.

China's imports and exports have both a price effect and a volume effect which have a differential impact on Latin America and the Caribbean because of the different composition of imports and exports of the two regions. China's dramatic economic growth has had limited impact on growth in the Caribbean, in stark contrast to the experience of Latin America. The potential displacement of production in the Caribbean has not materialized in a discernible way although imports from China have increased across a wide range of products. While it is hard to demonstrate statistically, Chinese goods have replaced traditional supplies from the US and Europe in a manner similar to the impact of Japanese and Korean suppliers in an earlier period. Electronics and household appliances are lucid illustrations of the displacement experience. The traditional presences of products and brand names from the UK were rapidly displaced by supplies from the US starting in the 1960s and, in turn, there was penetration of Japanese and Korean brands from the 1970s to the point of dominance.

Table 2.7: Net Trade Effect of China

	CHINA	GLOBAL	CARIBBEAN	
			POTENTIAL	ACTUAL
1.	Increased import demand for commodities	Increased commodity prices	Increased price of commodity imports	Increased prices for oil and grains
2.	Increased import demand for non-commodities	Increased prices of non-commodities	Increased export earnings and cost of imports	Benefitted some existing agricultural products
3.	Increased import demand	Increased volume of import demand	Expanded export opportunities	Several export opportunities have not been met by increased or new production.
4.	Increased exports at lower prices	Lower prices	Lower costs of imports (inputs and final use)	Many products. Restraining inflation, the cost of living and the cost of production
5.	Increased exports at lower prices	Lower prices	Lower export earnings for competing products	Displaced some manufacturing
6.	Increased exports at lower prices	Lower prices	Displace local production	Limited overall impact due to the dominance of services and limited overlap in manufacturing except in the Dominican Republic and Trinidad and Tobago

Chinese-made products have increased their market share in the last ten years largely through lower prices.

The growth of China's exports can have a disruptive effect on developing economies, particularly on labour-intensive manufactured goods as has happened in Latin America.[92] A notable example is the displacement of Mexican manufactured textiles and electronics in the US market.[93] In most industries, China's export capabilities have improved relative to those of Mexico.[94] Brazil is heavily exposed because Kevin P. Gallagher and Roberto Porzecanski calculate that 84 per cent of its manufacturing exports, representing 28 per cent of its total exports, are under threat from Chinese-made goods.[95] An estimated 92 per cent of Latin America's manufacturing exports were threatened by Chinese products by 2009, representing 39 per cent of Latin America's total exports.[96]

The growth of exports from China has not displaced Caribbean exports in global markets, as has been the case of Latin America nor has China's demand for commodities had a major impact in the Caribbean as it has had in Latin America.[97] This is because the region, with the exception of the Dominican Republic and

Haiti, had lost most of its exports of labour-intensive manufacturing goods given its relatively high level of wages, for example, for apparel manufacturing in Jamaica. Almost 90 per cent of Haiti's exports of goods, mainly assembled apparel articles, including T-shirts, sweaters and men's or boys' suits go to the US.[98] China poses a threat to manufacturing in the Caribbean as it does in Latin and Central America because of its cost advantage.[99] Between 2003 and 2013, an estimated 92 per cent of manufacturing in the Caribbean was losing export competitiveness to China. Apparel exports to the US from Central America in 2009 were down to $5.6 billion, having declined from $7.5 billion in 2004 while China's exports amounted to $24.3 billion, an increase of 127 per cent since 2004. In 2001, China and Central America each accounted for approximately 12 per cent of the US market for clothing, but by 2009, Central America's share of US clothing imports had declined to 8.7 per cent, and China now holds 38 per cent of the US market.[100] Like Latin America and Central America, how the Caribbean meets the challenge of competition from China will be influenced by domestic policy[101] as well as factor endowments and labour costs.

Competition from China in their domestic markets and in export markets is not confined to labour-intensive manufactured goods because China is becoming increasingly sophisticated in technology. China is becoming more competitive in high-technology products and these goods comprise an increasing share of China's exports, displacing low-technology goods.[102] By 2005, so-called 'high-tech' exports amounted to US$220 billion, 'a stunning more than 100 fold increase compared to 1989' and accounted for one-third of total exports.[103]

> China's industrial strength could put pressure on manufacturing industries in middle- and low-income countries...survival in those economies will depend on achieving industrial and innovation capabilities that equals or exceeds China's...other countries must match or exceed China's own investment in its innovation systems.[104]

The technological prowess of China is going to increase as it puts more resources into higher education and scientific research and development. China is now the second-largest producer of scientific knowledge and, if the present momentum continues, will overtake the US by 2020.[105] China has been able to raise its productivity of labour so that even though wages have risen, output per worker has risen. During the decade 1995–2005, labour costs trebled, but labour productivity rose 500 per cent so that unit labour costs fell.[106] China has made a rapid transition from relying on labour-intensive exports to exports that are more technology intensive as competitiveness has improved relative to other countries' exports which are also technology intensive.[107] According to the Global Competitiveness Report, China was ranked 28th in the world in 2015–16, up from 54th just ten years previously.[108]

6. SERVICES

Chinese firms, employing Chinese workers, have been involved in several large construction projects in several Caribbean countries. This is a global enterprise for China involving almost four million Chinese workers in overseas projects,[109] mainly in construction. The Shanghai Construction Company has been involved in the construction of several buildings for the government of Trinidad and Tobago, including the Prime Minister's official residence and the National Academy for the Performing Arts. To date, Chinese firms have been responsible for the construction of buildings with a value of just over US$120 million, and are in the process of completing several other major construction projects. In Jamaica, a convention centre was built at a cost of US$45 million and a campus centre for the University of the West Indies at US$15 million is planned. In Barbados, Chinese firms built the St John's Polytechnic and the Sherbourne Conference Centre. In The Bahamas, China financed and built $59 million of roads and a National Stadium at a cost of $40 million. In Suriname, China has undertaken construction of houses, roads and the Ministry of Foreign Affairs. In 2011, China gave a commitment to build a $600-million deep-sea harbour, highway and port in Suriname.[110] China has also built productive capacity in the Caribbean. For example, the National Technology Import and Export Corporation (CNTIC) has built a state-of-the-art sugar factory in Guyana at an estimated cost of US$181 million. The new factory has the capacity to process 350 tons of cane per hour, and replaces an old factory that could only process 92 tons per hour.[111]

Chinese firms have employed workers from China in their construction projects in the Caribbean. These workers are either responsible for the whole project or they work alongside local workers. They are viewed as depriving locals of employment. This has caused frustration and complaints among local architects, engineers, contractors and trade unions.[112] Trinidad and Tobago has granted work permits for up to 2,827 Chinese nationals, of whom 82 per cent were engaged in construction-related activities and five per cent were employed in food services occupations.[113] Chinese workers were also employed, in Jamaica, in building part of the Trelawny 25,000-Seat Trelawny Stadium for the World Cup Cricket Tournament and, in previous years, in apparel manufacturing. Chinese workers are often lauded for their productivity, such as when 400 Chinese workers built a 20,000-seat stadium in Antigua and completed it ahead of the deadline for the World Cup Cricket Tournament in March 2007. Chinese firms using Chinese workers were introduced to finish a hospital in Tobago when a local company lagged behind on the schedule for completion. Chinese labour built an $8-million international convention centre in Guyana.[114]

The China Harbour Engineering Company (CHEC), a subsidiary of China Communications Construction Company (CCCC), has been active in the construction sector in the Caribbean. CHEC has 31 overseas offices and projects in 70 countries valued at US$9.5 billion, employing 6,000 people. In 2010, it had revenue turnover of US$2.3 billion which yielded a profit of US$200 million. CHEC's operations in Latin America began, in Panama, in 2002 (container terminal) and subsequently carried out projects in Venezuela, Colombia, Argentina and Mexico (LNG terminal). It has made Kingston its regional office from which it supervises projects in 14 countries. In Jamaica, CHEC has two programmes involving road construction and repair, and bridge construction, both of which commenced in 2010. It will execute a five-year public works programme in Jamaica funded by a loan of US$400 million from the Export/Import Bank of China at an interest rate of three per cent with repayment over 20 years. CHEC is undertaking road construction in The Bahamas and is contracted to build a cruise ship port in the Cayman Islands.[115]

Firms from China are becoming internationally competitive in several service areas, especially in construction, engineering and architectural design. Chinese firms initially made their entry based on tied aid from the government of China, but have now started to win contracts through competitive bidding. For example, a Chinese firm won the contract to build the Pogson Hospital in St Kitts, a project that was funded by the World Bank. In Grenada, engineers and workers from China have commenced building a series of low-income housing schemes.[116] China is even a threat to industries regarded as uniquely Caribbean. Trinidadian costume designers and producers have been increasingly outsourcing to China some aspects of the production of costumes for Carnival because of its cheaper labour and the prices, accessibility and variety of materials.[117] There has been a similar experience in Brazil.[118]

7. DEVELOPMENT ASSISTANCE

China's development assistance takes the form of grants, loans, lines of credit, technical assistance and donations in kind. Loans from China are attractive because while terms and interest rates are on commercial terms they are dispensed without policy conditionality unlike loans from Western bilateral agencies and multilateral development institutions. The increase in Chinese aid in the Caribbean region is consistent with a substantial escalation of development aid to developing countries, especially oil-rich African countries. China has substantially increased its development assistance (grants and loans) from approximately $1.5 billion in 2002 to an estimated $25 billion in 2007[119] and $189.3 billion 2011. The *Financial Times* has made the startling revelation that China's lending to developing countries in the two years, 2009 and 2010, was more than that of the World Bank.[120] At the end of 2009, China had provided aid to 123 developing countries and over 30 international and regional organizations. Beneficiary countries include 51 in

Africa, 30 in Asia, 18 in Latin America and the Caribbean, 12 in Oceania and 12 in Eastern Europe. Approximately 80 per cent of China's foreign aid is given to Asia and Africa where the largest populations of the extreme poor are to be found.

The increase in Chinese aid is taking place at a time when aid from traditional sources such as the US is declining. Consequently, one observer articulates the widespread view in the region when he states that 'China has filled a void left by the United States and other Western nations'.[121] In 2007, China promised to provide the Caribbean economic assistance of ¥4 billion in low interest loans and for training related to the promotion of trade.[122]

Apart from its contribution to economic development in the Caribbean, development assistance is the principal means of influence employed by China in its foreign policy in the Caribbean. The amount and allocation are related to the rivalry with Taiwan for diplomatic recognition. The government of China is also willing to extend aid to those countries that switch diplomatic allegiance from Taiwan. For example, when Dominica switched its diplomatic recognition from Taiwan to China, it benefited from the construction of a $17-million cricket stadium and a promise of $122 million in economic assistance.[123] Those countries that have chosen to recognize Taiwan have done so for pecuniary motives rather than ideological reasons. Dr Denzil Douglas, Prime Minister of St Kitts and Nevis, explained: 'We took an informed position that we would prefer to support Taiwan because Taiwan at the moment can bring the greater support in the advancing of the economic, social and political development of the people.'[124] The Prime Minister of St Vincent expressed similar sentiments.[125]

Accurate and up-to-date statistical data on China's aid are extremely difficult to find, and it is an enigma to decipher the different forms of aid. Available data indicate that development assistance to Caribbean countries amounted to US$87 million in 2005, with the largest recipients Suriname ($23.6 million), Jamaica ($16.3 million), Belize ($10.1 million), Guyana ($9.9 million) and Dominica ($9.3 million). Aid to individual countries is shown in table 2.8 based on the latest data that is publicly available, which is seriously out of date. China significantly increased its aid in 2006 when it provided considerable resources – human and financial – in building several stadiums to enable the region to meet the requirements for hosting the World Cup Cricket Tournament in 2007. The construction of critical infrastructure such as bridges and important and highly visible buildings such as hospitals has earned the gratitude of several Caribbean governments. Chinese aid has prompted former Antigua and Barbuda Prime Minister, Baldwin Spencer, to declare, 'China has time and time proven that it is a true friend of Antigua and Barbuda and is prepared to assist us as we develop this country. For this we are eternally grateful.'[126] Such laudatory comments are no surprise given China's agreement to construct a new terminal at the airport at a cost of $45 million.

Table 2.8: China's Development Assistance to Caribbean Countries (US$)

Country/Region	**2004**	**2005**
Global Total	**21,368,980,000**	**26,776,050,000**
Caribbean	70,980,000	87,200,000
Antigua and Barbuda	12,910,000	7,990,000
The Bahamas	7,510,000	930,000
Barbados	11,800,000	6,480,000
Belize	14,180,000	10,140,000
Dominica	430,000	9,330,000
Dominican Republic	-	-
Grenada	-	1,480,000
Guyana	4,540,000	9,950,000
Jamaica	5,640,000	16,250,000
St Lucia	410,000	1,010,000
St Vincent and Grenadines	400,000	-
Suriname	11,560,000	23,590,000
Trinidad and Tobago	1,600,000	50,000

Source: China Statistical Yearbook 2006

Chinese aid to the Caribbean has evolved and includes some non-traditional forms of development assistance. In July 2007, China introduced debt forgiveness as a form of assistance, similar to that provided to the least developed countries of Africa. China agreed to write off over $15.3 million in debt owed by Guyana for loans accumulated between 1975 and 1993.[127] This precedent could be important because of the high level of external debt in most to the Caribbean countries[128] and because these states are middle-income economies that do not qualify for debt relief under HIPC. Haiti and Guyana are the only Caribbean countries that are eligible for relief provided for under the HIPC. Looking ahead, if the countries continue to borrow from the government and financial institutions of China at the current rate, then debt to China could assume some prominence.

Another departure in China's aid to the Caribbean has been the provision of funds to the Jamaica Defense Force (JDF) which has, since its formation, relied on assistance from the US, UK and Canada. In August 2011, the government of the People's Republic of China committed to providing military aid worth eight million Remnimbi (RMB) (US$1.1 million). The specific uses for which the aid can be used are yet to be defined.[129] This step is in keeping with China's expansion of cooperation with the military in Latin America[130] and is related to furthering its diplomatic, political and commercial interests rather than being motivated primarily by security concerns.

Throughout its relationship with the Caribbean countries, China has provided some development assistance starting with projects executed by technical assistance, e.g., shrimp farming and bamboo weaving in Trinidad and Tobago.[131] China has increased its development assistance to Caribbean countries, focusing resources on large, highly visible infrastructure projects such as the construction of national stadiums in Dominica, Grenada and St Lucia, and a community-based stadium in Sligoville, Jamaica. Schools have been built in several countries, a hospital in St Lucia, a multi-purpose sports arena in Barbados and a cricket stadium in Jamaica (US$30 million). The Chinese government also provided funding for the Montego Bay Convention Centre in Jamaica in the amount of US$45.2 million at a concessionary rate of interest through the Ex-Im Bank of China. Jamaica also benefited from a US$400 million loan for road construction and repair. In Suriname, Chinese companies will undertake US$600 million of construction projects, including a new deep-sea harbour, a railway from Paramaribo to Brazil, an east-west sea wall, a new highway to the airport and 8,000 low-cost houses.[132]

Apart from bilateral development assistance, China has become a development partner in regional and multilateral development finance institutions that service the Caribbean. China is a non-regional member of the Caribbean Development Bank (CDB) with US$56 million in shares and US$33 million in the CDB's Special Development Fund. All borrowing members of the CDB are eligible for these resources regardless of whether their diplomatic relations are with China or Taiwan. These resources can be accessed by all Caribbean countries except Cuba and the Dominican Republic because these countries are not members of the CDB.

China became the 48th member country of the Inter-American Development Bank[133] (IDB) in October 2008 when it purchased 184 shares, the equivalent of 0.004 per cent of the IDB's ordinary capital, which became available after the breakup of Yugoslavia. Simultaneously, China became the 44th member of Inter-American Investment Corporation when it acquired 110 shares or 0.16 per cent of its subscribed capital of the IIC. On joining, China contributed $350 million to the IDB Group allocated in: (a) $125 million to the IDB's Fund for Special Operations, which provides soft loans to Bolivia, Guyana, Haiti, Honduras, and Nicaragua; (b) $75 million to several IDB grant funds to strengthen the institutional capacity of the state, including municipal governments and private sector institutions; (c) $75 million is for an equity fund to be administered by the Inter-American Investment Corporation (IIC), which lends to small and mid-sized private businesses; and (d) $75 million to the Multilateral Investment Fund which focuses on microenterprises. In March 2013, IDB and the People's Bank of China (PBC) established the China Co-financing Fund for Latin America and the Caribbean, the objective of which is to finance public and private sector projects that promote sustainable economic growth. The Fund, the first of its kind established by China and a multilateral development bank, is designed to co-finance $500 million public sector loans and $1.5 billion to private sector entities.

The growth of the Chinese economy and foreign policy outreach proffers opportunities for Chinese investment. Foreign investment would provide Chinese firms with a production platform for exporting to the European Community, the US and Canada, where CARICOM has preferential trade arrangements. As these trade and investment interests grow, China, cognizant of Taiwan's aggressive competition in the region, will increase its foreign aid to Caribbean countries. Governments in the Caribbean are likely to be receptive to offers of development aid, including loans and lines of credit, even if these are tied to procurement in China and to execution by Chinese firms and workers. Interest in development assistance from China will be high, given the fiscal situation and debt profile of several governments, exacerbated by the global economic crisis.

Loans from China are generating opportunities for Chinese firms and workers. Activities in Dominica provide a lucid illustration of the nexus between Chinese development aid and construction projects. On signing a Framework Agreement, the government of Dominica and the government of China were able to finalize loan arrangements with the Export-Import Bank of China. The loan of up to US$40 million has an interest rate of two per cent per annum with a repayment period of 20 years, including a grace period of five years. It will be used for the construction of the Dominica State College, the State House, the office building of the Electoral Commission, and the rehabilitation of major roads.[134] Chinese aid has not been welcomed by some traditional bilateral donor agencies and multilateral development institutions. They have complained that Chinese aid is pushing them out of certain sectors such as road construction in which they have been traditional sources of development aid. They have claimed that while the interest rate on loans from China is lower, use is tied to employment of Chinese workers who ignore environmental standards and deliver shoddy construction. Still, many beneficiary governments have been pleased with the speed with which urgently needed facilities have been completed.

8. FOREIGN DIRECT INVESTMENT

China is the second largest economy in the world and has grown at an average rate of ten per cent per year during the period 1990–2005, the highest growth rate in the world. It is one of the engines of growth in the new global economy, accounting in recent years for 12 per cent of all growth in world trade.[135] China has continued to grow in spite of the global economic crisis of 2008, achieving a growth of 9.2 per cent in 2011,[136] although growth has since slowed. Foreign direct investment

(FDI) contributed to China's economic growth. Indeed, by 2002, when total FDI inflows reached US$53 billion, China had become the largest recipient of FDI, surpassing the US.[137] As China's economy has grown and become more integrated into the global economy, it is not only a major destination for FDI but has emerged as a source of foreign direct investment, especially in developing countries, and particularly in energy and raw materials.

a. Emergence of China as a Source of FDI

Outward FDI from China was authorized in 1979, when the first joint venture law was passed, and particularly after the Sixteenth Congress of the Chinese Communist Party promulgated the 'Go Global Strategy'. Starting from a low level, FDI has grown slowly throughout the 1980s and 1990s, increasing rapidly during the last decade. The impetus for FDI emanates from both the state and the enterprises, and the state and large enterprises are either in tandem or at least in alignment.[138] While the state has an overarching role, it is not possible to control all FDI given the number of firms involved in FDI. Based on a survey of executives of Chinese companies, it is reported that: 'The first primary push factor propelling the internationalisation of Chinese SOEs (state-owned enterprises) is the central government's "global" policy and related incentives, while the second relates to the business strategies adopted by enterprise leaders.'[139] The government of China has also relaxed the bureaucratic processes which enterprises have to go through to get permission to make a foreign investment. In February 2011, the National Development and Reform Commission raised the threshold on overseas direct investment (ODI), requiring government approval from $30 million to $300 million for investments in resources and concomitantly from $10 million to $100 million in non-resources projects.[140]

China's outward FDI flows have increased steadily since 2006 when it amounted to $21.2 billion in spite of the global recession which began in late 2008. In 2013, China with $101 billion was the third largest source of foreign direct investment after the US and Japan.[141] The stock of Chinese FDI has increased dramatically during that period from $90.6 billion to $531.9 billion.[142] In 2012, China's outward FDI accounted for 6.3 per cent of global FDI and 2.3 per cent of global stock of FDI, which put China third behind the US and Japan in global FDI and 13th in the stock of global FDI.[143] This trend is likely to continue as President Xi Jinping in November 2014 proclaimed that Chinese 'offshore' investment will reach $1.25 trillion over the next decade.[144]

By 2002, when total FDI inflows reached US$53 billion, China had become the largest recipient of FDI, surpassing the US.[145] The flow of investment to China is not at the expense of the Caribbean because the motivations for FDI in the two regions are different. The Chinese market is vast and the possible scale of production is conducive to realizing economies of scale and scope employing comparatively inexpensive labour. In contrast, the Caribbean countries, except for Guyana and Haiti, are middle-income developing countries with small national markets. There may have been some displacement of light manufacturing that benefited from proximity to the US. This effect would be quite small, given that manufacturing for export in the Caribbean is limited except in Trinidad and Tobago and the Dominican Republic. The industrial base of Trinidad and Tobago is based on natural gas and energy, and it has its own niche in the global market, hence the displacement would not have been significant. Manufacturing of consumer goods, and food processing, have the advantage of locale, brand recognition and traditional taste.

In a market-based economy, the state does not control investment decisions whereas in China, which is a mixed economy, the state dominates decisions about investment, including FDI. The Chinese state has been implementing a deliberate strategy of creating internationally competitive state-owned companies that operate as multinational corporations. According to the 2009 Statistical Bulletin of China's Outward Foreign Direct Investment, centrally controlled, state-owned enterprises (SOEs) were responsible for 68 per cent of the total Chinese outward direct investment compared to less than one per cent by private enterprises, with another 30 per cent by a variety of other economic entities owned by regional and provincial authorities.[146] An estimated 87 per cent of Chinese OFDI in Latin America and the Caribbean during the period 2000–11 emanated from public companies.[147] Given its large international reserves invested in low-yielding government paper and its need for raw materials, the Chinese state created a sovereign wealth fund, the China Investment Corporation, in 2007, with an initial capitalization of $200 billion.[148] During the period 2002–11, Chinese FDI grew at an annual average of 45 per cent. In 2011, FDI increased by 8.5 per cent to reach a total of $74.7 billion, with developing countries attracting $61.2 billion representing 82 per cent of China's FDI in that year.[149] China's outbound direct investment from 2011 to 2015 is expected to register double-digit annual growth to reach US$560 billion.[150]

Inducing investment from China inevitably requires state to state relations with the government of China. This engagement can be complicated because the catenation between the state in the form of the Department of Foreign Economic Cooperation of the Ministry of Commerce[151] and Chinese firms varies, resulting in different types of firms. Some are state enterprises under the direct control of the state, either the central government or at the provincial level, and some are private firms; these include multinational enterprises, large firms which have expanded overseas, and small and medium-sized firms that are involved in international trade and looking to invest abroad.[152]

China's outward investment activities are often directed by the state, especially for investments in oil, minerals and telecommunications. Investments in these sectors are under the control of the state and, in any case, the investments are in most instances being made by state enterprises.[153] The state gives explicit direction to overseas investment priorities. For example, a 2004 joint directive from the National Development and Reform Commission (NDRC) and the Export-Import Bank of China (EIBC) emphasized projects that mitigate the domestic shortage of natural resources, promote the export of domestic products, equipment and labour, and 'enhance the international competitiveness of Chinese enterprises and accelerate their entry into foreign markets'.[154] The superintending institutions include the State-owned Assets Supervision and Administration Commission (SASAC) which oversees large state-owned enterprises, the State Administration for Foreign Exchange (SAFE) and the Ministry of Commerce (MOFCOM). Entities regulated at the provincial level are allowed to make foreign investments since 2009, when the Ministry of commerce granted them this right.[155]

b. Identifying Chinese FDI

To establish the value of Chinese FDI in the Caribbean, it is necessary to first differentiate FDI from other capital flows from China. The literature labels all capital flows as investment, and this is particularly misleading in the case of the Caribbean because capital flows are almost entirely development loans from the Chinese state and its agencies and institutions. Data compiled from sources other than the government of China does not differentiate the two types of capital flows and therefore it is not possible to identify FDI. Second, care has to be exercised when interpreting the data on FDI available from the government of China both at the aggregate level and the disaggregated flows.[156] This is even more complicated in the case of Chinese FDI in the Caribbean because of funds held in Caribbean financial centres such as the Cayman Islands and the British Virgin Islands are listed as DFI when in fact they are being routed to other destinations. These large pools of funds exist in large measure because Caribbean destinations are used for 'round-tripping', i.e., the practice of sending capital out of China to bring it back as foreign investment and thereby gain the benefits of special concessions and lower taxes. An additional explanation for these flows is capital flight that is being repatriated, and this flow, which mainly exited to Hong Kong, may have accounted for 20–30 per cent of FDI.[157] Yet another complication is determining the actual source and destinations of the FDI, because some investment flows have been routed through some Caribbean jurisdictions[158] and, therefore, could be misinterpreted as originating in those states. Estimates vary; some sources have estimated that by 2006 the Cayman Islands accounted for one-fifth of the total FDI,[159] the British Virgin Islands is the second largest source of FDI to China.[160] Other calculations suggest that in 2009 the Cayman Islands and the British Virgin Islands together accounted for 12 per cent.[161] Palan, Murphy and Chavagneux state that 'round-tripping' accounts for 'a considerable portion of FDI into China.'[162] However, D.

Sutherland and B. Matthews suggest that 'round-tripping' alone cannot explain the net inflows because far more is invested in China from the Cayman Islands and the British Virgin Islands than emanates from China.[163] Sharman has suggested the transaction cost reducing efficiencies is a motivation of Chinese investors routing their money through offshore financial centres.[164]

Third, information on Chinese FDI is not complete as it does not capture small private investments. There are several small enterprises owned and operated by Chinese migrants which fall under the proverbial radar screen of registration by the state in China. These are settler-type investments in which the investor and their capital move to the Caribbean. These enterprises are a result of migrants, in some instances, workers who have not returned to China after employment in construction projects carried out by Chinese firms. They are mainly involved in restaurants and in the importation and retail distribution of consumer goods imported from China.

c. Stock of Chinese FDI

China's foreign direct investment in Caribbean countries is small, both as a share of China's FDI and as a share of the stock of FDI in the Caribbean. By 2013, the total stock of Chinese FDI in the Caribbean amounted to $493.2 million, having increased from $81.2 million in 2005. Data for the period 2005–13 are shown in table 2.9.

Table 2.9: Chinese FDI Stock in the Caribbean by Country 2005–13 (US$ millions)

	2005	2006	2007	2008	2009	2010	2011	2012	2013
Antigua and Barbuda	0.4	1.3	1.3	1.3	1.3	1.3	4.8	5.4	6.3
The Bahamas	14.7	17.5	56.5	0.6	1.6	1.6	1.6	0.6	0.6
Barbados	1.7	2.01	2.4	3.3	6	3.9	3.1	4.0	5.0
Belize	-	0.02	0.02	0.08	0.08				0.35
Cuba	33.6	59.9	66.5	72.1	85.3	70.0	146.4	135.7	111.3
Dominica	-	0.7	0.7	0.7	0.7	4.15	8.2	8.2	8.5
Dominican Republic	-	-	-	0.6	0.12	0.12	0.1	1.1	1.1
Grenada	-	4.0	7.5	7.65	7.65	14.25	14.5	14.5	14.5
Guyana	5.6	8.6	68.6	69.5	149.6	183.7	135.1	151.9	225.2
Haiti	-	-	-	-	-	-	-	-	-
Jamaica	-	0.02	0.02	2.16	2.16	4.37	39.1	74.9	79.7
St Kitts and Nevis	-	-	-	-	-	-	-	-	-
St Lucia	-	-	-	-	-	-	-	-	-
St Vincent and the Grenadines	12.27	14.92	20.8	32.5	23.03	36.2	36.2	36.2	36.2
Suriname	13.02	32.21	65.3	67.7	68.8	78.8	78.8	45.6	111.9
Trinidad and Tobago		0.8	0.8	0.8	0.8	0.8	0.9	1.1	3.9
Caribbean	81.2	142.0	290.4	258.8	347.1	398.1	468.9	479.2	604.45
Caribbean without Cuba	47.6	82.1	123.9	186.8	262.8	332.5	322.5	343.5	493.15

Source: Chinese Statistical Bulletin of Outward Foreign Direct Investment, various years.

They do not appear to include the largest investment by a Chinese firm in the Caribbean – the $2.6-billion port facility in Freeport, Bahamas, built and operated since 2000 by the Hong Kong-owned Hutchison Whampoa.[165] This firm is the largest Chinese company in the Caribbean although in a strict definition it would be regarded as a company from Hong Kong. Employing Dunning's typology of investment drivers, China's direct foreign investment in the region has been raw-material seeking and market seeking with little driven by efficiency and strategic-asset seeking.[166]

d. Inventory of Chinese FDI

A full inventory of Chinese-owned businesses is not possible because of the number of small trading companies and restaurants and the difficulty of distinguishing foreign Chinese from Caribbean citizens of Chinese origin. In March 2014, the Zhanghao Shipyard owned by Chinese nationals has completed the construction of its first vessel since its establishment in 2012. According to *Stabroek News*, the shipyard in Coverden has a 200,000-tonne barge for the purpose of transporting logs from its logging concession. The steel plates, engines and equipment were imported from China.[167]

The Chinese company, Bosai Minerals Group, purchased a controlling stake of 70 per cent in Omai Bauxite Mining, Inc. in Linden, Guyana, in December 2006 for $100 million,[168] with the government of Guyana retaining 30 per cent ownership. Bosai Mining, a privately owned firm based in China's Chongqing Municipality, will link its Guyana operations to its annual production capacity of 400,000 tons of refractory bauxite, making the company the largest producer in the world.

Negotiations between the government of Jamaica and a Chinese company, Zhuhai Hongfan, for the sale of its 45 per cent stake in bauxite producer and alumina producer Clarendon Alumina Production Limited (CAP) did not come to fruition.[169] The government of Jamaica has signed a memorandum of understanding with the Xinfa Group Company to examine taking over the plant formerly operated by Reynolds Mines.[170] It is, however, indicative of China's interest in securing supplies of certain raw materials. Chinese firms have made investments in the mineral sector in Bolivia, Brazil, Chile and Peru.[171]

The China National Complete Plant Import and Export Corporation (Complant), in a joint venture with private investors, established the Pan Caribbean Sugar Company which purchased three sugar factories and leased associated lands from the government of Jamaica. These include the Monymusk and Bernard Lodge factories for US$9 million and the lease of 30,000 hectares of cane-growing lands. Starting in August 2011, Complant began investing a proposed $156 million in improvements in fields and factories over a four-year period.[172] Complant also contemplates making additional investment in the new sugar refinery to process

200,000 tonnes of raw sugar per annum, and an ethanol plant. Complant's previous projects in Jamaica included the construction of the Trelawny Multi-Purpose Stadium and the Rose Hall Convention Centre. A Chinese firm, China Zhong Heng Tai Investment Company (CZHT), has invested $4.5 million guaranteed by the government of China in the production of palm oil from Patamacca plantation in Marowijne, Suriname. The project involves cultivation on 2,000 hectares that had been destroyed by civil war and disease. The first phase will involve replanting with disease resistant seedlings imported from Malaysia and the rehabilitation of a factory which was closed in 2004.[173]

China has had a strong interest in securing supplies of energy, and it has pursued that interest in the Caribbean as it has in Africa and Latin America. However, Chinese FDI in Trinidad and Tobago is small although there is involvement in the energy sector and expressions of interest. In May 2009, Chaoyang Petroleum (Trinidad), a wholly owned subsidiary of Chaoyang BVI, acquired from Talisman (Trinidad Block 3A) Limited, a 25.5 per cent interest in the production sharing contract under Block 3A offshore of Trinidad and Tobago for US$780,000. In August 2011, China Investment Corporation (CIC) acquired the ten per cent stake of French firm GDF Suez in Train 1 of the Atlantic LNG natural gas plant, as well as production payments associated with Trains 2, 3 and 4 for €600 million. ECLAC reports the value of this transaction at $850 million.[174] CIC will also acquire 30 per cent of GDF Suez's Exploration and Production division.[175] In February 2014, The National Gas Company of Trinidad and Tobago (NGC) signed a Memorandum of Understanding with the Chinese engineering company, ENN, one of China's largest private companies to develop compressed natural gas (CNG).[176] In 2012, a $5.3 billion joint venture between SABIC of Saudi Arabia and Sinopec of China for a methanol refinery in Trinidad and Tobago did not come to fruition,[177] but it certainly indicates the scale of investment which is possible.

The first major Chinese FDI has taken place in The Bahamas. The China State Construction Engineering Corporation, a state enterprise purchased the British Colonial Hilton[178] in October 2014. Major refurbishing is planned and when that is completed Hilton will continue to manage the hotel. The significance of this purchase is that it is a first for a Chinese corporation, albeit a state enterprise, and could be the forerunner of other Chinese DFI in tourism.

The demand for resources is one of the most compelling drivers of China's foreign economic policy,[179] including foreign direct investment. The Chinese company, Bosai Minerals Group, purchased a controlling stake of 70 per cent in Omai Bauxite Mining, Inc. in Linden, Guyana, in December 2006 for $100 million[180] with the government of Guyana retaining 30 per cent of ownership. Bosai Mining, a privately owned firm based in China's Chongqing Municipality, will link its Guyana operations to its annual production capacity of 400,000 tons of refractory bauxite, making the company the largest producer in the world.

Table 2.10: Chinese FDI in the Caribbean by Country, Company, Sector and US$ Value

Country	Company	Sector	Investment	
			Value	**Date**
Guyana	Bosai Mining[1]	Mining Investment	$100mn	2006
	Haier Computer Store[2]	Computer Service Center		2012
		Computer and TV Assembly Plant	$10 mn	Deferred indefinitely
	Bai Shan Lin/China Forest Industry Group[3/]	Forestry		
		Wood Processing Factory	$70mn	delayed
		Gold Mining		2014
		Housing and Mall Development		2014
	Datang[4] (20% shares in GT&T)	Telecommunications	$30 mn	2012
Jamaica	Xinfa[5]	Mining	In discussion	
	China National Complete Plant Import-Export Corporation[6]	Agriculture (cane farming)	$156mn.	2011
		Manufacturing (sugar)	$9mn.	2011
	China Harbour Engineering Co[7]	Transport	$600mn.	2014
		Tourism –Hotels		
Suriname	China Zhong Heng Tai Investment[8]	Agriculture/Mfg (Oil Palm)	$4.5mn.	
Trinidad and Tobago	Chaoyang BVI (25.5% share)	Energy (Oil production)	$0.78mn.	2009
	China Investment Corporation	Energy (Natural gas)	$850mn.	2011
	China Investment Corporation (30% share)	Energy (Exploration)	In discussion	
	ENN[9]	Energy(Compressed Natural gas)	MOU signed	2014
	SINOPEC/SABIC JV[10]	Alt Energy (methanol)	aborted	
The Bahamas	China State Construction Engineering[11]	Tourism	N/A	2014
Antigua	Yida International Investment Group[12]	Tourism	$1bn	2015

Sources:

1. *'Bosai Mining acquires South America bauxite mining company,' Mining Top News, 2006. Retrieved on November 23, 2009.*
2. *'Haier service centre opens in Guyana,' Guyana Times International, February 24, 2012.*
3. *Kaieteur News online edition*
4. *Stabroek News, 'US$25 mn from Sale of GT&T Shares Going to NICIL,' November 23, 2012.*
5. *Balford Henry, 'God Returns,' Jamaica Observer, 7 May, 2014, 1.*
6. *Luke Douglas, 'Govt. Seals Sugar Deal with Complant: Chinese Company Investing US$156m in Industry,' Jamaica Observer, August 16, 2011 and 'J$8b Sugar Divestment Agreements Signed between Government and Chinese Investors,' August 2, 2010, http://www.jis.gov.jm/news/opm-news/24875.*
7. *Karena Bennett, 'CHEC Adds 1,400 more rooms to planned North South Highway Hotels,' Jamaica Observer, May 9, 2015, 1.*
8. *R. Evan Ellis, 'Suriname and the Chinese: Timber, Migration, and Less-Told Stories of Globalization,' SAIS Review XXXII, no. 2 (Summer/Fall 2012): 91 and 'Suriname's Palm-oil Sector to be Rehabilitated,' http://agritrade.cta.int/Agriculture/Commodities/Oil-crops/Suriname-s-palm-oil-sector-to-be-rehabilitated.*
9. *Sasha Harrinanan, 'NGC signs agreement with China,' Trinidad and Tobago Newsday, February 24, 2014.*
10. *R. Evan Ellis, China on the Ground in Latin America: Challenges for the Chinese and Impacts on the Region (New York: Palgrave Macmillan, 2014), 141.*
11. *'Nassau's British Colonial Hilton Sold.' http://www.caribjournal.com/2014/10/...british-colonial-hilton-sold.*
12. *'Soil Turned, Jobs On,' Antigua & Barbuda News, May 1, 2015.*

Negotiations between the government of Jamaica and a Chinese company, Zhuhai Hongfan, for the sale of its 45 per cent stake in bauxite producer and alumina producer, Clarendon Alumina Production Limited (CAP), did not come to fruition. It is, however, indicative of the interest in China to secure supplies of certain raw materials. Chinese firms have made investments in the mineral sector in Bolivia, Brazil, Chile and Peru.[181]

Chinese FDI is beginning to grow in the Caribbean, but as indicated by the Economic Commission for Latin America and the Caribbean (ECLAC), Chinese FDI is still small compared to traditional sources of FDI such as Canada, the US, and the UK.[182] The sectors in which there has been Chinese FDI are agriculture, tourism, minerals and energy. Chinese FDI to date is shown in table 2.10.

The Caribbean countries have sought to induce direct foreign investment by establishing bilateral investment treaties with countries identified as likely sources of investment. Caribbean governments have signed 82 bilateral investment treaties with countries mainly in Europe and North America. This policy has been applied to China, starting well before China became a major source of investment. Jamaica signed a Bilateral Investment Agreement (BIT) with China in 1994 and a Double Taxation Avoidance Agreement (DTA) with China in 1996. Barbados signed a BIT in 1998 and a DTA in 2000. Trinidad and Tobago signed a BIT on July 22, 2002 and a DTA in 2003. In 2003, Guyana signed an Agreement for the Encouragement and Reciprocal Protection of Investment. These BITs vary as they relate to coverage of assets, dispute resolution, expropriation and compensation. How important the existence of BITs is to encouraging FDI is open to debate.[183] In this regard, it is interesting that the US has BITs only with Grenada, Haiti and Jamaica, but the stock of US investment is largest in The Bahamas, Barbados, and Trinidad and Tobago.[184]

Foreign investment in China has grown exponentially since 1979 when the first joint venture law was passed. By 2002, when total FDI inflows reached US$53 billion, China had become the largest recipient of FDI, surpassing the US.[185] There is concern that the amount of direct foreign investment going to China could be crowding out other developing countries. This is certainly a possibility where Caribbean countries are producing similar goods, for example, in some manufacturing in the Dominican Republic and Trinidad and Tobago. It is unlikely that there has been serious investment diversion from the Caribbean because of China's 'pull', since FDI in the Caribbean during the last decade has been primarily in tourism, which accounted for over 50 per cent of GDP in the smaller economies of the eastern Caribbean[186] except in Trinidad and Tobago and the Dominican Republic. Certainly, China has several advantages over the Caribbean, notably in attaching market-seeking investment given the enormous size of its domestic economy and inducing efficiency-seeking investment given its less costly labour, its economies of scale and its being the fastest growing economy in the world.

Although China constitutes a huge pool of potential foreign investment for the Caribbean, efforts by Caribbean governments and firms have been limited to investment promotion missions rather than a sustained and planned campaign. As China becomes more economically involved in the region, its investment interests could expand, but the extent to which FDI increases will depend in part on the economic environment in the Caribbean and the policies of governments in the Caribbean. For example, investment promotion missions have been mounted by Barbados, Guyana, Jamaica, Suriname, and Trinidad and Tobago at the 13th China International Fair for Investment and Trade (CIFIT), September 2009 in Xiamen of Fujian Province.[187] Similarly, there was the Trinidad and Tobago Business Forum held in Shanghai in September 2010 at the Shanghai Expo. The follow up to contacts resulting from these fledgling sorties is left to their embassies whose staff complement is not trained for this task. The embassies, however, could facilitate Chinese investors since, for example, the inordinately bureaucratic and time-consuming process of issuing visas for business travel to Jamaica has been eliminated.

Caribbean investment in China is virtually non-existent and is likely to remain that way for the foreseeable future. There is a Jamaican company that operates some restaurants serving Jamaican food. Trade has flourished at arm's length without Caribbean firms establishing themselves in China. Investment would be more likely to grow if it involved partnerships, joint ventures and strategic business alliances between Chinese and Caribbean firms. Government investment promotion agencies could encourage these by disseminating information and brokering strategic corporate alliances.[188] In September 2007, China announced that it would provide $530 million in concessional loans over three years to Chinese companies investing in the Caribbean.[189] Perhaps a fund could be established within the Caribbean Development Bank to advise and assist Caribbean companies to invest in China. Such a fund has been established in the Inter-American Development Bank.

As China increasingly becomes a source of foreign investment, there has been a willingness to employ direct investment in order to secure long-term supplies of raw materials. Securing sources of raw materials on a long-term basis has been a driving force in China's foreign policy, particularly in regard to supplies of oil.[190] To date, in 2010, global oil demand has fallen, but the International Energy Agency is forecasting that oil demand in China will rise by 2.8 per cent to 8.1 million barrels a day, and demand in 2011 will increase by four per cent to 8.4 million barrels a day.[191] Demand is predicted to reach 30 million barrels per day by 2030,[192] and this is certain to spur resource-seeking foreign investment. The Caribbean has some raw materials that are of interest to China, in particular fairly large reserves of bauxite, some natural gas and fish stocks. Indicative of China's interest in mineral supplies was its willingness to finance and construct a US$400-million aluminum smelter in Trinidad.[193] However, the current government of Trinidad and Tobago has decided not to proceed with this project. The possibilities of discovering oil and mineral deposits in the vast expanses of Guyana, as well as unexplored marine and seabed resources of the Caribbean, is unlikely to have escaped the attention of China's long-term planning.

Investment, aid and provision of construction services will continue to be an important nexus and mechanism of Chinese participation in Caribbean countries. Most of China's projects have been funded by preferential loans from state-owned Chinese banks with the Chinese Development Bank being the most important.[194] For example, in Suriname where the government has agreed on several infrastructure projects with two Chinese enterprises, Cheng Don International and China Harbour, involving the financing and execution of projects. Cheng Don International will construct 8,000 public housing units, and China Harbour will be engaged in road and railroad links between Paramaribo to Brazil, a deep-sea harbour, a sea dam from Albina to Nickerie and a high-way to Zanderij.

There may also be opportunities for Chinese foreign investment in tourism, agriculture, forestry, construction, infrastructure, education and healthcare. Chinese firms are being encouraged by both their own government and those of the Caribbean to examine investment prospects in the region. The government of Trinidad and Tobago held a promotion event in Beijing in April 2010 to attract investment and tourists from China. Demand for food in China will increase with population growth and rising income levels and, consequently, food imports will escalate. This could induce Chinese investment in agricultural production in other countries. The fertile, well-watered lands of Guyana, Belize and Suriname are attractive possibilities, as much of this land is suitable for food crops, including rice. China Zhong Heng Tai Investment Company (CZHT)[195] has made an investment which will resurrect palm oil production in Suriname which was seriously affected by disease. China has concluded an agreement with the government of Jamaica to purchase the three largest sugar plantations and the associated factories. China's need for lumber for construction could impel investment in the timber reserves of Belize, Guyana and Suriname.

Manufacturing possibilities could induce Chinese foreign investment because Caribbean countries could be attractive as production platforms for exports to the US, Canada, and the European Union. Caribbean countries have preferential trade arrangements, including the Caribbean Basin Economic Recovery Act[196] which has been extended to 2020 by the Haiti Economic Lift Program (HELP) Act of 2010, the Caribbean–Canada Trade Agreement (CARIBCAN),[197] the Dominican Republic–Central American–United States Free Trade Agreement[198] and the CARIFORUM–EU Economic Partnership Agreement.[199] This opportunity is beginning to elicit interest from Chinese investors, for example, Mindray, a Chinese–US joint venture manufacturing electro-medical equipment in China for sale in more than 60 countries across the world, is currently exploring the possibilities of investing in Jamaica. In addition to a logistics and distribution centre in Jamaica to serve export markets in the Western Hemisphere, it is also assessing the establishment of a manufacturing, assembly and/or repair and after-sales facility.[200]

Tourism is a distinct possibility for Chinese foreign investment given the growth of world tourism and the forecast of significant increase in foreign travel by Chinese. This started to emerge in February 2011 with the construction of the Baha Mar, a 3,800-room, $3-billion resort in Nassau, Bahamas, which is being financed by the Export-Import Bank of China, and its construction will involve about 5,000 Chinese workers. The Baha Mar Resort will include six hotels, a new casino and an 18-hole golf course.[201] The Bank of China and the Foreign Trade Bank of China will provide $462 million in financing for the Punta Perla tourism complex in the Dominican Republic which is being undertaken by Spanish investors.[202] The transaction marks the first Chinese investment in the Dominican Republic and is all the more remarkable because of its diplomatic affiliation with Taiwan.

Two new trends in Chinese foreign investment could appear in the Caribbean in the near future. First, mergers and acquisitions account for 30 per cent of China's total outward direct investment.[203] Chinese firms are increasingly taking over foreign firms in order to expand overseas[204] and may acquire Caribbean firms and/or Caribbean export products that are established global brands, as they have done with some US firms. The acquisition of IBM's personal computer division by a virtually unknown Chinese computer manufacturer and the purchase of Volvo from Ford by the Zhejing Geely Holding Company are examples. Second, an interesting and potentially important possibility for the future is portfolio investment. This type of investment is emerging, e.g., as in Chinalco's acquisition of a stake in the Anglo-American mining giant, Rio Tinto. In addition, the government or the central bank of China could purchase bonds issued by governments in the Caribbean. This is new but not unprecedented as China agreed to buy $300 million in 12-year bonds at two per cent from the government of Costa Rica as part of a deal for switching its diplomatic allegiance from Taiwan to the People's Republic of China.[205]

9. TOURISM

Nearly 46 million Chinese travelled abroad in 2008,[206] and spent $30 billion. These numbers will increase significantly as incomes rise and as the middle class continues to grow. China's middle class in 2000 numbered 56 million, and is predicted to reach 361 million by 2030.[207] China is expected to become the world's fourth largest source of tourists by 2020, generating 100 million outbound tourists each year, according to the World Tourism Organization. In 2005, 71 per cent of all outbound travel from the Chinese mainland was to Hong Kong and Macau, and a further 17 per cent travelled within Asia. Of the rest, five per cent went to Europe.[208] The demand for tropical vacations is yet to be developed and, in this regard, the Caribbean will encounter vigorous competition from Pacific destinations. It is interesting to note that Chinese visitor arrivals are extremely small – 976 in Jamaica in 2006, of total arrivals of 1,678, 905 in that year, with 55 per cent staying in private homes.[209]

All Caribbean states that have recognized the potential of the Chinese travel market[210] and have established diplomatic ties with China have received 'approved destination status'. It is understood that a lot more has to be done to break into the tourism market in China and establish the Caribbean as a desirable destination.[211] Products and marketing programmes have to be specifically designed and mounted to entice tourists from China. Increasing Chinese tourist arrivals to the Caribbean should be possible as over 50,000 Japanese tourists a year travel to the region, covering a distance and travel time similar to that faced by potential Chinese tourists. These arrivals occurred without direct flights, little marketing presence and despite competition from Hawaii. This suggests that the potentially gigantic Chinese market can be developed with improved air links and specialized promotion. If the Caribbean could garner even a small share of the growing number of Chinese tourists, it would have a substantial economic and cultural impact.

10. CONSTRUCTION

In recent years, Chinese companies have successfully carried out numerous construction projects in the Caribbean, involving buildings and infrastructure. However, there have been complaints and allegations about the quality of work performed by Chinese companies, implying that they do not adhere to accepted standards. Chinese companies have also been accused of ignoring damage to the natural environment in construction and agriculture and forestry. The common theme is that Chinese companies do shoddy work and have a disregard for damage to the natural environment. These allegations have occurred in an atmosphere of prejudice and suspicion about the standards adhered to by Chinese firms in the execution of construction and infrastructure projects. This amounts to a worldwide smear of Chinese businesses because statements are often not supported by any verifiable empirical evidence. Much of what appears in the media is speculative, and the media regularly predict that Chinese firms will flout the accepted standards of the countries in which they work – be it environmental or structural. Many believe that Chinese construction work will be shoddy and soon show signs of premature degradation while others believe that Chinese firms will show a wholesale disregard for damage to the natural environment. These environmental concerns gain credence because of the many environmental problems in China[212] that lead people to assume the Chinese will transplant their environmental woes to the locations in which they operate.

a. Buildings and Infrastructure

Predictions of poor quality work usually emanate from interest groups who feel that the Chinese firms and Chinese workers have pre-empted the use of their services and usurped their employment opportunities. In several instances, local trade unions such as the Barbados Workers Union;[213] contractors such as the Barbados Association of Contractors; architects such as the Trinidad and Tobago Institute of Architects; and engineers have complained about the employment of Chinese workers on projects being executed by Chinese firms and financed by the government of China. There have been protests against the use of Chinese workers, complaining that locals are not employed in sufficient numbers. These protests occurred at Hutchinson Port Holdings in The Bahamas, China Harbour Engineering Company in Jamaica, China Jiangsu in Trinidad,[214] Shanghai Construction Group in Guyana[215] and in the China State Construction Engineering Corp. in The Bahamas.[216] There has even been speculation in the media that convicts have been brought in from China to work on construction in Guyana.[217] This was subsequently proven to be untrue. The Caribbean is not alone in this respect as there have been similarly unproven allegations in Africa.[218]

Over time, Chinese firms have been responsive to these criticisms in the Caribbean whether by enlightened self-interest, learning or by the insistence of governments. Construction projects undertaken by Chinese firms now employ a combination of Chinese and local workers. Both sets of workers appear to get along well based on the absence of reports of friction and my own observation at the Pan-Caribbean Sugar Company in Jamaica.

The China Railway Construction Caribbean Company was awarded the contract for construction of a hospital in Trinidad and was alleged to be under investigation for corruption.[219] The parent company, the China Railway Construction, is one of the largest construction companies in China and one of the top 500 enterprises in the world that has carried projects in many countries across the globe. The corruption allegations were subsequently found to be false. In the case of Amila Falls in the Guyana, it was reported in the press that the intended Chinese firm, China Railway Construction Caribbean Company, was being probed in China for shoddy railway work.[220]

People protested the Chinese company which was building the Marriott hotel in Guyana after they believed they were employing only Chinese workers.[221] There were also accusations that the Chinese company was doing shoddy work. The government of Guyana denied this and expressed it satisfaction, pointing out that both the government and Marriott had supervisory teams in place to ensure standards.[222] The company involved was the Shanghai Construction Group, the same company that built the National Academy for the Performing Arts (NAPA), in Port of Spain where there were issues about the quality of the work.

The Trinidadian government was forced to close the doors to its National Academy for the Performing Arts (NAPA) in Port of Spain because of shoddy works undertaken by its contractor, Shanghai Construction Group. The government of Trinidad and Tobago explained that there was a combination of issues, including design flaws, maintenance and defects and that the company worked with the government to correct those issues.[223] In March 2016, the Occupational Safety and Health Authority (OSHA) ordered the closure of a part of the facility, citing badly secured lighting fixtures, shattered glass panes, and issues with air quality.[224] The company has gone on to construct the Children's Hospital, the Cycling Velodrome and Aquatic Centre in Couva. At Southern Academy for the Performing Arts (SAPA), some 300 problems were identified requiring an estimated TT$20 million in renovation.[225] It is important to note the media's perspective on the issue of SAPA, the *Express* stated:

> It is clear from China's foreign policy adventurism in Africa and the Caribbean that the Asian behemoth is intent on replacing American hegemony over the world in the fullness of time. For that reason, the Chinese government will, hopefully, respond with alacrity to this embarrassing disclosure of its agents' lack of high standards and professional probity.[226]

These were fixable problems but in one instance building had to be demolished.

> Two Housing Development Corporation (HDC) apartment buildings, constructed by China Jiangsu International Economic Co-operation Corp (CJI) in Morvant at a cost of $26 million, are to be demolished because they have begun to collapse. The buildings are four-story HDC buildings in Morvant, which accommodate 48 three-bedroom units.[227]

There is empirical evidence to suggest that Chinese investors have shown 'an ability to exceed local standards'.[228] Case studies of Chinese investments in eight Latin America countries show that Chinese firms do not perform significantly worse relative to domestic or other international firms. This is also the case in Africa.[229] They have shown that they are flexible, able to adapt to new environments and perform up to local standards. In fact, in 'some instances of Chinese firms were outperforming their competitors, especially with proper incentives from governments and civil society'.[230] The Chinese government has been encouraging its companies operating overseas to observe environmental standards. In 2013, Ministry of Commerce and the Ministry of Environmental Protection for the first time issued guidelines to encourage enterprises investing abroad to follow local environmental laws. Admittedly, these guidelines are voluntary, but a growing number of Chinese state-owned enterprises and private companies have signed the United Nations Global Compact.[231]

b. Environment

The Jamaican incident was tentative because Chinese firms had expressed an interest in the construction of a logistics hub being planned by the government, and it was they who suggested locating the project on Goat Island, a very small island off the south coast of Jamaica. Even before the government had completed its preparatory work, including an environmental study, the non-governmental organizations, in particular, environmentalists began a campaign demanding that Goat Island not be considered because of the damage to the indigenous flora and fauna.

How to proceed with the development of a logistics hub is now a much discussed topic in Jamaica. The prospect of Chinese investors in Goat Island, an integral location for some of the activities of the proposed hub, has raised the issue of the impact of Chinese foreign investors on the natural environment. These concerns prompted the Prime Minister of Jamaica to give a public assurance that all regulations would be observed in a road construction project being executed by a Chinese company, China Harbour Engineering Company, which has satisfactorily completed several projects in Jamaica.[232] Some vociferous groups and individuals are arguing that development of Goat Island would destroy a unique natural environment. The government has all but dismissed this as patently false, claiming that there is nothing unique about the flora and fauna in that location. Some of those worried about the natural environment, having lost the debate on whether there should be development there or it should remain pristine, have raise the specter of Chinese investors ruthlessly constructing without any concern about the harmful impact on environment.[233]

c. Chinese Firms and Environmental Standards

Critics in Jamaica cite the operations of Chinese firms in Africa in mining and the polluted air in several cities in China. In this regard, they are tapping into a strong suspicion not confined to the Caribbean. There is global debate about the impact of the Chinese on the natural environment which resonates with nationalist sentiments in the Caribbean. The sensitivity and concern about this issue is high in the Caribbean because of its fragile natural environment and biodiversity vulnerable to natural disasters and climate change. There is a widely held suspicion that in their haste and need to sustain their rapid economic growth that the Chinese are rapaciously exploiting natural resources, recklessly destroying natural environments and using, if necessary, corruption without compunction and in disregard of democracy and human rights. Balanced assessment of this perspective by Elizabeth C. Economy and Michael Levi contradict the veracity of the propositions. They conclude:

> Pundits, scholars and policymakers have too often blown China's resource quest and its consequences out of proportion to reality: their warnings of intolerable rises in commodity prices, unprecedented social and environmental damage to countries where China invests, a competitive playing field ever more tilted against Western companies and inevitable resource-related conflicts even perhaps war between China and other powers are not supported by the facts on the ground.[234]

The details of the arrangements between the government of Guyana and a Chinese company, Bai Shan Lin, regarding the export of logs has not been made public. First, queries surrounded the terms under which the company imported 200 trucks, 60 bulldozers, 40 loaders and several luxury vehicles all duty-free. Duty-free imports of equipment are not unusual incentives given to attract foreign direct investment. Bai Shan Lin has been accused of exporting logs in excess of its authorized quota[235] and of harvested timber by illegally leasing land from third parties through joint 'venture agreements'. Guyana has a policy of discouraging the export of raw unimproved logs. It is estimated that Bai Shan Lin has been granted a logging concession of close to one million hectares of rainforest.[236] There is speculation that bribery of government officials and/or politicians, but there is no proof to date.

In 2003, the Chinese company, China Zhong Heng Tai, signed an agreement with the government of Suriname, involving a 38-year land concession of 98,800 acres to redevelop the palm oil industry in Patamacca. It was expected that the firm would invest US$116 million over 11 years to build a palm oil refinery. The rehabilitation of palm oil production was subjected to protests from the local community and environmentalist activists.[237] The opposition was in part due to the suspicion the real intention was to cut 40,000 acres of timber to export to China and that there was no intention of then cultivating palm oil.[238]

It is unnoticed that many local businesses exercise no more care than the much criticized foreign enterprises. Locals have been just as rapacious and destructive to the natural environment as the foreign firms they are wont to lambast. The other misperception is that foreign investors are different and the Chinese, in particular, are bent on development with no regard for the natural environment.[239] This topic is currently being debated in the Caribbean, particularly in regard to the possible Chinese involvement in a major infrastructure project being contemplated in Jamaica. It was voiced in the press that:

> The Jamaican government is preparing to sell the Goat Islands to the China Harbour Engineering Co. to build a "megafreighter" seaport and industrial park. China Harbour is part of a conglomerate blacklisted by the World Bank under its Fraud and Corruption Sanctioning Policy.[240]

The discussion is clouded by conflating opposition to the Chinese and opposition to any development of the particular natural environment.[241] Certainly, some firms are better corporate citizens than others, but entire nationalities should not be branded as bad or irresponsible. Locally owned firms and foreign companies, including American, Canadian and European firms have, at times, caused damage to the natural environment in the Caribbean. The red mud lakes which are the residue of alumina plants operated in Jamaica by American and Canadian mining companies are an example. In any case, it is only fair to acknowledge that any human activity has an impact on the natural environment, some more than others. It is the responsibility of governments as custodians of the natural environment on behalf of the Caribbean people to put in place regulations, safe-guards and monitoring to ensure the proper conduct of companies both local and foreign. In another regard, trade with China could help with preserving the environment. China's production of solar PV panels could be instrumental to Caribbean efforts to make more use of solar power as has been the case in Chile.[242]

d. Ensuring Standards

Ensuring that constructions fulfil the contracts they are awarded involves specifying in the contract what standards have to be met and monitoring the construction process and inspection on completion of construction. This approach applies to both foreign and local contractors. In this respect, the comments of the former Jamaican Minister of Transport, Works and Housing are instructive. Dr Omar Davies, Jamaica's Minister of Transport, Works and Housing during the period December 2012–March 2016, conducted negotiations with officials of the government of China and the China Harbour Engineering Construction (CHEC) on several major construction projects and attested that the work done by Chinese contractors was consistently of a high and satisfactory standard. Indeed, a Chinese company was able to complete a road construction project that had stalled when the original contractor, a European company, was not able to solve certain engineering problems. The Chinese were able to resolve the issues and complete the project on schedule and to the standards specified by the government of Jamaica. Dr Davies noted that in negotiating with the Chinese, a government must be well prepared and know exactly what it wants done and stipulate the standards to be attained by the contractors. The inference is that Chinese will work to standards demanded, and that is up to the country. He also observed that Chinese companies take great pride in their work. The comments of Dr Davies serve to dispel the accusations that Chinese companies do 'shoddy work' and disregard environmental standards.[243]

11. CHINA'S DISTINCT PRESENCE IN THE CARIBBEAN

China's economic presence in the Caribbean has increased significantly in the last decade, as is evident in the enlarged trade deficit with the Caribbean which is a consequence of the growth of China's exports to the region, outpacing that of the Caribbean. There has also been a substantial increase in Chinese development assistance to countries that recognize the People's Republic of China instead of Taiwan. The profile of China in the Caribbean has risen because China has funded and constructed several stadiums and prestigious buildings. The growth of China's economic presence is also beginning to be seen in an embryonic increase in foreign direct investment and loans to governments. This presence is likely to continue to increase, particularly in the expanding range of exported goods. Development assistance levels will be maintained and could be increased, while the rivalry with Taiwan for diplomatic recognition continues.

In the next 20–30 years, there will be a progressive reordering of global affairs in which China, along with Asia as a whole, will be prominent. This will translate into more assertive engagement and influence in all aspects of international affairs. The enormous growth of China has changed – and will continue to change – the pattern of trade and investment in the world economy. China is forecast to become the world's largest economy in 30 years. The rise toward economic dominance, together with its enormous military prowess ranging from nuclear weapons to the largest army in the world, will ensure that China's influence and power in international politics increase dramatically. This outlook is propitious for the continued rapid growth of China's economic presence in the Caribbean region. Growing Chinese presence in the Caribbean will become more varied in the future as its private-sector firms become more active in trade and infrastructure and construction projects. This shift towards increased private-sector involvement relative to official engagement has happened in other regions, for example, Africa.[244]

The developments and trends that characterize the growing economic presence of China in the Caribbean are different from those described in the literature on Latin America in several important respects: (a) Trade between China and Latin America has expanded rapidly, with both sides increasing their exports[245] whereas in the Caribbean the growth in trade has been almost entirely in imports from China; (b) the most important trading partner for the Caribbean remains the US, and the performance of the US economy is a significant influence on growth in the Caribbean. In contrast, China's impact on growth in Latin America has increased significantly while that of the US has declined;[246] (c) financial flows between China and the Caribbean are dominated by development assistance, whereas in Latin America[247] this flow is far less important except in Central America. The rivalry between China and Taiwan for diplomatic recognition is a major factor in China's foreign and economic policy in the Caribbean and Central America, and is reflected in the amount and destination of development assistance; (d) loans are important in both the Caribbean and Latin America as China increases lending for infrastructure, energy and construction. In August 2010, Ecuador signed a $1-billion loan with China for oil and infrastructure projects. The China Development Bank has lent $10 billion to Brazil to secure guaranteed oil supplies[248] Petrobras will supply Sinopec, China's largest refiner, 200,000 barrels per day from 2010, and they will cooperate on oil exploration;[249] and (e) foreign investment in energy and raw materials are prominent in Latin America. For example, the energy sector in Venezuela[250] amounting to $20 billion, represents a new venture for China and this is not replicated in the Caribbean, which has fewer energy resources.

12. CONCLUSION

China's presence in the Caribbean has grown significantly in the last ten years after a gradual build-up since the 1970s. The presence has been concentrated in those countries that have diplomatic relations with China. The countries that recognize Taiwan have no diplomatic relationship with China and receive no development aid or FDI. However, they purchase imports from China. The growth of the Chinese presence is evident in: (a) the closer diplomatic ties reflected in the increased frequency of high level visits involving the President of China to the Caribbean and the visits of several heads of government from the Caribbean; (b) the substantial expansion of Chinese development aid and loans resulting in several high profile construction projects which has generated goodwill for China; and (c) a substantial increase in imports from China and China's development assistance to some governments in the Caribbean.

CHAPTER 3

Factors Explaining the Expanded China–Caribbean Relationship

OBJECTIVE

In recent years, the People's Republic of China (China) has expanded its economic relations with the countries of the Caribbean. This is evident in the increase in trade and development assistance. The objective of this chapter is to explain the expanded and intensified economic presence of China in the Caribbean region. In order to accomplish this, it is necessary to identify the motives for China's conduct in the region and the factors that account for the receptivity of the Caribbean to economic relations with China. Although the focus is primarily on the economic relationship between China and Caribbean countries, this aspect of China's involvement in the region cannot be separated from the political dimension. China's motives for a growing presence in the region are both economic and political, and have to be examined in the wider context of China's overall foreign policy, its shifting world view, its superpower status and the geopolitics of the current global conjuncture. Similarly, the Caribbean's conduct has to be located in the wider context of its overall foreign policy.

Section I outlines the history and current status of China–Caribbean relations. This is followed by an exposition of the extent and increase in economic interaction between China and the Caribbean. The third section provides an examination of China's motives for the conduct of its foreign policy in Caribbean countries. These motives are partly influenced by economics, and partly by politics and hence have to be understood in the global geopolitical context. A fourth section is devoted to explaining the Caribbean's receptivity to increased economic relations with China. The final section provides a brief outlook for China–Caribbean economic relations.

I. HISTORY, STATUS AND MODALITIES

Formal diplomatic relations between the People's Republic of China and Caribbean states began with the establishment of diplomatic ties with Guyana and Jamaica in the latter half of 1972. Not all Caribbean countries have official diplomatic links with China; some have chosen instead to have a relationship with Taiwan. Deciding on a relationship between the two nations has been plagued by ambivalence and opportunism. Some Caribbean states have switched their allegiances (sometimes more than once) between the Republic of China (Taiwan) and the People's Republic of China. This has happened as recently as 2007 when St Lucia reversed its recognition in favour of Taiwan. From 1984 until 1996, St

Lucia recognized Taiwan, but switched allegiances in 1996 when the government changed. To their credit, Barbados, Guyana, Jamaica and Trinidad and Tobago have been unwavering in their commitment to the One China Policy. Countries recognizing the People's Republic of China and Taiwan are shown in table 3.1.

There is still a reservoir of ignorance and suspicion in the region about China compared to ongoing comfort with a foreign policy still focused primarily on traditional European and North America allies. This perpetuation is a vestige of a colonial past and the more recent hegemonic American presence, which in the Caribbean has remained remarkably immune to change despite profound economic and political change in global power configurations. This state of affairs cannot continue as China's economic, political and military power escalates, inexorably shifting the centre of gravity of the world economy[1] in conjunction with the Asian Tigers and Japan. Some have argued that the region should fear the rise of China because of what they regard as the ominous failure to push political reform to the point of transformation of its political system to democracy of the Western type.[2] The syncretic coexistence of a single-party communist political system with a mixed economy, which each day becomes more market driven, is a curious and unique social formation, which is best described as 'Market Leninism'.

Table 3.1: Caribbean Countries Recognizing China

Country	**China**	**Taiwan**
Antigua	Since January 1983	
The Bahamas	Since May 1997	
Barbados	Since May 1977	
Belize	1987–89	Since 1989
Dominica	Since March 2004	
The Dominican Republic		Since 1952
Grenada	Oct. 1985–Aug. 1989, Jan. 2005	1989–2005
Guyana	Since June 1972	
Haiti		Since 1956
Jamaica	Since November 1972	
St Kitts andvNevis		Since 1983
St Lucia	1997–2007	1984–97, 2007
St Vincent and the Grenadines		Since 1981
Suriname	Since May 1976	
Trinidad and Tobago	Since June 1974	

China's relations with Caribbean countries have been conducted on a bilateral basis rather than a regional one. China does not have an agreement with the Caribbean as a whole because all member states do not have diplomatic relations with China. There are institutional arrangements between China and those countries that recognize the People's Republic of China. Institutionalized arrangements exist in the form of the China–Caribbean Economic and Trade Cooperation Forum (CCF) and the China–Caribbean Joint Business Council (CCBC). The CCF encompasses Caribbean countries which have diplomatic relations with China, as well as Haiti which recognizes Taiwan, the Dominican Republic and Cuba. The CCF has been convened three times, first in Kingston in February 2005, then, in July 2007, in China and in September 2011, in Port of Spain, in conjunction with a third meeting of the China–Caribbean Joint Business Council attended by 56 Chinese companies looking for export and investment opportunities and seeking investment.[3]

The differences among Caribbean governments regarding diplomatic allegiances with China and Taiwan have not affected Caribbean unity because, whilst formally committed to common or joint foreign policy positions,[4] in reality, the group has been divided on several issues on many occasions. Those countries which have relations with China collaborate in certain meetings and encounters with China such as the Biennial China–Caribbean consultations which took place in September 2002, June 2004 and July 2006. On a daily basis, seven Caribbean countries have embassies in Beijing, namely, The Bahamas, Barbados, Dominica, Grenada, Guyana, Jamaica and Suriname.

In its bilateral focus, Beijing has accorded Jamaica pride of place because it sees Jamaica as exerting an influential leadership role in Caribbean affairs and in the formulation and execution of Caribbean collaboration on foreign policy. Therefore, China views Jamaica as the platform from which to engage the rest of the Caribbean, and hence its campaign to enhance relations with Caribbean sates has been spearheaded by the strengthening of its relations with Jamaica. China opened an embassy, in Kingston, in 1973, and Jamaica has had non-resident ambassadors to China since 1992 until Jamaica opened an embassy, in Beijing, in July 2005 in order to consolidate a more intensive relationship. Numerous delegations have visited both countries, including visits by Prime Minister P.J. Patterson to China in 1998, Prime Minister Bruce Golding in February 2010 and Prime Minister Portia Simpson Miller in August 2013. Vice President Zheng Qinhong led the delegation to the 1st China–Caribbean Economic and Trade Cooperation Forum and the first China–Caribbean Trade Fair hosted by Jamaica in February 2005. In recent years, high-level Chinese delegations have visited several Caribbean countries and, in turn, have received heads of government from countries that have diplomatic relations with China. In June 2013, Xi Jinping, the President of China, met in Port of

Spain with Caribbean leaders from Antigua and Barbuda, Barbados, The Bahamas, Dominica, Grenada, Guyana, Jamaica, Suriname and Trinidad and Tobago to 'inject new and strong vitality' into relations with the Caribbean countries.[5]

Economic assistance is the principal means of influence employed by China in its foreign policy in the Caribbean. Economic assistance takes the form of grants, loans, lines of credit, technical assistance and donations in kind. Projects are executed in many instances by different forms of assistance. Some of these projects are highly visible buildings, sports facilities and stadiums, which have boosted the prestige of several governments. This high-profile expansion of development assistance has taken place in the context of a sharp decline in US foreign aid to Caribbean countries. The increase in Chinese aid in the Caribbean is consistent with a substantial escalation of development aid to developing countries, especially oil-rich African countries.

II. GOALS OF CHINA'S FOREIGN POLICY[6]

In order to discuss the place of the Caribbean in China's current and future foreign policy, it is necessary to understand the goals and priorities of China's foreign policy. China has certain enduring goals, but the manner in which they have been pursued has changed over time, particularly since the end of the Cold War. The modalities of foreign policy execution and implementation will continue to change in response to both internal changes and external circumstances. Among the current goals are, first, expanded involvement in the global economy in order to promote rapid and sustainable economic development while maintaining a monopoly of political power by the Chinese Communist Party and social order. To secure the benefits of engagement in the global economy, there has been a moderation in resolving international issues and a more cooperative approach to participation in multilateral organizations and the process and institutional arrangements for global governance. The flavour of this approach can be gleaned from the 'Going Global' strategy which speaks about:

- Supporting qualified enterprises to engage in outward direct investment and global operations;
- giving priority to competitive industries;
- providing guidance to enterprises to engage in overseas processing trade;
- promoting the diversification of products' places of origin;
- cultivating and developing Chinese multinational corporations through international mergers and acquisitions, equity participation, public listing, restructuring and consolidation, etc.;
- enhancing cooperative development of overseas resources based on the principles of complementary strengths, equality and mutual benefits;

- encouraging enterprises to participate in infrastructure construction overseas;
- improving the level of project contracting overseas, and steadily develop labour cooperation;
- improving the outward investment promotion and security system; and
- strengthening the coordination of overseas investments, risk management and the supervision of state-owned assets overseas.[7]

Second, the Chinese are riveted to the view that their interaction in international affairs must not compromise the unity of a holistic China as a country, culture and territory. Preserving the integrity of its territory, culture and civilization is of paramount importance. China will not relinquish that which it regards as part of China, for example, Taiwan is held to be a breakaway province of China. The Great Wall built on and off between the third and seventeenth centuries was for national security, customs and migration control, but it also functioned as a psychological barrier[8] protecting Chinese civilization.

Third, Chinese foreign policy, while pragmatically engaged in current international issues, views the attainment of goals and the resolution of issues in a much longer time span than the Western World. The Chinese are often misunderstood as vacillating and viewed as excessively patient by their Western counterparts. An example of China as a whole and its long view of time is its approach to Taiwan. China first laid claim to Taiwan in 605 and the small island became a protectorate of the Chinese empire in 1206[9] and, hence, 1949 until the present is not a long time in which to reunite Taiwan with China.

Fourth, China has firmly and steadily asserted its presence in Asia while seeking to assure its neighbours that this does not portent a dominance. Asia is not only important because of its physical proximity and long history of acrimonious disputes but it is the most dynamic and rapidly growing region of the world economy. Indeed, the centre of gravity of the global economy has shifted to Asia. This phenomenon has a number of implications: (a) it furnishes opportunities for exports and foreign direct investment on an increasing basis; (b) it offers synergies in which the value chains can continuously be disaggregated and reallocated across the countries of the region; and (c) it is a region of fierce competitors in national and international markets.

Fifth, China avoids, as far as possible, a head-on collision with the US while establishing that they cannot be ignored on major decisions affecting its national interests or the international community. China has conducted its foreign policy in a non-confrontational manner which increasingly indicates that it accepts, for the most part, a role as a responsible power but in its own way and at its own pace. China's position on human rights and democracy indicate that these are areas in which it has its own distinctive view and that it will not be bullied or persuaded. The events of Tiananmen Square in 1989 was an embarrassing episode, but shows that China will go its own way when necessary in spite of international opprobrium. Yet, China has shown a willingness to accept the norms of international diplomacy and the basic rules of international law.

Sixth, the Chinese go to great lengths to assure the developing countries that their rise as a superpower is not a threat, but relations would be respectful of their sovereignty, sensitive to their development needs and an opportunity for fraternal relations on common issues as a country that still has many features of a poor, developing country. China has, since the beginning of the communist era, been active in the G-77 and the Non-Aligned Movement. It has provided aid to developing countries without interfering in their domestic politics. This approach has generated considerable goodwill and, by 1971, was a factor in The United Nations membership voting China into a permanent seat on the Security Council.

III. CHINA'S MOTIVES

In recent years, China has intensified its efforts to expand economic interaction and consolidate diplomatic and political ties in the region. China's expanded involvement in the Caribbean is reflected in its increased development assistance, technical assistance, the continued expansion of trade, emerging foreign investment and the involvement in construction projects. This enhanced presence is a manifestation of political and economic motivations. The pursuit of both motives is taking place against the background of a re-dimensioning of China's involvement in world affairs commensurate with the role and status of a superpower.

a. Political and Diplomatic Motives

The longstanding rivalry with Taiwan for the allegiance of governments in the region has traditionally been the driving force behind China's involvement in the Caribbean and Central America. Twelve of the 22 countries that continue to recognize Taiwan in preference to China are in Latin America and the Caribbean, and hence the rivalry is particularly intense in this region. The principal foreign policy employed by China and Taiwan is the provision of development assistance, and this has been the main factor that has induced some governments to switch their allegiance. Juan Gabriel Tokatlian refers to 'checkbook diplomacy' in which 'Taiwanese dollars compete with Chinese renminbis for diplomatic recognition.'[10] Apart from the ability to extract development aid in exchange for diplomatic recognition and advocacy in international fora such as the United Nations, the countries that recognized Taiwan were also mindful that it was the policy favoured by the US. The normalization of relations between the US and China from the

1970s on eased the political pressure of countries to maintain recognition of Taiwan. The diplomatic recognition of even a few small countries is the basis on which Taiwan can maintain the claim that it is an independent country. In the UN General Assembly, all countries have one vote so a small country can be a valuable ally. As an illustration, Timothy Harris, Prime Minister of St Kitts and Nevis, in his inaugural address to 70th UN General Assembly in September 2015, called for the inclusion of Taiwan in discussions on climate change on the basis that 'Taiwan with its advanced renewable energy technologies should be allowed to participate in relevant international meetings and mechanisms such as the UNFCCC and the UN Environmental Assembly.'[11] Harris made his eight visit and first as prime minister to Taipei just the month before his UN speech.

Belize, Haiti, St Vincent and the Grenadines, St Lucia and St Kitts and Nevis continue to recognize Taiwan, while the rest of the Caribbean has diplomatic relations with China. Guyana established diplomatic relations with China on June 27, 1972 and Jamaica, on November 21, 1972.[12] Trinidad and Tobago established diplomatic relations with China on June 20, 1974, Suriname on May 28, 1976, and Barbados on May 30, 1977. Antigua and Barbuda established diplomatic relations with China on January 1, 1983, while Grenada followed suit in October 1985. China decided to suspend its ties with Grenada in August 1989. However, the two countries resumed diplomatic relations on January 20, 2005. The Bahamas and Dominica commenced their relationship with China on May 23, 1997 and March 23, 2004 respectively, having previously pledged their allegiance to Taiwan. It is reported that China promised Dominica $122 million over five years for revoking its recognition of Taiwan which it had maintained for 21 years.[13]

b. Economic Motives

Although trade between China and the Caribbean has increased, for China this is miniscule and therefore economic motives remain secondary to political and diplomatic goals. Economic interests have assumed more significance in recent years and increasingly involve international trade and investment.

(1) Securing supplies of raw materials on a long-term basis has been a driving force in China's foreign policy, particularly in regard to supplies of oil.[14] The visit of the president of China to Trinidad in June 2013 is motivated, in part, by the opening of bids for exploration rights on new off-shore natural gas fields, bearing in mind that the newly opened expanded Panama Canal will make shipping easier, quicker and less costly.[15] The Caribbean has raw materials, in particular, fairly large reserves of bauxite, some natural gas and fish stocks. The possibility of discovering oil and mineral deposits in the vast expanses of Guyana as well as unexplored undersea resources of the Caribbean Sea has not escaped the attention of China's long-term

planning. Ironically, Taiwan has signed an oil exploration agreement with Belize.[16]

The potential of the blue economy will not go unnoticed by China. The countries of the Caribbean are not that small and not as deprived of resources if they are measured by their marine space and not by their population and land area. For example, the land area of The Bahamas is 5,383 square miles, but its exclusive economic zone (EEZ) is 242,970 square miles. St Kitts and Nevis is only 100 square miles of land area, but its EEZ is 7,900 square miles. This expanse of sea is a vast unexplored resource. In addition, the Caribbean Sea is crisscrossed by major sea lanes, hence, the potential for maritime transport, bearing in mind that 90 per cent of all international trade is transported by sea. The Caribbean is also one of the world's largest and busiest cruise ship arenas. Fish and fish products are an important sector of global trade. In 2013, total world exports of fish and fishery products was estimated to reach US$136 billion, increasing at an average of 12 per cent per annum over the previous ten years.[17] The aquaculture potential of the Caribbean can be gauged by what other small island developing states (SIDS) have gained from exploiting their maritime space. In 2012, exports of fish products from SIDS was valued at US$1.75 billion GDP.

(2) Although small in recent times, the expansion of Chinese exports has been steady with encouraging prospects for the future. It would be a mistake to assume that because exports to the Caribbean are infinitesimal in China's total exports that these small export markets will be overlooked. It is firms that trade and not countries and, hence, the small Caribbean export markets will be of interest to some firms in China, albeit smaller firms. In any case, the growth of exports from China is dependent on importers in the Caribbean knowing of Chinese products and finding easy ways to import from China. The export of services from China to date has been almost entirely in construction of buildings and infrastructure. These projects have been substantial for the Caribbean, and Chinese firms could continue in construction and could expand into other services such as medicine and engineering.

(3) As China increasingly becomes a source of foreign investment, there has been an increasing willingness to employ direct investment in order to secure supplies of raw materials. There may be opportunities for Chinese foreign investment in tourism, construction, infrastructure, education and health care. Chinese firms are being encouraged by both their own government and those within the Caribbean to establish themselves in the region. The

drivers of Chinese FDI in the Caribbean are the same as those operative in the global spread and, hence, the Caribbean does have prospects for garnering FDI from China in tourism, agriculture, energy and mining. Some of the opportunities in the small developing Caribbean economies are not unique, and Chinese investors will have alternatives elsewhere in the world. Caribbean governments should identify factors beyond those common to all investment venues such as the attractiveness of the policy environment and the ease of doing business that would influence Chinese decisions about FDI in the Caribbean. In this regard, Caribbean countries should realize that their small size is not necessarily a disadvantage because not all Chinese FDI is executed by large state enterprises or Chinese multinational corporations. Despite the enormous size of the Chinese economy, there are a range of firms of different sizes and for some of these firms, the Caribbean economies will be a suitable fit. Firm heterogeneity is very complex in China, involving differences between foreign-owned firms and local firms, and the latter differing between publicly owned and privately owned firms. Public firms are state-owned or communally owned. The variety is further complicated by whether they are regulated by the central government or provincial authorities. The mix and relative weight of different types of firms has changed dramatically in the last 20 years, with the decline in the number of publicly owned companies being a pronounced trend.[18] Firm heterogeneity has important implications for production, value chains and patterns of international trade.[19]

(4) Another aspect to be recognized is that it is not necessarily what business a firm does in the Caribbean but what business it does from its Caribbean location. In this regard, the Caribbean has some locational advantage being close to the largest market in the world, the US. Caribbean countries could be a production platform for exports to the US, Canada and the European Union because of preferential trade arrangements. These include the Caribbean Basin Economic Recovery Act (CBERA), Caribbean–China Trade Agreement (CARIBCAN) and the CARIFORUM–EU Economic Partnership Agreement with the European Union.[20] Trinidad and Tobago with its low energy costs could be of interest to Chinese firms engaged in manufacturing in the CARICOM market and more significantly the US, Canada and the EU. Trinidad has several internationally established brands which invited the interest of large Chinese corporations interested in taking over already established brands rather than the more arduous task of building brand recognition. These brands include the world famous Angostura Bitters and high-end rums made by Angostura Limited. Purchase of world renowned

brands has occurred elsewhere in the Caribbean, notably with the sale of Red Stripe beer. There are several other food products which, while not enjoying global demand, are entrenched in the Caribbean diaspora markets.

(5) China has a growing need to import food as its population of 1.37 billion grows, a trend likely to continue now that the one-child per family rule has been rescinded after 35 years and as food consumption per capita has increased as incomes have risen. The fertile, well-watered lands of Guyana, Belize and Suriname are an attractive possibility for food production. Much of this land is suitable for rice production which is likely to interest Chinese investors because of the increased demand for this dietary staple in China. It is not only the increase in food consumption per capita but that the demand is shifting towards a more diverse range of foods and to more expensive foodstuffs as a result of population growth and the increased food consumption due to increased per capita income. The food market and patterns of consumption have changed dramatically in the last decade. Previously imported foods were not widely available nor much in demand both because of taste and high price. Today, many imported goods are no longer expensive and hard to find. They are widely available and no longer the preserve of cosmopolitan cities such as Beijing and Shanghai. There are now shops that specialize in selling imported food, and are purveyors of fine foods and wines from all over the world.

c. Superpower Assertion

As a superpower, China wants to have a presence in all regions of the globe and, therefore, the Caribbean, despite its small size and remoteness from China, has a place in China's foreign policy. The Caribbean is not a region where China could confront the US physically as an aspect of China's national security policy. The political significance of the Caribbean derives from the unresolved rivalry with Taiwan as opportunistic Caribbean governments openly barter their political recognition for development assistance. Retaining and expanding support in the region involves funds, aid in-kind and technical assistance which are miniscule in China's foreign aid outreach. The motivations behind the growing Chinese presence in the Caribbean will become more varied in the future as its private sector firms become more active in trade, infrastructure and construction projects.[21]

If, as thought by some in the US, the reigning, lone superpower, is declining relatively and there is a burgeoning of China, then this portends a bi-polar or multi-polar world. Waning global powers are typically wary of rising powers, especially if they aspire to a more powerful role and the commensurate status.[22] How the relationship between the US and China evolves will be critical in determining the evolution of the global economy and the reconfiguration of power in international affairs. An important factor will be willingness of the US to modify its 'affinity for unipolar policy'.[23] Many American foreign policy cognoscenti feel that the bilateral relationship is froth with 'mismatched interests, values and capabilities'.[24] A strong current of opinion sees China as set on global domination and, therefore, a threat to and in conflict with the US.[25] The prescription which emanates from this perspective is to counter China's rising influence in every region, including the Caribbean.

In reality, China's rise is a rebalancing of world affairs to take account of a nuclear power with the largest population in the world. For China, it is destiny fulfilled by the inevitable and long-awaited turning of the 'wheel of fortune', returning it to a position held for centuries[26] before the usurpation by 'barbarian' European powers. As recently as the early nineteenth century, China accounted for 36 per cent of the gross domestic product (GDP) of the world before beginning the 'Century of Humiliation' with the nadir at five per cent in 1950.[27]

By its sheer size and phenomenal growth, China's integration into the world economy will seriously affect the level and pattern of world trade and investment. This development will have positive and negative effects on a variety of countries. China's exports can have a disruptive impact on the economies of developing countries, particularly in labour-intensive manufactured goods, for example, the displacement of Mexican manufactured textiles and electronics in the US market.[28] It has even been suggested that Chinese competition was in some way a contributing factor to the Asian financial crisis of 1997–98.[29] Where China's expansion causes trade diversion and dislocation, it has prompted a backlash such as the attempts in the US to use phyto-sanitary and safety concerns to block Chinese exports, especially food items. As China's profile and tangible presence increases, it will have to work assiduously through its foreign policy to prevent resentment and ensure harmonious trading relationships.[30] While not challenging US dominance, China's increased economic and diplomatic involvement in Latin America and the Caribbean has not gone unnoticed in Washington, DC.[31] The US was sanguine about China's deployment of 143 peacekeepers, in Haiti, in 2007, which constituted a precedent in the Western Hemisphere.[32]

The degree of assertiveness in international affairs is still debated in Beijing, including the extent to which China would go to prevent Taiwan's independence.[33] Jiange Shixue states that in the conduct of foreign policy, 'a consensus has never been reached on the balance between keeping a low profile and taking action.'[34] The growth of economic ties between Taiwan and China, less virulent nationalism in Taiwan and a long-term perspective in Beijing have ameliorated the tensions that could ignite a military conflict with serious implications for US–China relations.[35]

As Richard C. Bush and Michael E. O'Hanlon point out, US–China military conflict is neither impossible nor inevitable.[36] Meanwhile, the keenly contested rivalry between China and Taiwan continues over recognition in a limited number of states concentrated in Central America and the Caribbean and the small island states of the Pacific.[37]

IV. THE CARIBBEAN'S RECEPTIVITY

The countries of the Caribbean have evinced receptivity to the expansion of economic relations with China. The response is a combination of motives some of which are tangible benefits and the immediate prospects of additional benefits, and others reflect the possibilities of benefit. Development aid is an actual benefit whilst trade, tourism and investment are possible benefits. The general favourable awareness of China by the public is due to the increase in the quantity and range of goods imported from China and the quality of those goods. In the past, Chinese products were regarded as cheap and there was scepticism about their durability.

1. Aid-Seeking Foreign Economic Policy

Governments in the Caribbean region have been the beneficiaries of development assistance since the colonial era, and are reliant on this type of resource transfer to fund a substantial part of the public sector capital expenditure. Traditional sources of development assistance have been the US, Canada, Britain and the EU. There has been stagnation in development assistance from the US to Caribbean countries, except Haiti and Guyana. US aid to the Caribbean (and to the Dominican Republic) amounted to $458.9 million in 1985, dropping to $136.3 million in 1998 and recovering to $317.3 million in 2006, with Haiti receiving 50–60 per cent of the total.[38] Particularly, the smallest countries in the Caribbean are in a situation of a structural fiscal incompetence in which the tax base is extremely narrow, and these countries genuinely need external development aid to sustain public administration and to support economic development. Given the small size and structural characteristics of these economies, the options for economic development are very limited. Governments in these countries have little alternative but to resort to certain policies that large and more developed countries may eschew. The pursuit of foreign aid in these circumstances becomes an overriding policy objective. Prime Minister of St Kitts, Dr Timothy Harris, explains that these efforts 'should not be characterized in condescending terms as dollar diplomacy but be aptly described for what they are: economic diplomacy at work'.[39]

Caribbean Governments recognized that the decline in development assistance from traditional partners underscores their lack of geopolitical significance and the small size of their markets. The end of the Cold War and the decline in the popularity of state-led development strategies have culminated in the decline in possibilities of aid from socialist countries.[40] This cutback in bilateral development assistance is compounded by the fact that many Caribbean countries are middle income and consequently have become ineligible for certain concessionary financing facilities. The per capita income of many of the countries, notably The Bahamas ($29,600), Trinidad and Tobago ($23,600), Antigua ($19, 600) and Barbados ($19,600)[41] places them among the middle-income countries and makes them ineligible for certain types of concessionary development aid. These trends appear to Caribbean governments to be irreversible, and hence there has been an increased willingness to explore new sources of development assistance from non-traditional sources such as China, India and Venezuela.

Caribbean governments are aware that China has been a donor country to the developing world since the early 1950s. From 1950 to 1985, China provided aid to 87 countries, including 20 in Asia, 46 in Africa, 16 in Latin America and five in Europe. China's 'economic cooperation with foreign countries or regions' was $27 billion for 2005, up from US$1.6 billion in 1989.[42] The vast majority is provided through bilateral channels, although more aid is channelled through multilateral organizations. Approximately half of China's aid takes the form of grants and half takes the form of loans, some of which are at concessionary rates. The geographical distribution of the aid reflects a focus on Asia, which receives about one-half and, in recent years, increasing amounts have been allocated to Africa.[43] China has also been generous in constructing buildings and infrastructure which are granted to countries as gifts, and it has provided free technical assistance to developing countries in a wide range of activities. China has also largely eliminated tariffs on imports from 29 of the least developed African countries.[44]

In the Joint Declaration of the 2nd China Caribbean Economic and Trade Cooperation Forum, China gave its commitment to increase its assistance to the Caribbean countries over three years by (a) providing preferential loans worth RMB four billion yaun for bilateral cooperation in infrastructure construction, resource development, industrial production, agriculture, tourism and telecommunications and (b) allocating a total quota of 2,000 trainees for the Caribbean to assist in training of government officials and technical professionals.

The countries of the Caribbean region will increasingly look to China for economic assistance, knowing of China's foreign aid deployment and their possession of the largest international reserves in the world. Many governments in the Caribbean are heavily indebted[45] and face tight fiscal situations and difficulties with debt sustainability. The global economic crisis has exacerbated the economic situation of Caribbean countries, which have experienced severe declines in tourist arrivals, tourist expenditure and remittances. Caribbean countries are grappling with difficult global economic circumstances while facing graduation from the more concessionary multilateral and bilateral forms of development assistance because of their relatively high per capita incomes. The possibility of development assistance in loans and grants, trade financing and lines of credit in the midst of the global financial crisis is enticing.

The possibility of access to development assistance with less and more flexible conditionality will make Chinese development assistance attractive relative to that of the developed countries and the multilateral development institutions. A comparison of the terms and conditions of loans from the China Development Bank with those from the World Bank and the Inter-American Development Bank reveals that rates of interest are similar, but there are no policy conditions on Chinese loans.[46] This is a crucially important difference, making loans from China less onerous to Caribbean governments. The China Export-Import Bank charges lower interest rates than the US Export-Import Bank.[47] In any case, bilateral aid donors have traditionally tied aid,[48] in one form or another, even if procurement rules have reduced the extent of the practice. Oxfam reports that 68 per cent of US aid was tied in 2005.[49] Tied aid can increase the costs of projects by as much as 30 per cent,[50] but this is likely to be much less in construction projects carried out by tied Chinese loans because Chinese construction is comparatively inexpensive compared to local and other foreign contractors. Chinese loans are tied, in part or whole, to the purchases of goods and services from China. This is not viewed as a disadvantage by Caribbean beneficiaries because, in many instances, suppliers from China are the least expensive.

Caribbean governments also find Chinese aid attractive because it is not accompanied by several of the conditions which are integral aspects of Western bilateral donor agencies and multilateral development finance institutions. China's 'White Paper on Foreign Aid' explicitly states that it is based on 'Imposing no political conditions' and 'respects recipient countries' right to independently select their own path and model of development, and believes that every country should explore a development path suitable to its actual conditions.'[51] This approach means a lot to small developing countries which feel that their development policy options are foreclosed by the conditionality that is a part of loans from international financial institutions. As further assurance, China has promulgated the principles which guide their aid policy in 'China's Eight Principles for Economic Aid and Technical Assistance to Other Countries'.[52]

1. The Chinese government always bases itself on the principle of equality and mutual benefit in providing aid to other countries. It never regards such aid as a kind of unilateral alms but as something mutual.
2. In providing aid to other countries, the Chinese government strictly respects the sovereignty of recipient countries, and never attaches any conditions or asks for any privileges.

3. China provides economic aid in the form of interest-free or low-interest loans and extends the time limit for the repayment when necessary so as to lighten the burden on recipient countries as far as possible.
4. In providing aid to other countries, the purpose of the Chinese government is not to make recipient countries dependent on China but to help them embark step by step on the road of self-reliance and independent economic development.
5. The Chinese government does its best to help recipient countries complete projects which require less investment but yield quicker results, so that the latter may increase their income and accumulate capital.
6. The Chinese government provides the best-quality equipment and materials manufactured by China at international market prices. If the equipment and materials provided by the Chinese government are not up to the agreed specifications and quality, the Chinese government undertakes to replace them or refund the payment.
7. In giving any particular technical assistance, the Chinese government will see to it that the personnel of the recipient country fully master the technology.
8. The experts dispatched by China to help in construction in recipient countries will have the same standard of living as the experts of the recipient country. The Chinese experts are not allowed to make any special demands or enjoy any special amenities.

These principles are not merely platitudes but constitute real guidelines. China's non-alignment and non-intervention polices have their roots in the psyche of the Chinese which dates back to antiquity. China has always believed itself not just to be a civilization but *the* civilization, and hence avoiding contact with other nations was a sense of superiority. China does not claim the universality of its values, culture and institutions.[53] This is different from the Western sense of superiority which mandates the proselytization of other nations, cultures and peoples. There is one condition or prerequisite for eligibility for aid from China and that is adherence to the 'One China Policy'. Interestingly, even this is resented as the Foreign Minister of a Central American country famously remarked that China's insistence on not having relations with Taiwan was no different from the Americans telling them not to have relations with Cuba.[54]

2. Less Expensive Imports

Goods from China have proven very attractive to Caribbean importers because of their prices and, consequently, they have been increasingly substituted for goods from traditional trading partners such as the US. The market penetration of Chinese goods is across all product categories. Indeed, many of the souvenirs purchased by tourists visiting the region originate in China. So rapid and pervasive has been the increased consumption of Chinese products in the Caribbean market that in some areas this reliance has reached the point where normal life cannot be conducted without products from this source as is the case in the US.[55] The Caribbean is likely to import increasingly capital goods from China, including automobiles traditionally sourced from Japan, Europe and the US. This trend is likely to be experienced across a wide range of machinery and equipment as China has the capacity to produce high-tech exports which already account for 30 per cent of total exports.[56] Imports from China are likely to grow if Chinese firms establish themselves in distribution and retail sales as has happened in Guyana. The Haier Service Center was established in 2012 to facilitate a contract with the government of Guyana to provide 27,000 laptops.[57]

3. Export Possibilities

Prior to the global economic crisis, the Caribbean's leading exports to China were experiencing growth and prospects were encouraging. However, this momentum has not continued although China has maintained slower but still relatively high rate of economic growth. The lack of growth in Caribbean exports is, therefore, not caused by a lack of demand or even a decline in demand and, hence the explanation must be related to (a) the international competitiveness in price and quality. Caribbean-based producers have competitive, high quality products, but have not adequately exploited the opportunities for exporting products such as coffee[58] and rum. Rum exports to China declined between 2001 and 2005 while China's expenditure on this product increased. This is also the case with mass market consumer items such as dried fish, smoked fish, rock lobster, frozen fish fillet and frozen shrimp and molluscs. If there are good products for which there is demand in China but little or no exports, then the problem is in (b), the export marketing. Penetrating and establishing in the Chinese market is a challenge, and a learning experience is involved. However, strategic alliances with Chinese distributors could solve this problem. This will take some initiative which some potential exporters do not expend because of being intimidated by the Chinese market. One of the misconceptions that fosters intimidation is the belief that the Chinese market is dominated by a few giant enterprises. This is certainly not the case, for example, in the market for food snacks, the top five companies account for only eight per cent of the total market value with the largest having less than three per cent.[59] Given the size of any of the top firms in China, exporting only requires negotiating and arranging business with one Chinese firm. For example, exporting processed food products may only require a contract to supply China Resource Enterprise, China's largest supermarket chain that has 4,400 stores.[60]

A major opportunity to export services is not being exploited by Caribbean producers. There is enormous potential for sale of entertainment services, primarily music. The worldwide popularity of Jamaican reggae music is such that it is established as a distinctive genre of popular music. China is a market waiting to be tapped, and the feasibility of marketing reggae indicated by the sale of reggae recordings and performance in Japan makes China a promising market.[61] The market for reggae grew after a slow start in the late 1970s and, today, there are Japanese reggae performers and annual reggae festivals such as the Yokohama Reggae Sai. The popularity of Trinidadian steel pan music is also well established. For example, there are several Japanese steel pan bands, and steel pans are even being manufactured in Japan. Trinidad's annual Carnival is world-renown and only needs to be promoted in China. There are possibilities for the export of other services from the Caribbean, for example, the athletes of the Caribbean have excelled and this creates an entrée into coaching in track and field. The Caribbean has considerable expertise in oil and gas engineering and hotel management which could be of interest to Chinese firms as they spread across the world.

4. Tourism Prospects

In 2009, nearly 47.7 million Chinese travelled abroad[62] and these numbers will increase significantly as incomes rise and as the middle class continues to grow. The middle class in 2000 numbered 56 million, but by 2030 it is projected to reach 361 million.[63] China is expected to generate 100 million outbound tourists annually by 2015 according to the World Travel and Tourism Council[64] and expenditure is projected to be $120 billion by 2020.[65] In 2005, 71 per cent of all outbound travel from the Chinese mainland was to Hong Kong and Macau; a further 17 per cent travelled within Asia, and five per cent went to Europe.[66] The demand for tropical vacations is yet to be developed and, in this regard, the Caribbean will encounter vigorous competition from Pacific destinations. The lack of direct airline service between China and the Caribbean has hindered the development of tourist arrivals from China. A direct airline service is to be established between China, Cuba and Jamaica. Representatives of the People's Republic of China and the government of Jamaica have signed a Memorandum of Understanding (MOU) with the intention of concluding an air services agreement.[67] Cuba and China had entered into an arrangement for Air China to fly directly to Cuba.[68]

5. Foreign Direct Investment Prospects

China is the fourth largest economy in the world and has grown at an average rate of ten per cent per year during the period 1990–2005, the highest growth rate in the world. It is one of the engines of growth in the new global economy, accounting in recent years for 12 per cent of all growth in world trade.[69] China has continued to grow in spite of the global economic crisis since late 2008, making it a robust export opportunity for the Caribbean, particularly if firms in the region are provided with the support needed to navigate the bureaucratic obstacles to market penetration.[70] The economic size and growth of China makes it an enormous opportunity for Caribbean-based firms to invest there, both to supply the region and the global economy.

China is a huge pool of potential foreign investment for the region, particularly in minerals and agriculture. China planned to be involved in the financing and construction of a US$400-million aluminium smelter in Trinidad and Tobago.[71] However, this particular project has been halted.[72] As China becomes more economically involved in the region, its investment interests will widen as was evident in the interest of Air China in the heavily indebted, loss-making Air Jamaica.[73] Chinese foreign direct investment in the Caribbean would be more likely to grow if it involved partnerships, joint ventures and strategic business alliances with Chinese entities. There is a deal-promoting and brokering role for governments to jump start the forging of corporate links, investment and trade.[74]

The Caribbean has been slow to entice wealthy Chinese to invest in real estate, particularly in luxury resort properties. The alacrity with which Chinese investors are buying luxury properties in the US and Europe is indicative of an appetite for luxury real estate. For countries to transfer this latent appetite into actual investment requires the right approach. Sales in the US have been accomplished by flying Mandarin-speaking salespersons to China to meet prospective purchasers[75] and incorporating Chinese culture into the design and outfitting of properties. Chinese investors have also shown a marked affinity for the acquisition of brands as a faster method of market penetration than introducing and popularizing their own brands.

6. Shifting Global Geopolitics

An enhanced relationship between the Caribbean states and China portends both opportunities and challenges. Robert Kaplan expresses this appositely as: 'the rise of China makes Beijing intimidating and appealing at once'.[76] Further engagement with China is unavoidable, indeed inevitable, and in any case most of the Caribbean governments view further engagement as advantageous. Developing a closer relationship with China can diversify the foreign relations of Caribbean countries individually and collectively. This will require re-balancing relations with all partners especially the traditional allies who have significantly supported the region over the last 50 years. This diversification of partners can increase the limited leverage of the region in international affairs. A good relationship with a superpower like China can be enormously valuable to the small states of the Caribbean. As Prime Minister Mitchell of Grenada explains: 'it is in the long term best interest of Grenada to ensure that it does not become an isolated small state within the polarized but wider global community.'[77]

The task is made more complex by the entrenched divided diplomatic affiliations in the region. They seem likely to persist for the foreseeable future, signalled by a further strengthening of ties between Taiwan and St Lucia with the appointment of St Lucia's first resident ambassador to Taiwan in October 2015.[78] China and Taiwan have both shown some pragmatic flexibility while holding fast to the policy of countries having to choose relations with either but not tolerating diplomatic relations with both simultaneously. For example, China did not let the Dominican Republic's relations with Taiwan get in the way of financing a major construction project in that country. In October 2010, the Bank of China and China's Foreign Trade Bank approved US$462 million in financing for a multi-hotel complex in Punta Perla. At the time, the Ministry of Foreign Affairs of Taiwan stated that 'the Republic of China does not oppose trade relations between the private sectors of our allies and those in China.'[79] Taiwan, through increasing levels of aid, has consolidated relations with its few remaining allies such as St Kitts. Small though the numbers are, they are invaluable to Taiwan. For example, Prime Minister of St Kitts and Nevis, Timothy Harris, speaking at the 2015 General Assembly of the United Nations, declared his country to be 'perhaps Taiwan's most consistent and reliable friend in the Caribbean region', and he committed to provide strong advocacy for Taiwan in all agencies of the UN.[80]

The geopolitics is continually shifting in terms of the players and the issues. The visit of Prime Minister Abe to the Caribbean in 2015 is part of a global shift by Japan from what has been described as the 'self-imposed, pacifist oriented' foreign and security policies.[81] Japan's re-entry centred on finance to help the Caribbean SIDS with coping with climate change. This is new both in regard to the country and the issue involved. This illustrates the fluidity of the international scene, the difficulty it poses for predicting the future and how Caribbean governments will handle these new situations and challenges.

CHAPTER 4

Opportunities and Challenges

The outlook for China–Caribbean relations involves political, diplomatic and economic issues which are simultaneously opportunities and challenges. The Caribbean in meeting the challenges and seizing the opportunities must be proactive and strategic in its engagement. The first major challenge will be consolidating and strengthening the relationship with China in a changing geopolitical environment in which there is no guarantee that China's interest in the region will remain unchanged, particularly if the issue of Taiwan is settled. The small states of the Caribbean will have to pursue relations individually and collectively, hampered in this latter respect by the divided diplomatic loyalties in the region. Foreign policy towards China has to be an integral part of an overall foreign policy towards the world, in which much of the assumptions that were the foundation of past and present foreign policy are no longer valid. This is the case even in relations with long-standing partners such as Britain and the European Union. In developing the relationship with China, Caribbean states must recognize the inter-connectedness of relations with all countries and take account of how the complex dialectic of the relationship with China affects other countries. Relations with China will of necessity be part of a general re-balancing and re-calibration of relations with all other countries both in the bilateral and multilateral arenas. The second major challenge is to make fuller use of the opportunities of increased economic interaction with China. It will be incumbent on the Caribbean to diversify the economic relations beyond development loans from China to seek export markets for it exports of goods and services, notably entertainment. Third, to strengthen and develop the relationship with China is vitally important to the Caribbean and will necessitate a far better understanding of China's history, culture and policies and, on that basis, formulate a strategic plan of engagement on which to execute foreign policy in the future.

A. RELATIONS WITH CHINA IN A NEW GEOPOLITICAL CONTEXT

Chapter one provided an analysis of the main features and trends in the international scene and analysed the repercussions of the global re-dimensioning of China that is already in progress.

1. Caribbean Navigation of the New Conjuncture

How the Caribbean conducts its relations with China will have an impact on relations with other countries, in particular the US and, in turn, the China–Caribbean relationship could be affected by the approach taken to the region by other countries. The position of the Caribbean could be made more complex if some of the parties view with alarm the economic and political emergence of China, globally and in the region. If, on the other hand, other countries find acceptable China's prominence in the Caribbean, a more vibrant China–Caribbean relationship may inject some energy into traditional allies whose residual interests have led to what many in the region regard as neglect or scaled down engagement. However, the EU and the US may regard China's increased presence in the Caribbean as benign or even a welcomed relief in what they see as the burden of providing aid to the Caribbean for an indefinite future. Traditional powers such as the UK, the EU and the US feel in varying degrees 'aid fatigue' in their relations with the Caribbean and might welcome China's provision of loans and aid.

A key factor is how the US views and approaches China's role in the Caribbean. The US reaction could be influenced by factors beyond the China–Caribbean relationship, but this exogenous factor could lead to a US policy in the Caribbean which is unfavourable or even antagonistic to the strengthening of China–Caribbean relations. Meanwhile, as discussed in chapter 1, the Obama administration has managed the relationship with China without major conflicts. Although there have been differences which persist on many issues, these have been managed amicably. Yet, this cordiality cannot be assumed to continue. There is a wide spectrum of views on China in the US political arena. Some of the views expressed in the conservative wing of the Republican Party on enhanced relations with China could be viewed in Washington, DC with some concern, even alarm and possibly with antagonism. This a distinct possibility when there is a change of administrations, as recent history has demonstrated in the transition from Carter to Reagan and from Clinton to Bush. Fortunately, pragmatism has tempered or prevailed over foreign policy positions advanced during the 'heat' of the campaigns for the presidency.[1]

Balancing a variety of interests and a range of relations in a harmonious way will depend on how other countries view China's growing presence in the Caribbean. The formulation and execution of the foreign policies of the Caribbean will have to be diversified and re-balanced to accord greater significance to Asia, in particular China and India.[2] The future engagement with China will require a more substantial diplomatic deployment in Beijing and the policy towards China must be based on a more sophisticated understanding of the enigma that is China, its goals and its foreign policy. This is no easy task given the complexities of China, its culture and history. More important is to build a capacity to respond to changes in China which are difficult to anticipate. A crucial starting point is to avoid imbibing the notions that China is eventually or even shortly going to move in the direction of traditional Western democracy or some variant of Western capitalism. As capitalism spreads, it is argued Western democracy will follow. Although it has become a widely held view among US policymakers,[3] this scenario is only one possibility among many, and some, like James Mann[4] and Minxin Pei,[5] have argued that this will not happen. Some doubt that there will be political order whether authoritarian or democratic, indeed they foresee the diametrically opposed position that the world is destined to degenerate into political chaos.[6] It would be unwise for Caribbean governments to posit their policy towards China on either the inevitability of a Western-style democracy premise or the collapse into political chaos. Indeed, one of the lessons which emerge from the study of China is that it will evolve uniquely in a way that cannot be adequately grasped or interrogated by current models and concepts in common use in the Western World.

Among the many incorrect forecasts or perhaps wishful thinking in some quarters is that China's phenomenal economic growth will shortly grind to a halt because of internal economic and political contradictions and unsustainable demographic, environmental and social problems. The continuation of a high rate of economic growth is not without challenges which some like Nicholas R. Lardy argue will require fundamental market-oriented reform.[7] Justin Yifu Lin, the former chief economist of the World Bank, is convinced that despite several problems China can continue the rapid growth of the last 20 years for 'another two decades or even longer'.[8] Kermal Dervis and Karim Foda foresee continued rapid economic growth in East Asia region during the next decade.[9]

2. Keeping Old Friends/Making New Friends

The revamped foreign policy of China towards Caribbean countries poses challenges and opportunities for the Caribbean group and has implications for the region's relations with traditional friends. How the EU and the US react[10] to China's expanded contact with Caribbean countries will also have an impact on the Caribbean. The traditional powers in the region are unlikely to passively relinquish their traditional role, albeit a sphere of influence of declining importance. On the other hand, it may revive the interest of the EU and US in the region. In this milieu, the Caribbean must devise and implement a strategy of winning new friends and influencing old friends. As small powerless developing countries, the Caribbean has to maintain good relations with all the superpowers and the key, developed countries even if there are frictions among these countries or clashes over their respective roles in the Caribbean region.

The EU does not view the Caribbean as a vital partner of significant economic or strategic value and has no antagonistic inclinations regarding increased involvement of China and India in the Caribbean. This is not the case in other areas such as Africa where China's aggressive scramble for minerals and raw materials could unnerve the Europeans in a continent which has traditionally been their preserve and where they retain a feeling of lingering paternalism and responsibility. The US, although preoccupied with Iraq, Afghanistan and the Middle East, will come to resent the increasing intrusion as Chinese aid and exports continue to displace that of the US. China is now Africa's largest trading partner sourcing more than one-third of its oil imports from Africa and receiving 13.8 per cent of its outward investment during 2005–2010.[11] The Chinese presence is so pervasive that one observer remarked that:

> Time and again travelling in Africa I found myself in a remote village where I wondered if I was the first foreigner to reach it. Then I would be offered Coca-Cola. Now it is the Chinese and their products who reach everywhere.[12]

Indeed, 'almost every manufactured thing I can see has been made in Asia'.[13] The Chinese involvement in Africa is deepening because of China's development aid and loans which, although tied like aid from Western countries, has less conditionality such as human rights practice and electoral democracy.

3. Avoiding the Friendly Fire from US–China Rivalry

Part of the Caribbean's receptivity to China is the strong feeling that the interest in and attention to the Caribbean has waned consequent on preoccupations and involvements elsewhere in the world. Prime Minister Patrick Manning of Trinidad and Tobago criticized the US for 'studiously ignoring'[14] the Caribbean region, in general, and its security, counter narcotics and trade needs, in particular. He referred specifically to the Third Border Initiative which he said was eloquently articulated but had 'not gotten off the mark in any significant way'.[15] Others in the region opine that particularly since the end of the Cold War, the Caribbean has declined in importance in US foreign policy, and worry that 'the region will continue to be ignored, and, sadly, it will take chaos or grave upheaval before it is paid attention.'[16] The meeting in late 2012 in Montego Bay, Jamaica, between former Secretary of State Hillary Clinton and the Caribbean did not assuage this perception. This is in sharp contrast to the laudable statements for Chinese aid from grateful Caribbean leaders, for example, the Prime Minister of Antigua and Barbuda. Former Antiguan Prime Minister, Baldwin Spencer, speaking of Chinese aid, stated 'China has time and time proven that it is a true friend of Antigua and Barbuda and is prepared to assist us as we develop this country. For this we are eternally grateful.'[17] No surprise since the Chinese built a stadium and funded a power plant among other projects.

The US and the Caribbean have different perspectives on what are the priorities for US–Caribbean relations. The US focuses on security issues, including narcotics trafficking while the Caribbean sees economic development as inextricably linked to security and, therefore, looks to the US for economic support. Dr Denzel Douglas, former Prime Minister of St Kitts and Nevis, speaking about the US position on the EU preferential banana regime, said that Washington must not 'see everything within the crucible of narcotics. There are other social problems that exist in the Caribbean, and a lot of these social problems, to some extent, the United States can help and has not helped."[18]

How the Caribbean conducts its relations with China will impact its relations with other countries. Balancing a variety of interests and relations in a harmonious way is made more complex when some of those parties view with alarm the economic and political emergence of China globally and in the region. This is particularly the case in the US where concern about the rise of China in world affairs in some quarters borders on paranoia.[19] *Newsweek* magazine has argued that China is a fierce and fragile superpower. 'Conflict and competition particularly in the economic realm between China and the United States is inevitable. But whether this turns ugly depends largely on policy choices that will be made in Washington D.C. and in Beijing.'[20] Calmer voices recognized that genuine friendship may not exist but the interests are so intertwined that cooperation is the best option.[21] G. John Ikenberry has suggested that China's rise will end the 'United States' unipolar moment', but the US can remain dominant in the international order while integrating China.[22]

The prospect of a more vibrant China–Caribbean relationship may inject some energy into traditional allies whose residual interests have led to what many in the region regard as neglect or a scaled-down engagement. At the presidential, vice-presidential and ministerial levels, China has been far more active in Africa,[23] Latin America[24] and the Caribbean. The Chinese have stepped up their diplomatic visits to the Caribbean, starting in 2009 and 2011, Vice-President Xi Jinping and Vice-Premier, Hui Lingyu, visited Jamaica and Jamaican Prime Ministers, P.J. Patterson, Bruce Golding and Portia Simpson Miller visited Beijing. Neither US President George W. Bush nor Vice-President Cheney visited the Caribbean, nor did UK Prime Ministers Tony Blair or Gordon Brown. However, David Cameron visited in October 2015. President Obama attended the Summit of the Americas, in April 2009, in Port of Spain, Trinidad and visited Jamaica in April 2015 and Cuba in March 2016. President Xi Jinping visited Trinidad and Tobago from May to June 2013.

China's enhanced engagement in the Caribbean might prompt other developed countries to give more attention to the Caribbean, e.g., Japan (which China has surpassed as an exporter to world market[25]) and instigate greater involvement by traditional allies by making them less complacent about their positions in Caribbean markets and their comparative influence. The US during both the Bush and Obama administrations has regarded the increased involvement of the Chinese in the Caribbean as benign. In a similar manner, the US has not been worried by increased trade between China and Latin America and the Caribbean. There does appear to be concern about loss of markets to the Chinese perhaps because the preoccupation has been on the impact of imports from China displacing production for the US domestic market and loss of manufacturing jobs in the US.

The continuation of China's growth in exports and investment despite the global economic crisis poses problems for both developed and developing countries. How these countries adjust to the new challenging realities will affect global economic trends and will have implications for the Caribbean. There is apprehension about the unavoidable adjustment to China's exports and competition for raw materials, energy, food and export markets. Apprehension in the developed countries, in particular the US, is being spurred by speculation about whether 'cheap' products from China will gut whole sectors of the US economy.[26] China threatens other countries not only by the export of cheap manufactured goods but increasingly China is developing a capacity of high-tech exports. By 2005, so-called 'high-tech' exports amounted to US$220 billion, 'a stunning more than 100-fold increase compared to 1989', and accounted for one-third of total exports.[27] This development is a reflection of advances in science and technology and expenditure on research and development. China is a rapidly expanding supplier of advanced technology research and high technology products. Chinese scientists have produced 55,000 material science papers in the last five years compared with 30,000 US papers.[28]

While producers for domestic markets are increasingly apprehensive, some potential exporters salivate at the prospect of what a fraction of the Chinese market can mean to the exports of a company or country despite the difficulties of doing business in China.[29] This approach requires more attention with resources and ingenuity being focused on seeing China as an opportunity requiring improved competitiveness rather than leading inevitably to the demise of domestic manufacturing. It would be unfortunate and ultimately counterproductive for the policy response to economic competition with China to be distorted by those in the US who posed in the issue as China's economic progress as being at the expense of the US.[30]

The overriding concern voiced by many is the difficulty of competing with Chinese-made goods because of low wages and unfair practices, in particular counterfeiting.[31] These apprehensions are not assuaged by the commitments made on intellectual property rights on accession to the World Trade Organization

(WTO).[32] The claim that China is guilty of widespread unfair trade practices and exchange rate manipulation[33] has been employed by some as the justification for their advocacy of protectionism and retaliatory measures to shield vulnerable domestic producers. An extension of this position is that temporary protectionism will allow China's internal economic, social, demographic, environmental and political problems[34] eventually stymie its exceptional growth and emergence in global affairs.[35] Demographics prompt Eberstadt to venture: 'China's continued rise, if it does occur, could be decidedly more qualified than the smart money today seems to think'.[36] These problems do pose real and pressing challenges for China, but there is no reason to assume that China will not cope with them and continue its economic growth.

4. Rebalancing China and Europe

Caribbean countries and the region as a whole have become less important to the US since the end of the Cold War. This is reflected in the very substantial reduction in US development assistance to the Caribbean. Canada has maintained a very close relationship with the region although trade and investment have declined relative to that of the US. Venezuela and China have increased their engagement in the last ten years; they have not removed European influence. The EU with some countries whose relationship with the Caribbean dates back over 500 years has remained engaged. With the conclusion of the CARIFORUM–EU Economic Partnership Agreement[37] the EU confirmed its continuing relationship with the region and the maintenance of high levels of development assistance. The EU is the world's biggest donor of official development assistance. The 28 EU member states and the European institutions together provided €58.2 billion ($64.2 billion) of development assistance in 2014.[38] This is certainly enough to enable the bloc to remain a pre-eminent actor in international affairs and allow it to continue its long partnership with the Caribbean. After all, there are islands in the Caribbean which are part of some European countries such as France.

The Caribbean region is not of sufficient political weight in international affairs nor valued as a strategic geographic location to be courted as a major ally by the US and the EU. The Caribbean is too small a market to be of significant economic interest and is too small for any of its problems, e.g., drug trafficking, migration and debt to have global implications. Democracy has operated successfully in the region and, with few exceptions, per capita incomes are relatively high and therefore the region does not attract the attention of major powers, with the exception of China. Caribbean countries, in this milieu, are understandably receptive to increased economic relations with China.

The revamped foreign policy of China poses challenges and opportunities for the Caribbean group and has implications for the region's relations with traditional friends. How the EU and the US react[39] to China's expanded contact with Caribbean countries will also have an impact on the region. The traditional powers in the region are unlikely to passively relinquish their traditional role although the region is a sphere of influence of declining importance. China's presence may revive the interest of the EU and US in the region. British Prime Minister David Cameron's one-day visit to Jamaica in September 2015 was described in an article in the *Guardian* as:

> ...not altruism or slavery guilt, but a bid to regain relevance and geopolitical capital in the Caribbean. Britain and the US have largely ignored the region, while China's booming economy has driven its appetite for buying influence and power in America's backyard.[40]

The European countries will understand the Caribbean's engagement with China as many of them are intensifying their own engagement. For example, in Britain, China's President Xi Jinping's four-day visit in October 2015 signalled a new closeness between the two countries. Earlier in the year, Britain set the tone by joining the Asian Infrastructure Investment Bank to the chagrin of the US. British motivation is not hard to understand when Chinese investment in Britain has shot up from $511 million in 2011 to $8.5 billion in 2014.[41] Britain will certainly be looking to increase its exports to China which currently amount to only 3.6 per cent of total exports of goods and service making China the sixth most important trade partner.[42] China, in turn, has discerned a growing export market for a wide range of consumer and capital goods.

5. Harmonizing China Policy and Asia Policy

Asia is destined to become more prominent in global affairs and will offer interesting economic possibilities as the centre of gravity of the world economy shifts towards Asia. Nina Hachigian and Mona Sutphen[43] have argued that China and India have no desire to be confrontational but should have a vested interest in a stable world order in which they can be prosperous while exerting increased influence commensurate with their size and view of their place in the world. The US may well view their increased presence in the Caribbean as burden-sharing in a region where there are no military or security concerns arising from an enlarged engagement by India and China. China has even provided peacekeepers in Haiti, but having set that precedent, Beijing wants to reform UN peacekeeping.[44] Apart from displacing US exports, the only contentious issue is US support for Taiwan, a dispute whose lineage and dimensions go far beyond the issue that some Caribbean states still recognize Taiwan instead of China. The US will have long ago realized that the recognition issue is not ideological but related to development assistance.

As China assumes greater importance in the affairs of Caribbean states, the governments in these countries will inevitably devote more attention to relations with China. This, in turn, will entail adjustments to foreign policy priorities, rebalancing of the relative weights of different countries and a redeployment of foreign policy personnel and assets. The increased attention to China is likely to be accompanied by a diversion of attention to other Asian countries such as Japan, South Korea and Singapore. One longstanding relationship for the Caribbean has been ties with Japan. Relations between the Caribbean and Japan have been relatively low-profile, with Tokyo maintaining a presence in the region simply to keep global trade channels open. This modest ambit is not at this time a reflection of China's rise but more an indication of the relative contraction of Japan's role in world affairs. In the 1980s, there was a view that Japan's economic prowess was at the expense of the US.[45] In the 1990s, Japan experienced severe economic contraction which 'shattered the vision of Japan dominating Asia through economic preeminence with as much finality as World War II shattered Japan's effort at military leadership'.[46]

Japan is an aging economic power[47] with limited trade, investment and aid in the Caribbean and its position in the Caribbean could be overshadowed by the rise of China. In recent years, Japan has raised its profile in the Caribbean and this change in posture is indicated by the visit of Japan's Prime Minister Abe to Trinidad and Tobago in July 2014 and to Jamaica in September 2015. It was the first such visit and involved a summit meeting with the leaders of 14 CARICOM member states and nine bilateral meetings. The series of meetings built on the regular meetings between the two sides most recently the 15th Japan–CARICOM Consultation and the15th Japan–CARICOM Consultation in July 2012. The significant outcome of the meeting was the signing of the Grant Aid for Environment/Climate Change Countermeasure Programs 'The Project for Japan-Caribbean Climate Change Partnership' in coordination with the United Nations Development Programme and signing of the 'Memorandum for Cooperation' concerning cooperation in the field of renewable energy among the Japan International Cooperation Agency, Inter-American Development Bank and Caribbean Development Bank.

In deciding to visit the Caribbean, Japanese Prime Minister Abe was cognizant of the visits by Chinese President Xi Jinping in 2013 and US President Obama in 2015. An editorial in the *Jamaica Observer* opined: 'The rising sun of Japan has been waning in the Caribbean for a long time and is now eclipsed by China.'[48] In this context, the motives for the visit which were part of a sweep through Latin America and the Caribbean were like those of most oil-importing countries: Japan was looking for energy resources. Indications are that a Japanese corporation is considering a huge investment in energy-related production in Trinidad. Second, Japan needs to strengthen its diplomatic ties with a group that has 15 votes in the

United Nations that could prove useful in its potentially explosive dispute with China over the Senkaku Islands in the East China Sea. China's relationship with CARICOM countries has been lucrative for several countries in the region, and Japan realizes that this could sway the Caribbean in China's favour. Uppermost in the mind of Prime Minister Abe is Japan's campaign for election in October 2016 to a non-permanent seat on the United Nations Security Council. Third, and not a very important motive, is Japan's belated concern to retain its pre-eminent position of supplier of motor vehicles, electronics and manufactured goods in Caribbean markets, which has come under pressure from a surge of imports of Chinese goods.

China's prominence in Caribbean affairs is in contrast to the oversight of the possibilities of the relationship with India. China's economic transformation over the last 20 years has been unprecedented, and some are already calling this century the 'Chinese Century' and acknowledging China as one of the world's oldest and greatest civilizations. Nowadays, the news across the world is dominated by what China has done, what it is doing and what it might do in the near future. In the Caribbean, prestigious projects funded and executed by China make headlines. Relations with India are uneven across the region with Guyana and Trinidad and Tobago giving most attention to this relationship. Why other Caribbean countries have not given more attention to relations with India is an enigma. India is a civilization as old as China with one of the largest populations in the world and it is a large, rapidly growing economy, making the country a major player in international affairs. Citizens of Indian descent have contributed to development in the Caribbean in every walk of life and constitute almost half of the population of Guyana and Trinidad and Tobago.

India and Trinidad and Tobago have had diplomatic relations since 1962 and both have resident high commissions. A trade agreement was signed in January 1997, a Double Taxation Avoidance Agreement was signed in February 1999 and a Bilateral Investment Promotion & Protection Agreement signed in March 2007. Former Prime Minister, Kamla Persad-Bissessar with a delegation, including seven Cabinet Ministers and 160 business representatives, visited India in January 2012.[49] Guyana has had diplomatic relations with India since the independence of Guyana in May 1966 and was favoured in 1968 with a visit by the late Indira Gandhi, then Prime Minister of India. Under the Indian Technical & Economic Cooperation, 40 scholarships are granted every year for university-level training. India provides a variety of forms of development assistance. Most notably, it helped in the construction of a national cricket stadium in time for the Caribbean's hosting of the Cricket World Cup. Compared to Guyana and Trinidad and Tobago relations with the rest of the Caribbean has been relatively limited.

India is a case of untapped potential on both sides of the relationship, and whatever rivalry there is between China and India does not seem to affect their bilateral relations in the Caribbean. There are untapped trade and investment opportunities and technology transfer for the Caribbean, but development aid from India is extremely limited. India is the world's largest democracy, the second most populous country and a nuclear power. Indian multinational corporations are major global players, e.g., Mittal is the largest steel producer in the world and the Reliance Group is one of the world's largest manufacturers of textiles. More recently, Indian companies have started to acquire global brands such as Jaguar, Land Rover and Tetley Tea while Indian brands have gone global, e.g., the TATA Group. India dominates certain industries and accounts for 65 per cent of the global market in offshore information technology and 45 per cent of the world market in information technology-enabled services.

In its preoccupation with China, the Caribbean has not given enough attention to relations with India as it should. A country like Jamaica does not have a resident ambassador and embassy in New Delhi, but has had one for many years in Beijing. India is destined in the coming 20 years to be a global economic power which already has nuclear capability. Its economy produces every good and service comparable in quality and less expensive than some of our current suppliers, yet trade between the Caribbean and India has remained limited and there is even less investment. If the governments of Caribbean countries were less preoccupied with borrowing, they could develop important exchanges with India to garner foreign direct investment and transfers of appropriate technology.

6. Choice, Switching and Credibility

The farce that the Republic of China known as Taiwan is the legitimate government of China has been maintained by a small and declining number of countries since the beginning of the People's Republic of China in 1949. Taiwan has been able to maintain this ludicrous situation by providing generous economic aid to secure and maintain the diplomatic allegiance of small developing countries desperately in need of financial assistance.[50] A handful of countries that recognized Taiwan has never changed their commitment, for example, St Kitts since 1983; St Vincent since 1981; the Dominican Republic since 1957; and Haiti since 1956. Grenada recognized China during 1984–89 and switched to Taiwan during 1989–2004 and then back to China again in 2005. The Bahamas switched from Taiwan to China in 1997 and so did Dominica in 2004. Switching is often described as governments opportunistically switched their allegiance between Taiwan and China depending on which relationship seems the most beneficial. The Prime Minister of St Kitts and Nevis, Dr Timothy Harris, has explained that:

> The term 'Dollar Diplomacy' is often used in the pejorative as a description of countries engaged in the 'sale' of their vote or allegiance. In the context of evolving diplomacy it can be argued that the so called dollar diplomacy behaviour of states is a form of evolving economic diplomacy in which states consciously pursue relations that redound in tangible ways to their economic benefit.[51]

St Lucia maintained diplomatic relations with Taiwan from 1984 to 1997, but the Kenny Anthony-led administration switched recognition to China in 1997, and this was the status quo until 2006 when the opposition led by John Compton returned to office and reversed the diplomatic ties by reinstituting Taiwan on May 1, 2007. This was followed almost immediately by the suspension of diplomatic relations by the People's Republic of China. At that time, Foreign Ministry spokesman Liu Jianchao said the resumption of ties was a 'flagrant violation' of a 1997 declaration establishing ties between China and St Lucia, Xinhua news agency said. Dr Anthony became Prime Minister in 2011. In September 2012, St Lucia decided after discussions based on a report prepared by former Prime Minister, Professor Vaughn Lewis, to maintain relations with Taiwan while seeking simultaneous diplomatic ties with the People's Republic of China. This came as a surprise since it was the administration of Dr Kenny Anthony which severed relations with Taiwan in 1997 and had opened diplomatic relations with China.

By way of explanation, the government of St Lucia headed by Dr Anthony stated that it would keep diplomatic relations with Taiwan, surprising many who expected the new government to switch to China. The ruling Labour Party has always allied itself with China, but Prime Minister Anthony said St Lucia needed to stop jumping from one country to another every few years. Prime Minister Anthony stated that he still wanted fraternal relations with China, but the People's Republic of China has not agreed to entertain this overture. The pronouncement is not consistent with Dr Anthony's statement in 1997 that he was making the switch to China for reasons of principle based on a pragmatic assessment of global geo-politics. The choice is even more enigmatic since Anthony's party accused the former ambassador of Taiwan of flooding the island with money to support the Stevenson King administration and had Ambassador Tom Chou withdrawn. Prime Minister Anthony stated that: 'The Foreign Minister disclosed that his Government would henceforth make available to the Government of Saint Lucia, a sum of US$12 million or EC$32.6 million annually for the funding of projects.'[52] An editorial in the *Jamaica Observer*[53] in a parody on a popular love song uncharitably states that it:

> seems that St. Lucia is torn between two donors. The problem is that while St. Lucia wants to have relations with both simultaneously, each donor wants exclusive rights. It is all or nothing at all which raises the question of whether what the Government of St. Lucia is proposing is pragmatism

> or opportunism. It could be a recipe for getting little or nothing from both of them.

St Lucia's decision does indicate that the choice of relations with China or Taiwan along with the awkwardness and seeming opportunism of switching allegiances, is a very real dilemma. In recent years, Taiwan and China reached an informal understanding to not compete for allegiance. This unwritten agreement exists in an atmosphere of decades of animosity and is at best fragile. Ever closer economic integration and a lowering of the militaristic rhetoric do not mean the end of the rivalry for diplomatic allegiance. Prime Minister Anthony explained in a statement to the nation that the decision took into account the 'peaceful coexistence' between China and Taiwan. Prime Minister Anthony explained:

> In the past few years, Taipei has had to undergo fundamental changes in its foreign policy and its relations with Beijing and indeed, the rest of the world. After 60 years of hostility across the straits that divide China and Taiwan, the two sides have, in the past four years, entered into an era of co-operation and peaceful co-existence and shared understanding. They have signed many bilateral agreements based on peaceful cooperation in everything, from trade to tourism, travel, science and technology. Under the current Taiwan Government, China and Taiwan are rapidly building bridges across the straits that have hitherto divided them.[54]

This Taiwan–China rapprochement which reached a new level with a face-to-face meeting in Singapore in November 2015 does not mean that either country will countenance a switch in allegiance. The aggressive tactics of Taiwan during 2012 to force Grenada to repay its debt is directly related to Grenada's switch to China a few years before and belies the notion of peaceful coexistence. Taiwan later reduced Grenada's $36 million debt to its Export-Import Bank by 50 per cent.[55]

7. China and CARICOM

A relation between China and the Caribbean consists of a series of bilateral relations between individual Caribbean countries and China. This seems to have worked for both China and the Caribbean judged by the amount of development aid and the frequency of diplomatic exchanges. Government officials, in particular the Caribbean ambassadorial group in Beijing, do exchange ideas among themselves on pertinent issues but not on a regular or systematic basis. Bilateral diplomacy raises the questions whether this is the most effective way to engage China, whether there are any advantages to a coordinated regional approach to relations with China and whether given the split in diplomatic ties such a regional approach is possible.

One of the problems with China's relations with the Caribbean is that when it meets with Caribbean countries as a group it only does so with those countries that have relations with Beijing. For example, the Third China–Caribbean Economic and Trade Cooperation Forum held in Port of Spain, Trinidad and Tobago, on September 12–13, 2011, was only attended by Antigua and Barbuda, Grenada, Guyana, Jamaica, Suriname and Trinidad and Tobago. The Bahamas, Barbados and Dominica did not attend although they were eligible because of their diplomatic relations with the PRC. Countries aligned with Taiwan were not included. Similarly, when President Xi Jinping visited Trinidad and Tobago from May 31 to June 2, 2013, he met with the prime ministers and presidents of the CARICOM states that have diplomatic ties with China. These meetings were not serviced by the CARICOM Secretariat although the Secretary General and senior staffs of the CARICOM Secretariat attended the meetings. Joint CARICOM positions and engagement coordinated by the CARICOM Secretariat has been standard operating procedure for the region. A regional approach has certain advantages for CARICOM, including (1) the leverage of dealing with China as a group, (2) development assistance for regional projects which can strengthen the integration process by encompassing all member states on CARICOM, (3) the preparation and coordination of common regional positions by CARICOM Secretariat, (4) the administrative and logistical savings for both sides and (5) providing a voice for those countries that do not attend or cannot afford bilateral representation.

The Revised Treaty of Chaguaramas in Article 6 (g) and (h) establishes as objectives 'the achievement of a greater measure of economic leverage and effectiveness' in external relations and 'enhanced coordination of Member States' foreign and (foreign) economic policies'.[56] The countries of the region have practised common positions in joint external representation even before the establishment of the formal integration dating back to the West Indies Federation of the late 1950s. The absence of a coordinating role for the CARICOM Secretariat is in contrast to the relationship with other regional groups such as the EU and most countries, including the US, Canada and the UK and China's Asian neighbour, Japan. Diplomatic relations with Japan date back to 1964 in the case of Jamaica (March) and Trinidad and Tobago (May). Since 1993, CARICOM and Japan have been engaged in regular consultations after the first meeting was held in Jamaica. There have been 16 meetings of the CARICOM–Japan Consultation Mechanism since that date. In addition, there have been joint ministerial-level meetings with the Fourth Japan–CARICOM Ministerial-Level Conference held in Tokyo during November 14–15, 2014.

There is the fascinating question of whether, in the case of relations with China, CARICOM countries are better off dividing their diplomatic affiliations between China and Taiwan and hence keeping the competition for diplomatic allegiance, which has been an important source of aid. In the case of Taiwan, it has been the sole basis for its aid and engagement in the Caribbean. If all CARICOM governments pursued a One China Policy, would Taiwan cease or continue to induce CARICOM countries to grant diplomatic recognition by offering increasing amounts of aid? Would China provide less aid if it had the allegiance of all of CARICOM? In the long term, would the CARICOM countries not be better off by having relations only with the PRC given that it is already a superpower with a large pool of resources and global influence certainly for the foreseeable future? Should those countries now affiliated with Taiwan make the switch to China as a precaution of the possibility that Beijing and Taipei arrive at an accommodation for their relations to change, e.g., Taiwan in a status similar to Hong Kong or to remain *in situ*?

B. OPPORTUNITIES

China's emergence as one of the largest and fastest growing economies complements its status as a global political and military superpower. The resulting re-dimensioning of its role in the world economy has allowed a steadily growing exercise of political and diplomatic influence commensurate with its economic size. The Caribbean has become less important to its traditional partners, in particular the US, Canada and the countries of the European Union, but remains an important arena for China because of its ongoing rivalry with Taiwan. China has expanded its presence in the region by increasing its foreign aid while US aid has declined except for that given to Haiti. Many Caribbean countries are urgently looking for new sources of aid, investment and trade. There are many aspects of achieving greater economic benefits from the relationship with China, one of which is to manage and minimize potential frictions.

1. Increased Exports

China is an increasingly important trade partner and its relatively less expensive goods replace those of the Caribbean's traditional partners. The region's imports from China are poised to expand significantly. In particular, China has become a major source of manufactured goods. At the same time, there are good prospects for exporting to the vast Chinese market. Indirectly, China's growth has also created buoyancy in resource markets, including aluminium, energy and forestry, which have benefited various Caribbean economies. Apart from energy, raw materials, agricultural products, manufactured goods, food in general and seafood in particular, there are also numerous market niches which are new to the Caribbean but which can be exploited, for example, the export of scrap metal that has become a sizeable industry in Jamaica. The Caribbean has high-end products and globally renowned brands that could be exported to China. As the rapidly growing middle class in China is exhibiting a taste for internationally renowned brands, this creates the possibility of importing Caribbean brands as Jamaica Blue Mountain Coffee[57] and such world-famous rums of the Caribbean such as Mount Gay of Barbados, Appleton of Jamaica and Angostura of Trinidad and Tobago. Caribbean exporters have not utilized franchise opportunities for those with strong brands such as the various rums to command a premium. However, exporting to China is not as easy as exporting to traditional markets and will require a learning process. Undoubtedly, importers habituated to purchasing from the US, Japan, Great Britain and the EU will take time to learn the intricacies of trading with Chinese entities. Other developing countries have significantly expanded their exports to China, so it is possible to learn to sell into the Chinese market. Mastering the intricacies of the Chinese system has to be matched by learning about the vast, heterogeneous and rapidly changing market in China. Chinese consumers vary widely in age, customs and income level, knowledge of new products, exposure to media and regional variations in taste.[58] Caribbean exporters have the advantages of the uniqueness of some of their products and services, e.g., entertainment and the existence of nationals of Chinese descent in commercial activities in Caribbean countries who are natural interlocutors for trade with China.[59]

2. Increased Tourism

The rising standard of living and the rapid expansion of the middle class in China has set off a boom in foreign travel. The number of travellers is forecasted to climb to 53 million in the next decade, with an anticipated expenditure by 2020 of $120 billion annually.[60] This type of opportunity is not likely to escape the attention of Chinese investors willing to buy into hotel and cruise shipping. With some planning and marketing, the Caribbean could be early in capitalizing on these new trends, especially if the opportunities were designed specifically for the taste of Chinese tourists, e.g., shopping.[61] All Caribbean states that have recognized the potential of the Chinese travel market[62] and those that have established diplomatic ties with China have received 'approved destination status'. Increasing Chinese tourist arrivals to the Caribbean should be possible since over 50,000 Japanese tourists a year travel to the region, covering a distance and time of travel similar to that faced by potential Chinese tourists. These arrivals occurred without direct flights, little marketing presence and competition from Hawaii. This suggests that the potentially gigantic Chinese market can be developed with improved air links and specialized promotion. Most aspects of tourism by Chinese are at a fledgling stage, for example, cruise travel. It was not until April 2015 that the first cruise ship from China docked in the Caribbean when 1,000-plus Chinese tourists arrived in Ocho Rios, Jamaica as part of an 86-day round the world cruise.[63] Jamaica was the only Caribbean port of call. There are complementary industries which could create synergies with tourism, for example, retirement communities. The ambassador of

China to Barbados has said that Chinese people are looking at retirement facilities in the Caribbean for their elderly citizens because the weather is favourable.[64]

If the Caribbean region could garner even a small share of the growing number of Chinese tourists, it would have a substantial economic and cultural impact. A lot more has to be done to understand the Chinese tourism market,[65] break into the tourism market in China[66] and establish the Caribbean as a desirable destination.[67] Products and marketing programmes have to be specifically designed and mounted to entice tourists from China to these destinations. Accommodation designed to suit the taste of Chinese do not yet exist as is evident in the small number of tourists and that half of the Chinese tourists to Jamaica stayed in private homes, indicating that they were visiting with family.[68] Even before organizing a campaign to attract Chinese tourists is launched, the governments of the region must eliminate or minimize hindrances to travel, in particular, visas and air transportation issues.

The opportunity to develop a demand by Chinese for Caribbean destinations will face competition from all tourist destinations, all of which have seen the potential market that Chinese travellers present. No Caribbean country has a full-time tourism promotion officer or agency because of the cost entailed in such representation. They rely on the small staff of their embassies to market their tourism product. In the absence of a sustained marketing campaign, Caribbean governments have mounted displays at trade fairs and special events such as Jamaica at the 15th International Association of Athletics Federation's World Track and Field in Beijing, in August 2015. The Jamaica Tourist Broad capitalized on the success of the Jamaican athletes and the attention given to world champions, Usain Bolt and Shelly-Ann Fraser-Pryce.[69] The Caribbean governments and private sector have to quickly establish air links and expand their advertising campaigns. Cuba, although its infrastructure and hotel accommodation is not as good as the rest of the Caribbean, has established air links with China. Air China will operate flights between Beijing and Havana, with a stop-over in Canada. Cuba is promoting the island as a tourist destination, e.g., at the China–Latin America and the Caribbean Forum, 'Sharing the Future' in Shanghai to an audience of over 300 Chinese business representatives, tour-operators and tourist agencies.[70]

3. Transition from Debt to Investment

Capital flows from China to the Caribbean have been predominantly grants or loans. If the current trend continues, the feasible limits of debt payment capacity of the already heavily indebted Caribbean countries will soon be reached or breached. Caribbean countries should be turning their attention to attracting foreign direct investment from China. Foreign investment in China has grown exponentially since 1979 when the first joint venture law was passed and by 2002, when total FDI inflows reached US$53 billion, it became the largest recipient of FDI surpassing the US. There is concern that the amount of foreign direct investment going to China could be crowding out other developing countries. This would certainly be the case in the Caribbean in manufacturing and some services. Apart from differences in wage costs, China is more attractive than the Caribbean because the gigantic domestic market offers economies of scale not available in the minute Caribbean economies. The Caribbean still benefits from proximity to the US, and this is particularly so for firms supplying its Eastern coast. The command of the English language is an asset of diminishing value for the former British colonies in the Caribbean given that English is the second language of China and India and, therefore, call centres and back office operations are open to global competition. The Caribbean does have prospects of garnering foreign investment from China in tourism, agriculture and mining. A Chinese firm has invested in the bauxite mining industry in Guyana.

Chinese foreign direct investment is a possibility because despite the enormous size of the Chinese economy there is a range of firms of different sizes. Therefore, for some of these firms, the Caribbean economies will be attractive. Firm heterogeneity is very complex in China involving differences between foreign owned firms and local firms and the latter differing between publicly owned and privately owned firms. Public firms are state-owned or communally owned. The variety is further complicated by whether they are regulated by the central government or provincial authorities. The mix and relative weight of different types of firms has changed dramatically in last 20 years with the decline in the number of publicly owned companies being a pronounced trend.[71] Firm heterogeneity has important implications for production, value chains and patterns of international trade.[72]

The Caribbean receptivity to Chinese FDI derives from several factors. First, the Caribbean throughout history has received FDI from a variety of countries in all sectors of their economies. As private sector-led, market-driven economies, FDI has had an established and important role in investment. Second, like all developing countries, Caribbean economies are trying to accelerate economic growth by raising the level of investment. One way to increase the level of investment is by inflows of FDI. Third, capital flows from China to the Caribbean have been predominantly grants or loans, and Chinese aid to the region has grown in reflecting geopolitical concerns and the significant increase in Chinese aid.[73] If the political rapprochement and economic integration continue, China may be less willing to provide aid to the Caribbean. If China reduced its development aid to the Caribbean, governments in the region should formulate and implement strategies to shift from reliance on development aid to attracting FDI. Fourth, in addition to the possibility of a reduced amount of aid, some of the Caribbean countries will have to monitor carefully the amount of additional debt they contract. Debt in several Caribbean countries[74] has already reached levels that constrain economic growth.[75] If the current trend continues the debt payment of the already heavily indebted Caribbean countries could become unsustainable.

China's economic relationship with the Caribbean is on the threshold of transition as a consequence of changes in China not directly related to the Caribbean, and because the broader relationship with the Caribbean, is likely to expand beyond development assistance and exports. To date, the economic presence of China has not involved significant direct private investment in the Caribbean. The capital flows from China have been almost entirely development aid[76] in the form of loans to fund infrastructure projects built by Chinese enterprises in Caribbean countries. As China continues to increase its outward FDI on a global scale, it will examine investment opportunities in the Caribbean. Chinese delegations, including several from China Development Bank (CDB), make frequent trips to the Caribbean to investigate projects – including a recent casino bid, which was highly controversial in China. Chinese delegations and investment missions with participation by the CDB have made several trips to the Caribbean to identify projects. This is part of a strategic thrust into the global economy by the state in China. The Ministry of Commerce, Ministry of Foreign Affairs and the National Development and Reform Commission developed and published in 2011 a detailed guide for Chinese investors in Latin America and the Caribbean. This country-by-country and sector-by-sector enumeration of investment opportunities will undoubtedly assist Chinese enterprises looking to invest abroad. Opportunities of interest to Chinese planners and enterprises exist in tourism, manufacturing, agriculture, energy and raw materials. However, the Chinese preparedness has not been matched by a similar approach by Caribbean governments that have been slow to progress methodically from a ubiquitous but vague recognition of the possibilities for Chinese FDI.

C. CHALLENGES

1. Avoiding Negative Economic Impact

The growth of China in the world economy has implications for all countries and for the small, developing countries of the Caribbean it will be significant. The main issue for these countries in competing with China for export markets and inward private foreign investment will be that of productivity given the vast difference in wage levels. China's exports can disrupt the economies of developing countries particularly in labour-intensive manufactured goods, for example, the displacement of Mexican manufactured textiles and electronics in the US market. The rise of China has stimulated exports in a few countries in a narrow range of primary products,[77] but has had a negative impact on manufacturing. China is increasingly 'out competing' Latin American manufactured good exports in regional and global markets, and this is having and will have adverse effect on Latin American economies.[78] China's export has penetrated the markets of the North American Free Trade Agreement (NAFTA) countries[79] and has had a deleterious impact on Mexican exports to the US market.[80] Chinese exports to the Caribbean and to the US and EU could adversely affect the manufacturing sector in the Dominican Republic and Trinidad and Tobago.

China's demand for food, raw materials and oil drove up prices across a wide range of products. Asia's growing demand, in particular, India in recent years, has also contributed to the surge in prices. The rapid increase in the demand for oil by China and India is projected to continue. Indeed, one estimate is that it will quadruple by 2030. This expansion of demand will put upward pressure on oil prices and adversely affect the oil import dependent Caribbean, especially if there was any diminution or discontinuation of PetroCaribe from Venezuela. In addition, if demand from China and India drives up the price of food, it will have both negative and positive effects on the Caribbean. On the export side, there will be opportunities for Belize, Guyana, the Dominican Republic and Suriname to export food, fish and agricultural commodities to the vast Chinese market. Higher food prices would be beneficial to food exports from the region. Asian processed food products have entered the markets of Caribbean countries even where there is domestic production. In this regard, the Caribbean may face increased market penetration even for commodities such as rice. The overall effect will depend on whether countries are not importers or exporters of food and which food prices are affected. If the price of food imports which are staples of the diet of Caribbean people and which are not produced in the region increases, then it will lead to an escalation in the cost of living. The most notable items are wheat, corn, rice and soybean.

2. Chinese Workers, Traders and Migrants

It is not unusual for foreigners and immigrants in business to arouse nationalist sentiments about the de-nationalization of companies and foreigners being employed in jobs that qualified and experienced locals are willing to do. Resentment that is born of prejudice, racism and xenophobia are concerns that frequently accompany direct foreign investment and have occurred all over the world. There is a heightened sensitivity in small developing countries where as few as 100 jobs, an acre or two of prime real estate or a few managerial jobs can be an issue. This type of concern is also evident in large, developed countries such as the US. Japanese, Arab, and Chinese investments and attempted investments have experienced pushbacks, where these investments could not threaten to dominate or control whole sectors of such a large, highly developed economy. There has been a reoccurring view that foreigners are buying up America.[81] The objections include Mitsubishi 1989 purchase of Rockefeller Center in New York, the Tata Group's acquisition of the Pierre Hotel and Shuanghui International Holding's takeover of Smithfield Foods. Nationality is not the issue; it is all about foreigners. A lead article spoke for many Americans when it asked 'why are we allowing China to buy American companies?'[82] The sale of port management in six major US seaports by Dubai Port World, a company owned by the government of Dubai in The United Arab Emirates (UAE), was withdrawn after the proposal ignited a political firestorm over whether it would compromise US security.

While welcoming FDI, small developing economies such as those of the Caribbean can develop apprehension, and feelings of being overwhelmed can be aroused by a single investment, especially if it involves a multinational corporation. To avoid a sense of exclusion, governments try to insist on joint ventures and other forms of local partnership, e.g., in Jamaica from as far back as the 1970s.[83] Employment both in the construction phase and when the company is operational has been an issue with all foreign investors. It has been irksome to locals to see foreigners in jobs which they could be doing. In many instances, local trade unions, e.g., the Barbados Workers Union;[84] contractors, e.g., the Barbados Association of Contractors; architects, e.g., the Trinidad and Tobago Institute of Architects; and engineers have complained about the employment of Chinese workers on projects being executed by Chinese firms. There have been protests against Hutchinson Port Holdings in The Bahamas, China Jiangsu in Trinidad[85] and Shanghai Construction Group in Guyana.[86] Realizing that there is a sensitivity, some companies like China Harbour and Pan Caribbean Sugar Company in Jamaica have succeeded in finding a balance between local staff and Chinese staff.[87] A related issue which causes unease is the perception of Chinese buying up real estate prompting one commentator to suggest that the government was standing by allowing sales of property to Chinese, euphemistically referred to as 'Mr Chin', but there is no factual information.[88] There has always been a minority which has voiced in shrill tones the feeling that the Chinese are much larger in number than is in fact the case. For example, in 1911, when the Chinese were only 0.3 per cent of the total population of Jamaica, the *Daily Gleaner* carried an article about the so called 'Chinese invasion'.[89] There has also been some suspicion about the activities of the Chinese. For example, there are allegations in Trinidad and Tobago that Chinese restaurants are involved in gambling, money laundering and other forms of crime.[90] In Jamaica, the Chinese business community, especially the expatriates, complain that they are the target of extortion,[91]but there have not been acts of animosity in recent history.[92]

3. Sinophobia-Xenophobia

Chinese people have experienced prejudice and suspicion all over the world and this has not declined with the presence of more Chinese across the world. If anything, in some places it has led to an escalation of xenophobia. These feelings can turn to resentment when local populations believe the Chinese are usurping economic opportunities. For example, 'ignorance and fear regarding the Chinese threat remains strong in Mexico in the media and the private sector'.[93] It is not unusual for FDI to arouse nationalist sentiments about the de-nationalization of ownership and resentment born of prejudice, racism and xenophobia. In small developing economies such as those of the Caribbean, there is an awareness of the differences in size between governments and multinational corporations and hence feelings of being overwhelmed can be aroused. A single, large investment or project in a small developing country can and, in some cases, has aroused hostility. Anti-Chinese sentiments in the Caribbean are grounded in a loss of economic opportunities in employment and small-scale trading. In contrast to Latin America, where in addition to concerns about Chinese immigrants and the growing presence and influence of China, there is concern over how trade relations with China is impacting the pattern of economic development.[94]

Chinese transnational business networks in the Caribbean have two sources: Caribbean citizens of Chinese descent and recently arrived Chinese citizens. The newly arrived Chinese originate as workers who remain after the projects on which they were employed are completed or whose initial entry was illegal. Both those who are settler-type investors and those who are sojourning with the intention of going elsewhere, in particular the US, opt to establish small trading businesses. The new settlers have been so successful that local traders and small businesses are losing customers to them. This occurs because they are able to import goods from China more cheaply than local traders because of their language capability and contracts. This has become an economic issue and a nascent source of social friction in Africa[95] and in parts of the Caribbean. The President of the St Lucia Manufacturers Association described the situation as the threat of the influx of Chinese businesses.[96] Migration has arisen as an issue because of undocumented Chinese immigrants, some of whom have remained after construction projects are completed. The Chinese community has become visible because it is approaching ten per cent of the population in Suriname.[97] R. Evan Ellis observed that in Suriname 'the influx of the undocumented itself has created social tensions with other (ethnic) groups'[98] and initially led to opposition to Chinese investment in palm oil production.[99] Chinese immigrants have faced some hostility, notably there have been incidents in which Chinese shopkeepers were victims of looting and property loss. These tensions might have inhibited the process of social integration and led the new migrants to be more tightly knit. This is reflected in the operation of two newspapers and one TV station in Mandarin.[100]

Some accusations have been made about Chinese migrants involved in undesirable and even criminal activities. Although the evidence is anecdotal, concerns have been expressed about human trafficking of Chinese in Dominica, Grenada, Trinidad and Tobago, and Suriname.[101] The concern about new Chinese migrants/settlers is also evident in the US because the US government is concerned about Chinese workers entering from The Bahamas rather than staying there or returning to China.[102]A recent development that has aroused resentment has been the alleged involvement of Chinese in illegal gambling and possible money laundering in Trinidad. Chinese migrants, because of language difficulties and unfamiliarity with banking regulations, have established gambling through unregulated and unlicensed gaming machines, and the speculation voiced by several local business associations is that the profits are converted to US dollars and sent to China.[103]

In spite of all the various types of adverse publicity about Chinese migrants, some countries are willing to include the Chinese in the programmes of sale of economic citizenship. In St Kitts, citizenship is granted to those who spend $400,000 on real-estate investment or donate $250,000 to the country's Sugar Industry Diversification Fund.[104] Similar programmes exist in Antigua, Dominica, Grenada and St Lucia. Incidentally, nearly every country has some sort of investment for citizenship scheme and Chinese millionaires and billionaires have a high propensity to migrate. The preferred destinations are the US, Canada, Australia and some European countries. For example, Portugal, where the requirement is a property investment of €500, 000, has garnered €900 million during 2012–14 and its inflows are projected to reach €2 billion by the end of 2015. Since 2012, some 81 per cent of these visas have been issued to Chinese.[105] Under the US's EB-5 program, which has operated since 1990 to benefit the US economy by attracting investments from qualified foreign investors, an investor is required to demonstrate that at least ten new jobs were created or saved as a result of a minimum investment of $1 million, or $500,000 if the funds are invested in certain high-unemployment or rural areas. Estimates of total investments made through the EB-5 program range from $3.58 billion and 41,000 US jobs to $4.2 billion and 77,150 jobs.[106] At the other end of the spectrum, the least expensive place to buy citizenship is Dominica where for $100,000 plus sundry fees, a new citizen can travel to 50 countries, including Switzerland, without a visa.[107]

4. Debt Accumulation and Repayment

The judicious borrowing is a financing option that can contribute to economic development as long as it does not become excessive. The rationale being that borrowed resources productively invested increases both current GDP and expands the capacity for further economic growth and hence repayment is made possible. The problem with borrowing is that it can become addictive in the quest for economic growth and in response to the social pressure for poverty alleviation programmes. Don Harris[108] has warned that a strategy of 'debt financed growth' must be short-term because beyond certain limits it becomes a barrier to economic growth. Countries could end up borrowing to repay thereby creating a 'vicious circle of foreign indebtedness.'[109] Debt is not a new problem in the Caribbean,[110] but the recent escalation has its origin in the very severe adverse impact of the global economic crisis. Indeed, the Caribbean economies were the hardest hit of all the economies in the world including other small island developing states.[111] Average annual growth rates of real GDP were negative for eight of 13 CARICOM members in the period 2008–13. Bilateral and multilateral development finance receipts decreased after 2010. In 2014, several countries had debt-GDP ratios in excess of 100 per cent. Debt service absorbs over 25 per cent of government revenue in Antigua and Barbuda, The Bahamas, Barbados, Grenada, Jamaica, St Lucia, and St Vincent and the Grenadines.[112] The pressure to borrow emanates from the need to alleviate poverty, provide social services such as education and help and to make infrastructure investments, e.g., roads. Debt restructuring exercises have already been undertaken in Antigua in 2010, Belize in 2012, Dominica in 2004, Grenada in 2005 and 2013 and Jamaica in 2010 and 2013, but have had 'limited impact on debt to GDP or on the debt service burden'.[113]

In this context, loans from China have assumed considerable importance and have grown in recent years. They will have to be repaid at some time, and Caribbean governments need to manage the debt to China as part of their overall external debt management strategy. One possibility to limit the amount of new external borrowing from China is to increase the inflow of Chinese foreign direct investment. Another possibility is that China could grant some debt relief in the form of reduction, cancellation or lengthening repayment periods. China's Policy Paper on Latin America and the Caribbean states that the:

> Chinese Government will, based on its consistent policy on debt reduction and cancellation, discuss with relevant Latin American and Caribbean countries ways to relieve their debts as China's ability permits. The Chinese Government will also continue to call upon the international community, developed countries in particular, to take more concrete steps to reduce and cancel debts owed by Latin American and Caribbean countries.[114]

This position was not lost on the Caribbean and when China announced $3 billion for investment at the First Ministerial Meeting of the CELAC–CHINA (Community of Latin American and Caribbean States) Forum in Beijing China in

January 2015, CARICOM made a pitch for debt relief. Perry Christie, Prime Minister of The Bahamas, speaking on behalf of the region, signalled that CARICOM would like to use the new funds 'for budget support, as well as debt restructuring and refinancing'.[115] He was reiterating the position put forward by CARICOM at the meeting of the Heads of States and government of China and CELAC on July 17, 2014 in Port of Spain, Trinidad. In making a plea for debt relief, the leadership of the Caribbean will recall that China cancelled debt owed to it by Guyana.

5. Enhancing and Promoting the Business Environment

More trade and investment between the Caribbean and China can result from enhancing the business environment in the Caribbean and promoting foreign investment.

a. Caribbean Business Environment

The small developing economies of the Caribbean are interested in raising the level of private investment and one way of doing that is to attract foreign direct investment. Caribbean governments have traditionally sought to induce FDI by incentives and by the operation of national investment promotion agencies. Several factors will have an impact on the ability of Caribbean countries to attract FDI from China. The extent to which Chinese FDI takes place in the Caribbean is a function of both the motivation and drivers of Chinese investors and the receptivity of the Caribbean. The more attractive and easier it is for Chinese firms to make investments, the more likely it is that the Caribbean will receive such flows. Since some of the investment opportunities in the Caribbean are not unique to the region, Caribbean countries are in competition with other destinations. It is imperative that governments in the region minimize the bureaucratic inconveniences and bear in mind that Chinese firms and their executives are new to foreign investment and therefore still learning. Chinese investors feel more secure in countries that have signed bilateral investment treaties (BITS) with China. China considers these BITs and Double Taxation Avoidance Agreement (DTAs) important, and in pursuit of what Davis describes as 'active investment diplomacy since the early 1980s', signed 127 BITs by June 1, 2010 and 112 DTAs by June 1, 2009.[116]

The Doing Business Index tracks changes in ten areas: starting a business, dealing with construction permits, getting electricity, registering property, access to credit, protecting investors, paying taxes, trading across borders, enforcement of contracts and resolving insolvency. Of the 189 countries from which data was collected, the easiest Caribbean country in which to do business is St Lucia at 64, down from 52 in 2008, and the most difficult is Haiti at 177, not much behind Suriname at 161. Of the countries that have relations with China, Trinidad and Tobago is at 66, Jamaica is at 94 (down from 88), Barbados is at 91 and Guyana is at 115. There are over 100 countries where it is easier for Chinese firms to do business.[117] The Global Competitiveness Index for 2015–16 surveys 140 countries (not all Caribbean countries are included) and ranks the Dominican Republic at 98, Guyana at 131, Haiti at 138, Jamaica at 86, and Trinidad and Tobago at 89.[118] This certainly indicates that there is room for improvement especially since many other developing countries that are natural competitors for Chinese FDI are ranked higher up the scale. The natural competitors for Chinese FDI are other small economies, but Caribbean countries compare unfavorably. Inder Ruprah, Karl Melgarejo and Ricardo Sierra found that 'Caribbean businesses face higher time-costs in terms of starting a business, dealing with construction permits, enforcing contracts, and resolving insolvency.'[119]

When it comes to the ease of doing business, compared to the rest of the world, the Caribbean is not doing as well as it could to encourage local and foreign investment. The comparatively less competitive business environment retards local economic activity and it makes Caribbean economies less attractive in the competition in the global environment for investment. The Caribbean has to compete with other economies across the globe to retain its existing business and to attract investment to establish new businesses, expand existing ones and improve international competitiveness. Putting in place the institutional and policy components of a modern globally integrated business environment is not rocket science.[120]

b. Investment Promotion

The Caribbean has received numerous delegations from China seeking trade and investment opportunities, and countless individual investors and enterprises have conducted reconnaissance missions to identify economic possibilities. Similarly, Caribbean countries have sent private-sector delegations to explore the Chinese market during the past ten years. For example, in April 2002, in response to an invitation from the China Council for the Promotion of International Trade, a 13-member delegation from the Barbados Private Sector Association visited Beijing, Shanghai and Guangzhou and participated in the Canton Fair. But there needs to be a systematic and consistent campaign rather than the sporadic visit. Perhaps the establishment of some institutional arrangement for organizing regular exchanges would facilitate more investment. In this regard, the China Council for the Promotion of International Trade (CCPIT) and InvesTT have signed a co-operation agreement to arrange the exchange of trade and investment delegations. Caribbean countries need to make use of their own investment promotion missions mounted as public/private partnerships and constant facilitation efforts by embassies, although the staff complements are very small and there is no specialist commercial attaches. The Caribbean relies on special trade missions, e.g., the delegation of businessmen that accompanied the Prime Minister of Trinidad and Tobago on her visit to China in 2014.

The Caribbean as a group of small investment destinations should do collective or joint investment promotion in China for the obvious economies of scale and scope. Marketing the region as a whole also has the advantage of presenting a larger market to Chinese investors. The efficacy of presenting the Caribbean as a region in which there are broad similarities and commonalities has been proven with respect to tourism in the region, without obscuring the uniqueness of each country. Regional collaboration could help in branding the region as an investment destination to attract foreign direct investments. A start has been made by the Caribbean Association of Investment Promotion Agencies (CAIPA) which has membership of the investment promotion agencies of 19 countries and territories in the Caribbean.[121] CAIPA has participated in the China Outbound Investment Forum in Beijing, China. Missions from both sides is a necessary step to increasing investment, but the prospects for private foreign investment could be enhanced by a strategic targeting of sectors and companies. Investment would be more likely to grow if there were a focus on the formation of partnerships, joint ventures and strategic business alliances between Chinese and Caribbean firms. Government investment promotion agencies could encourage these by disseminating information and brokering strategic corporate alliances.[122]

6. Learning Process

The process of Chinese FDI is more complicated than the process for a private foreign company investing in the Caribbean. First, FDI is a relatively new phenomenon in China and hence, there is a learning process, particularly when many Chinese enterprises are young, i.e., coming into existence in the 1980s and 1990s[123] and making their first overseas investment. Second, Chinese firms are unique and are not adequately covered by the existing theories of the firm which assume that firms internationalize to exploit competitive advantages, but Chinese firms are generally making such investments in order to address competitive disadvantages.[124] Third, there is also a learning process on the side of the country receiving the investment. Caribbean countries do have some experience in dealing with state enterprises from socialist countries such as Cuba and the then Soviet Union,[125] but the experience is primarily among officials of the government and public enterprises. Few in the Caribbean private sector have had dealings with Chinese firms outside of arms-length trade, almost entirely by importing from China. However, the Jamaican-owned Sandals hotel chain has successfully operated a hotel in Cuba for many years and has built up experience and expertise in doing business in a socialist country. Thirdly, Chinese FDI inevitably involves state-to-state negotiations, which add a parallel layer of negotiations, complicating what in a private enterprise transaction would be negotiations between private entities. Given the state control of the Chinese economy and governance process, the involvement of the state in some form, national, provincial, or local, is inevitable, even when it involves a private enterprise. Adam Hersh observes: 'There is often no clear distinction between "privately owned" and "government-owned" enterprises in terms of government support,' and cites a US diplomat who opines: 'In the United States you can do whatever you want unless the government says you can't. In China you can only do what the government permits you to do.'[126]

Mergers and acquisitions are motivated in part because Chinese firms are inexperienced in operating in foreign countries;[127] hence, Chinese firms are increasingly employing mergers and acquisitions to take over foreign firms in order to expand overseas.[128] Mergers and acquisitions up to the end of 2009, account for 30 per cent of China's total Overseas Foreign Direct Investment (OFDI)[129] and account for the vast majority of Chinese investment in the US during 2010 and 2011.[130] The majority of mergers and acquisitions have been in oil, gas and minerals.[131] Mergers and acquisitions is one way in which Chinese firms have sought to shorten the learning process in investing in the Caribbean, gaining market acceptance through the acquisition of an established brand or renowned firm. Chinese investors may acquire Caribbean firms and/or Caribbean export products that are established global brands as they have done with some US firms. The acquisition of IBM's personal computer division by Lenovo, a virtually unknown Chinese computer manufacturer, and the purchase of Volvo from Ford by the Zhejiang Geely Holding Company and Rover by Nanjing Automobile Corporation obviated the need to establish a product in a new market. It is important for both the host country and the foreign investor that strategic business alliances and mergers are ones with positive externalities in which the local enterprise is an opportunity investor and not a necessity investor and that they help to internationalize local businesses rather than merely encapsulate local firms at the lowest levels in global value chains. Corporate alliance can be very beneficial to foreign investors as it integrates local knowledge-based competitive advantage and furnish immediate access to local networks of suppliers and customers.

7. Performance of Vanguard Companies

New areas and sectors for trade and FDI, in some instances, only develop momentum and increase exponentially only after the entry of a 'vanguard company'. Once it is established and operating successfully, the company has a demonstration effect and sometimes a pull effect as other firms see that problems of entry are not insurmountable and want to be sure that the first firm to establish does not foreclose entry. There is a Chinese company that could play this role and whose activities are already a vanguard in operating in the Caribbean. If the company transitions from doing business to making direct investments it could have a demonstration effect.

China Harbour Engineering Company Ltd (CHEC), a subsidiary of China Communications Construction Company Ltd (CCCC), has carried out several construction projects throughout the Caribbean, operating from its regional head office in Kingston, Jamaica. CHEC has 40 overseas offices with business involving activities in more than 70 countries. CHEC is focused on basic infrastructure construction, such as marine engineering, dredging, reclamation and the construction of buildings, roads, bridges, railways, airports and ports. CHEC is now the major international operating division of the CCCC Group, which was ranked 211st among the Global 500 Companies in 2011, the 11th in 225 Top International Contractors (ENR) and first among all Chinese international contractors.[132] CCCC is the large state-owned transportation infrastructure group. Among the 127 enterprises governed by SASAC, it ranks 12th in revenue, 14th in profit, has 34 wholly-owned or controlled subsidiaries and has 112,719 employees.[133] The CCCC has announced its intention to establish an office in Jamaica.

8. China and the Natural Environment

There is a widely held assumption that Chinese firms do not adhere to best practices and the highest environmental standards. This is now a much discussed topic in deciding how to proceed with the development of a logistics hub in Jamaica. The prospect of Chinese investors in Goat Island, an integral location for some of the activities of the proposed hub, has raised the issue of the impact of Chinese foreign investors on the natural environment.[134] Some vociferous groups and individuals are arguing that development of Goat Island would destroy a unique natural environment. The government has all but dismissed this as patently false, claiming that there is nothing unique about the flora and fauna in that location. Some of those worried about the natural environment, having lost the debate on whether there should be development there, have raised the spectre of Chinese investors ruthlessly constructing without any concern about the harmful impact on the environment.[135] They cite the operations of Chinese firms in Africa in mining and the polluted air in several cities in China.

The debate is certainly not confined to the Caribbean although the sensitivity and concern about this issue should be high in the Caribbean because of its fragile natural environment and biodiversity vulnerable to natural disasters and climate change. For example, the National Association of Manufacturers (NAM), the largest manufacturing association in the US, ran a media campaign declaring that the new Environmental Protection Agency (EPA) measures contemplated by the Obama administration would amount to punishing manufacturers in the US for China's failure to curb air pollution. NAM suggested that:

> According to the EPA, ground-level ozone is down nearly 20 percent over the past decade and by 33 percent since 1980. Out west, states have

> reduced their ozone production by 21 percent in recent years. Despite these substantial improvements, a recent study by researchers affiliated with NASA concluded that air pollution from China is offsetting emission-reduction measures in the United States.[136]

This campaign ran in the weeks immediately before the presidents of the US and China met in Washington, DC and announced stronger commitments on greenhouse gas emissions. President Xi Jinping of China announced in late September 2015 the creation of a national programme of cap-and-trade to start in 2017.[137]

There is empirical evidence that shows that stricter environmental standards do not harm productivity. Joshua D. Margolis and James P. Walsh,[138] in a comprehensive review of the empirical literature between 1972 and 2002, concluded that 54 of 61 studies, reveal a significant positive relationship between environmental responsibility and competitiveness. Adam B. Jaffe et al.,[139] in a study on the impact of environmental regulations on the competitiveness of the US manufacturing industry, conducted an exhaustive review of the empirical evidence to find that environmental regulations can be beneficial not only in terms of their impact but also have a positive effect on the competitive position of industries. The study finds no evidence that environmental regulations and the costs associated with pollution abatement have had an adverse effect on competitiveness. A study by Silvia Albrizio et al.[140] on the empirical evidence of the effects of environmental regulation on European productivity growth also concludes that the enforcement of strict environmental policies has had no adverse effect on factor productivity growth. Michael E. Porter and Claas van der Linde,[141] and Francesco Testa, Fabio Iraldo, and Marco Frey[142] confirm that environmental regulations favour investments in advanced technologies and bolster corporate economic performance.

All development of the built environment and all economic activity have some impact on the environment, and it need not always be harmful. Sometimes, development actually protects the environment. Every industry has some cost to the environment. For instance, the red mud lakes in Jamaica are the cost of the alumina and bauxite industry. Government regulation, building codes and monitoring should seek to minimize this. Regulation and enforcement of Caribbean governments has improved, but there has already been damage, for example, the destruction of the coral reefs by tourists, fishermen and cruise ships. Poor supervision and inadequate enforcement can be costly, e.g., sand mining in riverbeds and clearing land by burning, which has deforested valuable watershed areas. All investors, local and foreign (regardless of their country of origin) should be made to operate in a manner that facilitates development with minimal adverse impact on the natural environment. The policy issue is how to strike a balance between the regulation of foreign investors to ensure that their operations do not cause permanent damage to the environment, while also allowing them to maximize their efficiency and profitability.

Empirical evidence suggests that Chinese investors have shown 'an ability to exceed local standards'.[143] Case studies of Chinese investments in eight Latin American countries show that Chinese firms do not perform significantly worse relative to domestic or other international firms. They have shown that they are flexible, able to adapt to new environments and perform up to local standards. In fact, in 'some instances…Chinese firms outperformed their competitors, especially with proper incentives from governments and civil society.'[144] In another regard, trade with China could help with preserving the environment. China's production of solar PV panels could be instrumental to Caribbean efforts to make more use of solar power as has been the case in Chile.[145]

D. POTENTIAL OPPORTUNITIES

There are potential opportunities for increased and diversified Chinese FDI in Caribbean countries. Such possible developments have the benefit of a long, stable and supportive relationship with those Caribbean governments that have established diplomatic relations during the 1970s, e.g., Guyana, Jamaica and Trinidad and Tobago. The length of the relationship and the diplomatic support given to China in the early years, after it became a member of the United Nations, has not been forgotten by the Chinese. More needs to be done on the Caribbean side to enhance the prospects for Chinese ODFI. Indeed, Trinidad and Tobago only established an embassy in Beijing in 2013,[146] almost 40 years after establishing diplomatic ties and the visit of Prime Minister Eric Williams to Beijing in 1974.

There may also be opportunities for Chinese investment in tourism, agriculture, forestry, construction, infrastructure, education, real estate and healthcare. Chinese firms are being encouraged by both their own government and those of the Caribbean to examine investment prospects in the region. The government of Trinidad and Tobago held an investment promotion event in Beijing in April 2010, and Jamaica has sent several tourism promoting delegations to events such as Shanghai Trade Show to attract tourists from China. Only 2,420 Chinese tourists arrived in Jamaica in 2013 out of a total of over two million tourists. In March 2014, Jamaica has waived visa requirements for tourists from China[147] in the hope that by making it easier there will be an increase in arrivals.[148]

As its population continues to increase, China will need to increase the amount of food it imports. This will be a driver of Chinese investment in agricultural production in other countries. The fertile, well-watered lands of Guyana, Belize and Suriname are attractive possibilities as much of this land is suitable for food crops, including rice. China's need for lumber for construction could impel investment in the timber reserves of Belize, Guyana and Suriname. China Zhong Heng Tai Investment Company (CZHT)[149] has made an investment that will resuscitate palm oil production in Suriname. China purchasing and leasing land is likely to continue given the rapidly increasing demand for food in China. There have been some concerns in sections of the media suggesting that Arab countries and China are involved in a neo-colonial 'land grab' in Africa.[150] It is certainly a compulsion for China which has 20 per cent of the world's population, but only eight per cent of the arable land and about six per cent of the world's water reserves. However, the facts do not support such exaggerated concerns.[151]

Manufacturing possibilities could induce Chinese foreign investment because Caribbean countries could be attractive as production platforms for exports to the US, Canada and the European Union. Caribbean countries have preferential trade arrangements, including the Caribbean Basin Economic Recovery Act[152] which has been extended to 2020 by the Haiti Economic Lift Program (HELP) Act of 2010, the Caribbean–Canada Trade Agreement (CARIBCAN),[153] the Dominican Republic–Central American–United States Free Trade Agreement[154] and the CARIFORUM–EU Economic Partnership Agreement.[155] This opportunity is beginning to elicit interest from Chinese investors, for example, Mindray, a Chinese–US joint venture manufacturing electro-medical equipment in China for sale in more than 60 countries across the world, is currently exploring the possibilities of investing in Jamaica. In addition to a logistics and distribution centre in Jamaica to serve export markets in the Western Hemisphere, it is also assessing the establishment of a manufacturing, assembly and/or repair and after-sales facility.[156] Lake Asphalt signed a memorandum of understanding in May 2013 with Chinese firm Beijing Oriental Yuhong Waterproofing Technology Co. Ltd, to explore the possibility of establishing a manufacturing plant in La Brea in Trinidad.[157] Chinese companies may also be interested in producing in the Caribbean for export markets where Chinese goods face non-tariff barriers[158] and phyto-sanitary barriers.

China has made a strong push for involvement in ports across the globe and activities related to shipping and shipyards. Chinese companies have investments in ports in Bangladesh, The Bahamas, Belgium, Dijbouti, Greece, Nigeria, Pakistan, Singapore, Sri Lanka, Togo and the US (Los Angeles and Seattle).[159] Chinese companies have shown interest in upgrading the port of Kingston and the proposed logistics hub.

Tourism is a distinct possibility for Chinese investment given the growth of world tourism and the forecast of significant increase in foreign travel by Chinese. To date, Chinese firms have been involved in the construction of hotels financed by China. A Chinese firm is building the Baha Mar resort complex in The Bahamas which will include six hotels with 2,250 rooms, a convention centre and attractions, including a casino, a golf course, a water park, shopping facilities, restaurants and spas. The US$3.5 billion complex is being financed by US$2.5-billion loan from the Export-Import Bank of China, with the construction work being done by China State Construction Engineering Corporation (CSCEC), one of the largest construction companies in China. Construction will involve up to 8,000 Chinese workers.[160] The Bank of China and the Foreign Trade Bank of China will provide $462 million in financing for the Punta Perla tourism complex in the Dominican Republic, which is being undertaken by Spanish investors.[161] The transaction marks the first Chinese investment in the Dominican Republic and is all the more remarkable because of that country's diplomatic affiliation with Taiwan. Chinese FDI might be prompted by the exponential growth in overseas travel. This so called 'travel craze' is projected to climb to 53 million in the next decade, with an anticipated expenditure by 2020 of $120 billion annually.[162] This type of opportunity is not likely to escape the attention of Chinese investors willing to buy into hotel and cruise shipping. With some planning and marketing, the Caribbean could be early in capitalizing on these new trends, especially if the opportunities were designed specifically for the taste of Chinese tourists, e.g., shopping.[163]

A Chinese enterprise has purchased the building housing the Hilton Hotel in Nassau, Bahamas and is refurbishing it to facilitate its continued operation as a Hilton hotel. In Jamaica, lands transferred to a Chinese company operating a toll road in Jamaica will in part be used for the construction of hotels. There is Chinese interest in a company with plans to construct hotels on the outskirts of Havana.

China is a huge pool of potential foreign investment for the region, particularly in minerals and agriculture. The breadth of China's interest is indicated not only by actual investment but also by the interest expressed in projects which did not actually result in an investment. The Caribbean has some raw materials that are of interest to China, in particular, bauxite, natural gas and fish stocks. China has a strong interest in bauxite because it consumes over 40 per cent of the world's aluminum production,[164] up from roughly five per cent in 1990. Indicative of China's interest in mineral supplies was its willingness to finance and construct a US$400 million aluminum smelter in Trinidad.[165] However, the current government of Trinidad and Tobago has decided not to proceed with this project for reasons unrelated to China's potential involvement. The possibilities of discovering oil and mineral deposits in the vast expanses of Guyana, as well as unexplored marine and seabed resources of the Caribbean, are unlikely to have escaped the attention of China's long-term planning. China is already the second largest importer of hydrocarbons and demand is projected to grow, playing 'a major role in shaping long-term global energy trends'.[166]

Chinese firms expressed strong interest in the financing and construction of a US$400-million aluminum smelter in Trinidad,[167] which has subsequently been shelved.[168] Another example of the widening of investment interests was Air China's interest in the heavily indebted, loss-making Air Jamaica.[169] Chinese investment in the Caribbean would be more likely to grow if it involved partnerships, joint ventures and strategic business alliances with Chinese entities. In this regard, there is a deal-promoting and brokering role for the investment promotion agencies of Caribbean governments and private investment firms to jump-start the forging of corporate links, investment and trade.[170]

The Caribbean has been slow to entice wealthy Chinese to invest in real estate, particularly in luxury resort properties. The alacrity with which Chinese investors are buying luxury properties in the US and Europe is indicative of an appetite for luxury real estate. For countries to transfer this latent appetite into actual investment requires the right approach. Real estate firms in the US have sent Mandarin-speaking salespersons to China to meet prospective purchasers,[171] and builders have incorporated Chinese culture into the design and outfitting of properties.

Chinese investors have also shown a marked affinity for the acquisition of brands as a faster method of market penetration, rather than introducing and popularizing their own brands.[172] For example, Shuanghui International's purchase of the US brand/company, Smithfield, the world's largest producer of pork products, was motivated not by importing pork from China but assuaging food safety concerns in China with US-produced pork products.[173] The Minister of Commerce is quoted as stating: 'We will encourage the best firms to acquire or build up overseas operations and to license or acquire famous global brands in order to obtain international recognition and improve the image and competitiveness of Chinese products.'[174]

Unexpected opportunities will always emerge, for example, the possibility of the extraction of rare earth metals from the residue of alumina plants in Jamaica a possibility being explored by a Japanese company. China will be interested in this possibility because it is currently the world's largest producer of rare earth metals,[175] accounting for 90–95 per cent, mostly in Inner Mongolia, and Japan imports 60 per cent of China's production. The Jamaican possibility is also attractive because rare earth elements are typically dispersed and not often found concentrated in economically exploitable ore deposits. The rapid increase in demand in recent years has led to a shortage, and if production is not increased the shortage will result in price increases. Apart from the natural scarcity of rare earth metals, China has, since 2009, instituted measures to limit supply so as to conserve scarce resources.

The provision of education and training, particularly in science and technology, by Chinese institutions, including universities, is a possibility in the same way that US universities operate in Grenada and St Kitts. There are opportunities for cooperation between universities in the Caribbean and those in China in language training, research and teaching with student exchanges as part of the collaboration. This could be an important part of China's soft power outreach, and could be expanded as only a small number of students from the Caribbean have taken up scholarships to study in China. The return and employment of these graduates could be extremely beneficial to the efforts of Caribbean governments to deepen diplomatic relations and to the private sector to enhance their capacity to seize business opportunities in China. It is enigmatic that these graduates have not been engaged in the Caribbean's relations with China, for example, in the embassies of Caribbean countries in China.

1. Foreign Direct Investment

China's FDI seems very likely to increase significantly in the future as China's economy continues to experience economic growth and become more integrated into the global economy. Chinese FDI is spreading to all parts of the world in pursuit of opportunities in a wide range of sectors, but particularly in energy, raw materials, and food production. China has established a growing political and economic presence in the Caribbean, primarily through development assistance. A limited amount of Chinese FDI has taken place in the Caribbean in recent years; however, the number of investments and the amount of FDI might increase in the future. An increase in Chinese FDI in the Caribbean is possible in the future because of interest in China and the receptivity of Caribbean governments to Chinese FDI. Chinese interest in FDI opportunities in the Caribbean is prompted by a combination of the traditional drivers of Chinese FDI and factors peculiar to the Caribbean. The expansion and spread of Chinese FDI could be an important development for the countries of the Caribbean and their economic circumstances and may assume some urgency if there were a reduction in Chinese aid and loans. Such an eventuality may arise because China may not continue its current level of development assistance to the Caribbean if the diplomatic dispute with Taiwan remains unresolved. Given the possibility of reduced aid from China, the current economic circumstances and the growth of FDI from China, Caribbean countries should be trying to attract direct foreign investment from China.

E. THE CARIBBEAN IN CHINA'S FUTURE GLOBAL RELATIONS

China is the world's largest economy and is the country with the largest land area, the largest population and the largest standing army. The precedent economic growth of China over the last 30 years has changed and will continue to influence the performance and evolution of the global economy. Consequently, a tectonic redistribution of global power has occurred giving rise to a bi-polar world in which the US and China are the most powerful countries. China has gradually and quietly pursued a policy of more assertive engagement and influence in all aspects of international affairs. For the foreseeable future, the small states of the Caribbean will operate in this new international environment. Caribbean countries need to understand the new international political environment and make the appropriate adjustment to their respective foreign policies. An issue that affects relations among the Caribbean, the US and China is the diplomatic recognition of China and Taiwan. That the Caribbean is divided on this issue affects China's approach to the Caribbean. The relationship with China could influence US foreign policy towards the Caribbean because issues between the US and China outside of the region could impact the bilateral relationships. How the Caribbean handles the key relationships with the US and China has to be part of an approach to international affairs in general.

1. China's Foreign Policy Template[176]

In order to discuss the likely place of the Caribbean in China's future foreign policy, it is necessary to understand the goals and priorities of China's foreign policy. China has certain enduring goals, but the manner in which they have been pursued has changed over time, particularly since the end of the Cold War. The modalities of foreign policy execution and implementation will continue to change in response to both internal changes and external circumstances. Among the current goals are first: expanded involvement in the global economy in order to promote rapid and sustainable economic development while maintaining a monopoly of political power by the Chinese Communist Party and social order. To secure the benefits of engagement in the global economy, there has been a moderation in resolving international issues and a more cooperative approach to participating in multilateral organizations and the process and institutional arrangements for global governance. The flavour of this approach can be gleaned from the 'Going Global' strategy which speaks about:

- Supporting qualified enterprises to engage in outward direct investment and global operations;
- Giving priority to competitive industries, providing guidance to enterprises to engage in overseas processing trade and promoting the diversification of products' places of origin;
- Cultivating and developing Chinese multinational corporations through international mergers and acquisitions, equity participation, public listing, restructuring and consolidation, etc.;
- Enhancing cooperative development of overseas resources based on the principles of complementary strengths, equality, and mutual benefits;

- Encouraging enterprises to participate in infrastructure construction overseas, improving the level of project contracting overseas and steadily developing labour cooperation; and
- Improving the outward investment promotion and security system, strengthening the coordination of overseas investments, risk management and the supervision of state-owned assets overseas.[177]

Chinese interaction in international affairs must not compromise the unity of a holistic view of China as a country and the integrity of its territory, culture and civilization. China will not relinquish that which it regards as part of China, for example, Taiwan. China, while pragmatically engaged in current international issues, views the attainment of goals and the resolution of issues in a much longer time frame than the Western World. The Chinese are often misunderstood as vacillating and viewed as excessively patient by their Western counterparts. An example of China as a whole and its long view of time is its approach to Taiwan. China first laid claim to Taiwan in 605, and the small island became a protectorate of Chinese empire in 1206[178] and hence 1949 until the present is not a long time in which to reunite Taiwan with China.

China has firmly and steadily asserted its presence in Asia while seeking to assure its neighbours that this does not portend dominance. China is avoiding, as far as possible, a head-on collision with the US while at the same time establishing that they cannot be ignored on major decisions that affect the international community. The Chinese go to great lengths to assure the developing countries that their rise as a superpower is not a threat and relations would be respectful of their sovereignty, sensitive to their development needs and opportunities for fraternal relations on common issues as a country which still has many features of a poor, developing country. In China's Policy Paper on Latin America and the Caribbean,[179] China describes itself as 'the largest developing country in the world' and states that 'To enhance solidarity and cooperation with other developing countries is the cornerstone of China's independent foreign policy.' It reiterates that: 'China is ready to establish and develop state-to-state relations with all Latin American and Caribbean countries based on the one China principle.'

Specifically in regard to Latin America and the Caribbean, China states that: 'The two sides are at a similar stage of development and face the common task of achieving development.' This is to be accomplished by the expansion and intensification of political, diplomatic, educational, cultural and economic cooperation and exchanges. From the Caribbean point of view, the policy paper encourages Chinese tourists to visit the region, encourages Chinese companies to invest, provide technical assistance to the region, combat climate change and address debt reduction and cancellation.

2. US Reaction to the Growing Presence of China

By its sheer size and phenomenal growth, China will seriously affect the economics, politics and culture of the world. This development will have implications for the Caribbean's exports, imports, foreign investment, aid and tourism. How the relationship between the US and China evolves will be critical in determining the evolution of the global economy and the reconfiguration of power in international affairs. An important factor will be the willingness of the US to modify its traditional affinity for unipolar policy. Economic interdependence will override any lingering Cold War animosity because the US is the largest export market for China's phenomenal growth, and China is the largest foreign lender to the US with implications for the exchange rate of the US dollar and funding the fiscal deficit. How US–China relations evolves will have and important impact on the relations between China and the Caribbean. China has economic and political motives for expanding its presence and influence in the Caribbean. So far the US does not appear to be perturbed, but in a global strategy an event in another region or a dispute over an issue unrelated to the Caribbean could prompt one or others to react in the Caribbean. In his regard, there are different contending approaches to relations with China and, depending on which school of thought prevails there will be implications for US foreign policy.

Security concerns have a central place in US politics and foreign policy[180]after a long history of a yin and yang of competing currents of 'isolationism' and 'intervention'. Since being drawn into the Second World War by the Pearl Harbour attack, the US has been involved in several military engagements. Almost immediately after the Second World War it was involved in the Korean War and from then on was locked into combating communism whether in the form of the Soviet Union or the Vietnam War until the end of the Cold War Era when the Soviet Union imploded in 1991. In these circumstances, national security became the central leitmotif in American thinking. The currency of this perspective on national security was perpetuated, in part, by the existence of and 'unwarranted influence' of what President Dwight Eisenhower in his farewell address described as the 'military-industrial complex'.[181] The security template remained intact even after the US became the single superpower because it was reinforced by the widespread belief that the US was exceptional and, therefore, obliged to play a role in leading, stabilizing and managing world order to ensure peace, democracy and human rights. The 9/11 attacks gave the security tendency renewed mission in the form of the War on Terrorism. It is understandable that, against this background and in keeping with this type of outlook, China as a communist country would continue to be seen as an enemy of American national security and world stability[182] and an evitable contestant for supremacy.[183] In this defence-infused political environment, the extreme manifestation of the preoccupation with national security in US politics, spending on security can never be enough as there is a need felt for new weapons such as missile-defence systems and drones and a build-up of the stockpile of nuclear weapons. This security-dominated view is in contention with those who eschew isolationism but advocate coexistence ideally with the US as decisive arbiter. The majority of the Americans in all elite categories thought the world would be more stable if the US remains the leading superpower, but Chinese elites felt that a balance of power between Washington and Beijing would be more conducive to global stability.[184] Those opposed to cooperation portray this disposition as appeasement; the worse moniker to be labelled with is being an 'appeaser'.

In this state of mind, it is always possible to identify enemies and even conjure up and exaggerate others into full-scale threats. In the former case, there does not have to be absolute certainty about an enemy, but what is followed is the policy articulated by Dick Cheney which states that even a one per cent chance of a possible threat to the US should be met with maximum caution. In the latter case, Umberto Eco explains that:

> Having an enemy is important not only to define our identity but also to provide us with an obstacle against which to measure our system of values and, in seeking to overcome it, demonstrate our own worth. So when there is no enemy, we have to invent one.[185]

He adds that:

> The people who become our enemies are often not those who directly threaten us...But those who someone has an interest in portraying as a true threat even when they aren't. Rather than a real threat highlighting the ways in which these enemies are different from us, the difference becomes the symbol of what we find threatening.[186]

3. China's Consolidation of its Relations with the Caribbean

China has significantly increased its engagement in the Caribbean and this is evident in the substantial increase in development assistance and the construction of projects of political importance to Caribbean governments such as sports stadiums. The Chinese have flattered these small states by the number of visits of high-level delegations, e.g., at the presidential, vice-presidential and ministerial levels. The President of China, Xi Jinping, visited Trinidad in June 2013 en route to meeting President Obama in Washington, DC. China has been very active in the developing countries in Africa,[187] Latin America[188] and the Caribbean. This might prompt traditional allies and other developed countries to give more attention to the Caribbean, e.g., Japan, which China has surpassed, as an exporter to world markets,[189] and make them less worried about their positions in Caribbean markets such as, the US. The Caribbean is not a region where China and the US confront each other on security issues and hence the US is not overtly concerned by a growing Chinese presence. The political significance of the Caribbean derives from the unresolved rivalry with Taiwan; however, the motivations behind the growing Chinese presence in the Caribbean will inevitably become more varied in the future as its private sector firms become more active in trade, infrastructure and construction projects.[190]

China has built goodwill in the countries which are of strategic value such as oil exporting countries that are important in the ongoing campaign over diplomatic recognition of Taiwan by some countries. The provision of aid, especially to finance infrastructure, has been an important means of initiating, building or consolidating good relations with developing countries, including those in the Caribbean. The most notable way of creating goodwill has been the practice of 'stadium diplomacy',[191] i.e., the construction of stadiums which are highly visible symbols of China's assistance and a lasting source of pride for the beneficiary country. Chinese firms are beginning complement government-to-government goodwill through donations to sport and education to parallel the campaign of their government. China Harbour in September 2012 made a very substantial financial contribution to bolster the professional soccer league in Jamaica.[192] Recently arrived Chinese migrants who have established businesses in Suriname have begun to make links with Surinamese business persons of Chinese descent or who are part Chinese. Even more interesting is that this engagement was the result of the initiative of the Chinese ambassador employing the celebration of the Chinese New Year as an occaision for socializing and networking.

4. China's Future Interest in the Caribbean

China is in the process of momentous uncharted transformation. China is gaining in power and as Robert Kagan points out, this will change China:

> Power changes nations. It expands their wants and desires, increases their sense of entitlement, their need for deference and respect. It also makes them more ambitious. It lessens their tolerance to obstacles, their willingness to take no for an answer.[193]

China's role in international affairs is increasing and changing, and this is a factor influencing global change and, in turn, being influenced by changes in the world. What these changes will, along with the status of relations with Taiwan, portend for the Caribbean is difficult to foresee, but the governments of Caribbean states should not assume the current high level of interest will last. The principal concern of the Caribbean must be how to retain China's interest in the region, in particular to retain the levels of development assistance and to increase and diversify the forms of economic engagement and political support. The critical determinant of how the relationship develops is the China–Taiwan rivalry. Whether China's particular interest in the small states of the Caribbean continues, and for how long, depends on the intensity of the rivalry with Taiwan for diplomatic recognition. To the extent that there is an abatement of the rivalry or agreed truce between China and Taiwan, the importance in China's foreign policy of the countries that opt for the One China policy could wane. This could precipitate a reduction in development assistance to these countries. Such a contraction in Chinese aid would be a very serious loss to and dislocation in small island developing states of the Caribbean. It is likely that China would continue some level of aid, even if reduced, to the Caribbean countries in order to maintain the exclusion or prevent the re-entry of Taiwan as a competitor for diplomatic recognition.

China's economic interests in the Caribbean should not be dismissed because China is such a huge economy and the countries of the Caribbean are very small developing economies. The drivers of global spread of Chinese trade and investment are operative in the Caribbean and hence the Caribbean does have prospects of garnering FDI from China in tourism, agriculture, energy and mining. Some of the opportunities in the small developing Caribbean economies are not unique, and Chinese investors will have alternatives. This prompts the question of what factors beyond those common to all investment venues such as the attractiveness of the policy environment and the ease of doing business would influence Chinese decisions about FDI in the Caribbean. One such often overlooked factor is that not all Chinese FDI is executed by giant state enterprises or Chinese multinational corporations. Despite the enormous size of the Chinese economy, there is a range of firms of different sizes and for some of these firms the Caribbean economies will be a suitable fit. Firm heterogeneity is very complex in China, involving differences between foreign-owned firms and local firms, and the latter differing between publicly owned and privately owned firms. Public firms are state-owned or communally owned. The variety is further complicated by whether they are regulated by the central government or provincial authorities. The mix and relative weight of different types of firms have changed dramatically in the last 20 years, with the decline in the number of publicly owned companies being a pronounced trend.[194] Firm heterogeneity has important implications for production, value chains and patterns of international trade.[195]

A second factor which makes the Caribbean an unusual opportunity is that the countries of the region are beneficiaries of several preferential trade arrangements with the US through the Caribbean Basin Economic Recovery Act, Canada through CARIBCAN and the European Union through the CARIFORUM–EU Economic Partnership Agreement.[196] Preferential market access, together with the geographic location of the region, the value of which will soon be enhanced by the expanded Panama Canal, make the Caribbean economies possible platforms for export production to these markets or for a niche in global value chains.

Employing John H. Dunning's typology of investment drivers of raw-material seeking, market-seeking, efficiency-seeking and asset-seeking to China's FDI in the Caribbean reveals that, to date, most investment has been raw-material seeking and market-seeking, with little driven by efficiency- and strategic-asset seeking.[197] Chinese investment is not likely to be highly motivated by market-seeking, given the small size of Caribbean economies, but investors could see the region as a platform for exports to the global market. This has happened in apparel and textiles in Africa, making use of special trade arrangement such as the EU's 'Everything but Arms Agreement' of the European Union and the US' 'American Growth and Opportunity Act'.[198] Huajian, one of China's largest manufacturers of shoes for export, is investing in Ethiopia to take advantage of lower labour costs and preferential access to the markets of the EU and the US.[199]

Resource-seeking FDI is more likely to occur if, in addition to the availability of resources, there is a need for large capital investment to extract and export the raw material. Empirical analysis by Luke Hurst shows that Chinese FDI in developing nations' assets has been driven by 'natural resources, lower levels of property rights and the potential for trade relationships'.[200] In some cases, Chinese companies have been willing to explore for raw materials, particularly for energy deposits. This is evident in China's involvement in the energy sector in Africa and Latin America. During 2000–10, 87 per cent of Chinese FDI in Latin America and the Caribbean went into projects in energy and raw materials.[201] Labour-seeking investments are not likely to occur; these tend to be undertaken when manufacturing and service-providing firms, from countries with high real labour costs establish or acquire subsidiaries in countries with lower real labour costs. Labour costs in China are lower than those in the Caribbean.

A relatively new development, the implications of which are not yet clear, is the normalization of relations between the US and Cuba, which has been accelerating and could continue now that diplomatic relations have been restored after more than 50 years. The resumption of diplomatic relations portends the eventual full normalization of relations. Most pundits are, however, prognosticating that normal relations are still far in the future because of the continued application of the Helms-Burton Act and the Republican control of Congress. These predictions have not learnt from one of the peculiar lessons of US political history: policy change can happen literally overnight. A Republican administration could reverse its traditional stance because the Cuban vote in Miami is no longer a determining factor in winning the state and, indeed, the new generation of Cuban-Americans is not interested in returning to Cuba. Many are in favour of normal relations with Cuba so that they can come and go freely to the ancestral home. In addition, the corporate lobby particularly the exporters of agricultural products have been pressing to open the Cuban market. The American business community is salivating at investment opportunities in Cuba and a new export market.

Normal relations between Cuba and the US will change the Caribbean and could also have an impact on China's involvement in the rest of the Caribbean. The first impact will be on tourism and almost immediately in cruise-ship travel where access to Cuba could divert tourists who would have chosen other Caribbean destinations. The Caribbean Hotel and Tourism Association (CHTA):

> Expects that those islands and countries nearest to Cuba will feel the greatest ripple effects and believes it would be wise for them to begin planning ways to mitigate those effects now. As for the other destinations in the Caribbean, the CHTA is of the view that the consequences might be more muted but in the end the total Caribbean travel landscape will be changed forever. There is ample time and opportunity for the net effects to be positive for the Caribbean as a whole. But as for the individual effects by country, those will depend on both individual and collective action in avoiding the longstanding Caribbean malaise of "business as usual".[202]

The Caribbean has been contemplating tapping into the coming world-wide surge in Chinese tourists, but have not yet established the region in the Chinese travel market. However, the Chinese are already showing interest in Cuban tourism with the twice weekly Air China service between Beijing and Havana via Montreal, Canada,[203] which started in September 2015.

Beyond tourism, Cuba will become a growth pole attracting foreign direct investment, bearing in mind the size of the Cuban market and the educated low-wage labour force in Cuba. Foreign investment to Cuba could be at the expense of the rest of the Caribbean, diverting particularly foreign direct investment in the vital tourism sector. Cuba at some stage may wish to join regional development banks especially the Inter-American Development Bank and even the Caribbean Development Bank.[204]

The implications of Cuba–US normalization are not all negative. Continued reform[205] and developments in Cuba could act as catalyst to economic activity in the northern and western Caribbean, concentrated around Miami, Cuba, Jamaica, Panama and the Dominican Republic. This would create opportunities for the Caribbean[206] and countries external to the region, including China. It is for Caribbean governments to create synergies between themselves and Cuba, e.g., multi-destination tourism and Chinese investors. There are also the possible political repercussions for current forms of institutional arrangements of regionalism. A key to the future of CARICOM is whether Cuba joins or stays out. If

CARICOM expands its membership to include Cuba and the Dominican Republic (made more difficult by recent problems with Haiti), then it will have a much larger critical political mass of almost 40 million people. If Cuba joins then the Dominican Republic and some countries in Central America might seek membership.

F. BUILDING AND STREGTHENING RELATIONS WITH CHINA

Given the reality of China's global re-dimensioning, a continuing and enhanced relationship could be beneficial to the region and to a certain extent unavoidable. This could involve an increased engagement by those states that have relations with China and the possibility that some will switch their allegiance from Taiwan. If the Caribbean countries want to deepen and strengthen its relations with China, it must learn more about China and its history, foreign policy and culture. This will involve an enhanced strategic diplomatic engagement, learning to do business with China and transnational ethnic business networks.

1. Not Misunderstanding China

The first step to staying engaged with China is to avoid misunderstanding China by not imbibing the misinformation of which there is considerable amount and avoiding old ways of thinking and the prejudices which cloud objective thinking. Much misleading thinking and writing about China is predicated on the assumption that the integration of China into the world economy would transform nascent tendency towards capitalism into full-blown capitalism and that this, in turn, would lead to prosperity which would foster democracy of the two-party electoral type and that would lead to world peace because prosperous, democratic countries tend not to fight each other. This is more fable than fact-based analysis as it is the political rather than the sociological interpretation of the 'McDonaldization' process. In this perspective, the theory it portents harmonization of political systems to Western electoral democracy. It would be a mistake to conflate China's political system and its evolution as a self-correcting mutation. Indeed, the increasing role of capitalism in the Chinese economy is not a variation of capitalism but, for want of a better description, it is 'Market Leninism' in which a mixed economy has coexisted with a one-party, authoritarian state. The apogee of this theory is the so-called 'Golden Arches Theory of Conflict Prevention' advanced by Thomas Friedman in his book, *The Lexus and the Olive Tree*. Put succinctly, that with a few exceptions, no two countries that both had McDonald's had fought a war against each other since each got its McDonald's. He explains that when a country reaches the level of economic development where it has a middle class big enough to support a McDonald's network, it becomes a McDonald's country. And people in McDonald's countries don't like to fight wars anymore'.[207] As much as China has adjusted to make the most of globalization, there is no inevitability of either electoral democracy or capitalism of a type which has existed before, and it would be a grave mistake to try to understand China by squeezing that country's reality into the existing concepts and theories.

2. Enhanced Diplomatic Engagement

Building and/or strengthening relations with China will require serious and sustained application to learning about China and the Chinese. Some countries are off to a late start in this regard. Trinidad and Tobago established an embassy, in Beijing,[208] in 2013, almost 40 years after establishing diplomatic ties.

Relations with traditional Western allies, i.e., Britain, Canada and the US, benefits from familiarity with culture, institutions and traditions. Knowledge of the West is pervasive because the education system in most Caribbean countries is based on a Western curriculum and the years of constant exposure to US and British print and electronic media. In addition, the leaders of the government, private sector and civil society have invariably lived, worked or studied in a Western country. This is definitely not the case for knowledge of China, which is a unique civilization. Henry Kissinger captures it well when he speaks of the 'singularity' of China and illustrates how this has given rise to different conceptions of international relations.[209] Knowing Chinese institutions, traditions and ways of thinking is not a matter of a visit to Beijing or reading Sun Tzu's *The Art of War*[210] or recalling a few gems of thought from I Ching. Gaining an acquaintance with things Chinese requires immersion in the history of China with attention to Confucianism, an appreciation of the thought of Mao Tse-tung and the reforms which have taken place since 1979.

Mao Tse-Tung's thought and policies were emblematic of the self-confidence and awareness that the Chinese have in the uniqueness of their civilization and their place in the world. Mao articulated a distinctively Chinese brand of Marxism despite the Soviet Union's attempts to have a monolithic Marxist-Leninism as interpreted by Joseph Stalin. Mao argued that that the revolutionary class in not the proletariat in countries that are not industrialized and posited the peasantry as the moving force in history. Apart from being a major revision of Marx, it made China's brand of Communism more appealing to non-industrialized countries, which were the majority of countries in the world. He went further than pointing to a new way of applying Marxism in circumstances not anticipated in the writings of Marx and argued for a new interpretation to dialectic methodology of Marxism and Marxist-Leninism. Mao Tse-tung in his treatise: 'On Contradiction' proposed an extension and interpretation of the Hegelian concept of 'contradiction'. [211]

It will be hard to grasp the differences in thought and perspective when countries that were under colonial rule and attained political independence during the last 50 years and whose recorded history is about 500 years try to comprehend civilization that can trace its recorded back thousands of years before the birth of Jesus Christ. History is a very important contextualizing influence in contemporary policy, for example, the 'century of humiliation', the nineteenth century which is still an influence[212] on foreign policy. The shame and humiliation of intervention in China by European countries in the nineteenth century and Japan in the twentieth century is deep in the psyche of the Chinese and is a motivational factor in the politics and intellectual life of China.[213] Chinese policymakers look to history for lessons which can be useful in the present. Kissinger in his book, *China*, recounts how Mao drew events which took place thousands of years previously in formulating a strategy during a military conflict with India. No statesman, regardless of their political acumen and experience, can depend on a few face-to-face meetings with Chinese leaders. The famous meeting between Mao and Richard Nixon in Beijing lasted only an hour, but the success was the results of extensive preparatory diplomatic exchanges and assiduous work.[214]

Jacques Barzun's dictum from his 1965 article in *Foreign Affairs* is particularly pertinent in dealing with China because of China's 'exceptionalism'. 'To see ourselves as others see us is a rare and valuable gift, without a doubt. But in international relations what is still rarer and far more useful is to see others as they see themselves.'[215] China's view of itself consists of a core of ideas based on the past such as recovery from the 'century of humiliation' and ideas about the future such as how China will gain the sovereignty it seeks and the return to a situation akin to the centuries of pre-eminence. The core of ideas is a framework within which there are differences of strategy, tactics and pace. These questions are being actively debated and it would therefore be a mistake to not recognize different and contending currents in China which could affect foreign policy. The literature on China that emanates in the West, while informative in many respects, does not give sufficient coverage of the various perspectives.[216] For example, the nuanced arguments of Hu Angang[217] exhibits confidence in China's rise and its surpassing the US as the world's largest economy while cognizant of the problems which are inherent in this process. This is contrasted with the more nationalistic, hortatory call for a deliberative and assertive rise by Hu Anang who foresees China to be a new type of superpower. However, Liu Mingfu is more concerned to emphasize that strong military power as a indispensable complement to China's economic prowess is the basis for coexisting with the US.[218]

Caribbean governments and their business community will have to become more knowledgeable about all aspects of China. This will require first, a deliberate policy of continuous learning which involves an attitude, willingness and an institutional capacity. Second, marshalling existing human resources consisting of Caribbean people who have lived, worked or studied in China. Third, engage the local community of Chinese-descended citizens and recent Chinese migrants to build non-government contacts. Of particular interest will be the role of transnational ethnic business networks.

3. Managing Potential Frictions

In any relationship there are actual and/or potentially discordant issues which, if not handled well, can be disruptive even among the best of partners.

a. Avoiding Negative Economic Impact

The growth of China in the world economy has implications for all countries, and for the small, developing countries of the Caribbean, it will be significant. The main issue for these countries in competing with China for export markets and inward private foreign investment will be that of productivity given the vast difference in wage levels. China's exports can disrupt the economies of developing countries particularly in labour-intensive manufactured goods, for example, the displacement of Mexican manufactured textiles and electronics in the US market. The rise of China has stimulated exports in a few countries in a narrow range of primary products,[219] but has had a negative impact on manufacturing. China is increasingly 'out competing' Latin American manufactured good exports in regional and global markets, and this is having and will have adverse effect on Latin American economies.[220] Mexico is a clear example of the deleterious impact of China's exports on exports to the US market.[221] Chinese exports to the Caribbean and to the US and EU could adversely affect the manufacturing sector in the Dominican Republic and Trinidad and Tobago as well.

4. Learning to do Business with China

In a market-based economy, the state does not control investment decisions, whereas in China, which is a mixed economy, the state dominates decisions about investment, including trade and investment. The Chinese state has been implementing a deliberate strategy of creating internationally competitive state-owned companies that operate as multinational corporations. According to the 2009 Statistical Bulletin of China's Outward Foreign Direct Investment, centrally controlled SOEs were responsible for 68 per cent of the total Chinese outward direct investment compared to less than one per cent by private enterprises, with another 30 per cent by a variety of other economic entities owned by regional and provincial authorities.[222] Approximately 87 per cent of Chinese OFDI in Latin America and the Caribbean during 2000–2011 came from public companies.[223] Given its large international reserves invested in low-yielding government paper and its need for raw materials, the Chinese state created a sovereign wealth fund, the China Investment Corporation in 2007 with an initial capitalization of $200 billion.[224]

The state dominates economic decision-making in China, and there is considerable complexity of institutional arrangements, decision-making, and administrative practices.[225] The involvement of the state has a direct bearing on the objectives and strategies of the firm[226] because, in addition to profit maximization the firm has to be cognizant of the state's economic strategy and policies. Therefore, increasing trade and investment with China inevitably requires state-to-state relations with the government of China, obviously for state-owned enterprises but also for private firms. The difference being that private firms take the initiative that can benefit from the support of the state whereas there is state involvement in initiation and execution in the case of SOEs. This engagement can be complicated because the catenation between the state in the form of the Department of Foreign Economic Cooperation of the Ministry of Commerce[227] and Chinese enterprises varies, resulting in different types of firms. Some are enterprises under the direct control of the state, either the central government or at the provincial level, and some are private firms; these include multinational enterprises, large firms which have expanded overseas, and small- and medium-sized firms that are involved in international trade and looking to invest abroad.[228] Beyond these issues, the willingness of the Chinese state to direct and/or encourage OFDI in a country is a reflection of relations between China and that country and the place of that investment in the overall strategy of OFDI. Good relations with China are a necessary though not sufficient condition for mobilizing Chinese ODFI whereas in conventional FDI the key decisions are at the firm level.

China's foreign economic activities are directed by the state through direct involvement in deal making and by the provision of financing as is evident in the role of the China Development Bank in Africa and Venezuela,[229] especially for investments in oil, minerals and telecommunications. Investments in these sectors are under the control of the state and, in any case, the investments are in most instances being made by state enterprises.[230] For example, the three leading Chinese investors in Africa are state-owned oil companies: China Petrochemical Corp., China National Petroleum Corp., and China National Offshore Oil Corp.[231] The state gives explicit direction to overseas investment priorities. For example, a 2004 joint directive from the National Development and Reform Commission (NDRC) and the Export-Import Bank of China (EIBC) emphasized projects that mitigate the domestic shortage of natural resources, promote the export of domestic products, equipment and labour, and 'enhance the international competitiveness of Chinese enterprises and accelerate their entry into foreign markets'.[232] The superintending institutions include the State-owned Assets Supervision and Administration Commission (SASAC), which oversees large SOEs, the State Administration for Foreign Exchange (SAFE) and the Ministry of Commerce (MOFCOM). Entities regulated at the provincial level have been allowed to make foreign investments since 2009 when the Ministry of Commerce granted them this right.[233]

The private sector in Caribbean countries will have to learn to do business with China and that entails understanding the process of trading with a mixed socialist economy, appreciating the culture and some competence in language. The process of trade and investment with China is more complicated than the process for a private foreign company investing in the Caribbean. First, foreign economic relations as a mode of economic activity are still not widespread in China as in capitalist economies. FDI, in particular, is a relatively new phenomenon in China and hence, there is a learning process, particularly when the Chinese enterprise is making its first overseas investment. Second, the learning process on the side of the Caribbean countries can seem daunting as these have limited experience with socialist countries, for example, Jamaica's export of bauxite to the Soviet Union. The experience in dealing with state enterprises from socialist countries such as Cuba and the then Soviet Union[234] is primarily among officials of the government and public enterprises. Thirdly, Chinese trade and investment inevitably involves state-to-state negotiations, which add a parallel layer of negotiations complicating what in a private enterprise transaction would be negotiations between private entities. Given the state control of the Chinese economy and governance process, the involvement of the state in some form, national, provincial, or local is inevitable, even when it involves a private enterprise. Adam Hersh observes: 'There is often no clear distinction between "privately owned" and "government-owned" enterprises in terms of government support,' and cites a US diplomat who opines: 'In the United States you can do whatever you want unless the government says you can't. In China you can only do what the government permits you to do.'[235] There are ways to accelerate the leaning process, for example, firms offering internet gaming from Jamaica hired Mandarin-speaking Chinese staff to service the business from Chinese customers across the globe. Mergers and acquisition is also a means of combining skills and knowledge between Chinese and Caribbean private firms. Mergers and acquisitions are motivated, in part, because Chinese firms are inexperienced in operating in foreign countries;[236] hence, Chinese firms are increasingly employing mergers and acquisitions to take over foreign firms in order to expand overseas.[237] Mergers and acquisitions up to the end of 2009 account for 30 per cent of China's total OFDI[238] and account for the vast majority of Chinese investment in the US during 2010 and 2011.[239] One way in which Chinese firms can shorten the learning process in the Caribbean and gain market acceptance is through the acquisition of an established brand or renowned firm. Chinese investors may acquire Caribbean firms and/or Caribbean export products that are established global brands as they have done with some US firms.

5. Transnational Ethnic Business Networks

New aspects and modalities will emerge in relations between China and the Caribbean. One such possibility is the expansion of non-state relations, specifically between the business communities in China and the Caribbean; such relations already exist. These transnational ethnic business networks are an important determinant of the growth of trade and investment with China.[240] Research has shown that most Chinese private enterprises depend on the local overseas Chinese network and other networks to facilitate their entry into overseas markets.[241] Peter Drucker was prompt to describe the overseas Chinese network as a 'new economic superpower'.[242] Kao suggests that Chinese businesses, many of which are located outside of China, constitute the 'world's fourth economic power'.[243] Chinese business networks are a global phenomenon[244] and have been important in the development of commerce in several countries, e.g., in Asia.[245] The government of China has mounted a strategy to engage Chinese diaspora communities in an effort to strengthen political relations and promote business ties. Chinese officials met with representatives of 25 Chinese organizations, in Havana, in October 2009, and mooted their role in fostering closer relations between China's embassies and the local businesses.[246]

Starting in the 1990s, there was a steady increase in immigration from China creating a new, culturally and linguistically diverse Chinese migrant group whose numbers are overwhelming the small Surinamese Chinese community primarily of Hakka origin.[247] In Suriname, the Chinese community accounts for eight per cent of the population, a figure which has increased by recent migration. According to R. Evan Ellis, they have been 'local' partner in investment projects with Chinese companies, and play 'a leading role in the business and political structures of the country'.[240] Some in Suriname are becoming sensitive about their widespread involvement across a range of economic sectors and worry that their numbers will continue to increase. The estimates of the number of Chinese are understated because it includes only migrants from China and does not include the indigenous Chinese community. There is a growing interaction between the businesses operated by migrant Chinese and local Chinese and that, in turn, acts as links to China.

Elsewhere the number of Chinese migrants is not large, but they do attract attention when they are in competition with local enterprises. The existence of a strong business community of Jamaicans of Chinese descent with links to Hong Kong and recent immigrants from China has contributed to a social and cultural comfort level that has allowed China to step up its relations with Jamaica and then to extend from there to the rest of the Caribbean. The Chinese-Jamaicans have always been involved in trade with Hong Kong, including using relatives and family friends. A common practice was to bring relatives from China to work in Jamaica who would save enough to start their own businesses.[249]

In recent years, the number of imports and range of imports has outgrown what in the 1960s and 1970s was near-monopoly on what was then a very small trade. The Chinese-Jamaican business community, like Chinese social networks elsewhere in the world[250] has the comparative advantage of family links, knowing both cultures, having a command of both English and Mandarin, and knowledge of supply and demand in both countries. This allows them to develop relations of trust[251] and overcome information asymmetries that would inhibit other traders, allowing them to achieve lower transaction costs. This type of business connection between people of Chinese ethnic background could be important in the development of trade and investment between China and the Caribbean. For example, Hong Fan, a Chinese company specializing in the production and sale of metallic elements, had indicated its interest in buying the government of Jamaica's 45 per cent ownership of the 1.4 million tonne Jamalco Alumina plant in Jamaica. The interlocutor between the company and Jamaica was a Jamaican-Canadian businessman, Ray Chang, who operates a firm specializing in investments to and from China.[252]

Caribbean business interests both in the region and in the diaspora and private Chinese firms are exploring business opportunities with the instigation of governments, e.g., through investment conferences in places like New York.[253] The business connection is being nurtured by the Jamaica China Friendship Association and the Chinese Benevolent Society, which in conjunction with the Embassy of the People's Republic of China, has mounted seminars on doing business with China. Some Caribbean firms seem to have no particular difficulty in importing from China, for example, a large distribution and manufacturing group headed by a Jamaican of Chinese descent expressed that doing business with China was no more difficult than with other countries.

Chinese transnational business networks in the Caribbean exist in two forms, resident transnational business networks, i.e., between Caribbean citizens of Chinese descent and settler transnational business networks, i.e., Chinese citizens who came as construction workers or who entered illegally and opened small trading businesses. The new settlers have been so successful that local traders and small businesses are losing customers to them. This occurs because they are able to import goods from China cheaper than local traders because of their language capability and contracts. This has become an economic issue and nascent source of social friction in Africa[254] and in parts of the Caribbean, e.g., the President of the St Lucia Manufacturers Association described the situation as the threat of the influx of Chinese businesses.[255] There is the issue of migration which has arisen because undocumented Chinese immigrants have remained after construction projects are completed. In Suriname, Ellis observed that 'the influx of the undocumented itself has created social tensions with other (ethnic) groups'[256] and the Chinese community is approaching ten per cent of the population.[257] The issue of new Chinese settlers extends to the US because the US government is concerned about Chinese workers entering the US from The Bahamas rather staying there or returning to China.[258]

6. Chinese Firms in the Caribbean

The number of Chinese companies in the Fortune 500 has increased dramatically, indicating China's increased role in the global economy. China's corporations are rising in the global economy. According to the 2015 list of Fortune Global 500 Companies, 89 Chinese companies made the list compared to 34 in 2008. Three companies made it to the top ten at positions two, four and seven.[259] As of 2010, there were 13,000 Chinese-owned overseas enterprises in 177 countries.[260] Most of the Chinese firms operating in the Caribbean have been service providers and not investors. These firms have been almost exclusively involved in the provision of construction services to governments in the Caribbean. The funding for the construction projects in which Chinese firms have been involved has come from agencies and financial institutions of the Chinese government. Investment, aid and provision of construction services have been a nexus and a mechanism for the introduction of Chinese firms into Caribbean countries. Most of China's projects have been funded by preferential loans from state-owned Chinese banks, with the Chinese Development Bank being the most important.[261] For example, in Suriname, where the government has agreed on several infrastructure projects with two Chinese enterprises, Cheng Don International and China Harbour, involving the financing and execution of projects, Cheng Don International will construct 8,000 public housing units, and China Harbour will be engaged in road and railroad links between Suriname and Brazil, a deep-sea harbour, a sea dam from Albina to Nickerie, and a high-way to Zanderij.

China is interested in promoting or at least facilitating and supporting OFDI because it sees the obvious benefits of this type of development in terms of expansion of exports, outsourcing production and control of raw material supplies. In September 2007, China announced that it would provide $530 million in concessional loans over three years to Chinese companies investing in the Caribbean. These funds from state-owned financial institutions have been used to fund projects in which Chinese firms have been awarded the contract for construction financed by loans to governments in the Caribbean. China is providing financing for a special fund in the Inter-American Development Bank (IDB) to assist small firms in Latin America and the Caribbean and promote investment in energy, transportation and infrastructure.

There is a learning experience which Chinese firms inevitably have to undergo, especially because of their very limited experience with FDI in the Caribbean. The learning is not confined to the Caribbean as it is also taking place in Latin America[262] but is complicated in the Caribbean because of the differences in the investment environments among the countries. The necessity for learning to establish and operate foreign direct investment is a national phenomenon in China[263] because in recent years the state has intensified its encouragement and facilitation of Chinese enterprises to invest abroad.

7. Attracting Chinese FDI

The contribution of FDI and its efficacy in promoting economic growth and economic development is a longstanding debate in development economics[264] and in Caribbean economic policy.[265] The generally accepted conclusion which has emerged from the debate on FDI in developing countries is that FDI can make a positive economic contribution under the appropriate conditions. The appropriate conditions vary from country to country, but the commonality is that a critical component of the country-specific appropriateness are the laws, regulations, guidelines, institutions and policy framework within which FDI operates. The policy issue for the host country is to ensure that the benefits are maximized and exceed the costs.[266]

FDI can contribute to the economic growth of developing countries, increasing production, exports, foreign exchange, tax revenue and employment and by the productivity-boosting spillover effects of the diffusion of technology, managerial practices and innovation spurred by integration into global value chains.[267] The extent to which spillovers occur depends on the development of backward and forward linkages[268] and the domestic factor of productivity, in particular human capital.[269] Governments in developing countries recognize that FDI can alleviate the investment, foreign exchange and trade constraints;[270] hence, they seek to attract as much FDI as they can mobilize in an effort to raise the level of gross investment above that which is financed from national savings. FDI has costs and benefits for the host country,[271] especially when that country is a developing economy. The small developing countries of the Caribbean, while welcoming FDI, are always sensitive about foreign direct investment especially when such investments are made by large companies, in particular multinational corporations,[272] whose sales dwarf their GDP. FDI involves ownership and control of assets, including land, and foreign firms often attain monopoly or oligopoly status in the small markets of Caribbean economies. Concerns have also been expressed about the outflow of profits, the amount of tax paid, loss of control over key decisions about resource allocation and whether the operations of foreign investors are harmful to long-term development prospects.

Due to both reality and perception, considerable misunderstanding and resentment can build up between foreign investors, the government and in the populace at large. The impression of the inexorable rise of China and the frequently expressed view that China is literally buying up the world is greatly exaggerated and emotive but unfounded;[273] nonetheless, it can arouse nationalist sentiment against FDI. The experience with Chinese FDI is not without real problems. UNCTAD reports Chinese FDI as

> the average Chinese firm operating on the continent is a large state-owned enterprise and tends to enter new markets by building new facilities, is highly vertically integrated, rarely encourages the integration of its management and workers into the African socioeconomic fabric, conducts most of its sales in Africa with government entities, and exploits its ability to out-compete other bidders for government procurement contracts.[274]

Interestingly, Africans by a two-to-one majority view China's investments favourably rather than negatively.[275]

The question of how to strike a balance between the regulation of foreign investors to ensure that their operations do not do permanent damage to the environment, while also allowing them to maximize their efficiency and profitability, is now a much discussed topic in deciding how to proceed with the development of a logistics hub in Jamaica. The prospect of Chinese investors in Goat Island, an integral location for some of the activities of the proposed hub, has raised the issue of the impact of Chinese foreign investors on the natural environment.[276]

Several myths have to be dismissed, starting with the recognition that all development and economic activity has some impact on the environment, and it need not always be harmful. Sometimes development actually protects the environment. Every industry has some cost to the environment. Government regulation, building codes and monitoring should seek to minimize this. Unfortunately, this has not been a strong point of successive governments, the most glaring example being the destruction of the island's coral reefs by hotels and cruise ships. Poor supervision and inadequate enforcement can be costly, e.g., sand mining in riverbeds and clearing land by burning, which has deforested valuable watershed areas.

All foreign investors, regardless of their country of origin, should be made to operate in a manner that facilitates development with minimal adverse impact on the natural environment. The task of the government in facilitating investment is to create a business environment that encourages the maximum private investment, both foreign and local, and ensures that investors operate in the best interest of the country. In order for Caribbean governments to ensure their economies gain the maximum from the operations of direct foreign investment, they must establish a regulatory regime involving the following:

> First, in their investment promotion programmes, Caribbean governments must screen and identify the 'right' foreign investors. The considerations here go beyond the financial capacity of the firm to make the initial investment, and include the encouragement (not enforcement) of technology transfers, joint ventures and the utilization of local labour, raw material and local suppliers. There must be adequate institutional arrangements to conduct careful due diligence of foreign investors expressing an interest in operating in Caribbean countries. The financial records and history of operations must be examined to only allow entry to foreign companies of the highest repute and to prevent money laundering. We must never assume that every cash-rich investor is a desirable investor capable of being a good corporate citizen.

Second, Caribbean countries must create and maintain a business environment that provides the incentives that maximize the benefits of FDI, such as encouraging joint ventures, local sourcing of inputs and collaborations with local institutions, e.g., in research and development. In this regard, the stable, democratic traditions and the high quality of human resources in most Caribbean countries will be an asset.

Third, establish rules and regulations, in addition to the laws of the land, to regulate the conduct of foreign investors. The government must never let its desperation for foreign investment cause it to wave these crucial guidelines. A harmful investment, local or foreign, is worse than no investment. This must be kept in mind when examining investment proposals for the logistics hub; otherwise Jamaica is destined to repeat the experience of its first logistics hub, Port Royal, once a haven for pirate-foreign investors. Governments must have adequate arrangements to continuously monitor foreign investors and ensure they are operating within the laws and stipulated regulations, adhering to proper labour practices, paying taxes and import duties and respecting the environment. Caribbean government must exercise surveillance and when necessary enforce regulations and imposing penalties on foreign and local investors who violate these regulations. If all else fails, the government must also be prepared to institute the ultimate remedial action of closing down undesirable operations.

Caribbean countries have sought to induce FDI by establishing bilateral investment treaties with countries identified as likely sources of investment. Caribbean governments have signed 82 bilateral investment treaties with countries mainly in Europe and North America. This policy was applied to China starting before China became a major source of investment. Jamaica signed a Bilateral

Investment Agreement (BIT) with China in 1994 and a Double Taxation Avoidance Agreement (DTA) with China in 1996. Barbados signed a BIT in 1998 and a DTA in 2000. Trinidad and Tobago signed a BIT on July 22, 2002 and a DTA in 2003. In 2003, Guyana signed an Agreement for the Encouragement and Reciprocal Protection of Investment. These BITs vary as they relate to coverage of assets, dispute resolution, expropriation and compensation. How important the existence of BITs is to encouraging FDI is open to debate.[277] In this regard, it is interesting that the US has BITs only with Grenada, Haiti and Jamaica although the stock of US investment is largest in The Bahamas, Barbados, and Trinidad and Tobago.[278]

Cuba has traditionally been reticent about the role of FDI in its economy,[279] but attitudes have been changing in recent years. Increased Chinese interest in Cuba might be prompted by that country's new investment law[280] (March 2014) which provides exemption from tax on profits for eight years for joint ventures with the Cuban state and between foreign and Cuban companies. It also allows for 100 per cent foreign ownership, but these investments are not eligible for tax exemptions. Foreign investment will be allowed in all sectors except health care and education. Foreigners doing business will be exempted from personal income tax.

Although China constitutes a huge pool of potential foreign investment for the Caribbean, efforts by Caribbean governments and firms have been limited to investment promotion missions rather than a sustained and planned campaign. As China becomes more economically involved in the region, its investment interests could expand, but the extent to which this occurs will be influenced by the information and marketing of the Caribbean. For example, investment promotion missions have been mounted by Barbados, Guyana, Jamaica, Suriname, and Trinidad and Tobago, at the 13th China International Fair for Investment and Trade (CIFIT), September 2009, in Xiamen of Fujian Province.[281] Similarly, there was the Trinidad and Tobago Business Forum held in Shanghai on September 2010, at the Shanghai Expo. The follow-up to contacts resulting from these fledgling sorties is left to their embassies whose staff complement is not trained for this task. The embassies, however, could facilitate Chinese investors, by reducing, bureaucratic and time-consuming processes for issuing visas for business travel. Investment would be more likely to grow if it involved partnerships, joint ventures, and strategic business alliances between Chinese and Caribbean firms. Government investment and promotion agencies could encourage these by disseminating information and brokering strategic corporate alliances.[282]

The Caribbean, as a group of small investment destinations, should present the region as a cluster development opportunity by collective or joint investment promotion in China for the obvious economies of scale and scope. Marketing the region also has the advantage of presenting a larger market to Chinese investors. The efficacy of presenting the Caribbean as a region in which there are broad similarities and commonalities has been proven with respect to tourism in the region, without obscuring the uniqueness of each country.

Epilogue

Here in this final chapter an epilogue is presented which highlights salient points for the purpose of emphasis and adds some very recent information which captures the latest developments on issues discussed earlier in the book. This chapter consists of four sections, first, a very brief summary of the gravamen of chapters 1–4, second, selected points of emphasis, third, latest developments on some pertinent issues and fourth, a closing word on the approach by the Caribbean to its relations with China.

1. OVERVIEW

Chapter one discussed China's global re-dimensioning which is manifested primarily in global trade and investment trends. Economic changes have been accompanied by a concomitant rise in influence in international affairs. Whether or not China becomes as dominant as Britain and the US in their halcyon eras is debatable, but there is no denying a new global reality in which China is one of the dominant countries. The analysis in this first chapter sets the context in which to examine China's relations with the Caribbean.

Against the background of China's global prominence, chapter two examined and analysed the nature and the extent and character of the growing economic and political presence of China in the Caribbean. The focus of the chapter is a review of development assistance, trade and foreign investment. The trend in aid and investment is constrained by the limited availability of statistical data on development assistance and foreign direct investment. The information on trade is more detailed and reveals the sharp increase in imports from China and the paucity of exports to China. The resulting adverse trade deficit is both a challenge and an opportunity. The challenge is multifaceted, involving financing the growing volume of imports, the possible displacement of local production and making more use of the vast export market in China.

The motivations of China and the countries of the Caribbean for deepening and widening their relationship are identified and explained in chapter three. China, as a global power, inevitably extends its diplomatic reach across the globe and ultimately in the Caribbean, spurred on by the desire to be rid of the embarrassment of some countries continuing to recognize Taiwan as an independent sovereign state. China values a unified state, and the goal of reunification will not be relinquished. Caribbean states are fully cognizant of the centrality of the rivalry between China and Taiwan and have deliberately designed their respective foreign policy choice to maximize the benefits to be derived. The future of the rivalry is not clear, but even if it persists, it is likely not to be as virulent as in the past, which could mean a reduced interest in the Caribbean and a reduced dispensation of aid.

This growing presence by China in the Caribbean appears to be an anomaly because, in general, superpowers find little interest in ties with small states. Indeed, relations with small states are a low priority for superpowers preoccupied with global perspectives. Apart from the unusual display of interest by a superpower, especially one that has not held a traditional hegemonic role in this region of the world, the subject is of interest because relations with China have assumed prominence in the international relations of Caribbean states. The relationship merits in-depth examination and analysis and this study fills a lacuna in the literature and establishes the specificity of the relationship.

Given the importance of China to the Caribbean now and in the future, chapter four discussed the challenges and opportunities for the Caribbean that the relationship with China presents, which warrant careful attention. The complexity of these issues is compounded by possible changes in the relationship between China and Taiwan. Amelioration could result in a cessation of Chinese interest in the region given the small markets and natural resources which are not unique nor in short supply. Whatever happens between China and Taiwan will not obviate the need for the Caribbean countries to be proactive in identifying ways to engage China's interest. One such potential driver of future economic relations is private foreign direct investment.

2. POINTS OF EMPHASIS

A few points are briefly brought to the attention of the reader to emphasize their importance.

Mindset

When a customer purchases a bottle of 'Ethos' brand of water it bears under the label a map of the world in which the Atlantic Ocean is at the centre of the globe flanked by the US, to the west and Europe, to the east. The map of the world produced in China long before European countries came to dominate the world showed China at the centre of the globe. The centre of gravity of the world economy has shifted to the East with China now the largest economy in the world. This change does not mean that China will be the dominant economic power but it does mean that the world economy will be multi-centric. There is no point living in the mindset portrayed on the Ethos bottle. All of this implies that as difficult as it may be to shed old thinking and ingrained perceptions, it is necessary to recognize the changes, try to understand them and re-think policy in response to this new situation. Those countries, organizations and governments that are the quickest to adjust to the reality will have an advantage over their slower compatriots. Apart from outdated thinking, there is also an unconscious prejudice which tends to assign blame to China not supported by the facts.[1] These run the gamut from accusations of environmental damage to illegal migrants and gambling. This tendency is not confined to the Caribbean.

Relinquishing Old Concepts

In formulating policy in the recent international context, it is necessary to disregard the old conceptual lens used in previous eras, in particular that in a multipolar world the economic competition and political rivalry between China, the rising power, and the US, the dominant but waning power, must lead to conflict. The China–US relationship is certainly not of the kind of the Cold War between the US and the former Soviet Union. China's rapid economic growth has benefited from capitalizing on opportunities in the globalization of the world economy and therefore is largely dependent on the global economy. China does not threaten the West or global capitalism although its competitive advantage in manufacturing has eroded some industrial lines of production in Western capitalist countries[2] and Latin America.[3] China's ever closer integration into the global economy has had an impact on global capitalism, but it does not undermine the capitalist system. Ironically, China's rapid economic growth has liberated millions from poverty, and this prosperity has reinforced the Communist Party in power. It has saved the Communist Party from the internal economic failures and international political contradictions that precipitated the implosion of the Soviet Union.[4]

Deepening China–Caribbean Relations

The relationship between China and the Caribbean has become one of the most important and topical issues in the region, both in countries that have diplomatic relations with the People's Republic of China and those that opt for ties with Taiwan. China's relations with the Caribbean has grown in importance as is indicated by the increase in imports from China and the substantial amount of development aid which has been contributed to the Caribbean especially at a time when traditional donors are determined to wean middle-income developing countries from the 'drip' of financial aid, primarily in the context of an ongoing global economic crisis. The receptivity to China's willingness to provide aid in grants and loans has come at a time when many governments in the region are highly indebted and are confronted with the urgent need to implement a policy of fiscal consolidation. Those countries that continue the fallacy of diplomatic recognition of Taiwan have also benefited from China's growing presence in the Caribbean because it has prompted Taiwan to maintain and, in some cases, increase its financial aid to its Caribbean allies. As the economic ties between Taiwan and China intensify and consolidate, a process of rapprochement is proceeding with the two countries having their first ever face-to-face meeting in early 2014. If China and Taiwan reach an agreement and untie financial aid from diplomatic recognition, Caribbean countries might receive less foreign aid in the not too distant future. How governments in the region react if this does happen will be a major foreign policy issue for all the countries of the Caribbean.

From Loans to FDI

One distinct possibility is to attract foreign direct investment from China into key economic sectors as many other countries are already doing despite the sceptics. Indeed, a well-known scholar on US–China economic interaction advocated, in the *Washington Post*, that Chinese companies should buy American companies in an effort to maintain 'good relations'.[5] This will benefit the US economy. Some do not find this a compelling argument and call for scrutiny, especially since Chinese FDI was estimated at $15 billion in 2015 and is forecast to be as high as $30 billion in 2016.[6] The possibilities of garnering Chinese FDI are particularly propitious in the tourism sector. Major Chinese FDI in tourism is about to happen, and the Caribbean, whose economies are heavily dependent on tourism, must secure a part of this investment. Chinese investments in tourism are emerging. For example, Anbang Insurance Group Company of China's bid to buy Starwood Hotels & Resorts Worldwide, which includes the Sheraton, Westin, Four Points, W, Luxury Collection, St. Regis, Le Meridien and Aloft hotels. Anbang also sought to acquire the US luxury hotel line, Strategic Hotels & Resorts, for $6.5 billion. Two years ago, it purchased the Waldorf Astoria in New York for almost $2 billion.[7]

However, Anbang, along with other Chinese investors, must bear in mind that the number of Chinese tourists has been growing significantly. As such, they should look to invest in other regions such as the Caribbean to meet the growing demand. In 2015, Chinese tourists spent $215 billion on foreign travel. This represents an increase of over 53 per cent from 2014.[8] The World Travel & Tourism Council has forecasted annual growth of seven per cent over the next ten years.[9]

The prospects of sourcing tourists from China and inducing more foreign direct investment has galvanized nearly all of the governments of the Caribbean region to 'ramp up' interaction via a flurry of high-level visits by the political leadership. Nearly all the prime ministers and presidents of countries with relations with China have made visits to Beijing, including three prime ministers of Jamaica who made official visits. Such diplomatic forays were made almost mandatory as the reciprocity for the visit to the region by the President Xi Jinping of China in late 2013. Both in an operational sense and in recognition of China's superpower status, Caribbean governments have been strengthening the means for closer relations by appointing new ambassadors and, in the case of Trinidad and Tobago, finally opening an embassy in Beijing.

New Dimensions

During the last 10–15 years, China has expanded its economic and political relations with developing countries as it expanded its involvement in international affairs. In the case of the Caribbean, China's economic relationship with the countries of the region has grown significantly with a concomitant increase in political linkage between China and the Caribbean states. The relationship between China and Caribbean countries continues to evolve and is beginning to widen in scope beyond development, finance and trade. In March 2016, Barbados and China signed a Mutual Legal Assistance Treaty and an Extradition Treaty.[10] The former will allow collaboration in the investigation and prosecution of crime, and the latter formalizes co-operation on extradition. This action was timely following the 2016 capture and repatriation of two of China's most wanted fugitives in St Vincent.[11] China and Caribbean countries which have diplomatic relationships have become more knowledgeable about each other, and their relationship has been strengthened as a result. The China Harbour Engineering Company (CHEC) has announced that it will establish its regional headquarters in Kingston, Jamaica and will construct a building to house this office. CHEC's reasons for choosing Kingston were that 'Jamaica was the first Caribbean country to set up diplomatic relations with China in the early 1970s, yielding what is now a long history between the two countries.' Second, China has carried out several large construction projects in Jamaica before, so it was confident in continuing an economic partnership with Jamaica. Third, Jamaica is a mountainous island with many rivers and CHEC specializes in marine engineering, dredging and bridge building.[12]

People-to-People Contacts

There is more person-to-person contact than is commonly realized as Caribbean people are beginning to live and work in China. A small number of Jamaicans live and work in China, and a growing number frequently travel to China, including creative artists, entrepreneurs and students. Most Caribbean students speak favourably of their student days in China, and several have expressed an interest in returning to China. Some have married Chinese citizens. Some Jamaican artists regularly spend time in China and exhibit their paintings in China. Bryan McFarlane, whose wife is Chinese, is a professor of painting and drawing at the University of Massachusetts, Dartmouth, has sojourned in China on and off since 2007. McFarlane feels that 'China has recently become a very special part of my journey' and 'it is one which will unquestionably define a most important period of my life's work as an artist/painter.' Peter Wayne Lewis, Jamaican Professor of

Painting at Massachusetts College of Art and Design, Boston, has visited China several times and has mounted several exhibitions of his paintings which have been well received. Since 2012, he divides his time between Boston and Beijing.

Persons from the Caribbean who have studied in China have had good undergraduate and postgraduate experiences and gained a proficiency in Mandarin. The experience of living in China was said to be enriching and many expressed an interest in living and working in China. These people will be an invaluable asset in the relationship between their countries and China. Recollections and impressions of Lisandra Colley, a Jamaican who completed a PhD in international economics, are provided in an Appendix. Exchanges and collaboration in higher education are certainly going to expand. In this regard, the University of the West Indies (UWI) is leading the way with interesting new initiative. UWI, in collaboration with the Global Institute of Software Technology (GIST) in Suzhou, China, will establish the UWI–China Institute of Science and Technology. The Institute's first cohort of students will read for a bachelor's degree in Science and Technology starting in September 2016. Students of the Institute will do an internship in China.[13] This initiative is taking place at a time when it is being suggested that Chinese universities are improving relative to their US counterparts.[14]

While not being naive about the self-interest of all countries and peoples, both Chinese and Caribbean people must be conscious to not let prejudice and misinformation cloud and inhibit their relationship. The ability to discuss China intelligently and without the bias is seriously compromised by the misinformation that emanates from a lot of Western scholarship and the Western media. Countries and regions beyond the Western world are often portrayed in derogatory terms, their achievements disparaged and their contributions to Civilization almost completely ignored. Frank Frankopan goes to great lengths to show that what is now described as the Middle East and Central Asia is: 'Far from being at the fringe on global affairs, these countries lie at its very centre – as they have done since the beginning of history. It was here that Civilization was born.'[15] Foreign direct investment is usually welcomed except if the investors are Middle Eastern or Chinese. The venerable *Financial Times* while acknowledging that the integration of Chinese companies into the global economy is 'beneficial' and 'potentially great' and while eschewing the xenophobia in some quarters, advises: 'Western governments in particular should follow a policy of 'trust but verify' when it comes to vetting Chinese deals.'[16] It would be difficult, if not impossible, to find a similar statement about British or American foreign direct investment.

China's Future

China is not merely a state but it is an ancient civilization whose origins are still unknown. The US and European countries, perhaps with the exception of Greece, can date their origin in recorded history after the birth of Christ. China has never been conquered although parts have been under the control of Japan and various European trading nations for brief intervals. China has always had an attitude of superiority, expecting the world to come to it and has not sought to spread its culture across the globe nor created an empire of colonies. Expansion and the self-assurance to forcefully spread its systems and institutions and culture across the world is the hallmark of Western expansionism whether by formal colonialism or by policing the world through military interventions. The economy of China and its economic development are unique, and the pace, path and process it takes in the future will be unprecedented. The existing economic models of capitalism and socialism offer little use in predicting China's future; no one should assume an inevitable evolution towards some version of Western electoral democracy. The economic miracle in China faces both internal problems and external difficulties, but it would be simplistic to assume this is either implosion or continued exceptional economic growth.

The temptation to see China as a new imperialist intent on raping the resources of the developing countries as a new type of imperialism or neo-colonialism is largely fuelled by racial and cultural prejudice and must be resisted. The relationship with China is also not a panacea with a steady flow of investment from a bottomless reservoir. Chinese aid will not build every public building, finance unsustainable fiscal deficits nor fund every major transformational infrastructure project. Chinese investors are interested in profits just like American and European multinational corporations. Development aid from China, like PetroCaribe from Venezuela, has to be repaid at some time in the future. No Caribbean government should assume that it will benefit from aid and that when the debt is to be paid it will be cancelled. All bilateral aid from any foreign government is money used to win friends and influence governments.

Chinese FDI

China's FDI seems very likely to increase significantly in the future because China's economy continues to experience economic growth and as China becomes more integrated into the global economy. Chinese FDI is spreading to all parts of the world in pursuit of opportunities in a wide range of sectors, but particularly in energy, raw materials and food production. China has established a growing political and economic presence in the Caribbean, primarily through development assistance. A limited number of Chinese FDI has taken place in the Caribbean in recent years, however, and the number of investments and FDI could increase in the future, and this could happen quite quickly. The circumstances for increased Chinese FDI in the Caribbean are propitious. On China's side, there have been indications of interest by Chinese enterprises and entrepreneurs prompted by a combination of the existing drivers of Chinese FDI and factors peculiar to the Caribbean. On the Caribbean side, there is the well-established receptivity of Caribbean governments to FDI in general. The expansion and spread of Chinese FDI could be an important development for the countries of the Caribbean given their economic circumstances and may assume some urgency if there were a reduction in Chinese aid and loans. Such an eventuality could arise if the contentious diplomatic dispute with Taiwan abates.

Chinese FDI clearly is growing with the encouragement of the political directorate. The impulses for Chinese FDI arise from the level of the enterprises and from the overarching policy by the state of enhanced engagement with the global economy. This does not mean that all aspects FDI will be subject to the general direction and priorities of the state. The Caribbean provides a range of investment opportunities and a policy framework which, although it can always be made more investor friendly, seeks to induce FDI. The favourable disposition and interest of both sides is conducive to Chinese FDI, but there is an unavoidable economic, political, social and psychological learning process on both sides. Among the considerations which will determine the amount, sectoral distribution and pace of Chinese FDI are factors internal to China and the Caribbean and those prevailing in the global economy. The global context impinges on the possibility of Chinese FDI being involved with transforming opportunities in the Caribbean into actual investments because most of the opportunities are not unique to the Caribbean. Caribbean countries are competing with other countries, especially other developing countries, for Chinese FDI.

Strengthening Relations with China

Whether or not China replaces the US as the dominant superpower, it will still be a major and increasingly influential superpower. By now it should be pellucid to even the most Sinophobic person in the Caribbean that the region can benefit from a strong relationship with China if this relationship is handled properly. If the relationship is not handled with skill based on sound strategic thinking, then most benefits will accrue to China. After all, China, like every other country, has to pursue its national interests. Consolidating on a long relationship dating back, in some instances, to the early 1970s when the independent countries of CARICOM adopted the 'One China Policy' recognizing the People's Republic of China as the sole and rightful government of China has been advantageous. Since 2000, China has become an important source of development, financing Chinese enterprises to construct roads, infrastructure and buildings. However, there is much more that can be gained from the region's economic interaction with China. China, the second largest source of foreign direct investment, also represents an enormous opportunity for exports and is also soon to become the second largest source of tourists.

3. UPDATES

A few updates have been made necessary by recent developments and the availability of new information.

Corporate Dimension

New aspects and modalities will emerge in relations between China and the Caribbean. One such possibility is the expansion of non-state relations, specifically between the business communities in China and the Caribbean; such relations already exist. These transnational ethnic business networks are an important determinant of the growth of trade and investment with China. There is going to be a learning process on both sides. Chinese enterprises operating in the Caribbean have to understand and exhibit sensitivity to local culture and institutions as do foreign firms of all nationalities that operate in the Caribbean. This acculturation will be necessary where Chinese companies are supervising construction and infrastructure projects. As the Chinese population and enterprises in small Caribbean countries continue to grow, tensions could arise if the Chinese are perceived as displacing employees in the local workforce. In the past, the Chinese have used their own workers on construction projects and among small-scale vendors which met the disapproval of the local labour force.

China's Economic Slowdown

The future of relations between China and Caribbean countries faces challenges as the government, enterprises, organizations and the people learn more about each other. The challenges are not insurmountable but will require learning, strategic thinking and sound policies. The urgency for strategic thinking and action is made more necessary by changes emerging in the Chinese economy. The Chinese economy is beginning a transition from export-led economic growth to a growth process in which domestic demand plays a greater role. This transition is accompanied by a slowing in the rate of economic growth which has been a phenomenal ten per cent per annum for the last 30 years. The deceleration in the rate of growth should not be interpreted to be the frequently predicted demise of the Chinese model and economy. Real GDP growth in China has declined falling from 10.4 per cent in 2010 to 7.8 per cent in 2012 and to 7.3 per cent in 2014. It is likely that the trend line of economic growth per annum will average between five and seven per cent per annum. A process of rebalancing internal and external factors has begun. The International Monetary Fund has described the process as China moving to a 'new normal' of slower yet safer and more sustainable growth.[17] The authorities in China have recognized that its economy is caught in an interaction between some long-term structural problems and short, cyclical factors. It has sought to cauterize the effects of speculative exuberance in its stock exchange, avoid a real estate 'bubble' and counteract changes in its relative international price competitiveness by exchange rate adjustment.

China's central bank has also cut its benchmark interest rate and allowed banks to lend more in an attempt to turn around the slowing economic growth. In the short run, the Chinese will seek to stabilize the economy, but the medium-term outlook is difficult to predict because of the unique nature of China's economy whose performance has confounded economic pundits over the last 30 years. Whatever happens will have an impact on the world economy. The deceleration of economic growth is beginning to adversely affect the rest of the world, starting in Asia but manifested globally by the prices for commodities which has had an impact on world trade, particularly commodity exporting countries in Africa and Latin America. The adverse impact of the slowdown in China's economy is particularly pronounced in Latin America where, from 2003 to 2013, there was a China Boom which Kevin Gallagher calls the 'era of the largest per capita grow rate in over 100 years'.[18] The ability of China to sustain high rates of economic growth over the short, medium and long run will depend on formulating and implementing a comprehensive package of economic reforms which blend policies to address the internal and external factors. It is hoped that Chinese authorities will be able to stabilize the economy and maintain high growth rates because this has been one of the engines of economic growth for the global economy which is still in the doldrums.

Implications of the Evolution of China's Economy

From the Caribbean point of view, the implications of the fortunes of China's economy do not seem to be too ominous at this time. Jamaica does not depend on export commodities and therefore slumping commodity prices should have little impact. Tourism will be largely unaffected because the two most important source countries – the US and Canada – are doing reasonably well with the continuation of the nascent growth in the US. It appears that the Federal Reserve intends to maintain its policy of very low rates. Similarly, remittances should be unaffected although the UK's economy continues to struggle. Oil prices have remained low and that is not affected by China's demand for oil which has slowed in tandem with the decline in economic growth. There is plenty of supply capacity, and there is the prospect of Iran's resumption of more oil exports. This abatement in oil prices will ease the pressure on the exchange rate and help to keep inflation moderate. The ability and willingness of the government of China to fund construction projects in the countries that have committed to the 'One China Policy' will not be impaired by recent developments. The fluctuations in the Chinese stock market might even be positive if it prompts Chinese investors to move out of the financial markets and into real estate investment. If this switch occurred it might lead to more foreign direct investment, a prospect well worth investigation by the Caribbean countries.

South China Sea Flashpoint

Asian countries have been encouraging and supporting a greater US presence in the Pacific as a bulwark against what they regard as China's expansionism which cannot be halted, even acting collectively. Whether the US regards the Chinese enlarged islands in the South China Sea as a threat to its national security interests in this area of the world or Asian allies in their anxiety goad the US into action, the US will respond. The question is how? The nature of the US response could vary from verbal condemnation to deployment of naval vessels, but the situation is unlikely to escalate into some form of violent conflict involving military, naval or air force strike. However, while the continual 'joisting' by the Chinese and the Americans, primarily for political optics, there is always the possibility of an accident or misunderstanding. Both sides understand the importance of keeping up appearances, but it is a 'chess game' that can easily escalate especially when national pride is involved. The prevailing view in Washington, DC is that fears are 'overblown' because of their isolation and because China is not in a position to control the airspace and seas around the islands.[19]

The Chinese do not want to provoke a conflict with the US but will push just short of the ultimate provocation. While the leadership no longer subscribes to Mao's famous comment that with such a large population millions of Chinese would survive a global nuclear war,[20] they have continued to avoid being drawn into any military conflict since the jousting over the border with India and the support for communist forces in the Korean and Vietnamese wars. China, as the largest country in the world and with the largest population of any country, would be confident of surviving any sort of conflict. However, China has a vested economic interest in a global economy unhindered by military conflicts. The remarkable economic progress in China has in part been due to its increased participation in the global economy. In 1990, 61 per cent of the Chinese people lived on less than US$1.25 per day at a time when the global economy was of limited relevance to China; however, only four per cent[21] of the Chinese population lives in abject poverty and thus the global economy is vitally important. For many, this is perfectly understandable. According to Thomas Freidman, 'when a country reaches the level of economic development where it has a middle class big enough to support a McDonald's network, it becomes a McDonald's country. And people in McDonald's countries don't like to fight wars anymore.'[22] A more modest observation might be that economic progress and integration in the world economy, symbolized by the operation of McDonald's restaurants, predisposes a country to peace. The first McDonald's outlet opened in China in 1990, and today there are over 2,000 outlets, making it the country with the third largest number of outlets behind Japan and the US.

In any event, some will be reassured and others dismayed by the fact that the US in any military or naval measure is far more powerful than China and continues to outspend China in military expenditure. The US spent $596 billion on defence in 2014, which is more than the next eight biggest spenders whose expenditure totalled $567 billion and more than double China's estimate expenditure of about $250 billion.[23]

Nature of Future Engagement

In forging closer relations with China, the Caribbean must be careful how they view the future of China and the assumptions about China's policy. China's experience has been unique and what has happened in other countries is not necessarily a guide to what will happened in China. Because economic modernization has been accompanied by democratization does not mean that this pattern will be reproduced in China.[24] While studying China in depth, the guiding principle for Caribbean diplomats and policymakers should be, 'expect the unexpected', and to respond to changes in creative ways. For example, the Renminbi is now one of the widely accepted global currencies and given the growing imports from China, Caribbean governments would do well to explore the use of the Renminbi in international reserves and in international payments. In any relationship, Sun Tzu's adage from *The Art of War*, 'A small enemy that acts inflexibly will become the captive of a large enemy', is sage advice.[25]

An important aspect of the future engagement with China is patience. Patience both arises from the longer view of time which is part of Chinese culture and from bureaucracy which is an inevitable aspect of a state centred economy. Ground was broken in August 2016, for the Chinese to build a hospital in Dominica, a project first conceived of in 2004 and under negotiation from 2010.[26] For over 10 years Jamaica has been seeking Chinese investment in the bauxite industry. On July 19, 2016 Jiuquan Iron and Steel Company (JISCO) signed an agreement to purchase the ALPART alumina plant in Nain, St Elizabeth in Jamaica from Russian alumina firm, UC Rusal. The purchase price is US$299 million.[27] JISCO is expected to take over operations in November 2016 and will invest US$220 million in the modification and upgrading of the plant during the first year. When fully operational, it will generate an additional 700 jobs. A further 3,000 jobs over a four-year period are expected when JISCO invests US$2 billion to establish an industrial zone in the area around the plant.[28] The planned use of coal as an energy source for the re-opened plant has set off vigorous opposition from those concerned about the harmful effect on the natural environment.

4. PROACTIVE, STRATEGIC APPROACH TO RELATIONS WITH CHINA

The world is being transformed by a multidimensional process of reconfiguration in economic and political power, and the Caribbean's expanded relationship with China is a reflection of this process. China's relations with the small states of the Caribbean have expanded in the last decade indicative of its global re-dimensioning and its rivalry with Taiwan. The leitmotif of the enhanced and growing presence in the Caribbean is the exponential increase in development assistance, loans and trade. This development poses challenges and opportunities for the Caribbean. How the Caribbean adjusts to and addresses these challenges and opportunities will have a profound impact on the economic development of Caribbean countries and their international relations with the rest of the world, in particular, with the US.

Caribbean governments must take a more informed and strategic approach to consolidate and diversify their relationships with China. This approach will require a deeper and more comprehensive knowledge of Chinese policy and appreciation for China's history, culture, politics and economic development. A thorough knowledge of China is a prerequisite for Caribbean governments to begin forming a more nuanced and sophisticated strategy on which to base foreign policy towards China. The accumulated knowledge of diplomatic conduct is the result of relations with Western countries, relations which will be of marginal use in dealing with China. Thus, Caribbean states have to tailor their foreign policy to Chinese culture if they are to succeed. They have to appreciate China's uniqueness and to treat China as just another country would be ill-advised.

Caribbean countries should not be passive or reactive in dealing with China because experience has shown that small developing countries, including those in the Caribbean can influence the foreign policy of superpowers in bilateral relations and can influence international affairs through regional and multilateral institutions such as the United Nations. In this regard, the Caribbean has been well served by astute, persuasive political leaders and some outstanding diplomats.[29] However, future success should not assume the good fortune of having such individuals but should rely on strategic foreign policy planning and execution.[30] In forging a pragmatic and efficacious foreign policy to achieve a beneficial relationship with China on a sustainable basis, Caribbean governments must be conscious of the facts and misinformation about China which abound. It is necessary to differentiate between the myths and the reality of the rise of China and to decipher the actual challenges and opportunities from the ever increasing and changing information overload on China. Many opportunities exist for both China and Caribbean countries, and the governments in the Caribbean must seek out issues in which there is a mutuality of interests with China. In a rapidly changing world economy and fluid international affairs, the Caribbean needs to move decisively, proactively and quickly to seize the opportunities and meet the challenges.

Appendix

Economic, Trade and Technological Cooperation between CARICOM and China

Country	Year	High Level Mutual Visits*	Agreements and Projects#	Value	Funded By
Antigua and Barbuda	**1983**	Prime Minister Bird of Antigua and Barbuda (China)	Exchange of notes on providing a grant		Chinese government
	1984	Chinese Vice-Foreign Minister, Han Xu (Antigua and Barbuda)			
	1985	Deputy Prime Minister and Foreign Minister of Antigua and Barbuda, Lester Bird (China)	Exchange of notes on providing gratuitous assistance.		Chinese government
	1986	A Chinese government economic delegation, led by Chinese Vice-Minister of Foreign Economic Relations and Trade, Lu Xuejian (Antigua and Barbuda)	A protocol on using the grant		Chinese government
	1987		Rehabilitation of Creekside Bridge Project	RMB 5,000,000	China
	1988	Assistant Minister of Foreign Economic Relations and Trade, Wang Wendong (Antigua and Barbuda)	Agreement on economic and technological cooperation		
	1990	Vice-Foreign Minister, Liu Huaqui (Antigua and Barbuda)	Exchange of notes on providing gratuitous assistance.		Chinese government
	1991	An economic delegation of the government of Antigua and Barbuda, led by Minister Williams of Economic Development, Industry and Tourism (China)	Agreement on special loan for the construction of an exhibition centre, banking arrangement on accounting procedure and a project design contract	US$3,740,000 Exhibition Centre	China
	1992	A Chinese Government Delegation, led by Secretary General of the State Council, Luo Gan, and Assistant Minister, Tian Renzhi, of Foreign Economic Relations and Trade (Antigua and Barbuda)	Agreement and exchange of notes on economic and technological cooperation		
	1996	Assistant Foreign Minister, Yang Jiechi (Antigua and Barbuda)	Exchange of notes on providing gratuitous assistance		

Country	Year	High Level Mutual Visits*	Agreements and Projects#	Value	Funded By
Antigua and Barbuda Contd	1996	Assistant Foreign Minister, Yang Jiechi (Antigua and Barbuda)	Exchange of notes on providing gratuitous assistance		
	1997	Prime Minister and Foreign Minister, Lester Bird (China)	Framework agreement on preferential and subsidized loan		China
			Exchange of notes on providing gratuitous assistance		Chinese government
	1998		Greys Farm drain reconstruction	RMB 4,585,000	China
	1999		Disaster Relief – Shanxi Corporation	RMB 800,000	China
	2001	An economic and trade delegation, led by Vice-Governor, Wang Xianmin, of Heilongjiang Province (Antigua and Barbuda)	Held a press conference on inviting outside investment into Heilongjiang		
		A trade and economic delegation led by Vice-Minister of Foreign Trade and Economic Cooperation, Sun Guangxiang (Antigua and Barbuda)	Agreement on economic and technological cooperation		
			Government of Antigua and Barbuda	RMB 30,000,000	China
	2002	Permanent Secretary of Foreign Ministry of Antigua and Barbuda Mr Murdock and his wife (China)			
	2003	A Chinese Government Delegation, led by State Councillor, Wu Yi (Antigua and Barbuda)	Agreement on economic and technological cooperation		

Country	Year	High Level Mutual Visits*	Agreements and Projects#	Value	Funded By
Antigua and Barbuda Contd	**2003**		Exchange of notes concerning the transformation of a cricket entertainment ground		
	2004	Vice Chinese Foreign Minister, Zhou Wenzhong, and his delegation (Antigua and Barbuda)	Agreement on economic and technical cooperation		
	2006		Agreement on economic and technical cooperation		
	2008		Agreement on the provision of a Loan for a 30 MW Power Plant (Handed over in 2011)	RMB 300,000,000	China through EXIM Bank China
	2009		Final construction agreement for a grant the installation of hundreds of street lights (Completed in 2010)	EC$10,000,000	China
	2011		Letters of agreement on a concessional loan/grant finalizing arrangements for the construction of the new airport terminal building (Exp. 2014)	US$ 45,000,000 (Added an additional US$30M in 2013)	China
	2012	A Chinese delegation, led by Vice Minister of the Ministry of Commerce of the People's Republic of China, Gao Hucheng (Antigua and Barbuda)	Letter of exchange for the construction of the Five Island Secondary School		
			Agreement for economic and technical cooperation for the maintenance of the Sir Vivian Richards Cricket Stadium	RMB 6,400,000	China
			Agreement for economic and technical cooperation for development projects	RMB 30,00,000	China
	2013	Vice President of China Ex-Im Bank, Zhu Hongjie (Antigua and Barbuda)	Loan agreements on Antigua and Barbuda International Airport Terminal II		China
		President Xi Jinping met with Prime Minister Baldwin Spencer (during Xi's state visit to Trinidad and Tobago)			

Country	Year	High Level Mutual Visits*	Agreements and Projects#	Value	Funded By
Antigua and Barbuda Contd	**2013**	Minister of Agriculture, Lands, Housing and the Environment, Hilson Baptiste, attended the first China–Latin America and Caribbean Agricultural Ministers' Forum (China)	The Beijing Declaration of the China–Latin America and the Caribbean Agricultural Ministers		
	2013		Agreement on the renovation of a cricket stadium		China
	2014	Prime Minister, Gaston Browne (China)			
		President Xi met with Prime Minister Browne at the CELAC 'Quartet' meeting following the BRICS Summit (Brazil)	Preparation to establish the China–CELAC Forum		
			Antigua and Barbuda waives visa for Chinese tourists		
The Bahamas	**1997**	Bahamian Prime Minister Hubert Ingraham (China)	Agreement on the provision of aid gratis		
	1998	A Chinese Government Economic and Trade Delegation, led by Assistant Minister, Yang Wensheng, of Foreign Trade and Economic Cooperation (Bahamas)	Presented a draft proposal of a framework of preferential loan and signed a note concerning a grant aid		
	1999	A Chinese Government Economic and Trade Delegation, led by Vice-Minister, Liu Shanzai, of Foreign Trade and Economic Cooperation (Bahamas)	Exchange of notes on a grant aid		
	2000	An economic and trade delegation, led by the Vice-Governor, Wang Zhenchuan, of Heilongjiang Province (Bahamas)			
		Vice-President of China Council of the Promotion of International Trade, Wan Jifei (Bahamas)			
			Hand-over ceremony of providing teaching equipment and furniture	RMB 2,000,000	Chinese government
		Vice-Minister of Foreign Affairs, Yang Jiechi (Bahamas)	Donated 10 sets of computers and printers		

Country	Year	High Level Mutual Visits*	Agreements and Projects#	Value	Funded By
The Bahamas Contd	**2001**	A delegation, led by the General Manager of the Shipping Co. Ltd from the Tianjin Machinery Export-Import Group of China, Wang Hongjian (Bahamas)	Contract with the Bahamian ship-building consultancy company concerning the Bahamian order of a pleasure boat from China	US$3,500,000	China
	2002	Vice-Minister of Foreign Trade and Economic Cooperation, Ma Xiuhong (Bahamas)			
		Deputy Head of the International Liaison Department of the CPC Central Committee, Cai Wu (Bahamas)			
	2003	State Councillor, Wu Yi (Bahamas)	Exchange of notes on providing aid gratis		
		Vice-Minister of Communications, Hong Shanxiang (Bahamas)	Ocean shipping agreement between the government of the People's Republic of China and the government of the Commonwealth of The Bahamas		
	2004		Agreement on economic and technical cooperation		
	2005		Memorandum of understanding between The Bahamas and the National Tourism Administration of the People's Republic of China on the facilitation of group travel by Chinese tourists to The Bahamas		
	2009		Memorandum of Understanding between the Export-Import Bank of China and the Government of the Commonwealth of The Bahamas		

Country	Year	High Level Mutual Visits[3]	Agreements and Projects#	Value	Funded By
The Bahamas Contd	**2009**		Memorandum of understanding on agricultural cooperation between the Ministry of Agriculture and Marine Resources of the Commonwealth of The Bahamas and the Ministry of Agriculture of the People's Republic of China		
			Agreement regarding the waiver of visa requirements for holders of diplomatic passports		
			Two Agreements on economic and technical cooperation between the government of the Commonwealth of The Bahamas and the government of the People's Republic of China		
			The framework agreement on the provision of a concessional loan		
			Agreement on the promotion and protection of investments		
			Signed tax information exchange agreement (Entered into force 2010)		
	2011		The construction and operation a container port in Freeport, The Bahamas, just 60 miles from Florida, by Hong Kong-based conglomerate Hutchison Whampoa Ltd.	US$1,000,000,000	China
		Wang Qishan, Vice Premier of the State Council of the People's Republic of China (Nassau, Bahamas)	Agreement on economic and technical cooperation	up to US$5,000,000	China
		Mr Li Ruogu, Chairman and President of China EXIM Bank, Mr Liu Jinzhang, Vice President of CSCEC	Breaking ground of the Baha Mar Resort Project	US$3,600,000,000	China EXIM and China State Construction Engineering Corporation

Country	Year	High Level Mutual Visits*	Agreements and Projects#	Value	Funded By
The Bahamas Contd	**2012**	Wang Qishan, Vice Premier of the State Council of the People's Republic of China (Bahamas)	Nassau Airport Gateway Project Opening	US$58,000,000	Concessional loan from China
			Thomas A. Robinson National Stadium opening	RMB 30,000,000	China
	2013	Vice Chairman, Li Zhaozhuo, of the Chinese People's Political Consultative Conference (CPPCC) (The Bahamas)			
		President Xi Jinping met with Prime Minister Perry Christie (during Xi's state visit to Trinidad and Tobago)			
			Agreement on mutual visa exemption		
	2014	President of the Bahamian Senate, Sharon Wilson (China)			
	2015		Memorandum of understanding on air services		
		Prime Minister Perry Christie at the first China–CELAC Forum (China)	China–CELAC Cooperation Plan (2015–2019)		
Barbados	**1980**	A government delegation led by Barbados Prime Minister Adams (China)			
	1981	A NPC delegation led by Vice Chairman, Ngapoi Ngawang Jigme, of the Standing Committee of the National People's Congress (NPC) of PRC (Barbados)			
	1982	Barbados Foreign Minister, Louis Tull (China)			
		Chinese Vice Foreign Minister, Han Xu (Barbados)			
	1985		Embroidery and grass weaving project (1985–87)		Chinese government

Country	Year	High Level Mutual Visits*	Agreements and Projects#	Value	Funded By
Barbados Contd	**1986**		Agreement on the construction of a gymnasium in Barbados with chinese assistance		China
	1990	Chinese Vice Foreign Minister, Liu Huaqiu, visited Barbados	Exchange of notes on providing gratuitous assistance		
		Barbados Prime Minister Sandiford, visited China	Agreement on economic and technological cooperation		
			Sir Garfield Sobers Gymnasium Project (1990–1992)		Chinese government
	1992	A Chinese government delegation led by Secretary General, Luo Gan, of the Chinese State Council (Barbados)	Ceremony of the handing over of the Barbados Gymnasium and signed a new agreement on economic and technological cooperation and a new loan agreement		
			Feather Handicraft Project (1992–95)		Chinese government
	1993	An NPC delegation led by Vice Chairman, Chen Muhua, of NPC Standing Committee (Barbados)			
			Sherbourn Conference Center Fitting-up Project (1993–94) renamed the Lloyd Erskine Sandiford Conference and Cultural Centre		Chinese government
			Sir Garfield Sobers Gymnasium Redevelopment Project		Chinese government
	1996	Vice Minister, Li Beihai, of the International Department of the Central Committee of the Communist Party of China visited Barbados			
		Assistant Foreign Minister, Yang Jiechi, visited Barbados	Exchange of notes on providing gratuitous assistance		

Country	Year	High Level Mutual Visits*	Agreements and Projects#	Value	Funded By
Barbados Contd	**1998**	Vice Premier of the State Council, Qian Qichen, visited Barbados.	Agreement on the encouragement and mutual protection of investment		
		An NPC delegation led by Chairman, Wang Weicheng of the Law Committee of NPC Standing Committee (Barbados)			
	1999	A Chinese delegation of the State Administration of Taxation (Barbados)	An initialled draft agreement on the avoidance of double taxation.		
		A delegation led by Barbados Procurator-General and Minister of Interior Simmons (China)	To attend the Beijing Conference of the Universal Postal Union		
		President of the Senate of Barbados, Fred Gollop (China)			
	2000	A delegation of the International Liaison Department of CPC Central Committee led by Deputy Head of the Department, Liu Jingqin (Barbados)			
		Barbados Prime Minister Arthur (China)	Agreement on the avoidance of double taxation and the prevention of tax evasion		
		Deputy Director-General, Zhang Guoxian, of the International Department of All-China Federation of Trade Unions (Barbados)			
	2001	A Chinese trade and economic delegation led by Vice President of China Council for International Trade Promotion, Wan Jifei (Barbados)	Talks with Barbados industrial and business communities on bilateral trade and economic cooperation		
			Cheapside Market Renovation Project (2001–02)		Chinese government
	2002	A 13-member delegation, led by Chairman of the Barbados Private Sector Association, Allan Fields (China)	Participated in the Canton Fair		

Country	Year	High Level Mutual Visits*	Agreements and Projects#	Value	Funded By
Barbados Contd	**2002**	A delegation of the Chinese Chamber of Commerce for Overseas Contract Projects, led by Wang Wendong, Honorary Chairman of the Chamber and former Vice Minister of Foreign Trade and Economic Cooperation (Barbados)			
		Assistant Foreign Minister of PRC, Zhong Wenzhong (Barbados)			
	2003	A Chinese Government Delegation, led by State Councillor, Wu Yi, visited Barbados.	Exchange of notes on China providing Barbados with aid gratis and the certificate of handing over the Cheapside Market.		
		Barbados Minister of Industry and International Business, Dale Marshall, and CEO of Barbados Investment and Development Corporation, Vince Yearwood	Participated in the China–Caribbean Countries Ministerial Level Economic Management Official Workshop and the September 8th China International Fair for Investment and Trade in Xiamen, Fujian Province.		
	2004	Minister of Foreign Affairs of PRC, Li Zhaoxing, visited Barbados.	Unveiled the newly renovated Cheapside Market, and signed the Exchange of notes of Grant Aid of the People's Republic of China to Barbados.		
		Vice Chairman, Sun Baoshu, of All-China Federation of Trade Unions (Barbados)			
		Deputy Secretary General Wang Yunlong of the Standing Committee of the NPC (Barbados)			
		Deputy Prime Minister of Barbados, Mia Mottley, and Minister of State in the Ministry of Foreign Affairs and Foreign Trade, Kerrie Symmonds (China)			

Country	Year	High Level Mutual Visits*	Agreements and Projects#	Value	Funded By
Barbados Contd	2005	A 50-member delegation of Chinese entrepreneurs led by Vice Chairman Yu Ping of the China Council for the Promotion of International Trade (Barbados)	A Forum of China–Barbados Entrepreneurs was held		
			Memorandum of understanding between the National Tourism Administration of the People's Republic of China and the Ministry of Tourism of Barbados on the Facilitation of Group Travel by Chinese Tourists to Barbados		
		Ambassador Chen Shiqiu, representative of the Chinese Foreign Minister, Li Zhaoxing (Barbados)			
		Ambassador Qin Huasun, Special Envoy of the Chinese Government (Barbados)			
		A CPC delegation led by Vice Minister of the International Department of the Central Committee of CPC Ma Wenpu (Barbados)			
		A three-member delegation led by Vice Minister of the General Administration of Customs of the People's Republic of China, Mr Liu Wenjie (Barbados)			
	2006		Two agreements on economic and technological cooperation		
	2007	A 16-member delegation led by Barbados Deputy Prime Minister, Mia Mottley (China)	Attended the 2nd China–Caribbean Economic and Trade Cooperation Forum and the 11th China International Fair for Investment and Trade		

Country	Year	High Level Mutual Visits*	Agreements and Projects#	Value	Funded By
Barbados Contd	**2007**	Prime Minister Owen Arthur and Minister of Agriculture, Senator Erskine Griffith visited China	Feasibility Study Project for the Redevelopment of the Barbados National Stadium (2007–10)		
	2008	Barbadian Prime Minister, David Thompson, paid an official visit to China.	Agreement on economic and technological cooperation, gratis assistance and office and teaching equipment	RMB 21,000,000	China
	2013	President Xi met with Prime Minister Prime Minister Freundel Stuart (during Xi's state visit to Trinidad and Tobago)			
			Agreement on economic and technical cooperation and three banking agreements on accounting procedures	USD $8M	China
	2014		Barbados waives visa requirements for Chinese diplomatic and service passport holders		
Dominica	**2004**		Signed a memorandum of understanding		
	2005	China's Minister of Commerce, Liao Xiaogi (Bahamas)	Agreement to fund the csonstruction of the state-of-the-art Windsor Park Sports Stadium	US$12,300,000	China
	2006		Agreement of economic and technical cooperation		
	2008	Hon. Prime Minister Skerrit visited China			
		Her Excellency Gu Xiulian, Vice Chairwoman of the Standing Committee of the National People's Congress, paid her official visit to Dominica			

Country	Year	High Level Mutual Visits*	Agreements and Projects#	Value	Funded By
Dominica Contd	**2008**	Hon. Minister George, Hon. Minister Savarin and Hon. Minister Bannis-Roberts (China)	2nd China–Caribbean Economic and Trade Cooperation Forum in Xiamen, China.		
		Permanent Secretary in the Foreign Ministry, Mr. Ferrol (China)			
	2011		A loan agreement for the Dominica State College, the State House project and the housing programme at Bath Estate.	US$14,000,000	China
			A cricket stadium	US$17,000,000	Chinese government
			Economic assistance	US$122,000,000	Chinese government
	2012	The 25-member team led by Chen Changzhi, Vice Chairman of the Standing Committee of the National People's Congress (Dominica)			
			Chinese grant fund for the construction of the Dominica/China Friendship Bridge	EC$8,000,000	China
			Completion of the rehabilitation of Dominica's West Coast Road, now known as the Edward Oliver Leblanc Highway	$100,000,000	China
			Economic and technical cooperation agreement		
	2013		Gratuitous aid and concessionary financing for construction of a state-of-the-art new Princess Margaret Hospital and a new Primary School in New Town. (More projects are to be agreed upon using this agreement)	US$40,000,000	China

Country	Year	High Level Mutual Visits*	Agreements and Projects#	Value	Funded By
Dominica Contd	2013		Technical cooperation agreement focusing on the development of aquaculture, in particular prawn farming – also expected to assist Dominica in the production of vegetables, flowers and fruits.		
		President Xi Jinping met with Prime Minister Roosevelt Skerrit (during Xi's state visit to Trinidad and Tobago)			
			Dominica waives visa requirements for Chinese tourists		
		Matthew Walter, Minister for Agriculture Fisheries and Forestry attended the first China–Latin America and Caribbean Agricultural Ministers' Forum (China)			
	2015		Agreement on economic and technical cooperation	US$16M	China
			Chinese humanitarian aid to Dominica following tropical storm Erika	USD $300,000	China
		President Roosevelt Skerrit (China)			
Grenada	2005		Memorandum of understanding		
			A contract agreement for the construction of the national stadium		
	2006	Grenadian Deputy Prime Minister and Minister of Agriculture, Lands, Forestry, Fisheries, Public Utilities and Energy Gregory Bowen (China)			
		Grenadian President of the Senate Kenry Lalsingh and Speaker of the House of Representatives, Lawrence Joseph (China)			
	2008		Economic and technical cooperation agreement	Part of US$14,600,000	China

Country	Year	High Level Mutual Visits*	Agreements and Projects#	Value	Funded By
Grenada Contd	**2009**	Grenadian Prime Minister, Tillman Thomas (China)			
		Grenadian Prime Minister, Tillman Thomas (China)			
			Economic and technical cooperation agreement	Part of US$14,600,000	China
			a certificate of acceptance in respect of a grant of US$1.0M for 2009		
	2010		Inspection ofChinese-aided Agriculture Program		
			Inspection ofChinese-aided Grenadian Cricket Field		
			Donated sports goods to the Ministry of Youth and Sports of Grenada		
			Donated Chinese books to Public Library of Grenada		
	2011		Agreement on economic and technical cooperation		
		A delegation led by Vice Chairman of the National Development and Reform Commission, Xie Zhenhua (Grenada)	Ministerial Meeting of the Alliance of Small Island States		
		A delegation of ruling party members Nazim Burke led by Deputy Leader of the National Democratic Congress and Minister of Finance (China)			
		Prime Minister Thomas attended the CARICOM Day event of the Shanghai World Expo			
			Official Hand-over Ceremony of Farm Machinery & Agricultural Equipment		Chinese government

Country	Year	High Level Mutual Visits*	Agreements and Projects#	Value	Funded By
Grenada Contd	**2011**	China–Grenada Trade Mission (Grenada)	A letter of intent on investment between the Chairman of the board of Touchstone Capital Group Holdings, and Mr Michael Gunn, Director of Bacolet Bay Resort & Spa, Grenada		
			The First-phase Rehabilitation of St Paul Community Sports and Culture Centre		Chinese government
			Signing ceremony for inter-governmental cooperation agreement between China and Grenada		
			Donated new computer sets to The Carriacou Multipurpose Centre		
			Opening ceremony of the second phase of technical cooperation of Grenada Cricket Stadium and donated computers to Ministry of Youth Empowerment and Sports		Chinese government
			Opening ceremony of Tri-Centennial Park of St George		
			Economic and technical cooperation agreement		
	2012		Memorandum of understanding was signed between the National Development and Reform Commission of the People's Republic of China and the Ministry of Finance, Planning, Economy and Cooperatives of the government of Grenada concerning the provision of goods for addressing climate change in the state of Grenada, Carriacou and Petit Martinique		

Country	Year	High Level Mutual Visits*	Agreements and Projects#	Value	Funded By
Grenada Cont'd	**2012**		Economic and technical cooperation agreement		
	2013		Hand-over ceremony of farm machinery and agricultural equipment (4th batch)		
		Mr Chen Ribiao, Chinese Charge D'Affaires to Grenada	Exchange of notes regarding the Low-income Housing Project under the framework of the Sino-Grenada Economic Technical Cooperation Agreement		
			Agreement with Hon. Michael Pierre, Speaker of Parliament of Grenada, with regard to the fulfilment of the cooperation program between both countries' parliaments.		
			Economic Technical Cooperation Agreement		
		President Xi Jinping met with Prime Minister Keith Mitchel (during Xi's state visit to Trinidad and Tobago)			
		Minister of Agriculture, Lands, Forestry, Fisheries and the Environment of Grenada, Simon Steele, attended the first China–Latin America and Caribbean Agricultural Ministers' Forum (China)			
			Reconstruction and restoration of the National Athletic and Football Stadium		
			Agreement on economic and technical cooperation		
	2015		Housing and the refurbishment of the cricket stadium	USD $20M	China
			Agreement on mutual visa exemption		
		Prime Minister Keith Mitchell (China)			

Country	Year	High Level Mutual Visits*	Agreements and Projects#	Value	Funded By
Guyana	**1971**		Agreement on the development of bilateral trade and the mutual establishment of commercial offices		
	1972		Agreement on economic and technical cooperation		
	1975	Guyanese Prime Minister Burnham (China)	Agreement on economic and technological cooperation		
	1977	President Arthur Chung (China)			
	1978	Chinese Vice-Premier Geng Biao (Guyana)			
	1981	A NPC delegation led by Vice-Chairman of the Standing Committee of the NPC (National People's Congress) Ngapoi Ngawang Jigme (Guyana)			
	1984	President Burnham (China)	Signed five documents on economic cooperation, cultural exchange, the establishment of a joint commission on economic, trade, scientific and technological cooperation, transformation of the textile mill built with Chinese assistance, and the provision of cotton under loans by China		
		Chinese Vice-Foreign Minister Han Xu (Guyana)			
	1987		Agreement on economic and technical cooperation		
	1988		Agreement on scientific and technological cooperation		

Country	Year	High Level Mutual Visits*	Agreements and Projects#	Value	Funded By
Guyana Contd	**1984**	President Burnham (China)	Signed five documents on economic cooperation, cultural exchange, the establishment of a joint commission on economic, trade, scientific and technological cooperation, transformation of the textile mill built with Chinese assistance, and the provision of cotton under loans by China		
		Chinese Vice-Foreign Minister, Han Xu (Guyana)			
	1987		Agreement on economic and technical cooperation		
	1988		Agreement on scientific and technological cooperation		
	1989	Speaker of the Guyanese National Assembly, Sase Naraine (China)			
	1990	Chinese Vice-Foreign Minister Liu Huaqiu (Guyana)	Exchange of notes on providing grant		
		Guyanese Foreign Minister Esmond Rashleigh Jackson (China)	A protocol on the consultation mechanism between foreign ministry officials of the two countries and an agreement on economic and technical cooperation		
	1993	A NPC delegation led by Vice Chairman of NPC Standing Committee, Chen Muhua (Guyana)			
		Guyanese President Cheddi Jagan (China)	Agreement on economic and technical cooperation		
	1996	A Chinese governmental economic and trade delegation led by Zhenyu, Vice-Minister of the MOFTEC (Guyana)	China/Caribbean Economic and Trade Symposium in Georgetown		

Country	Year	High Level Mutual Visits[a]	Agreements and Projects#	Value	Funded By
Guyana Contd	**1996**	A governmental trade and economic delegation led by Guyanese Foreign Minister, Clement Rohee (China)	Sixth session of the China/Guyana Joint Commission on Economic and Trade Cooperation		
		A delegation of the Guyana/China Friendship Association led by Guyanese Prime Minister, Samuel Hinds (China)			
	1997		Framework Agreement on the Provision of Preferential Discount Interest Loan by China to Guyana		
	1998	Chinese Vice-Premier Qian Qichen (Guyana)	Agreement on the mutual exemption of visas for official tour		
		Director General of the Ministry of Foreign Affairs of Guyana Marilyn Miles (China)	Formally launched the political consultation mechanism between foreign ministry officials of the two countries		
	1999	Vice-Minister, Liu Shanzai, of the MOFTEC (Guyana)	Co-hosted the 7th session of the China–Guyana Joint Commission on Trade and Economic Cooperation and signed a summary of talks and exchanged notes on the personnel training of the TCDC technique and on the moratorium on three loans namely of 1972, 1975 and 1979		
		Desmond Hoyte, Leader of the Guyanese People's National Congress (China)			
	2000	A Jilin Provincial government delegation led by Deputy Governor, Wei Mingxue (Guyana)			
		A government delegation of journalists headed by Guyanese Information Minister, Nagamootoo, visited China			

Country	Year	High Level Mutual Visits*	Agreements and Projects#	Value	Funded By
Guyana Contd	2001	'Yun-12' plane sales promotion team led by Vice-President of China Import-Export Corporation of Aeronautical Technology, Wang Dawei (Guyana)	Memorandum of understanding on the sale and purchase of the plane		
		Chinese Charge affairs ad interim, Wang Xinping, and Director-General of the Guyanan Foreign Ministry Mme Ramlall on behalf of their respective governments	Exchange notes on extending the technological cooperation in Moco Moco hydro-power station for one year and providing the station with a small number of necessary spare-parts for wear and tear		
		Assistant Foreign Minister Zhou Wenzhong (Guyana)	Exchanged of notes on providing free aid		
		General Secretary of the Guyanese People's Progress Party Ramotar (China)			
			Trade agreement		
	2002		Exchange of notes concerning China dispatching four experts to Guyana to repair the Moco hydro-power station and the exchange of notes concerning Guyana dispatching six students to China for TCDC training		
			Exchange of notes concerning the Chinese government dispatching a group of experts to Guyana for an inspection tour of the Guyana International Conference Centre		
		A Fujian provincial economic and trade delegation led by Vice-Chairman of Fujian Provincial Political Consultative Conference, He Shaochuan (Guyana)	Reached understanding on the intent to import large yellow croakers and green-heart wood from Guyana and to process clothing in Guyana.		

Country	Year	High Level Mutual Visits*	Agreements and Projects#	Value	Funded By
Guyana Contd	**2003**	A Chinese Government Delegation led by State Councillor, Wu Yi (Guyana)	Agreement on economic and technological cooperation concerning providing aid gratis, a protocol on forgiving debts owed to the Chinese government by the Guyanese government and exchanged notes concerning dispatching sports coaches and notes concerning the Chinese side undertaking the international conference centre project in Guyana.		
		President Jagdeo of Guyana (China)	Agreement on the promotion and protection of investment and an agreement on economic and technological cooperation		
	2010		Guyana Power and Light Transmission and Distribution Project		
	2011		A $100-million purchase of a majority stake in Omai Bauxite Mining from the government of Guyana by Chinese mining company Bosai Minerals Group		
			Agreements for the provision of laptops, fire fighting equipment for the Ministry of Home Affairs and for the continuation of the Chinese Youth Volunteers		
			Contract for the delivery of 27,000 laptops	US$7,500,000	China

Country	Year	High Level Mutual Visits*	Agreements and Projects#	Value	Funded By
Guyana Contd	2012		Agreement to provide Guyana with two roll-on/roll-off ferries	US$14,400,000	China
			Two grant agreements	RMB ¥60,000,000	China
			Arrangement for the signing of a framework agreement for the e-governance project	RMB¥215,000,000	China
			Signed a concessional loan agreement to support the construction of a new terminal building and other facilities at the Cheddi Jagan International Airport	US$130,000,000	China
			NCN/CCTV Project		China
		Chinese Ambassador to Guyana, Zhang Limin, visited Guyana	An agreement on economic and technical cooperation	RMB¥1,000,000,000	China
	2013	President Xi Jinping met with President Donald Ramotar (during Xi's state visit to Trinidad and Tobago)			
	2014	Mrs Li Bin, Minister with the National Health and Family Planning Commission (Guyana)			
	2015	A Chinse government delegation led by Commercial Counsellor, Mr Chen Lin (Guyana)			
Jamaica	1974		Agreement on economic cooperation		
	1976	Deputy Prime Minister David Coore (China)	Trade agreement		
			A commodity loan agreement concerning China's assistance of 5,000 tons of rice to Jamaica		
			Protocol on a project of polyester cotton mill with Chinese assistance		

Country	Year	High Level Mutual Visits *	Agreements and Projects#	Value	Funded By
Jamaica Contd	**1978**	Vice-Premier Geng Biao of the State Council (Jamaica)			
			Commodity loan agreement between the government of the People's Republic of China and the government of Jamaica		
	1982	Vice-Foreign Minister Han Xu (Jamaica)	Attended the UN Conference on International Law of the Sea		
	1985	A Jamaican government Delegation led by Mr Hugh Lawson Shearer, Jamaican Deputy Prime Minister and Minister of Foreign Affairs and Foreign Trade (China)			
	1986	Chinese government economic delegation led by Vice-Minister, Lu Xuejian of MOFERT (Jamaica)			
	1990	Jamaican Parliamentary Delegation led by Mr Headly Cunningham, Speaker of the House of Representatives and Mr Courtney Fletcher, Deputy President of the Senate (China)			
		Chinese government delegation led by Madame Wu Wenying, Minister of Textile Industry (Jamaica)	Launching ceremony of the Polyester Cotton Mill, a Sino–Jamaican joint venture		
	1991	Jamaican Prime Minister, Michael Manley (China)	Agreement on economic cooperation and an agreement on the provision of loans		
	1992	Chinese government delegation led by Secretary-General Luo Gan of the State Council (Jamaica)			
	1993	Mr Paul Robertson, Jamaican Minister of Foreign Affairs and Foreign Trade (China)	Exchange of notes on the provision of a batch of general goods		
	1994	Vice-Foreign Minister, Liu Huaqiu (Jamaica)			

Country	Year	High Level Mutual Visits*	Agreements and Projects#	Value	Funded By
Jamaica Contd	1994		Agreement on encouragement and mutual protection of investment		
	1995		Agreement between the government of the People's Republic of China and the Government of Jamaica on mutual exemption of visas for official tour		
		Chairman Li Ruihuan of the Chinese People's Political Consultative Conference (CPPCC) National Committee (Jamaica)	Donated a batch of general goods to the Jamaican Ministry of Foreign Affairs and Foreign Trade and the Jamaican Parliament	RMB 1,000,000	
	1996	Jamaican Deputy Prime Minister and Minister of Foreign Affairs and Foreign Trade, Seymour Mullings (China)	Agreement on the avoidance of double income taxation and prevention of tax evasion and signed an exchange of notes on the provision of a batch of general goods		
		Leader of the Jamaica Labour Party and former Prime Minister, Edward Seaga (China)			
		Jamaican House Speaker Carl Marshall (China)			
	1997		Agreement on mutual exemption of visas between Hong Kong SAR of the People's Republic of China and Jamaica		
	1998	Vice-Premier Qian Qichen (Jamaica)	Exchange of notes on a grant aid		
		Jamaican Prime Minister Percival Patterson (China)	Framework Agreement of a preferential loan		
		Jamaican Minister of Industry and Investment, Paul Robertson (China)	Exchange of notes on the provision of grant		

Country	Year	High Level Mutual Visits*	Agreements and Projects#	Value	Funded By
Jamaica Contd	**2000**	A delegation led by Qi Huaiyuan, member of the Standing Committee of the CPPCC and former president of Chinese People's Association of Friendship with Foreign Countries (Jamaica)			
	2001	A Chinese economic and trade delegation led by Vice-President of China Council for the Promotion of International Trade, Wan Jifei (Jamaica)			
		Assistant Foreign Minister, Zhou Wenzhong (Jamaica)			
		Jamaican Minister of Industry, Commerce and Technology, Paulwell (China)			
	2002	Vice-Minister of Finance, Luo Jiwei (Jamaica)	Presented two computers to the Jamaican youth field and track tournament		
		An NPC delegation led by Xu Dengxin, Member of NPC Standing Committee and Vice-Chairman of its Foreign Affairs Committee, (Jamaica)			
		Deputy Head of the International Liaison Department of CPC Central Committee, Cai Wu (Jamaica)			
		President of Chinese People's Association of Friendship with Foreign Countries, Chen Haosu (Jamaica)			
	2003	A Chinese government delegation, led by State Councillor, Wu Yi (Jamaica)	Agreement on economic and technical cooperation concerning an interest-free loan, exchange of notes concerning aid gratis and the certificate of delivering audio-video and computer equipment by the Chinese government to the Jamaican National Archives		

Country	Year	High Level Mutual Visits*	Agreements and Projects#	Value	Funded By
Jamaica Contd	**2003**	Chinese Foreign Minister, Li Zhaoxing (Jamaica)			
	2004	Jamaican Minister of Foreign Affairs and Foreign Trade, Keith Desmond Knight (China)	Framework agreement on the provision of concessional loan, agreement on economic and technical cooperation and a letter of exchange for dispatch of two Chinese table tennis coaches to Jamaica		
		A Delegation of the Communist Party of China (CPC) led by the Head of the International Liaison Department of the CPC Central Committee Wang Jiarui (Jamaica)			
	2005	Vice President Zeng Qinghong (Jamaica)	Agreement on economic and technical cooperation	RMB 30,000,000[1]	China
			Framework agreement on the provision of concessional loan for the construction of the Green Field Sports Complex in Trelawny	RMB 150,000,000 (2% interest rate per annum for up to 20 yrs)[2]	EXIM China
			Memorandum of understanding between the National Tourism Administration of the People's Republic of China and the Ministry of Industry and Tourism of Jamaica on the facilitation of group travel by Chinese tourists to Jamaica		
			Agreement of cooperation between China Council for promotion of international trade and Jamaica Promotions Corporation		
			Water system rehabilitation and extension project between the Export-Import Bank of China and the Ministry of Finance and Planning of Jamaica	RMB 100,000,000 (2% interest rate per annum for 180 mths)[3]	EXIM China

Country	Year	High Level Mutual Visits*	Agreements and Projects#	Value	Funded By
Jamaica Contd	**2005**		Frame agreement between China Minmetals Non-Ferrous Metals Company Limited and government of Jamaica on Bauxite and Alumina Trade and Mining Cooperation		
			Commercial contract between China National Corporation for Overseas Economic Cooperation and the National Water Commission of Jamaica on Water System Rehabilitation and Extension Project		
			Memorandum of Understanding between The Port Authority of Jamaica and China Ocean Shipping (Group) Company for the Development of New Transhipment Port and Commercial Free Zone/Logistics Distribution Hub Facilities in Jamaica		
		Jamaican Prime Minister Percival J. Patterson visited China.	Agreement on economic and technical cooperation		
			Cooperation agreement between the Jamaica Cabinet Office (Development) and China Minmetals Corporation on Bauxite Mining and Alumina Refining Cooperation		
			Heads of agreement on the Jamaica Railway Transportation Systems		
			Exchange of notes on issuing each other's nationals multiple entry visas for purposes of business travels.		

Country	Year	High Level Mutual Visits*	Agreements and Projects#	Value	Funded By
Jamaica Contd	**2007**		Concessional loan agreement to build the Montego Bay Convention Centre (Handed over to former Prime Minister Bruce Golding in April 2011)	RMB ¥ 350,000,000	EXIM China
			Grant funding for Sligoville Sports Complex – multipurpose stadium (completed), as well as a new police station and post office in Sligoville, St Catherine.	US$3,000,0004	Chinese government
			Disaster Relief assistance for Tropical Storm Gustav to the Jamaican Red Cross Society	US$100,000 US$ 50,000	China and the Chinese Red Cross Society respectively
	2009	His Excellency Xi Jinping, the recent former Vice President of the People's Republic of China, now the President of China (Jamaica)	Agreement on economic and technical cooperation for the provision of Grant Aid	RMB ¥50,000,000	China
		His Excellency Xi Jinping, the recent former Vice President of the People's Republic of China, now the President of China (Jamaica)	Exchange of letters for a Chinese Garden – to be constructed at the Hope Botanical Gardens through grant aid stipulated in the Agreement on economic and technical cooperation signed on 1st February 2005. (currently being implemented)	US$3,000,000	
			Exchange of letters for the supply of agricultural equipment/machinery	RMB 7,500,000	China
			Exchange of letters concerning the upgrade of the water supply system and the repair of the road in the Sligoville Community – second phase of the Sligoville Project.		

Country	Year	High Level Mutual Visits*	Agreements and Projects#	Value	Funded By
Jamaica Contd	**2009**		Indicative terms and conditions between the Development Bank of Jamaica and the China Development Bank for the provision of concessional financing	US$10,000,000	
	2010		Memorandum of understanding between the China Harbour Engineering Co. Ltd and the Government of Jamaica (MTW/ National Works Agency) concerning Institutional Capacity Building through Training		
		A Chinese Delegation from the China National Complete Plant Import and Export Corporation (Group) – Complant, visited the NWC (Jamaica)			
			Disaster Relief assistance for Tropical Storm Nicole to the Jamaican Red Cross Society	US$ 30,000.00	Chinese government through the Chinese Red Cross
		Former Prime Minister Bruce Golding accompanied by the former Deputy Prime Minister and Minister of Foreign Affairs and Foreign Trade (China)	A Preferential buyer credit loan agreement on Jamaica Road Improvement and Rehabilitation Works Project between the Road Maintenance Fund of Jamaica and the Export-Import Bank of China		
			Jamaica economical housing project government concessional loan agreement between the government of Jamaica (Represented by the Ministry of Finance, Planning and the Public Service) and the Export-Import Bank of China		

Country	Year	High Level Mutual Visits*	Agreements and Projects#	Value	Funded By
Jamaica Contd	**2010**		Agreement between Jamaica (Ministry of Agriculture) and China (Complant Sugar International Limited) for the divestment of government's sugar assets (Exp. return of J$8 billion)		
	2011	A Jamaican delegation	Initialling of a draft text towards an air services agreement		
	2012	Chinese International Trade Representative and Vice Minister of Commerce, His Excellency Gao Hucheng (Jamaica)	Agreement on economic and technical cooperation	RMB20,000,000/ approximately US$3M	
			Two letters of exchange for the provision of a set of mobile x-ray scanning equipment to the Port Authority of Jamaica and the construction of early childhood institutions in Jamaica		
		Chinese Vice Minister of Commerce, H.E. Li Jinzao (Jamaica)	Agreement on economic and technical cooperation for grant aid	RMB 30,000,000/ approximately US$4.7M	
			Certificate of handing-over of the mobile container x-ray scanning equipment for the Port Authority of Jamaica	RMB 21,000,000/ approximately US$3.3M	
		A small team of officials led by the Minister of Industry, Investment and Commerce (MIIC), Anthony Hylton (China)	Promotion of Jamaica's logistics hub		
		A small team led by the Minister of Transport, Works and Housing, Dr. Omar Davis (China)			
		Jamaican Minister of Energy, Mining, Science and Technology, Phillip Paulwell (China)			

Country	Year	High Level Mutual Visits*	Agreements and Projects#	Value	Funded By
Jamaica Contd	**2013**	Jamaican Minister of Foreign Affairs and Foreign Trade, Arnold Nicholson (China)			
		Jamaican Minister of Agriculture, Roger Clarke, attended the first China-Latin America and Caribbean Agricultural Ministers' Forum (China)			
		President Xi Jinping met with Prime Minister, Portia Simpson Miller (during Xi's state visit to Trinidad and Tobago)			
		Prime Minister of Jamaica, Portia Simpson Miller (China)	Agreement on economic and technical cooperation		
			Preferential buyers' credit		China
		Jamaican Minister, Ronald Thwaites (China)			
		Jamaican Minister of Finance, Peter Phillips (China)			
	2014	Two visits of Jamaican Minister of Tourism and Entertainment, Wykeham McNeil (China)			
		Jamaican Minister of Energy, Mining, Science and Technology, Phillip Paulwell (China)			
		Chinese Vice Minister of Education, Liu Zhanyuan (Jamaica)			
		Vice Chairman Bai Lichen of the Chinese People's Political Consultative Conference (CPPCC) (Jamaica)			
			Agreement on the construction of a Child and Adolescent Hospital in Western Jamaica		
			Jamaica waives visa requirements for Chinese tourists		

Country	Year	High Level Mutual Visits*	Agreements and Projects#	Value	Funded By
Jamaica Contd	**2015**	Mr Zhang Baowen, vice-chairperson of the Standing Committee of the National People's Congress (Jamaica)			
			An agreement on economic and technical cooperation		
Suriname	**1979**	Permanent Secretary of the Ministry of Foreign Affairs of Suriname, Heinemann, and his wife (China)			
	1984		Agreement on loan provided by China to Suriname in the construction of a gymnasium		
	1986	Foreign Minister Herrenberg of Suriname (China)	Agreement on economic and technical cooperation		
	1987	A Chinese Government Economic Delegation led by Vice-Minister of Foreign Trade and Economic Cooperation, Lu Peijian (Suriname)	Completion and hand-over ceremony of the gymnasium		
	1990	Vice-Foreign Minister Liu Huaqiu (Suriname)	Exchange of notes on providing gratuitous assistance		
		Assistant Minister of Foreign Trade and Economic Cooperation, Li Yan (Suriname)	Agreement on economic and technological cooperation		
	1992	Surinamese Foreign Minister, Subhas Mungra (China)			
	1993	An NPC Delegation led by Vice-Chairman Chen Muhua of NPC Standing Committee (Surinam)			
	1994	President Venetiaan of Suriname (China)	Agreement on loans		
			Exchange of notes providing a batch of general goods		

Country	Year	High Level Mutual Visits*	Agreements and Projects#	Value	Funded By
Suriname Contd	**1994**		Exchange of notes postponing the reimbursement of Chinese loan in the construction of a gymnasium in Suriname		
		A Chinese Government Forestry Delegation led by Vice-Minister of Forest, Wang Zhibao (Suriname)			
	1995	A Surinamese parliamentary delegation led by Mr. Lachmon, Speaker of the National Assembly (China)			
		A Chinese Government Economic Delegation led by Liu Shanzai, Vice-Minister of Foreign Trade and Economic Cooperation (Suriname)			
	1996	Vice-Foreign Minister Li Zhaoxing (Suriname)			
	1997	Special Envoy of the Surinamese President and Chairman of National Democratic Party, Desi Bouterse (China)			
			Exchange of notes concerning mutual exemption of visa between Hong Kong SAR and Suriname		
			Agreement on economic and technological cooperation		
	1998	Surinamese President Jules Wijdenbosch (China)	Trade agreement		
			Agreement on economic and technical cooperation		
			A framework agreement on providing a preferential loan		
	1999		Agreement on economic and technological cooperation		
		Vice-Foreign Minister Yang Jiechi (Suriname)			

Country	Year	High Level Mutual Visits*	Agreements and Projects#	Value	Funded By
Suriname Contd	**1998**	Surinamese President Jules Wijdenbosch (China)	Trade agreement		
			Agreement on economic and technical cooperation		
			A framework agreement on providing a preferential loan		
	1999		Agreement on economic and technological cooperation		
		Vice-Foreign Minister, Yang Jiechi (Suriname)			
	2001	An Economic and Trade Delegation of the Chinese Government led by Vice-Minister of Foreign Trade and Economic Cooperation, Sun Guangxiang (Suriname)	Agreement on economic and technological cooperation		
		A Jilin economic and trade delegation led by Vice-Chairman of Jilin CPPCC, Liu Xilin (Suriname)			
	2002	Vice-President of China Council for International Trade Promotion, Wan Jifei (Suriname)			
		Surinamese Permanent Secretary of Foreign Ministry Ewald Limon (China)	Agreement on economic and technological cooperation		
		A CPC delegation led by Deputy Head of the International Liaison Department of the CPC Central Committee, Cai Wu (Suriname)			
	2003	State Councillor Wu Yi	Agreement on economic and technological cooperation		
	2008		500-Kilometer road asphalt project both inside and outside paramaribo	US$200,000,000	China
			200 low-cost houses in Tout Lui Faut (Exp 2009)		China

Country	Year	High Level Mutual Visits*	Agreements and Projects#	Value	Funded By
Suriname Contd	2009		Handing over of the container scanning system in the New Harbour		
			Launching ceremony of the cargo ship 'ZHONGMU 1' (technicians, materials and equipment were all from China)		
			Two Agreements on economic and technical cooperation – a grant and interest-free loans		
	2011		Commitment by Beijing to build a $600-million deep-sea harbour, highway and port in Suriname	US$600,000,000	
			Agreement has been signed between the government of Suriname and Chinese company China Zhong Heng Tai Investment (CZHT) to rehabilitate Suriname's palm-oil sector.	US$4,500,000	
	2013	President Desire Bouterse of Suriname at the World Peace Forum in China (China)			
		President Xi Jinping met with President Desire Bouterse of Suriname (during Xi's state visit to Trinidad and Tobago)			
		Agriculture Minister Hendrik Setrowidjojo attended the first China-Latin America and Caribbean Agricultural Ministers' Forum (China)			
			Agreement on mutual visa waiver for diplomatic and service passport holders		
	2015		Currency swap	USD $160M	China

Country	Year	High Level Mutual Visits*	Agreements and Projects#	Value	Funded By
Trinidad and Tobago	1974	Prime Minister Eric Williams of Trinidad and Tobago (China)			
	1975	A Chinese petroleum delegation led by Vice-Minister of Fuel Chemical Industry, Tang Ke (Trinidad and Tobago)			
		Prime Minister Eric Williams (China)			
	1978	Vice-Premier Geng Biao (Trinidad and Tobago)			
	1981	A Chinese NPC delegation led by Vice-Chairman, Ngapoi Ngawang Jigme (Trinidad and Tobago)			
	1982	Vice-Foreign Minister Han Xu (Trinidad and Tobago)			
	1984	A Chinese economic and trade delegation led by MOFERT Vice-Minister, Jia Shi (Trinidad and Tobago)	Initialled an agreement on trade, economic, scientific and technical cooperation		
	1985	Prime Minister George Chambers (China)	Agreement on trade, economic, scientific and technical cooperation		
	1986	Vice-Foreign Minister Zhu Qizhen (Trinidad and Tobago)			
	1987	A Trinidad and Tobago parliamentary delegation led by House Speaker, Nizam Mohammed (China)			
	1990	Vice-Foreign Minister Liu Huaqiu (Trinidad and Tobago)			
	1992	A Chinese Government delegation led by Secretary General of the State Council, Luo Gan (Trinidad and Tobago)			
	1996	A Caribbean parliamentary leaders' delegation led by House Speaker, Hector McClean (China)			
	1997	A Chinese parliamentary delegation led by Vice-Chairman Buhe of NPC Standing Committee (Trinidad and Tobago)			

Country	Year	High Level Mutual Visits#	Agreements and Projects#	Value	Funded By
Trinidad and Tobago Contd	**1997**	Senate President Ganace Ramdial (China)			
		Minister of Finance Brian Kuei Tung (China)			
	1998	Vice-Premier Qian Qichen (Trinidad and Tobago)	Exchange of notes on China's gratuitous assistance		
	1999	Minister of Public Administration Wade Mark (China)			
		A delegation led by Minister of Trade and Industry, Mervyn Assam (China)			
		A delegation led by Chairman of the Foreign Affairs Committee of the NPC Standing Committee, Zeng Jianhui (Trinidad and Tobago)			
	2000	Chairman of the Chinese People's Political Consultative Conference (CPPCC), Li Ruihuan (Trinidad and Tobago)			
	2001	Assistant Foreign Minister Zhou Wenzhong visited Trinidad and Tobago	Exchange notes on providing free aid		
	2002	A governmental economic and trade delegation led by Vice-Minister of Foreign Trade and Economic Cooperation, Ma Xiuhong (Trinidad and Tobago)	Agreement on mutual promotion and protection of investment		
	2003	A Chinese Government Delegation led by State Councillor, Wu Yi (Trinidad and Tobago)			
			Agreement on avoidance of double taxation		
	2005		Agreement of economic and technical cooperation between government of the Republic of Tobago and China.		
			Framework agreement on providing preferential loans		

Country	Year	High Level Mutual Visits*	Agreements and Projects#	Value	Funded By
Trinidad and Tobago Contd	**2006**		Agreement on inter-free diplomacy, business and official passport's visa		
	2010		Upcoming 3rd China–Caribbean Trade and Economic Co-operation Forum to be held in Trinidad		
	2011	His Excellency Wang Qishan, Vice Premier of the PRC (Trinidad and Tobago)	3rd China–Caribbean Trade and Economic Co-operation Forum		
			The construction of Trinidad & Tobago's prime minister's official residence and the National Academy for the Performing Arts by the Shanghai Construction Co.		
	2012		Signing of the framework agreement for the provision of a concessional loan for the construction of the Children's Hospital in Central Trinidad		
	2013	President Xi Jinping (Trinidad and Tobago)	A number of cooperation documents covering trade, energy, education, health, agriculture, tourism, aviation, people-to-people and cultural exchanges.		
			China to donate cargo and container scanners to Trinidad and Tobago		
		Zhong Shan, Trade Representative and Vice Minister of Commerce (Trinidad and Tobago)			
		A delegation of the National Energy Administration (Trinidad and Tobago)			

Country	Year	High Level Mutual Visits*	Agreements and Projects#	Value	Funded By
Trinidad and Tobago Contd	**2014**	Wang Shenyang, head of the Cooperation Division of the Chinese Ministry of Commerce (Trinidad and Tobago)			
		Prime Minister Kamla Persad-Bissessar (China)			
	2015		Chinese donation of medical supplies to Trinidad and Tobago	Worth USD $400,000	

Notes

Introduction

1. Richard L. Bernal, 'China's Rising Investment Profile in the Caribbean,' *Economics Brief, Inter-American Dialogue*, October 2013.
2. Bernal., 'Dragon in the Caribbean: China-CARICOM Economic Relations,' *Round Table* 99, Issue 408 (June 2010): 281–302 and 'China's Growing Economic Presence in the Caribbean,' *The World Economy* 38, Issue 9 (September 2015): 1,409–37.
3. Bernal., 'China and Small Island Developing States,' *Africa-East Asian Affairs, The China Monitor* Issue 1 (August 2012): 3–30.
4. Robert Devlin, Antoni Estevadeordal and A. Rodriguez-Clare, eds., 'The Emergence of China: Opportunities and Challenges for Latin America and the Caribbean' (report, Inter-American Development Bank, Washington, DC, 2005); Claudio M. Loser, 'The Growing Economic Presence of China in Latin America' (report, Center for Hemispheric Policy, University of Miami, Miami, 2006); Osvaldo Rosales and Mikio Kuwayama, Latin America Meets China and India: Prospects and Challenges for Trade and Investment,' CEPAL Review, no. 93 (December 2007): 81–103; Rhys Jenkins, Enrique Dussel Peters and Mauricio Mesquita Moreira, 'The Impact of China on Latin America and the Caribbean,' World Development 36, no. 2 (2008): 235–53; Daniel Lederman, Marcelo Olarreaga and Guillermo E. Perry, 'Latin America's Response to China and India: Overview of the Research Findings and Policy Implications,' in China's and India's Challenge to Latin America: Opportunity or Threat, ed. Daniel Lederman, Marcelo Olarreaga and Guillermo E. Perry (Washington, DC: World Bank, 2009); Cynthia J. Arnson and Jeffrey Davidow, 'China, Latin America and the United States: The New Triangle,' (Washington, DC: Woodrow Wilson International Center for Scholars, 2011); Cynthia J. Arnson and Jorge Heine with Christine Zaino, eds., 'Reaching Across the Pacific: Latin America and Asia in the New Century' (Woodrow Wilson Center for International Scholars, Washington, DC, 2014), 'Latin America and the Caribbean and China: Towards a New Era in Economic Cooperation' (United Nations Economic Commission for Latin America and the Caribbean, Santiago, 2015) and Kevin Gallagher, The China Triangle: Latin America's China Boom and the Fate of the Washington Consensus (New York: Oxford University Press, 2016).
5. R. Evan Ellis, *China in Latin America: The Whats and Wherefores* (Boulder: Lynne Rienner, 2009), 236–49.
6. Osvaldo Rosales and Kuwayama, 'China and Latin America and the Caribbean: Building a Strategic Economic and Trade Relationship' (Economic Commission for Latin America and the Caribbean, Santiago, April 2012).
7. Daniel Lederman, Marcelo Olarreaga and Guillermo E. Perry, 'Latin America's Response to China and India: Overview of the Research Findings and Policy Implications', in *China's and India's Challenge to Latin America: Opportunity or Threat,* ed. Daniel Lederman, Marcelo Olarreaga and Guillermo E. Perry (Washington, DC: World Bank, 2009).

8. Bernal, 'Dragon in the Caribbean: China–CARICOM Economic Relations,' *Round Table* 99, no. 408 (2010): 1–22; and Richard L. Bernal, 'China and Small Island Developing States,' *Africa-East Asian Affairs, The China Monitor*, Issue 1 (August 2012): 3–30.
9. Cynthia J. Arnson and Jeffrey Davidow, 'China, Latin America and the United States: The New Triangle' (Woodrow Wilson International Center for Scholars, Washington, DC, 2011), Riordan Roett and Guadalupe Paz, eds., 'China's Expansion into the Western Hemisphere: Implications for Latin America and the United States' (Brookings Institution Press, Washington, DC, 2008) and Cynthia Aronson, Mark Mohr and Riordan Roett, 'Enter the Dragon: China's Presence in Latin America' (Woodward Wilson Center for Scholars, Washington, DC, 2007) and Eric Farnsworth, 'The New Mercantilism: China's Emerging Role in the Americas,' *Current History* (February 2011): 56–61.
10. R. Evan Ellis, *China in Latin America: The Whats and Wherefores* (Boulder: Lynne Rienner, 2009), 236–49. See also Daniel P. Erickson, 'China, Taiwan and the Battle for Latin America,' *The Fletcher Forum of World Affairs* 31, no. 2 (Summer 2007): 69–89.
11. Martin Jacques, *When China Rules the World: The End of the Western World and the Birth of a New Global Order* (New York: Allen Lane, 2009).
12. David Shambaugh, *China goes Global: The Partial Power* (New York: Oxford University Press, 2013).
13. Geoff Dyer, *The Contest of the Century: The New Era of Competition with China-and How America Can Win* (New York: Alfred A. Knopf, 2014).
14. Stephen Roach, *Unbalanced: The Codependency of America and China* (New Haven: Yale University Press, 2014).
15. There is a voluminous literature which does this and which the reader can peruse, e.g., Justin Yifu Lin, *Demystifying the Chinese Economy* (Cambridge: Cambridge University Press, 2012) and Susan L. Shirk, *China: Fragile Superpower: How China's Internal Politics Could Derail Its Peaceful Rise* (Oxford: Oxford University Press, 2007).
16. Gregory T. Chin, 'China and Small States of the Caribbean: Responding to Vulnerabilities, Securing Developmental Space,' Paper to be presented at The Centre for International Governance Innovation (CIGI) workshop, Tobago, April 3–4, 2008 and Richard L. Bernal, 'Dragon in the Caribbean: China–CARICOM Economic Relations,' *Round Table* 99, no. 408 (2010): 1–22.

Chapter 1

1. Guy Dinmore, 'Rome Negotiates with China for Lifeline from Financial Troubles,' *Financial Times*, September 13, 2011, 1; and Bob Davis, 'Beijing Rebuffs Hopes of Bailout,' *Wall Street Journal*, September 26, 2011, A15.
2. Robert S. Ross and Zhu Feng, 'Introduction,' in *China's Ascent: Power, Security, and the Future of International Politics*, ed. Robert S. Ross and Zhu Feng (Ithaca: Cornell University Press, 2008), 1–10.
3. In certain circumstances, small states can influence superpowers. See for example, Richard L. Bernal, *The Influence of Small States on Superpowers: Jamaica and U.S. Foreign Policy* (Lanham: Lexington Publishers, 2015).
4. Angus Maddison, *Chinese Performance in the Long Run* (Paris: Organization for Economic Cooperation and Development, 1998).
5. Ibid.
6. Kai Guo and Papa N'Diaye, 'Is China's Export-Oriented Growth Sustainable?' (IMF Working Paper WP/09/172, International Monetary Fund, Washington, DC, 2009), 3.

7. United Nations, 'Latin America and the Caribbean and China: Towards a New Era in Economic Cooperation' (United Nations Economic Commission of Latin America and the Caribbean, Santiago, 2015).
8. Jeffrey Sachs, 'Welcome to the Asian Century by 2050, China and Maybe India will Overtake the U.S. Economy in Size,' *Fortune*, January 12, 2004.
9. Kai Guo and Papa N'Diaye, 'Is China's Export-Oriented Growth Sustainable?'
10. IMF, 'World Economic Outlook, April 2015' (International Monetary Fund, Washington, DC, 2015).
11. Brahma Chellaney, *Asian Juggernaut: The Rise of China, India and Japan* (New York: Harper Collins Publishers, 2006), 1–53.
12. Robyn Meredith, ed., *The Elephant and the Dragon: The Rise of India and China and What It Means for All of US* (New York: W. W. Norton, 2007) and Bill Emmott, *How the Power Struggle between India, China and Japan Will Shape Our Next Decade* (New York: Harcourt, 2008).
13. Sachs, 'Welcome', 38–39.
14. Nikolas D. Kristof and Sheryl WuDunn, *Thunder from the East. Portrait of a Rising Asia* (New York: Knopf, 2000).
15. Sachs, 'Welcome', 38–39; and Morton Abramovitz and Stephen Bosworth, 'America Confronts the Asian Century,' *Current History: Ney York then Philadelphia* 105, no. 690 (April 2006): 147–52.
16. Minxin Pei, 'Asia Rise,' *Foreign Policy* (July/August 2009): 32–36.
17. Kishore Mahbubani, *The New Asian Hemisphere: The Irresistible Shift of Global Power to the East* (New York: Public Affairs, 2008).
18. Martin Jacques, *When China Rules the World: The End of the Western World and the Birth of a New Global Order* (London; Penguin Press, 2009).
19. Bill Emmott, *Rivals: How the Power Struggle between China, India and Japan will Shape Our Next Decade* (Orlando: Harcourt, 2008), 37.
20. Ibid.
21. This was a strong sentiment plaguing early attempts at intra-Asian dialogue. See, for example, Richard Wright's comments on the Bandung Conference in 1955. Richard Wright, *The Colour Curtin: The Bandung Conference* (London: Dobson, 1955).
22. Bill Emmott, *Rivals*, 45.
23. Kevin Brown, 'Biggest regional trades deal unveiled,' *Financial Times*, January 1, 2010.
24. Liz Gooch, 'Asia Free Trade Raises Hopes and Fears about China,' *New York Times*, January 1, 2010.
25. James Lamont, 'China's Progress Provokes Border Envy in India,' *Financial Times*, January 10, 2010.
26. This is a widely held and frequently stated view including among informed sources. See Eric Hobsbawn with Antonio Polito, *On the Edge of the New Century* (New York: New Press, 2000).
27. Amy Kazmin and Edward Luce, 'India Feels Chill as US Courts China,' *Financial Times*, November 23, 2009.
28. 'Pakistan has nothing to fear from India,' *Washington Post*, November 22, 2009.
29. Baldev Raj Nayar and T.V. Paul, *India in the World Order: Searching for Major-Power Status* (Cambridge: Cambridge University Press, 2003), 115.
30. Stephen P. Cohen, 'India: Emerging Power' (The Brookings Institution, Washington, DC, 2001), 52.
31. Yasheng Huang and Tarun Khanna, 'Can India Overtake China?' *Foreign Policy* (July/August 2003).

32. Baldev Raj Nayar and T.V. Paul, *India in the World Order.*
33. Paul Kennedy, *The Rise and Fall of the Great Powers* (New York: Vintage Books, 1987).
34. Henry R. Nau, *The Myth of America's Decline* (Oxford: Oxford University Press, 1990).
35. Joseph S. Nye, *The Paradox of American Power: Why the World's Only Superpower Can't Go it Alone* (Oxford: Oxford University Press, 2002).
36. David P. Calleo, *Beyond American Hegemony: The Future of the Western Alliance* (New York: Basic books, 1987), 220.
37. Immanuel Wallerstein, 'The Incredible Shrinking Eagle: The End of Pax Americana,' *Foreign Policy* (July/August 2002): 60–68 and 'The Eagle Has Crash Landed,' *Foreign Policy* (July/August 2002): 60–68.
38. Fareed Zakaria, *The Post-American World* (New York: W.W. Norton, 2008).
39. Josef Joffe, *The Myth of America's Decline: Politics, Economics, and a Half Century of False Prophecies* (New York: Liveright Publishing, 2013).
40. David P. Calleo and Benjamin M. Rowland, *America and the World Political Economy* (Bloomington: Indiana University press, 1973), 197.
41. Ezra Vogel, *Japan as Number One: Lessons for America* (New York: Harper Colophon, 1979).
42. Clyde V. Prestowitz, Trading Places: *How We are Giving Our Future to Japan and How to Reclaim It* (New Yok: Basic Books, 1988), 493.
43. Robert O. Keohane, 'Hegemony and After: Knowns and Unknowns in the Debate over Decline,' *Foreign Affairs* 91, no. 4 (July/August 2012): 114.
44. Robert Kagan, *The World America Made* (New York: Knopf, 2012).
45. For support of American exceptionalism see Seymour Martin Lipset, *American Exceptionalism: A Double-edged Sword* (New York: W.W. Norton, 1997). For a critique of American exceptionalism see Godfrey Hodgson, *The Myth of American Exceptionalism* (New Haven: Yale University Press, 2009).
46. Andrew Bacevich, *The Limits of Power: The End of American Exceptionalism* (New York: Metropolitan Books, 2008).
47. Charles Krauthammer, 'The Unipolar Moment,' *Foreign Affairs* (Winter 1990–91).
48. T.R. Reid, *The United States of Europe: The New Superpower and the End of American Supremacy* (New York: Penguin, 2005).
49. Mark Leonard, *Why Europe Will Run the 21st Century* (New York: Public Affairs, 2006).
50. Robert Kagan, *Paradise and Power: America and Europe in the New World Order* (New York: Vintage, 2004).
51. Niall Ferguson, 'Empire at Risk,' *Newsweek*, December 7, 2009, 41–44.
52. Paul Kennedy, *The Rise and Fall of the Great Powers.*
53. Niall Ferguson, *The Ascent of Money: A Financial History of the World* (New York: Penguin Press, 2008), 335–39.
54. Joseph Nye, *The Paradox of American Power.*
55. Zbigniew Bzerzinski, 'The Group of TWO that could change the world,' *Financial Times*, January 13, 2009.
56. David M. Gordon, 'Do We Need To Be No. 1?' *Atlantic Monthly*, April 1986, 100–108.
57. Niall Ferguson, 'A World Without Power,' Fo*reign Policy* (July/August 2004): 32–39. For more on the implications of the vacuum see Niall Ferguson, *Colossus: The Price of America's Empire* (New York: Penguin Press, 2004).
58. Bruce Jones, *Still Ours to Lead: America, Rising Powers, and the Tension between Rivalry and Restraint* (Washington, DC: Brookings Institution, 2014).
59. Thomas Friedman and Michael Mandelbaum, *That Used to Be Us: How America Fell Behind in the World It Invented and How We Can Come Back* (New York: Farrar, Straus and Giroux, 2011).

60. Fareed Zakaria, *The Post-American World 2.0*, 2nd ed. (New York: W. W. Norton & Company, 2011).
61. Daniel Gross, Better, *Stronger, Faster: The Myth of America's Decline and the Rise of a New Economy* (New York: Free Press, 2012.
62. Edward Luce, *Time to Start Thinking. America in an Age of Decline* (New York: Atlantic Monthly Press, 2012).
63. Michael Mandelbaum, The Road to Global Prosperity (New York: Simon & Schuster, 2104), 19.
64. Ian Bremmer, *Superpower: Three Choices, for America's Role in the* World (New York: Portfolio/Penguin, 2015), 125–62.
65. Martin Sieff, *Shifting Superpowers: The New and Emerging Relationship between the United States, China and India* (Washington, DC: The Cato Institute, 2009), 4.
66. Francis Fukuyama, *The End of History and the Last Man* (New York: Free Press, 1992).
67. Robert Kagan, *The Return of History and the End of Dreams* (New York: Knopf, 2008).
68. Ezra Vogel, *Japan as No. 1: Lessons for America* (Vermont: Tuttle Rutland, 1980), 21.
69. James Fallows, *Looking at the Sun: The Rise of a New East Asian Economic and Political System* (New York: Pantheon Books, 1994).
70. Jeffrey A. Frankel, 'Is Japan Creating a Yen Bloc in East Asia and the Pacific?' in *Asia Pacific Regionalism: Readings in International Relations*, ed. Ross Garnaut and Peter Drydale, 227–49 (Pymble, Australia: Harper Educational, 1994).
71. Aron Viner, *The Emerging Power of Japanese Money* (Homewood: Dow Jones-Irwin, 1988).
72. Clyde V. Prestowitz Jr., *Trading Places: How We Allowed Japan to Take the Lead* (New York: Basic Books, 1988).
73. Chalmers Johnson, *MITI and the Japanese Miracle: The Growth of Industrial Policy 1925–1975* (Stanford: Stanford University Press, 1982).
74. Fred Bergsten and Marcus Noland, *Reconciling Differences? United States–Japan Economic Conflict* (Washington, DC: Institute for International Economics, 1993).
75. Ronald McKinnon and Kenichi Ohno, *Dollar and Yen: Resolving Economic Conflict between the United States and Japan* (Cambridge: MIT Press, 1997).
76. Edward J. Lincoln, *Japan's New Global Role* (Washington, DC: Brookings Institution, 1993).
77. While recognizing this, Williams and Jain caution that it would be 'premature and unwise to write Japan's obituary yet'. See Brad Williams and Purnendra Jain, 'Japan: Descending Asian Giant?' in *Japan in Decline: Fact or Fiction?*, ed. Purnendra Jain and Brad Williams, xxiii (Folkstone: Global Oriental, 2011).
78. Robert J. Barbera, *The Cost of Capitalism: Understanding Market Mayhem and Stabilizing our Economic Future* (New York: McGraw Hill, 2009), 98.
79. Raymond Vernon, *In the Hurricane's Eye: The Troubled Prospects of Multinational Enterprises* (Cambridge: Harvard University Press, 1998), 141.
80. William Rees-Mogg, 'This is the Chinese Century,' The *Times*, January 3, 2005. For a contrary view, see Lester Thurow, 'A Chinese Century? Maybe It's the Next One,' *New York Times*, August 19, 2007.
81. Madeleine Albright, *Memo to the President Elect: How We Can Restore America's Reputation and Leadership* (New York: Harper, 2008).
82. James Kynge, *China Shakes the World: A Titan's Rise and Troubled Future-and the Challenge for America* (New York: Houghton Mifflin, 2006).
83. Jonathan Fenby, *Will China Dominate the 21st Century*? (London: Polity Press, 2014), 24.

84. Mel Gurtov, *Will This Be China's Century? A Skeptic's View* (Boulder and London: Lynne Rienner, 2013).
85. 'India Rising Growth Potential,' *Goldman Sachs*, 2007.
86. Bill Emmott, *Rivals*, 16.
87. Anne-Marie Slaughter, 'America's Edge: Power in the Networked Century,' *Foreign Affairs* 88, no. 1 (January/February 2009).
88. Joseph S. Nye, Jr., *Soft Power: The Means to Success in World Politics* (New York: Public Affairs, 2004).
89. R. Foot, 'Chinese Strategies in a US-hegemonic Global Order: Accommodating and Hedging,' *International Affairs* 82, no. 1 (January 2006): 77–94.
90. David P. Calleo, *Follies of Power: America's Unipolar Fantasy* (Cambridge: Cambridge University Press, 2009), 50.
91. Elizabeth C. Economy and Adam Segal, 'The G-2 Mirage: Why the United States and China are Not Ready to Upgrade Ties,' *Foreign Affairs* 88, no. 3 (May/June 2009): 2–6.
92. Steven W. Mosher, *Hegemon: China's Plan to Dominate Asia and the World* (New York: Encounter Books, 2006) and Bill Gertz, *The China Threat: How the People's Republic Targets America* (Darby, Penn.: Diane Publihing Company, 2002).
93. The long decline of China is traced in Will Hutton, *The Writing on the Wall: Why We Must Embrace China as a Partner or Face It as an Enemy* (New York: Free Press, 2006), Chapter 2.
94. Kenneth Pomeranz, *The Great Divergence: China, Europe and the Making of the Modern World Economy*, rev. ed. (Princeton: Princeton University Press, 2001). See also Andre Gander Frank, *ReOrient: Global Economy in the Asian Age* (Berkeley: University of California Press, 1998)
95. Angus Madison, *Chinese Economic Performance in the Long Run* (Paris: OECD, 1998).
96. Tim Summers, 'China's Global Personality' (Asia Programme Research Paper, London, Chatham House, June 2014), 9.
97. *The Emergence of China: Opportunities and Challenges for Latin America and the Caribbean* (Washington, DC: Inter-American Development Bank, 2005), 125–40 and Kevin P. Gallagher and Roberto Porzecanski, *Dragon in the Room: China and the Future of Latin American Industrialization* (Stanford: Stanford University Press, 2010), 83–97.
98. Kevin P. Gallagher and Roberto Porzecanski, *Dragon in the Room*, 39–82.
99. Chris Alden, *China in Africa* (London: Zed Books, 2007), 48–49.
100. Fred Bergsten, 'The Asian Monetary Crisis: Proposed Remedies,' Testimony to the US House Representatives, Committee on Banking and Financial Services, November 13, 1997 and 'When China and India Go Down Together,' The *Economist* 345, no. 22 (1997): 78–79.
101. Larry Weymouth, 'In Brazil, from Prisoner to President,' *Washington Post*, December 5, 2010, B5.
102. Robert D. Kaplan, 'A World with No One in Charge,' *Washington Post*, December 5, 2010, B1 and B4.
103. Zbigniew Brezezinski, *Strategic Vision: America and the Crisis of Global Power* (New York: Basic Books, 2012), 75.
104. Charles A. Kupchan, *No One's World: The West, the Rising Rest, and the Coming Global Turn* (New York: Oxford University Press, 2012).
105. William Rees-Mogg, 'This is the Chinese Century,' The *Times*, January 3, 2005. For a contrary view, see Lester Thurow, 'A Chinese Century? Maybe It's the Next One,' *New York Times*, August 19, 2007.
106. Martin Jacques, *When China Rules the World* (London: Allen Lane, 2009).

107. David Shambaugh, *China Goes Global: The Partial Power* (Oxford: Oxford University Press, 2013), 6.
108. Jonathan Fenby, *Will China Dominate the 21st Century*? (London: Polity Press, 2014), 53–77.
109. Thomas J. Christensen, *The China Challenge: Shaping the Choices of a Rising Power* (New York: W. W. Norton & Company, 2015), 63–94.
110. Kishore Mahbubani, *The New Asian Hemisphere: The Irresistible Shift of Global Power to the East* (New York: Public Affairs, 2008) and *India, China and Globalization: The Emerging Superpowers and the Future of Economic Development* (New York: Palgrave Macmillan, 2007).
111. Fareed Zakaria, *The Post-American World.*
112. C. Fred Bergsten, Charles Freeman, Nicholas R. Lardy and Derek J. Mitchell, *China's Rise: Challenges and Opportunities* (Washington, DC: Peterson Institute for International Economics and the Center for Strategic and International Studies, 2008), 8–32.
113. Ibid., 4.
114. Regina M. Abrami, William C. Kerby and F. Warren *McFarlan, Can China Lead? Reaching the Limts of Power and Growth* (Cambridge: Harvard Business School Publishing Corporation, 2014).
115. Nicholas Eberstadt, 'Will China (Continue to) Rise?' in *The Rise of China: Essays on the Future Competition*, ed. Gary J. Schmitt, 131–54 (see page 153) (New York: Encounter Books, 2009).
116. Robert D. Kaplan, *Asia's Cauldron: The South China Sea and the End of a Stable Pacific* (New York: Random house, 2014), 99.
117. David Shambaugh, *China Goes Global: The Partial Power* (Oxford: Oxford University Press, 2013), 9.
118. Henry Kissinger, *On China* (New York: Penguin Books, 2012).
119. Margaret MacMillan, *Nixon and Mao: The Week That Changed the World* (NewYork: Random House, 2008).
120. Zheng Bijian, 'China's Peaceful Rise to Great Power Status,' *Foreign Affairs* 84, no. 5 (September/October 2005): 18–24. See page 22.
121. Geoffrey Smith, 'China's Slowdown Pushes Commodity Prices to New Lows,' *Fortune*, July 24, 2015. http://fortune.com/2015/07/24/chinas-slowdown-pushes-commodity-prices-to-new-lows/.
122. *The Emergence of China: Opportunities and Challenges for Latin America and the Caribbean*, 125–40.
123. Yongzheng Yang, 'China's Integration into the World Economy: Implications for Developing Countries' (IMF Working Paper WP/03/245, International Monetary Fund, Washington, DC, December 2003), 6.
124. Keven P. Gallagher and Roberto Porzecanski, *The Dragon in the Room: China and the Future of Latin American Industrialization* (Stanford: Stanford University Press, 2010), 11–38.
125. Chris Alden, *China in Africa*, 8.
126. Patrick Jenkins, 'China Lenders Eclipse US rivals,' *Financial Times*, January 11, 2010.
127. Richard McGregor, 'Joining the Queue at the Beijing Cash Point,' *Financial Times*, January 27, 2010.
128. Steven Mufson, 'China Surpasses Germany as World's Top Exporter,' *Financial Times*, January 11, 2010.
129. Clive Cookson, 'China Set for Global Lead in Scientific Research,' *Financial Times*, January 26, 2010.

130. Andrew J, Nathan and Andrew Scobell, 'How China Sees America,' *Foreign Affairs* 91, no. 5 (September/October 2012), 32–47.
131. Edward Said, *Orientalism* (New York: Vintage, 1979).
132. Victor G. Kiernan, *The Lords of Mankind* (Harmondsworth: Penguin, 1969).
133. The term Eurocentricism is used in the two connotations of the term as explained by Blaut. First, 'false claims by Europeans that their society or region is, or was in the past, or always has been and always will be, superior to other societies or regions.' Second, 'an inordinate amount of attention- inordinate salience- given to Europe'. See J.M. Blaut, *Eight Eurocentric Historians* (London: Guildford Press, 2000), 4 and 17.
134. For a critique of some of the leading scholars whose work exhibit a Eurocentric approach, see J. M. Blaut, *Eight Eurocentric Historians.* See Also Samir Amin, *Eurocentricism,* 2nd ed. (New York: Monthly Review Press, 2009) and Andre Gunder Frank, *Re-ORIENT: Global Economy in the Asian Age* (Berkeley: University of California Press, 1998).
135. John M. Hobson, *The Eastern Origins of Western Civilization* (Cambridge: Cambridge University Press, 2004).
136. Kenneth Pomeranz, *The Great Divergence: China, Europe and the Making of the Modern World Economy* (Princeton: Princeton University Press, 2000).
137. Joseph Needham, *Science and Civilisation in China,* 24 vols. (Cambridge: Cambridge University Press, 1954–2004).
138. Stephen D. King, *Losing Control: The Emerging Threats to Western Prosperity* (New Haven: Yale University Press, 2010).
139. Robert Kagan, *The Return of History and the End of Dreams* (New York: Alfred A. Knopf, 2008), 86.
140. Simon Winchester, *The Man Who Loved China: The Fantastic Story of the Eccentric Scientist Who Unlocked the Mysteries of the Middle Kingdom* (New York: HarperCollins Publishers, 2008), 258.
141. 'Barack Obama in Asia,' The *Economist,* November 21–27, 2009.
142. Ross Terrill, *The New Chinese Empire and What It Means for the United States* (New York: Basic Books, 2004); Richard Bernstein and Ross H. Munro, *The Coming Conflict with China* (New York: Vintage, 1998); and John Bolton, 'America is far too soft in its dealings with Beijing,' *Financial Times,* January 19, 2011, 11.
143. Richard Bernstein and Ross H. Munro, *The Coming Conflict with China*; Ted Galen Carpenter, *America's Coming War with China: A Collision Course over Taiwan* (New York: Palgrave Macmillan, 2006); Hugo deBurgh, *China: Friend or Foe?* (Totem Books, 2003); Qiao Liang and Wang Xiangsui, *Unrestricted Warfare: China's Master Plan to Destroy America* (Pan American Publishing Company, 2002); Jed Babbin, *Showdown: Why China Wants War with the United States* (Regnery Publishing, 2006) and Michael Pillsbury, The Hundred-Year Marathon: China's Secret Strategy to Replace America as the Global Superpower (New York: Henry Holt and Co., 2015)..
144. James Bradley, *The Imperial Cruise: A Secret History of Empire and War* (Back Bay Books, 2010), 3.
145. Fareed Zakaria, 'The Rise of a Fierce Yet Fragile Superpower,' *Newsweek,* December 31, 2007/January 7, 2008, 12–13.
146. Wang Jisi, 'China's Search for Stability with America,' *Foreign Affairs* 84, no.5 (September/October 2005).
147. G. John Ikenberry, 'The Rise of China and the Future of the West,' *Foreign Affairs* 87, no. 2 (January/February 2008).

148. This is the argument made by among others Nina Hachigian and Mona Sutphen, *The Next American Century: How the US Can Thrive as Other Powers Rise* (New York: Simon & Schuster, 2008).
149. Robert G. Sutter, *U.S.–Chinese Relations: Perilous Past, Pragmatic Future* (London: Rowman & Littlefield Publishers), 154–56.
150. Martin Wolf, 'East and West Are in It Together,' *Financial Times*, January 19, 2011, 11.
151. The 'Peaceful Rise' school of thought has given way more assertive approaches, including an end to what some view as appeasement on the issue of Taiwan. See Mark Leonard, *What Does China Think?* (London: Fourth Estate, 2008), 88–90.
152. It is a mistake not to be aware of different views within China. These differences can be gleaned from Mark Leonard, *What Does China Think?* (New York: Public Affairs, 2008).
153. Jiang Shixue, 'The Chinese Foreign Policy Perspective,' in *China's Expansion into the Western Hemisphere: Implications for Latin America and the United States*, ed. Riordan Roett and Guadalupe Paz, 32 (Washington, DC: Brookings Institution Press, 2008).
154. This will have to be a priority for Chinese policy. Shahid Yusuf and Kaoru Nabeshima, *China's Development Priorities* (Washington, DC: World Bank, 2006), 78–79.
155. Fareed Zakaria, 'China is Not the World's Other Superpower,' *Washington Post*, 6 June, 2013, A15.
156. Cynthia A. Watson, 'U.S. Responses to China's Growing Interests in Latin America: Dawning Recognition of a Changing Hemisphere,' in *Enter the Dragon? China's Presence in Latin America* (Washington, DC: Woodrow Wilson International Center for Scholars, February 2007).
157. Since January 2007, China currently has 2,146 peacekeepers deployed in ten missions, mainly in Africa, with the heaviest concentration of peacekeeping troops in Liberia where there are a total of 563. See also Bill Gill and Chin-Hao Huang, 'China's Expanding Peacekeeping Role: Its Significance and the Policy Implications', Stockholm International Peace Research Institute, Policy Brief, February, 2009.
158. John Pomfret, 'As China rises, so does its influence on the Hill,' *Washington Post*, January 9, 2010.
159. Doreen Hemlock, 'Ready for China's Approach. Caribbean Wants to Enhance its Contacts,' *Sun-Sentinel*, Sunday, January 30, 2005.
160. Robert Kaplan, 'The Geography of Chinese Power,' *Foreign Affairs* 89, no. 3 (May/June 2010): 22–41.
161. Susan V. Lawrence and Thomas Lum, *US–China Relations: Policy Issues* (Washington, DC: Congressional Research Service, March 2011), 3.
162. 'Secretary Clinton's views of US rebalancing of relations with Asia are set out in Hilary Clinton, America's Pacific Century,' *Foreign Affairs*, November 2011. http://www.foreignpolicy.com/node/1002667.
163. Asia-Pacific Strategic Engagement Initiative-US Department of State. http://www.state.gov> Press Release, July 2012.
164. Geoff Dyer, 'Clinton Warns Beijing on Sea Dispute,' *Financial Times*, 13 July 2012, 4.
165. China's position and reaction is explained in Ely Ratner, 'Rebalancing to Asia with an Insecure China,' The *Washington Quarterly* 36, no.2 (Spring 2013): 21–38.
166. Aaron L. Friedberg, 'Bucking Beijing. An Alternative U. S. China Policy,' *Foreign Affairs* 91, no. 5 (September/October 2012): 48–58.
167. US–Korea Free Trade Agreement. http://www.ustr.gov/trade-agreements/free-trade-agreements/korus-fta/.
168. Yu Liu and Dingding Chen, 'Why China will Democratize,' The *Washington Quarterly* 35, no.1 (Winter 2012): 41–63.

169. For a critique of this notion see James Mann, *The China Fantasy: Why Capitalism Will Not Bring Democracy to China* (New York: Penguin, 2008).
170. Thomas J. Christensen, *The China Challenge: Shaping the Choices of a Rising Power* (New York: W. W. Norton & Company, 2015).
171. Robert E. Rubin and Jacob Weisberg, *In An Uncertain World* (New York: Random House, 2003), 227.
172. Stefan Harper, *The Beijing Consensus: How China's Authoritarian Model Will Dominate the Twentieth Century* (New York: Basic Books, 2010), 43.
173. 'The China Decade,' *Time magazine*, August 31, 2015, 39–42. See page 40.
174. Jeffrey A. Bader, *Obama and China's Rise: An Insider's Account of America's Asia Strategy* (Washington, DC: Brookings Institution, 2012), xvii.
175. Robert Keohane, 'The Theory of Hegemonic Stability and Changes in International Economic Regimes, 1967–1977,' in *Change in the International System*, ed. Ole R. Hoisti, Randolph M. Siverson and Alexander L. George, 131–62. See page 132 (Boulder: Westview Press, 1980).
176. Robert Gilpin, *The Political Economy of International Relations* (Princeton: Princeton University Press, 1987), 88.
177. Stephen D. Krasner and Michael C. Webb, 'Hegemonic Stability Theory: An Empirical Analysis,' *Review of International Studies* 15, no. 2 (1989): 183–98.
178. William Wohlforth, 'The Stability of a Unipolar World,' *International Security* 24, no. 1 (Summer 1999): 5–41. See page 23.
179. Peter Temin and David Vines, *The Leaderless Economy: Why the World Economic System Fell Apart and How to Fix It* (Princeton: Princeton University Press, 2013).
180. Effective October 1, 2016.
181. Cited in Andrew Walter, *World Power and World Money* (London: Harvester Wheatsheaf, 1993), 2.
182. Charles Kindleberger, *The World in Depression, 1929–1939* (Berkeley: University of California, 1973).
183. Barry Eichengreen, 'Hegemonic Stability Theories of the International Monetary System' (working paper No. 2193, National Bureau of Economic Research, March 1987), 58.
184. Robert J. Skidelsky, 'Retreat from Leadership: The Evolution of British Economic Policy, 1870 1940,' in *Balance of Power or Hegemony: The Interwar Monetary System*, ed. Benjamin M. Rowland, 177–92 (see pages 150–51) (New York: The Lehrman Institute/New York University Press, 1976).
185. Harold Van B. Cleveland, 'The International Monetary System in the Interwar Period,' in *Balance of Power or Hegemony: The Interwar Monetary System*, ed. Benjamin M. Rowland, 3–59. (New York: The Lehrman Institute/New York University Press, 1976).
186. Eswar Prasad and Lei Ye, *The Renminbi's Role in the Global Monetary System* (Washington, DC: Brookings Institution, 2012). Also see Eswar Prasad, *The Dollar Trap: How the U.S. Dollar Tightened Its Grip on Global Finance* (Princeton: Princeton university Press, 2014) for an analysis of why the US dollar retains its current role as a global reserve currency especially in a global economic crisis.
187. Chinese Renminbi to be Included in IMF's Special Drawing Right Basket, IMF Survey, December 1, 2015. http://www.imf.org/external/pubs/ft/survey/so/2015/NEW120115A.htm
188. 'IMF's Executive Board Completes Review of SDR Basket, Includes Chinese Renminbi.' Press Release No. 15/540 November 30, 2015. http://www.imf.org/external/np/sec/pr/2015/pr15540.htm.

189. Shawn Donnan, 'SDR Move Seen as Vote of Confidence in China's Leaders,' *Financial Times*, November 30, 2015.
190. Lucy Hornby and Tom Michell, 'China Pledges no More "sudden changes" after IMF Decision on Currency,' *Financial Times*, December 2, 2015, 4.
191. Susan Strange, *Mad Money: When Markets Outgrow Governments* (Ann Arbor: University of Michigan Press, 1998).
192. Susan Strange, *The Retreat of the State: The Diffusion of Power in the World Economy* (London: Cambridge University Press, 1996).
193. Benjamin J. Cohen, *Global Monetary Governance* (New York: Routledge, 2009), 207–24 and Benjamin J. Cohen, *The Geography of Money* (Ithaca: Cornell University Press, 1998).
194. Robert O. Keohane, *After Hegemony: Cooperation and Discord in the World Political Economy* (Princeton: Princeton University Press, 1984).
195. Hyman P. *Minisky, Stabilizing an Unstable Economy* (New York: McGraw-Hill Educational, 2008) and Hyman P. Minsky, *Can It Happen Again?: Essays on Instability and Finance* (Routledge, 1982).
196. Carmen M. Reinhart and Kenneth S. Rogoff, *This Time is Different: Eight Centuries of Financial Folly* (Princeton: Princeton University Press, 2009).
197. J.K. Galbraith, *A Short History of Financial Euphoria* (New York: Penguin Publishers, 1994).
198. Examples of this genre of literature include Liaquat Ahmed, *Lords of Finance: The Bankers Who Broke the World* (New York: Penguin Press, 2009) and Neil Irvin, *The Alchemists: Three Central Bankers and a World on Fire* (New York: Penguin, 2014).
199. Britain's dominance of global trade of which the colonial trade arrangements were an integral part was fundamental to its preeminent role in the Gold Standard. Marcello de Cecco, *Money and Empire: The International Gold Standard, 1890–1914* (Oxford: Basil Blackwell, 1974). Susan Strange explains: 'the political process of acquiring and empire and the financial process of acquiring an international currency were highly interactive.' See Susan Strange, *Sterling and British Policy: A Political Study of an International Currency in Decline* (London: Oxford University Press, 1971), 47.
200. Benjamin M. Rowland, 'Preparing the American Ascendancy: The Transfer of Economic Power from Britain to the United States, 1933–1944,' in *Balance of Power or Hegemony*, 195–224; David P. Calleo, *Beyond American Hegemony: The Future of the Western Alliance* (New York: Basic Books, 1987), 129–49; and Nicholas Mayhew, *Sterling: The History of a Currency* (New York: John Wiley, 2000).
201. Richard C. Gardner, *Sterling-Dollar Diplomacy in Current Perspective: The Origins and the Prospects of Our International Economic Order* (New York: Columbia University Press, 1980) and Benn Steil, *The Battle of Bretton Woods: John Maynard Keynes, Harry Dexter White, and the Making of the New World Order* (Princeton: Princeton University Press, 2014).
202. Fred Block, *The Origins of International Economic Disorder: A Study of United States International Monetary Policy from World War II to the Present* (Berkeley: University of California Press, 1978).
203. Randal D. Germain, *The International Organization of Credit* (Cambridge: Cambridge University Press, 1998).
204. Paul Cohen illustrates the 'overwhelming extent' of the application of western concepts. See Paul A. Cohen, *Discovering History in China: American Historical Writing on the Recent Chinese Past* (New York: Columbia University Press, 2010).

205. Martin Jacques, *When China Rules the World*, 142.
206. Wayne M. Morrison, *China's Economic Rise: History, Trends, Challenges, and Implications for the United State*s (Washington, DC: Congressional Research Service, March 4, 2013), 1.
207. Niall Ferguson, *The Ascent of Money*.
208. Zachary Karabell, *Superfusion: How China and America Became One Economy and Why the World's Prosperity Depends on It* (New York: Simon & Schuster, 2009).
209. See Sara Bongiorni, *A Year Without 'Made in China': One Family's True Life Adventure in the Global Economy* (New York: Wiley, 2007).
210. Charles Fishman, *The Wal-Mart Effect: How the World's Most Powerful Company Really Works--and How It's Transforming the American Economy* (New York: Penguin, 2006).
211. Joe Studwell, *The China Dream: The Quest for the Last Great Untapped Market on* Earth (New York: Grove Press, 2003).
212. 'Chinese Suspected over White House Cyber-attacks, Says Official,' *Financial Times*, November 7, 2008.
213. Ellen Nakashima, 'Chinese Leaders Ordered Google Hack, U.S. was told,' *Washington Post*, December 5, 2010, A16.
214. David E. Sanger, *The Inheritance: The World Obama Confronts and the Challenges to American Power* (New York: Harmony Books, 2009), 35–62.
215. Peter Nolan, *Is China Buying the World?* (Cambridge: Polity Press, 2012).
216. James Kynge, *China Shakes the World: A Titan's Rise and Troubled Future and the Challenge for America* (New York; Mariner Books, 2007); Ted C. Fishman, *China, Inc.: How the Rise of the Next Superpower Challenges America and the World* (New York; Scribner, 2006); and Susan L. Shirk, *China: Fragile Superpower: How China's Internal Politics Could Derail Its Peaceful Rise* (Oxford: Oxford University Press, 2007).
217. James McGregor, *One Billion Customers: Lessons from the Front Lines of Doing Business in China* (New York: Free Press, 2007).
218. Moises Naim, *Illicit: How Smugglers, Traffickers and Copycats are Hijacking the Global Economy* (New York: Doubleday Publishers, 2005), 119–130.
219. These are set out in *The Emergence of China: Opportunities and Challenges for Latin America for Latin America and the Caribbean*, 102.
220. C. Fred Bergsten, Bates Gill, Nicholas R. Lardy and Derek Mitchell, *China: The Balance Sheet: What the World Needs to Know Now about the Emerging Superpower* (New York: Public Affairs, 2006), 100.
221. Top Engineering Universities in the World. US News. http://www.usnews.com/education/best-global-universities/engineering.
222. Paul Krugman, 'Taking on China,' *New York Times*, March 14, 2010.
223. For the argument that China has been manipulating its currency and that this has had a deleterious effect on the US economy, see Peter W. Navarro, *Death by China: Confronting the Dragon: A Global Call to Action* (New York: Pearson Prentice Hall, 2011), 67–76.
224. Surjit S. Bhalla, *Devaluing to Prosperity: Misaligned Currencies and Their Growth Consequences* (Washington, DC: Institute for International Economics, 2012), 90.
225. Fred Bergsten and Joseph Gagnon, 'Time for a Fight Back in the Currency Wars,' *Financial Times*, September 4, 2012.
226. Lucy Hornby, 'Beijing to Lend Venezuela $5b to Boost Oil Production,' *Financial Times*, September 3, 2015, 3.
227. Joshua P. Meltzer, 'US–China Joint Presidential Statement on Climate Change: The Road to Paris and Beyond,' The Brookings Institution, September 29, 2015.

228. The BRICS Report, *A Study of Brazil, Russia, India, China and South Africa with special focus on Synergies and Complementarities* (New Delhi: Oxford University Press, 2012).
229. Nancy Birdsall, 'The World Bank: Toward a Global Club,' in *Global Governance Reform: Breaking the Stalemate*, ed. Colin I. Bradford and Johannes F. Linn, 50–59 (see page 57) (Washington, DC: Brookings Institution, 2007).
230. Peter B. Kenen, *Reform of the International Monetary Fund, CSR NO. 29* (New York: Council on Foreign Relations, May 2007).
231. Rakesh Mohan and Muneesh Kapur, 'Emerging Powers and the Global Goverance: Whither the IMF?' (IMF Working Paper WP/15/219, October 2015), 4.
232. Robert L. Ayres, *Banking on the Poor: The World Bank and World Poverty* (Cambridge: MIT Press, 1983), 230–32.
233. Sarah Babb, *Behind the Development Banks: Washington Politics, World Poverty and the Wealth of Nations* (Chicago: University of Chicago Press, 2009), 235.
234. Cheryl Payer, *The Debt Trap: The IMF and the Third World* (New York: Monthly Review Press, 1975); and Kevin Danaher, ed., *50 Years is Enough: The Case Against the World Bank and the International Monetary Fund* (Boston: South end Press, 1994).
235. Giovanni Andrea Cornia, Richard Jolly and Frances Stewart, *Adjustment with a Human Face: Protecting the Vulnerable and Promoting Growth* (Oxford: Oxford University Press, 1987).
236. Tony Killick, ed., *The Quest for Economic Stabilisation: The IMF and the Third World* (London: Heinemann Educational Books, 1984).
237. The Washington Consensus is a termed coined by John Williamson in John Williamson, 'What Washington Means by Policy Reform', in *Latin American Readjustment: How Much has Happened, ed. John Williamson* (Washington: Institute for International Economics, 1989). For a review, see Nancy Birdsall, Augusto de la Torre, and Felipe Valencia Caicedo, 'The Washington Consensus: Assessing a Damaged Brand', (working paper No. 213, Center for Global Development, Washington, DC, 2010). For criticism see Joseph E. Stigilitz, 'Is There a Post-Washington Consensus Consensus?' in *The Washington Consensus Reconsidered: Towards a New Global Governance*, ed. Narcís Serra and Joseph E. Stiglitz, 41–56 (Oxford: Oxford University Press, 2008).
238. Davison L. Budhoo, *Enough Is Enough: Dear Mr. Camdessus-Open Letter of Resignation to the Managing Director of the International* (Muscat, Oman: Apex Press, 1990); Joseph E. Stigilitz, *Globalization and its Discontents* (New York: W.W. Norton & Com,pany, 2002), 86–88.
239. Roy Culpeper, *The Multilateral Development Banks. Vol. 5 Titans or Behemoths?* (Blouder: Lynne Reinner Publishers, 1997); JoMarie Griesgraber and Bernhard G. Gunter, eds., *Promoting Development. Effective Global Institutions for the Twenty-First Century* (London: Pluto Press, 1995); and Edwin M. Truman, 'Overview on IMF Reform,' in Reforming the IMF for the 21st Century, ed. Edwin M. Truman (Washington, DC: Institute for International Economics, 2006), 31–126.
240. Cheryl Payer, *The World Bank: A Critical Analysis* (New York: Monthly Review Press, 1982).
241. Stuart Holland, *Towards a New Bretton Woods. Alternatives for the Global Economy* (London: Spokesman, 1994).
242. Jonathan R. Pincus and Jeffrey A. Winters, eds., *Reinventing the World Bank* (Ithaca: Cornell University Press, 2002), 1–25 and 222–26.
243. David A. Phillips, *Reforming the World Bank: Twenty Years of Trial and Error* (Cambridge: Cambridge University Press, 2009).

244. Dragoslav Avramovic, 'Financial Co-operation among Developing Countries: Issues and Opportunities,' in *The Rich and the Poor: Development, Negotiations and Cooperation-An Assessment*, ed. Altaf Gauhar, 205–225 (London: Third World Foundation, 1983).
245. Farooq Sobhan, 'Opportunities for South-South cooperation,' in *Crisis & Response: The Challenge of South-South Economic Cooperation*, ed. Noordin Sopiee, B.A. Hamzah and Leong Choon Heng, 63 (Institute of Strategic and International Studies Malaysia, 1988).
246. The South Commission Report, *The Challenge to the South: The Report of the South Commission* (Oxford: Oxford University Press, 1990), 171.
247. Sixth BRICS Summit – Fortaleza Declaration. brics6.itamaraty.gov.br/.../214-sixth-brics-summit-fortaleza-declaration (accessed March 23, 2015).
248. Rakesh Mohan and Muneesh Kapur, 'Emerging Powers and the Global Goverance: Whither the IMF?' (IMF working paper WP/15/219, October 2015), 7.
249. Ibid., 49.
250. Ibid., 8.
251. Prasanta Sahu, 'Brics Nations Broadly Agree on Capital Structure of Bank: Group Yet to Decide on Offering Stake in Joint Bank to Developed Countries,' *Wall Street Journal*, August 28, 2013.
252. While sharing common goals there are different motives and some anxiety among the BRICS about the possible predominance of China. Adriana Erthal Abdenur, 'China and the BRICS Development Bank: Legitimacy and Multilateralism in South–South Cooperation,' *IDS Bulletin* 45, no. 4 (July 2014): 85–101.
253. Fifth BRICS Summit Declaration and Action Plan, Paragraph 9. http://www.brics5.co.za/fifth-brics-summit-declaration-and-action-plan/. Accessed April 1, 2015.
254. Stephany Griffith-Jones, 'A BRICS Development Bank: A Dream Coming True?' UNCTAD Discussion Paper No. 2, March 15, 2014, 7.
255. Fifth BRICS Summit Declaration and Action Plan, Paragraph 10. http://www.brics5.co.za/fifth-brics-summit-declaration-and-action-plan/. Accessed 1 April, 2015.
256. Jamil Anderlini and Kiran Stacey, 'George Osborne Rejected Diplomatic Advice to Join China-led Bank,' *Financial Times*, March 26, 2015.
257. The decision has been viewed as pragmatic. See Martin Wolf, 'A Rebuff of China's AIIB Would be Folly,' *Financial Times*, March 2015.
258. Jamil Anderlini and Kiran Stacey, 'George Osborne Rejected Diplomatic Advice to Join China-led bank.'
259. 'China Gloats as Europeans Rush to Join Asian Bank,' *Washington Post*, http//www.washingtonpost.com/.../china-gloats-as-europea...(accessed March 19, 2015).
260. Robert Zoellick, 'Shunning Beijing's infrastructure bank was a mistake for the US,' *Financial Times*, June 7, 2015, 6.
261. David Pilling and Josh Noble, 'Bernake blames Congress for China's AIIB,' *Financial Times*, June 3, 2015, 4.
262. Stephany Griffith-Jones, 'A BRICS Development Bank: A Dream Coming True?' (UNCTAD Discussion Paper No. 215, March, 2014), 7–17.
263. Zhang Chunyan, Zhao Yinan and Chen Weihua, '46 countries apply to AIIB,' *China Daily*. http://usa.chinadaily.com.cn/world/2015-04/01/content_19965536.htm (accessed April 1, 2015).
264. Mainland welcomes Taiwan's participation in AIIB - China ... *China Daily*. http://www.chinadaily.com.cn/business/.../content_19967221.htm (Accessed April 1, 2015).
265. Patricia Anderson and Michael Witter, 'Crisis, Adjustment and Social Change. A Case Study of Jamaica,' in *Consequences of Structural Adjustment: A Review of the Jamaican Experience*, ed. Elsie Le Franc (Kingston: Canoe Press, 1994), 1–55.

266. Tyrone Ferguson, *Structural Adjustment and Governance: The Case of Guyana* (Georgetown: Public Affairs Consulting Enterprise, 1995).
267. Ngaire Woods, *The Globalizers: The IMF, the World Bank and Their Borrowers* (Ithaca: Cornell University Press, 2006), 2–3.
268. Paul Mosley, Jane Harrigan and John Toye, eds., *Aid and Power: The World Bank and Policy-based Lending*, vol. 1 (London: Routledge, 19991), 300.
269. Calculated from IMF, World Economic Outlook Database, April 2013. http://www.imf.org/external/pubs/ft/weo/2013/01/weodata/weorept.aspx.
270. Raj M. Desai and James Raymond Vreeland, 'What the New Bank of BRICS is All About,' *Washington Post*, July 17, 2014.
271. 'China's Silk Road Fund Announced Its 1st Investment Project,' *Live Trading News*. http://www.livetradingnews.com/chinas-silk-road-fund-announced-its-1st-investment-project-103415.htm#.Vava9_lVhBc. Accessed 12 July, 2015.
272. 'China and Cyber-Security: Political, Economic, and Strategic Dimensions' (Report, Workshops held at the University of California, San Diego, April 2012), 1.
273. Hajoon Chang, *Kicking Away the Ladder* (London: Anthem Press, 2002).
274. Sarah Rose, *For All the Tea in China: How England Stole the World's Favourite Drink and Changed History* (London: Penguin Press, 2011).
275. Kara Scannell and Gina Chon, 'Cyber Insecurity,' *Financial Times*, July 15, 2015, 8.
276. For example, David E. Sanger, 'U.S. Blames China's Military Directly for Cyberattacks,' *New York Times*, Mayb6, 2013; and Jack Gillum, 'Senate: China Hacked U.S. Military Contractor Networks,' *Huffington Post*, November, 17, 2014. http://www.huffingtonpost.com/news/china-hacking-us/.
277. Department of Defence, *The Military and Security Developments Involving the People's Republic of China, Annual Report to Congress, 2013* (Washington, DC: Department of Defence, 2013).
278. Greg Austin and Franz-Stefan Gady, *Cyber Détente Between the United States and China: Shaping the Agenda* (Washington, DC: East-West Institute, 2012).
279. Robert Wright and Andy Sharman, 'Cyber Hack Leads to Mass Car Recall,' *Financial Times*, July 25–26, 2015, 1.
280. Demetri Sevastopulo, 'US Set to Tackle Chinese Hackers with Sanctions,' *Financial Times*, September 1, 2015, 4.
281. Kenneth Lieberthal and Peter W. Singer, *Cybersecurity and U.S.-China Relations* (Washington, DC: Brookings Institution, 2012), vi. For a more general discussion, see Richard A. Clarke and Robert K. Knake, *Cyber War: The Next Threat to National Security and What to Do about It* (New York: HarperCollins, 2010).
282. Organization of American States, *Latin American + Caribbean Cyber Security Trends* (Washington, DC: Organization of American States, June 2014).
283. *Reducing Transatlantic Barriers to Trade and Investment: An Economic Assessment Final Project Report* (London: Centre for Economic Policy Research, March 2013).
284. David Rosnick, *TTIP: Are 40 Cents a Day Big Gains? Issue Brief* (Washington, DC: Centre for Economic Policy Research, 12 August, 2015).
285. Richard L. Bernal, *Globalization, Trade and Economic Development: A Study of the CARIFORUM–EU Economic Partnership Agreement* (New York: Palgrave MacMillan, December, 2013).
286. The reasons for the continued involvement of China and the US are succinctly set out in Fred Bergsten, *China Rises* (Washington, DC: Institute for International Economics, 2009), 169–89.

287. Martin Jacques, *When China Rules the World: The End of the Western World and the Birth of a New Global Order*, 2nd ed. (New York: Penguin Press, 2012), 570.
288. Margaret Macmillan, Nixon and Mao: The Week that Changed the World (New York: Random House, 2007), 233.
289. The possibility of a US–China military conflict is still felt by many to be a distinct possibility. See Steve Tsang, *If China Attacks Taiwan: Military Strategy, Politics and Economics* (London: Routledge, 2006); Ted Galen Carpenter, *America's Coming War with China: A Collision Course over Taiwan* (London: Palgrave Macmillan, 2006).
290. Richard C. Bush and Michael E. O'Hanlon, *A War Like No Other. The Truth About China's Challenge to America* (New York: Wiley, 2007); Steven W. Mosher, *Hegemon: China's Plan to Dominate Asia and the World* (New York: Encounter Books, 2006); and Bill Gertz, *The China Threat: How the People's Republic Targets America* (Darby, PA.: Diane Publishing Company, 2002).
291. David E. Sanger, *The Inheritance: The World Obama Confronts and the Challenges to American Power* (New York: Harmony Books, 2009), 353.
292. John Pomfret, 'Clinton Addresses China Spat,' *Washington Post*, January 12, 2010.
293. Kathrin Hille, 'China Attacks Taiwan Arms Deal,' *Financial Times*, September 23, 2011.
294. Robert D. Kaplan, 'A Power Shift in Asia,' *Washington Post*, September 25, 2011, A17.
295. Daniel H. Rosen and Zhi Wang, The Implications of China-Taiwan Economic Relations (Washington, DC: Institue for International Economics, 2011), 46.
296. Sun Shingling, 'Economic Relations across the Taiwan Straits and Beijing's Polciy Adjustment,' in *Cross-Taiwan Straits Relations since 1979: Policy Adjustments and Institutional Change Across the Straits*, ed. Kevin G. Cai, 51–86 (Singapore: World Scientif Publishing Co., 2011).
297. Ibid., 61.
298. Charles L. Glaser, 'A US–China Grand Bargain? The Hard Choice between Military Competition and Accommodation,' *International Security* 39, Issue 4 (Spring 2015): 49–90.
299. Martin Sieff, *Shifting Superpowers*, 75–103.
300. Piya Mahtaney, *India, China and Globalization: The Emerging Superpowers and the Future of Economic Development* (London: Palgrave, 2007) and L. Alan Winters and Shahid Yusuf, eds., *Dancing with Giants: China, India and the Global Economy* (Washington, DC: World Bank and Institute of Policy Studies, 2007).
301. Martin Sieff, *Shifting Superpowers*.
302. Anil K. Gupta and Haiyan Wang, *Getting China and India Right. Strategies for Leveraging the World's Fastest Growing Economies for Global Advantage* (San Francisco: Jossey-Bass, 2009).
303. 'Reshaping the World Economy,' *Business Week*, August 22, 2005.
304. Francine R. Frankel, introduction to *The India-China Relationship: What the United States Needs to Know*, ed. Kevin G. Cai, 13–24 (New York: Columbia University Press, 2004).
305. Baldev Raj Nayar and T.V. Paul, *India in the World Order*.
306. Mira Kamdir, *Planet India: The Turbulent Rise of the Largest Democracy and the Future of Our World* (New York: Scribner, 2008).
307. Sanjeev Sanyal, *The Indian Renaissance: India's Rise after a Thousand Years of Decline* (New York/New Delhi: Penguin, 2008), 12.
308. Henry Kissinger, *Diplomacy* (New York: Simon & Schuster, 1993), 23–24.
309. Samuel P. Huntington, *The Clash of Civilizations and the Remaking of World Order* (New York: Simon & Schuster, 1996), 121.

310. Amy Chua, *Day of Empire: How Hyperpowers Rise to Global Dominance and Why They Fall* (New York: Random House, 2007).
311. Parang Khanna, *The Second World. Empires and Influence in the New Global Order* (New York: Random House, 2008).
312. V.S. Naipaul, *India: An Area of Darkness* (London: Andre Deutsch, 1964).
313. V.S. Naipaul, *India: A Wounded Civilization* (New York: Alfred A. Knopf, 1977).
314. V.S. Naipaul, *India: A Million Mutinies Now* (New York: Viking, 1991).
315. Aaron Chaze, *An Investor's guide to the Next Economic Superpower* (New York: Wiley, 2006).
316. Kamal Nath, *India's Century* (New York: McGraw Hill, 2008).
317. Yasheng Huang, 'The Next Asian Miracle,' *Foreign Policy* (July/August 2008).
318. Daniel Lak, *India Express: The Future of the New Superpower* (New York: Palgrave Macmillan, 2009).
319. George Perkovich, 'Is India a Major Power?' The *Washington Quarterly* (Winter 2003–04): 134.
320. Nandan Nilekani, *Imagining India: The Idea of a Renewed Nation* (London: Penguin Press, 2009).
321. Kamal Nath, *India's Century*, 83.
322. For comprehensive treatment of this subject see Nandan Nilekani, *Imagining India: The Idea of a Renewed Nation.*
323. Robyn Meredith, *The Elephant and the Dragon*, 83.
324. Gordon Brown, *Beyond the Crash: Overcoming the First Crisis of Globalization* (New York: Free Press, 2010), 165.
325. Indrani Gupta, Bishwanath Golder and Arup Mitra, 'The Case of India,' in *International Trade in Health Services: A Development Perspective*, ed. Simonetta Zirrrilli and Colette Kinnon, 228 (Geneva: UNCTAD, 1998).
326. John Lancaster, 'Surgeries, Side Trips for India's Tourists,' The *Washington Post*, October 21, 2004.
327. Susan L. Shirk, 'One-Sided Rivalry: China's Perceptions and Policies towards India,' in *The India-China Relationship*, 75–100.
328. Robyn Meridith, *The Elephant and the Dragon*, 51.
329. 'Banyan. Land of Promise,' The *Economist*, November 21–27, 2009.
330. For example, 'Pushing Back,' The *Economist*, December 18, 2010, 67.
331. Matt Wade, 'Jealous India Jostles with China for US Favour,' *Sidney Morning Herald*, November 28, 2009.
332. Edward Timperlake, *Red Dragon Rising: Communist China's Military Threat to America* (Washington, DC: Regnery Publishing, 2002).
333. Henry Kissinger, *Does America Need a Foreign Policy? Toward a Diplomacy for the 21st Century* (New York: Simon & Schuster, 2001), 160.
334. Stephen P. Cohen, *India Emerging Power* (Washington, DC: Brookings Institution, 2001), 198–227.
335. Bill Emmott, *Rivals*, 61.
336. Edward Luce, *In Spite of the Gods: The Strange Rise of Modern India* (New York: Doubleday, 2007), 280.
337. Stephen P. Cohen, *India Emerging Power* (Washington, DC: Brookings Institution, 2001), 268–98.
338. Mark Kobayashi-Hilary, *Outsourcing to India: The Offshore Advantage*, 2nd ed. (New York: Springer, 2005); Kamal Nath, India's Century, 78–95; and Thomas L. Friedman, *The World is Flat: A Brief History* (New York: Farrer, Straus and Giroux, 2005).

339. Lou Dobbs, *Exporting America: Why Corporate Greed is Shipping American Jobs Overseas* (New York: Warner Business Books, 2004), 10. See also Ron Hira and Anil Hira, *Outsourcing America: What's Behind Our National Crisis and How We Can Reclaim American Jobs* (Amacon, 2005).
340. Cheryl Gay Stolberg and Jim Yardley, 'Obama Courts Emergent India as Deeper Ally,' The *New York Times*, November 9, 2010.
341. Robert D. Kaplan, *Monsoon: The Indian Ocean and the Future of American Power* (New York: Random House, 2010).
342. Shintaro Ishihara, *The Japan That Can Say No: Why Japan will be First Among Equals* (New York: Touchstone, 1992).
343. Edward J. Lincoln, *Japan's New Global Role* (Washington, DC: Brookings Institution, 1993).
344. Bill Emmott, *Rivals*, 96–134.
345. Jennifer Amyx, *Japan's Financial Crisis: Institutional Rigidity and Reluctant Change* (Princeton: Princeton University Press, 2006) and William W. Grimes, *Unmaking the Japanese Miracle: Macroeconomic Politics, 1985–2000* (Ithaca: Cornell University Press, 2001).
346. Wiliam H. Overholt, Asia, America and the Transformation of Geoplolitics (Cambridge: Cambridge University Press, 2008), 65–68.
347. Brahma Chelleney, Asia Juggernaut. The Rise of China, India, and Japan (New York: HarperCollins Publishers, 2010).
348. Kathrin Hille and Mure Dickie, 'Island Spats Threaten China-Japan Ties,' *Financial Times*, July 24, 2012, 6 and Chico Harlan and Jia Lynn Yang, 'Japan Stokes Territorial Tensions with Purchase of Islands,' The *Washington Post*, September 12, 2012, A11.
349. Chalmers Johnson, *Nemesis: The Last Days of the American Empire* (New York: Metropolitan Books, 2006), 200.
350. Remarks by President Obama and Prime Minister Abe of Japan in Joint Press Conference, April 28, 2015. https://www.whitehouse.gov/.../remarks-president-obama-an...
351. *The Budget and Economic Outlook: An Update 2009* (Washington, DC: The Congress of the United States, 2009).
352. Major Foreign Holders of Treasury Securities (Washington, DC: Department of the Treasury/Federal Reserve Board, November 17, 2009).
353. Narushige Michishita and Richard J. Samuals, 'Huggin and Hedging. Japanese Grand Strategy in the Twentith-First Century,' in *World Views of Aspiring Powers. Domestic Foreign Policy Debates in China, India, Iran, Japan and Russia*, ed. Henry R. Nau and and Deepa M. Ollapally, 146–80 (Oxford: Oxford University press, 2012).
354. Alice H. Amsden, *Asia's Next Giant: South Korea and Late Industrialization* (Oxford: Oxford University Press, 1992).
355. David Marsh, *The Euro: The Battle for the New Glogal Currency*, rev. ed. (New Haven: Yale University Press, 2011) and Johan van Overtveldt, *The End of the Euro: The Uneasy Future of the European Union* (Chicago: Agate Publishing, 2011).
356. Walter Laqueur, *After the Fall: The End of the European Dream and the Decline of a Continent* (Thomas Dunne Books, 2012).
357. Christopher Caldwell, *Reflections on the Revolution in Europe: Immigration, Islam and the West* (Archor, 2010).
358. T.R. Reid, *The United States of Europe: The New Superpower and the End of American Supremacy* (New York: Penguin Press, 2004) and John McCormick, *The European Superpower* (New York: Palgrave Macmillan, 2006).

359. David Stuckler, *The Body Economic: Why Austerity Kills* (New York: Basic Books, 2013); Florian Schui, *Austerity: The Great Failure* (New Haven: Yale University Press, 2014); and Mark Blyth, *Austerity: The History of a Dangerous Idea* (Oxford: Oxford University Press, 2015).
360. Robert Devlin, Antoni Estevadeordal and A. Rodriguez-Clare, eds., *The Emergence of China: Opportunities and Challenges for Latin America and the Caribbean* (Washington, DC: Inter-American Development Bank, 2005); Claudio M. Loser, *The Growing Economic Presence of China in Latin America* (Miami: Center for Hemispheric Policy, University of Miami, 2006); and Rhys Jenkins, Enrique Dussel Peters and Mauricio Mesquita Moreira, 'The Impact of China on Latin America and the Caribbean,' *World Development* 36, no. 2 (2008): 235–53.
361. *Latin America and the Caribbean and China: Towards a New Era in Economic Cooperation* (Santiago: United Nations Economic Commission of Latin America and the Caribbean, May 2015), 39.
362. *First Forum of China and the Community of Latin American and Caribbean States (CELAC): Exploring Opportunities for Cooperation on Trade and Investment* (Santiago: United Nations Economic Commission for Latin America and the Caribbean, January 2015), 6.
363. Cyntia J. Arnson and Jorge Heine, 'Reaching Across the Pacific: Latin America and Asia in the New Centurty,' in *Reaching Across the Pacific: Latin America and Asia in the New Centurty*, ed. Cyntia J. Arnson and Jorge Heine with Christine Zaino, 10 (Washington, DC: Wilson Center, 2014).
364. *Latin America and the Caribbean and China*, 37.
365. Ibid., 41.
366. Ibid.
367. *The Changing Nature of Asian-Latin America Economic Relations*, 9–10.
368. Osvaldo Rosales and Sebastian Herreros, 'Mega-regional Trade Negotiations: What is at Stake for Latin America?' (Inter-american Dialogue, Trade Policy Working Paper January, 2014), 4–5.
369. Kevin Gallagher and Roberto Porzecanski, *The Dragon in the Room*, 11–24.
370. R. Evan Ellis, *China on the Ground in Latin America: Challenges for the Chinese and Impacts on the Region* (New York: Palgrave Macmillan, 2014), 15–45.
371. For a discussion of the negative impact of imports from China on the manufacturing sector see among others Mauricio Mesquita Moreira, 'Fear of China: Is There a Future for Manufacturing in Latin America?' *World Development* 35, no.3:355–76; Rhys Jenkins, Enrique Dussel Peters and Mauricio Mesquita Moreira, 'The Impact of China on Latin America and the Caribbean,' *World Development* 36, no. 2 (2007): 235–53; Carol Wise and Cintia Quiliconi, 'China's Surge in Latin American Markets: Policy Challeges and Responses,' *Politics & Policy* 35, no. 3 (2007): 410–38; and Kevin Gallagher and Roberto Porzecanski, *The Dragon in the Room*, 39–56 and 136–48.
372. Kevin Gallagher and Roberto Porzecanski, *The Dragon in the Room*, 147.
373. Robert Devlin, Antoni Estevadeordal and A. Rodriguez-Clare, eds., *The Emergence of China*, 175–91.
374. Mauriceo Mesquito Moreira, in China, Latin America, and the United States: The New Triangle, ed. Cynthia J. Arnson and Jeffrey Davidow (Washington, DC: Woodrow Wilson International Center, 2011), 14.
375. The perception of erosion of Mexico's exports to the US may be worse than the reality maybe. It has been suggested that Mexico has maintained its market share in the US, See Ralph Watkins, 'Meeting the China Challege to Manufacturin in Mexico,' in *China*

and the New Triangular Relationships in the Americas: China and the Future of U.S.-Mexico Relations, ed Enrique Dussel Peters, Adrian H. Hearn and Harley Skaiken, 37–55 (Miami: Center for Latin American Studies, University of Miami, 2013).

376. Raul Prebisch, *The Economic Development of Latin America and Its Principal Problems* (New York: United Nations Economic Commission for Latin America, 1950); 'Commercial Policy in the Underdeveloped Countries,' *American Economic Review* 49, no. 2(May 1959): 251–73.
377. Celso Furtado, Development and Underdevelopment (Berkeley: University of California, 1974).
378. Theotonio Dos Santos, 'The Structure of Dependence,' American Economic Review 60, no. 2 (May 1970): 231–36.
379. Fernando Henrique Cardoso and Enzo Faletto, *Dependence and Development in Latin America* (Berkeley: University of California, 1979).
380. Osvaldo Sunkel, 'National Development Policy and External Dependence in Latin America,' *Journal of Development Studies 6, no. 1* (October 1969) and Osvaldo Sunkel, 'The Centre-Periphery Model,' Social and Economic Studies 22, no. 1 (March 1973): 132–76.
381. Luis Bértola and José Antonio Ocampo, The Economic Development of Latin America since Independence (New York: Oxford Univsercity Press, 2012), chapter 4.
382. 'No one even considered the possibility that Latin america's new industries might begin to export to the US: the region's industrialization focused on the domestic market.' Rosemary Thorp, *Progress, Poverty and Exclusion* (Washington, DC: Inter-American Development Bank, 1998), 131.
383. Rhys Jenkins and Enrique Dussel Peters, introduction to *China and Latin America Economic Relations in the Twenty-first Century*, ed. in Rhys Jenkins and Enrique Dussel Peters, 1–20 (see page 9) (Bonn & Mexico City: Deutsches Institut für Entwicklungspolitik (DIE), Universidad Nacional Autónoma de México and Centro de Estudios China-México, 2009).
384. Ruben Gnazales-Vincente, 'The Political Economy of Sino-Peruvian Relations: A New Dependency,' *Journal of Current Chinese Affairs* 4, no. 1 (2012): 97–131.
385. Kevin Edmunds, 'Guyana: Colonialism With Chinese Characteristics?' North American Congress on Latin America Jun 26, 2013. https://nacla.org/.../guyana-c...
386. 'Apec summit backs Beijing roadmap to vast Asia-Pacific free trade area,' The *Guardian*, November 11, 2014. http://www.theguardian.com/world/2014/nov/11/apec-summit-beijing-roadmap-asia-pacific-free-trade-area (accessed July 6, 2015).
387. Eric Farnsworth, 'Memo to Washington: China's Growing Presence in Latin America,' *Americas Quarterly*, vol, no. (Winter 2012).
388. Moises Naim, 'Does the Obama Administration have a foreign policy for Latin America?' *Americas Quarterly*, Vol. No. (Winter 2011).
389. John Ghazvinian, *Untapped: The Scramble for Africa's Oil* (New York: Mariner Books, 2008).
390. Yun Sun, 'China's Aid to Africa: Monster or Messiah?' *Brookings East Asia Commentary*, no. 75 (February 2014): 1.
391. Martin Jacques, *When China Rules the World*, 329 and Richard Dowden, *Africa: Altered States, Ordinary Miracles* (New York: Public Affairs, 2009), 497.
392. See a list in Stefan Halper, *The Beijing Consensus: How China's Authoritarian Model Will Dominant the Next Century* (New York: Basic Books, 2010), 101.
393. For an assessment of this aspect of China's Engagement in Africa, see Kenneth King, *China's Aid and Soft Power in Africa* (Woodbridge: Boydell & Brewer Ltd., 2013).

394. Dambisa Moyo, *Winner Take All: China's Race for Resources and What It Means for the Rest of the World* (New York: HarperCollins, 2012), 29.
395. Matt Grainger and Kate Geary, 'The New Forests Company and its Uganda plantations, Oxfam Case Study,' *Oxfam International*, September 22, 2011. http://www.oxfamamerica.org/explore/research-publications/the-new-forests-company-and-its-uganda-plantations/ (accessed July 11, 2015).
396. Fred Pearce, *The Land Grabbers: The New Fight Over Who Owns the Earth* (Boston: Beacon Press, 2012), 203.
397. Michael T. Klare, *Resource Wars: The New Landscape of Conflict* (New York: Henry Holt, 2002).
398. Michael T. Klare, 'The New Geography of Conflict,' Foreign Affairs 80, no. 3 (May/June 2001): 49–61.
399. Alex Prud'homme, *The Ripple Effect. The Fate of Freshwater in the Twenty-First Century* (New York: Scribner, 2011), 198.
400. *The Brics Report: A Study of Brazil, Russia, India, China and South Africa with Special Reference to Synergies and Complementarities* (New Delhi: Oxford University Press, 2012).
401. For a discussion of small island developing states, see Richard L. Bernal, *The Influence of Small States on Superpowers: Jamaica and U.S. Foreign Policy* (Lanham: Lexington Publishers, 2015), 34–37.
402. The World Bank and Commonwealth Secretariat employ a population threshold of 1.5 million to designate small states, but include larger countries such as Jamaica because they share many of the characteristics of smallness such as small size, high degree of openness, concentration on a few exports, narrow range of resources, remoteness and environmental vulnerability. The nomenclature of small island developing state encompasses countries that are not islands such as Belize and even some such as Guyana, which have relatively large land areas.
403. Richard L. Bernal, 'China and Small Island Developing States,' *Africa-East Asian Affairs, The China Monitor*, Issue 1 (August 2012): 3–30.
404. Richard Dowden, *Africa: Altered States, Ordinary Miracles* (New York: Public Affairs, 2019), 485.
405. Neil Shah, 'Immigrants to U.S.: From China Top Those From Mexico,' The *Wall Street Journal*, May 4, 2015, 1.
406. Nicholas D. Kristof and Sheryl Wudunn, *China Wakes: The Struggle for the Soul of a Rising Power* (New York: Vintage books, 1995), 44–45.
407. Joseph S. Nye, Jr., *Soft Power: The Means to Success in World Politics* (New York: Public Affairs, 2005).
408. Xi Jinping, *The Governance of China* (Beijing: Foreign Language Press, 2014), 180.
409. Tania Branigan, 'Chinese State TV Unveils Global Expansion Plan,' The *Guardian*, December 8, 2011.
410. Anne Nelson, *CCTV's International Expansion: China's Grand Strategy for Media?* (Washington, DC: Center for International Media Assistance, National Endowment for Democracy, October, 2013), 18.

Chapter 2

1. Dan P. Erickson and Janice Chen, 'China, Taiwan, and the Battle for Latin America,' *The Fletcher Forum of World Affairs* 31, no. 2 (2007): 69–89.
2. Richard L. Bernal, 'China and Small Island Developing States,' *The China Monitor*, Issue 1 (September 2012): 3–30.

3. Richard L. Bernal, 'The Integration of Small Economies in the Free Trade Area of the Americas, CSIS,' Policy Paper on the Americas, Vol. IX, Study No.1 (Washington, DC: Center for Strategic and International Studies, February 2, 1998).
4. Simon Kuznets, 'Economic Growth of Small National,' in *Economic Consequences of the Size of Nations*, ed. E.A.G. Robinson (London: MacMillan, 1960) and Paul Streeten, 'The Special Problems of Small Countries,' *World Development* 21, no. 2 (1993): 197.
5. Hollis B. Chenery and M. Syrquin, *Patterns of Development, 1950–1970* (London: Oxford University Press, 1975).
6. A Regional Integration Fund of the Free Trade Area of the Americas, ECLAC, LC/R. 1738, July 10, 1997
7. William Demas, *The Economics of Development in Small Countries with Special Reference to the Caribbean* (Montreal: McGill University Press, 1965), 2.
8. Richard L. Bernal, 'The Integration of Small Economies in the Free Trade Area of the Americas, CSIS.'
9. *Vulnerability: Small States in the Global Society* (London: Commonwealth Secretariat, 1985).
10. A Future for Small States: Overcoming Vulnerability (London: Commonwealth Secretariat, 1997), 8–9.
11. Walton Look Lai, *The Chinese in the West Indies 1806–1995: A Documentary History* (Kingston: The Press, University of the West Indies, 2000); Andrew R. Wilson, *The Chinese in the Caribbean* (Princeton: Marcus Wiener Publishers, 2004); and Kim Johnson, *Descendants of the Dragon: The Chinese in Trinidad 1808–2006* (Kingston: Ian Randle Publishers, 2006).
12. Walton Look Lai, *Indentured Labour, Caribbean Sugar: Chinese and Indian Migrants to the British West Indies, 1838–1918* (Baltimore: Johns Hopkins University Press, 2004) and Trev Sue-A-Quan, *Cane Reapers: Chinese Indentured Immigrants in Guyana* (Parksville: Riftswood Publishers, 1999).
13. Walton Look Lai, 'Origins of the Caribbean Chinese Community,' *Journal of Caribbean Studies* 14, no.1 (2000): 25–38.
14. Jacqueline Levy, 'The Economic Role of the Chinese in Jamaica: The Grocery Retail Trade,' *Jamaican Historical Review*, no. 5 (1986): 31–49 and Ray Chen, *The Shopkeepers* (Kingston: Periwinkle Publishers, 2004).
15. Wing Yin Tsang, 'Enterprise Development among Chinese Immigrants in Jamaica,' (Doctoral Thesis, Economic Development Policy, The University of the West Indies, Mona Campus, 2014), 135.
16. CARICOM, *Our Caribbean Community: An Introduction* (Kingston: Ian Randle Publishers, 2005), 279–372.
17. 'Restructuring Jamaica's Economic Relations with Socialist Countries, 1974–1980,' Development and Change 17, no. 4 (October 1986): 607–34.
18. Guyana – Relations with Communist Countries. *countrystudies.us/guyana/92.htm.*
19. Sino-Jamaica Ties – China CRIENGLISH.english.cri.cn/2238/2005-1.../110@198619.ht...
20. 'Patterson Leaves for Asia Today,' *Jamaica Observer*, June 9, 2005 http://www.jamaicaobserver.com/news/82044_Patterson-leaves-for-Asia-today, June 9, 2005.
21. Address by the Most Hon. P.J. Patterson, Prime Minister of Jamaica at the China/Jamaica Business Seminar, Shanghai, June 23, 2005. Jamaica Information Service. http://www.jis.gov.jm/address-by-the-most-honourable-.. June 23, 2005.
22. China's Policy Paper on Latin America and the Caribbean. http://www.chinadaily.com.cn/china/2008-11/06/content_7179488.htm

23. Chinese premier's speech at ECLAC. http://www.china.org.cn/world/2012-06/27/content_25752050.htm.
24. *China's* Xi Offers *Caribbean* Nations $3 Billion in Loans - Bloomberg. *http://www.bloomberg.com.*
25. 'Chinese Vice President Winds up Official Visit to Jamaica,' February 15, 2009. http://news.xinhuanet.com/english/2009-02/15/content_10820595.htm.
26. Richard L. Bernal, *The Influence of Small States on Superpowers: Jamaica and U.S. Foreign Policy* (Lanham: Lexington Publishers, 2015), 295–308.
27. Several Caribbean political leaders have expressed this sentiment. See examples in Richard L. Bernal, 'The Unimportance of the English Speaking Caribbean in US Foreign Policy as told by Presidents and Secretaries of State,' *Caribbean Journal of International Relations & Diplomacy* 1, no.1 (February 2013): 132–50.
28. Beijing Declaration of the First Ministerial Meeting of the CELAC, January 8–9, 2015. http://www.chinacelacforum.org/chn/zywj/t1230938.htm (accessed July 6, 2015).
29. Katrina Manson, 'Beware Tribalism-it Will Tear You Apart, Obama Tells,' *Financial Times*, July 27, 2015, 4.
30. Juliet Eilperin and Kevin Sief, 'Obama Finds a Kenyan Audience Receptive to His Critique,' *Washington Post*, July 27, 2015, A5.
31. Xi Jinping, *The Governance of China* (Beijing: Foreign Languages Press, 2014).
32. Full text: China's Policy Paper on Latin America and the Caribbean... news.xinhuanet.com/english/2008-11/05/content_10308117.htm.
33. Joseph S. Nye. Jr, *Soft Power: The Means to Success in World* Politics (New York: Public affairs, 2005) and Joseph S. Nye. Jr, *The Future of Power* (New York: Public affairs, 2011), 81–112.
34. Michael Barr, *Who's Afraid of China? The Challenge of Chinese Soft Power* (London: Zed Books, 2011), 27.
35. Shen Ding, *The Dragon's Hidden Wings* (Lanham, MD: Lexington Books, 2008), 16–17.
36. Joshua Kurlantzick, *Charm Offensive: How China's Soft Power is Transforming the World* (New Haven: Yale University Press, 2008).
37. The goals and mission of the Confucious Institutes. See Shen Ding, *The Dragon's Hidden Wings* (Lanham, MD: Lexington Books, 2008), 117–23.
38. Chad Bryan, 'Prime Minister Thanks China for Enjoyment Garden,' August 20, 2015. http://www.jis.gov.jm/prime-minister-thanks-china-for-e (accessed August 21, 2015).
39. 'China's Role in Jamaica: No Strings Attached,' *Jamaica Gleaner*, May 3, 2015, 1.
40. 'Ten to study in China,' August 21, 2014. http://www.barbadostoday.bb/2014/08/21/ten-to-study-in-china/.
41. 'China, Grenada Celebrate 10th Anniversary of Ties Resumption,' January 21, 2015. http://english.gov.cn/news/international_exchanges/2015/01/21/content_281475042278268.htm.
42. 'Grenada China Relation Is Stronger Than Ever,' January 22, 2015. http://on.grenadianbuzz.com/grenadainformer/2015/01/22/grenada-china-relation-is-stronger-than-ever/.
43. 'China Offers Eight More Scholarships in Medicine.' http://www.kaieteurnewsonline.com/2011/07/07/china-offers-eight-more-scholarships-in-medicine/.
44. Confucius Institute – University of the West Indies. http://www.mona.uwi.edu/.../confucius-institute-. University of the West Indies.
45. *Caribbean Insight, Caribbean Council* 38, Number 37, October 21 2015.
46. New Confucius Institute Location Officially Opens - The ...www.cob.edu.bs/.../Confucius Institute New Location...College of The Bahamas, Nov 12, 2013 -

47. Confucius Institute at the University of Guyana Officially Inaugurated 2014/05/22. embassy of the people's republic of china in the cooperative ...gy.chineseembassy.org/eng/.
48. The Barbados Advocate – Confucius Institute officially ...http://www.barbadosadvocate.com/newsitem.asp?... The *Barbados Advocate* Apr 21, 2015.
49. Fay Pickersgill, Jamaica China Friendship Association, July 2015.
50. Joseph S. Nye. Jr, 'China's Soft Power,' *Wall Street Journal*, May 8, 2012 and Michael Barr, *Who's Afraid of China? The Challenge of Chinese Soft Power* (London: Zed Books, 2011), 45–46.
51. Adam Clayton Powell III, 'Many Voices: Is Anyone Listening?' In America's Dialogue with the World, ed. William P. Kiehl (Washington, DC: Public Diplomacy Council, 2006), 115–28.
52. David Shambaugh, *China Goes Global: The Partial Power* (Oxford: Oxford University Press, 2013), 177.
53. 'Chinese foreign direct investment in Latin America and the Caribbean,' Working Document, Summit on the Global Agenda, World Economic Forum, Abu Dhabi, November 18–20, 2013, 7.
54. Jamil Anderlini, 'Lender with a Global Reach,' *Financial Times*, May 23, 2011.
55. 'China's Xi Offers Caribbean Nations $3 Billion in Loans.' *Bloomberg*. http://www.bloomberg.com/.../china-s-xi-offers-caribbean-nati... June 3, 2013.
56. R. Evan Ellis, 'Learning the Ropes,' *Americas Quarterly* 6, no. 4 (Fall 2012): 28–34.
57. Karl Sauvant, 'New kid on the block learning the rules,' *East Asian Forum Quarterly* 4, no.2 (April–June 2012): 11–12.
58. *Poverty Reduction and Economic Management Department, East Asia and Pacific Region, From Poor Areas to Poor People: China's Evolving Poverty Reduction Agenda* (Washington, DC: World Bank, March 2009), iii.
59. Fred G. Bergsten, Bates Gill, Nicholas R. Lardy and D. Mitchell, China: *The Balance Sheet. What the World Needs to Know Now about the Emerging Superpower* (New York: Public Affairs, 2006), 4.
60. Guyana, Suriname, Dominica, Jamaica, Grenada and The Bahamas have established Embassies in Beijing. St Kitts established an Embassy in Taipei in 2007.
61. Richard L. Bernal, 'Restructuring Jamaica's Economic Relations with Socialist Countries, 19741980,' *Development and Change* 17, no. 4 (October 1986):607–34.
62. Yongzheng Yang, 'China's Integration into the World Economy: Implications for Developing Countries' (IMF Working Paper WP/03/245, Washington, DC: International Monetary Fund, 2003), 4.
63. Deepak *Bhattasali, Li* Shantong and Will *Martin,* 'China's Accession to the World Trade Organization, Policy Reform, and Poverty Reduction: An Introduction,' *World Bank Economic Review* 18, Issue 1 (2004).
64. China Business Guide, Federation of International Trade Agencies. http://www.fita.org, February 7, 2007 (accessed September 9, 2009).
65. This is not surprising since China is now the top goods producing country. Peter Marsh, 'China Noses Back Ahead as Top Goods Producer to Halt 110-year US Run,' *Financial Times*, March 14, 2011, 4.
66. Economic and Social Survey Jamaica 2008 (Kingston: National Planning Institute, 2009), 11.7.
67. *Comparing Global Influence: China's and U.S. Diplomacy, Foreign Aid, Trade, and Investment in the Developing World* (Washington, DC: Congressional Research Service. August 15, 2008).

68. Alex Vines, *The Scramble for Resources: African Case Studies, South African Journal of International Affairs* 13, Issue 1(2006): 63–75.
69. H.G. Broadman, *Africa's Silk Road: China and India's New Economic Frontier* (Washington, DC: World Bank, 2007, 10–12.
70. T. Burgis, 'China in $23bn Nigeria Oil Deal,' *Financial Times*, May 15–16, 2010, 4.
71. Cynthia J. Arnson and Jeffrey Davidow, *China, Latin America and the United States: The New Triangle* (Washington, DC: Woodrow Wilson International Center for Scholars, 2011), 18.
72. Leslie Hook, 'High Coal Costs Force China to Ration Electricity,' *Financial Times*, May 18, 2011.
73. *The People's Republic of China and Latin America and the Caribbean: Towards a Strategic Relationship* (Santiago: Economic Commission for Latin America and the Caribbean, 2010).
74. Vivek Arora and Athanasios Vamvakidis, 'China's Economic Growth: International Spillovers' (IMF Working Papers WP/10/165 2010), 16.
75. Cynthia J. Arnson and Jeffrey Davidow, *China, Latin America and the United States: The New Triangle* (Washington, DC: Woodrow Wilson International Center for Scholars, 2011), 3.
76. Ibid., 2.
77. Sara Bongiorni, *A Year Without 'Made in China': One Family's True Life Adventure in the Global Economy* (New York: Wiley, 2007).
78. Robert Devlin, Antoni Estevadeordal and Andres Rodriguez-Clare, eds., *The Emergence of China: Opportunities and Challenges for Latin America and the Caribbean* (Washington, DC: Inter-American Development Bank, 2005), 83.
79. China grew at 9.1 per cent in 2009. See Cynthia J. Aronson and Jeffrey Davidow, *China, Latin America and the United States: The New Triangle* (Washington, DC: Woodrow Wilson International Center for Scholars, 2011), 1.
80. A. Ramdass, 'China, T&T Agree to US$49m Asphalt Deal,' *Trinidad Express*, September 23, 2011.
81. A. Collinder, 'The Coffee Industry Board (CIB), Targets China for New Coffee markets,' *Jamaica Gleaner*, November 22, 2009, 10.
82. P. Foster, 'Big Shipment of J'can Coffee off to China,' *Jamaica Observer*, April 6, 2011.
83. China Briefing 2011, http://www.china-briefing.com/news/2011/08/02/china-costa-rica-fta-comes-into-effect.html.
84. Murray Weidenbaum and Samuel Hughes, *The Bamboo Network* (New York Press: Free Press, 1996) and Constance Lever-Tracy, David Fu-Keune Ip and Noel Tracy, *The Chinese Diaspora and Mainland China: An Emerging Economic Synergy* (Houndmills: Macmillan Press, 1996).
85. '11 Jamaicans Begin Chinese Odyssey,' *Jamaica Observer*, September 12, 2010, 1.
86. Clive Cookson, 'China Set for Global Lead in Scientific Research,' *Financial Times*, January 26, 2010, 4.
87. Best Global Universities for Engineering.
88. http://www.usnews.com/education/best-global-universities/engineering.
89. 'Jamaica, China Sign Billion-dollar Pacts,' *Jamaica Gleaner*, February 13, 2009, 1.
90. Giles Chance, *China and the Credit Crisis: The Emergence of a New World Order* (Singapore: John Wiley & Sons, 2010), 25.
91. *Latin America and the Caribbean's Long-Term Growth: Made in China* (Washington, DC: World Bank, 2011), 22.

92. *Globalized, Resilient, Dynamic: The New Face of LAC* (Washington, DC: World Bank, 2010).
93. Cynthia J. Arnson and Jeffrey Davidow, *China, Latin America and the United States. The New Triangle* (Washington, DC: Woodrow Wilson International Center for Scholars, 2011), 14.
94. Robert Devlin, Antoni Estevadeordal and Andrés Rodriguez-Clare, eds., *The Emergence of China: Opportunities and Challenges for Latin America and the Caribbean* (Washington, DC: Inter-American Development Bank, 2005), 125–40.
95. Keven P. Gallagher and Roberto Porzecanski, *The Dragon in the Room: China and the Future of Latin American Industrialization* (Stanford: Stanford University Press, 2010), 6.
96. G.H. Hanson, G.H. and R. Robertson, 'China and the Recent Evolution of Latin America's Manufacturing Exports,' in *China's and India's Challenge to Latin America. Opportunity or Threat*, ed. Daniel Lederman, Marcelo Olarreaga and Guillermo E. Perry, 145–78 (Washington, DC: World Bank, 2009).
97. Shane Streifel, *Impact of China and India on Global Commodity Markets: Focus on Metals and Minerals and Petroleum* (Washington, DC: World Bank Development Group, 2006).
98. US International Trade Commission 2008. 'Caribbean Region: Review of Economic Growth and Development,' Washington, DC: Publication 4000, 4–74.
99. Robert Devlin, Antoni Estevadeordal and Andrés Rodriguez-Clare, eds., *The Emergence of China: Opportunities and Challenges for Latin America and the Caribbean* (Washington, DC: Inter-American Development Bank, 2005), 175–95.
100. Keven P. Gallagher, 'China Crashes Cafta's Party,' *Guardian*, June 5, 2010, 6.
101. Mauricio Moreira, 'Fear of China: Is there a future for manufacturing in Latin America?' INTAL-ITD Occasional Paper 36, April 2006.
102. Robert Devlin, Antoni Estevadeordal and Andrés Rodriguez-Clare, eds., *The Emergence of China: Opportunities and Challenges for Latin America and the Caribbean* (Washington, DC: Inter-American Development Bank, 2005) and S. Yusuf, K. Nabeshima and D.W. Perkins, 'China and India Reshape Global Industrial Geography,' in *Dancing with the Giants: China, India and the Global Economy*, ed. L. Alan Winter and Shahid Yusuf, 35–66 (Washington, DC: World Bank).
103. C. Fred Bergsten, Bates Gill, Nicholas R. Lardy and Derek Mitchell, *China: The Balance Sheet: What the World Needs to Know Now about the Emerging Superpower* (New York: Public Affairs, 2006), 100.
104. S. Yusuf, K. Nabeshima and D.W. Perkins, 'China and India Reshape Global Industrial Geography,' in *Dancing with the Giants: China, India and the Global Economy*, ed. L. Alan Winter and Shahid Yusuf, 35–66. See page 64 (Washington, DC: World Bank).
105. Clive Cookson, 'China Set for Global Lead in Scientific Research,' *Financial Times*, January 26, 2010.
106. Gordon Brown, *Beyond the Crash: Overcoming the First Crisis of Globalization* (New York: Free Press, 2010), 155.
107. J.Y. Lin and Y. Wang, 'China's Integration with the World: Development as a Process of Learning and Industrial Upgrading' (World Bank Research Working Paper No. 4799, (Washington, DC: World Bank, 2008).
108. *The Global Competitiveness Report 2015–16* (Geneva: World Economic Forum, 2015).
109. Bates Gill and James Reilly, 'The Tenuous Hold of China INC. in Africa,' *The Washington Quarterly* 30, no. 3 (Summer 2007): 41.

110. E. Fieser, 'Why is China spending billions in the Caribbean?' *Global Post of Canada*, April 22, 2011.
111. 'First Batch of Sugar Rolls off Skeldon Factory,' *Stabroek News*, May 5, 2010, 1.
112. B. Wilkinson, 'Caribbean: Influx of Chinese Workers Irks Local Unions,' *Inter Press Service*. http://ipsnews.net/news.asp?idnews=386912009 (accessed April 10, 2010).
113. 'Foreign Invasion,' *Trinidad and Tobago Guardian*, July 4, 2009, 2.
114. Bert Wilkinson, 'Caribbean: Influx of Chinese Workers Irks Local Unions,' *Inter Press Service*. http://ipsnews.net/news.asp?idnews=386912009 (accessed April 10, 2010).
115. Al Edwards, 'China Harbour Engineering Company: Building a Better Jamaica,' *Jamaica Observer*, September 2, 2011.
116. 'Arrival of Chinese Construction Workers.' http://www.gov.gd/egov/news/2010/mar10/17_03_10/item_3.
117. D.A. Dickson, 'Chinese Labour Making T&T Mas,' *Trinidad Guardian*, February 10, 2011.
118. Samantha Pearson, 'Carnival: Celebrated in Brazil but Made in China,' *Financial Times*, May 23, 2011.
119. T.H. Lunn, J. Fischer, A. Gomez-Granger and A. Leland, *China's Foreign Aid Activities in Latin America and South Asia* (Washington, DC: Congressional Research Service, 2009), 6 and Charles Wolf Jr, Xiao Wang and Eric Warner, *China's Foreign Aid and Government-sponsored Investment Activities: Scale, Content, Destinations and Implications* (Santa Maria: Rand Corporation, 2013).
120. G. Dyer, J. Anderlini, and H. Sender, 'China's Lending Hits New Heights,' *Financial Times*, January 18, 2011, 1.
121. Sir Roland Sanders, 'China's presence in Dominica,' April 28, 2011. http://www.caribbean360.com/index.php/opinion/389630.html#axzz1Kq0uuSct.
122. The Second China-Caribbean Economic and Trade Cooperation Forum, Xaimen, 2007.
123. E. Fieser, 'Why is China Spending Billions in the Caribbean?' *Global Post of Canada*, April 22, 2011.
124. 'St Kitts and Nevis PM Defends Diplomatic Relations with Taiwan,' http://www.cuopm.com/newsitem_new.asp?articlenumber=1553 (accessed May 18, 2011).
125. Prime Minister Gonzales of St Vincent has expressed a similar rationalization to justify diplomatic ties with Taiwan as the need to have relations with countries that would further enhance the island's socio-economic development. See 'St Vincent Defends Diplomatic ties with Taiwan,' *Jamaica Observer*, May 4, 2011, 17.
126. *Caribbean Insight* 33, no. 12 (March 26, 2010).
127. Jamaica Gleaner, 'China Cancels Debt Owed by Guyana,' *Jamaica Gleaner*, July 13, 2007.
128. 'Achieving Debt Sustainability and the MDGs in Small Island Developing States, United Nations Development Programme' (Discussion Paper, October 20, 2010).
129. 'JDF gets military aid from China,' *Jamaica Observer*, August 23, 2011.
130. R. Evan Ellis, 'China-Latin America Military Engagement: Good Will, Good Business and, Strategic Position,' Strategic Studies Institute, 2011.
131. Sahadeo Basdeo and Greame Mount, *The Foreign Relations of Trinidad and Tobago: The Case of a Small State in the Global Arena* (Port of Spain: Lexicon Trinidad Ltd., 2001), 178–79.
132. David Jessop, 'China-Caribbean Ties Offer Alternative Development Model,' *Jamaica Gleaner*, February 20, 2011 and, E. Fieser, 'Why is China Spending Billions in the Caribbean?' *Global Post of Canada*, April 22, 2011.
133. Information in this paragraph is derived from the IDB's website.

134. 'Dominica signs Framework Agreement with China.' http://www.dominicacentral.com/general/community/dominica-signs-framework-agreement-with-china.html (accessed May 13, 2010).
135. C. Fred Bergsten, Bates Gill, Nicholas R. Lardy, and Derek Mitchell, *China: The Balance Sheet: What the World Needs to Know Now about the Emerging Superpower* (New York: Public Affairs, 2006), 4.
136. The People's Republic of China and Latin America and the Caribbean: Dialogue and Cooperation for the New Challenges of the Global Economy (Santiago, Chile: Economic Commission for Latin America and the Caribbean, October, 2012), 12.
137. Yongzheng Yang, 'China's Integration into the World Economy: Implications for Developing Countries,' (IMF Working Paper WP/03/245, Washington, DC, International Monetary Fund, 2003), 6.
138. FDI by Chinese companies which are mostly state owned are 'in alignment' with the plans of the state. See P. J. Buckley, L. J. Clegg, A. Cross, X. Liu, H. Voss and P. Zhong, 'The Determinants of Chinese Outward Foreign Direct Investment,' *Journal of International Business Studies* 38, no. 4 (2007): 499–518 and Gaston Fornes and Alan Butt Philip, *The China-Latin America Axis: Emerging Markets and the Future* (London: Palgrave Macmillan, 2012), 84.
139. Ilan Alon, 'The Globalization of Chinese Capital,' *East Asian Forum Quarterly* 4, no. 2 (April–June 2012): 6.
140. 'What a Globalizing China Means for LatAm,' *HSBC South-South Special*, November 2013, 4.
141. *UNCTAD's World Investment Report 2014* (Geneva: United Nations Conference on Trade and Development, 2014), xv.
142. *2012 Statistical Bulletin of China's Outward Foreign Direct Investment*, 77.
143. *World Investment Report 2013* (Geneva: UNCTAD, 2013).
144. Jamil Anderlini, 'China Forsees $1.25tn in Outbound UInvestment,' *Financial Times*, November 10, 2014, 4.
145. Yongzheng Yang, 'China's Integration into the World Economy: Implications for Developing Countries' (IMF Working Paper WP/03/245, Washington, DC: International Monetary Fund, 2003), 6.
146. MOFCOM, *2009 Statistical Bulletin of China's Outward Foreign Direct Investment* (Beijing, 2010), 12.
147. Enrique Dussel Peters, 'Chinese FDI in Latin America: Does Ownership Matter?' (Working Group on Development and Environment in the Americas, Discussion Paper No. 33, November, 2012), 1.
148. Michael F. Martin, *China's Sovereign Wealth Fund* (Washington, DC: Congressional Research Service, January 22, 2008).
149. 'China's 2011 Outward Investment growth Slows to 8.5 percent,' *Reuters*. http://reuters.com/.../china-economy-investment-idINL4E8JU2MW2012... (accessed 19 March 2013).
150. 'Ministry predicts new surge in ODI.' www.china.org.cn. http://www.china.org.cn/.
151. This Ministry is responsible for supervising all firms with foreign investments over $10,000.
152. B. Gill, B. and J. Reilly, 'The Tenuous Hold of China Inc. in Africa,' *Washington Quarterly* 30, no. 3 (Summer 2007): 37–52.
153. Nargiza Salidjanova, 'Going Out: An Overview of China's Outward Foreign Direct Investment,' USCC Staff Research Report, US–China Economic and Security Commission, March 30, 2011, 4.

154. Ibid., 5.
155. Enrique Dussel Peters, 'Chinese FDI in Latin America: Does Ownership Matter?' Working Group on Development and Environment in the Americas, Discussion Paper No. 33 (November 2012).
156. For a discussion of the problems see Daniel H. Rosen and Thilo Hanemann, 'China's Changing Outbound Foreign Direct Investment Profile: Drivers and Policy Implications,' Policy Brief No. PBO9-14, Washington: Institute of International Economics, June 2009.
157. Geng Xiao, 'People's Republic of China's Round-Tripping FDI: Scale, Causes and Implications' (Asian Development Bank Discussion Paper No. 7, July 2004).
158. This difficulty can cause confusion and misleading data. For example, it would suggest that Chinese investment in the British Virgin Islands dwarfed Chinese investment in Great Britain. See Derek Scissons, 'Chinese Outward Investment: Acceleration Features the US, The Heritage Foundation,' Issue Brief No. 3656, July 9, 2002.
159. D. Sutherland and B. Matthews, 'Round Tripping or Capital Augmenting OFDI: Chinese Outward Investment and the Caribbean Tax Heavens,' Paper prepared for Leverhulme Centre for Research on Globalization and Economic Policy, University of Nottingham, 2009.
160. Ronen Palan, Richard Murphy and Christian Chavagneux, *Tax Havens: How Globalization Really Works* (Ithaca: Cornell University Press, 2010), 54.
161. Nargiza Salidjanova, 'Going Out: An Overview of China's Outward Foreign Direct Investment, US-China Economic and Security Review Commission Research Report,' March 30, 2011, 15.
162. Ronen Palan, Richard Murphy and Christian Chavagneux, *Tax Havens: How Globalization Really Works* (Ithaca: Cornell University Press, 2010), 54 and William Vleck, *Offshore Finance and Small States: Sovereignty, Size and Money* (New York: Palgrave Macmillan, 2008).
163. D. Sutherland and B. Matthews, 'Round Tripping or Capital Augmenting OFDI: Chinese Outward Investment and the Caribbean Tax Heavens,' Paper prepared for Leverhulme Centre for Research on Globalization and Economic Policy, University of Nottingham, 2009.
164. J.C. Sharman, 'Chinese Capital Flows and Offshore Financial Centers,' *The Pacific Review* 25, no. 3 (2012): 317–37.
165. J. Collins, 'China's Whampoa Ltd. Opens Port in Bahamas,' *Washington Times*, November 20, 2001.
166. John H. Dunning, *International Production and the Multinational Enterprise* (London, Allen & Unwin, 1981).
167. 'President opens Chinese-owned shipyard at Coverden,' *Stabrock News*, March 16, 2014, 1 and 'New Chinese-owned Shipyard Eyeing Guyanese Market,' December 23, 2013. http://www.caribnewsdesk.com.
168. 'Bosai Mining Acquires South America Bauxite Mining Company,' *Mining Top News*, 2006. Retrieved on November 23, 2009.
169. The Chinese community in the Caribbean could be instrumental in promoting the expansion of economic relations between Jamaica and China. For example, it was a Chinese-Jamaican who is also a citizen of Canada who identified a Chinese company to purchase the shares of the government of Jamaica in a bauxite company in Jamaica. C. Raymond Chang is president of CI Financial and is founder of companies involved in promoting investment from China. He founded the Chinese Investment Club and is vice-president of Trinity Investment Corp, which is engaged in several Asian countries.

170. Balford Henry, 'God Returns,' *Jamaica Observer*, 7 May, 2014, 1.
171. *Opportunities for Trade and Investment between Latin America and Asia-Pacific* (Santiago: Economic Commission for Latin America and the Caribbean, 2008), 61.
172. Luke Douglas, 'Govt. Seals Sugar Deal with Complant: Chinese Company Investing US$156m in Industry,' *Jamaica Observer*, August 16, 2011 and 'J$8b Sugar Divestment Agreements Signed between Government and Chinese Investors.' August 2, 2010 http://www.jis.gov.jm/news/opm-news/24875 (accessed March 16, 2011).
173. R. Evan Ellis, 'Suriname and the Chinese: Timber, Migration, and Less-Told Stories of Globalization,' *SAIS Review* XXXII, no. 2 (Summer–Fall 2012): 91 and 'Suriname's Palm-oil Sector to be Rehabilitated.' http://agritrade.cta.int/Agriculture/Commodities/Oil-crops/Suriname-s-palm-oil-sector-to-be-rehabilitated.
174. Olaf De Groot and Miguel Perez Ludena, *Foreign Direct Investment in the Caribbean: Trends, Determinants and Policies, Studies and Perspectives Series No. 35* (Santiago: United Nations Economic Commission for Latin America and the Caribbean, February 2014), 16.
175. Julia Jhinkoo, 'Highlighting the China-Caribbean Relationship,' *Caribbean Centre for Money and Finance Newsletter* 6, no. 10 (October 2013): 1–3.
176. Sasha Harrinanan, 'NGC Signs Agreement with China,' *Trinidad and Tobago Newsday*, February 24, 2014.
177. R. Evan Ellis, *China on the Ground in Latin America: Challenges for the Chinese and Impacts on the Region* (New York: Palgrave Macmillan, 2014), 141.
178. 'Nassau's British Colonial Hilton Sold.' http://www.caribjournal.com/2014/10/... british-colonial-hilton-sold.
179. David Sweig and Bi Jianhai, 'China's Global Hunt for Energy,' *Foreign Affairs* 84, no. 5 (2005): 25–38.
180. 'Bosai Mining Acquires South America Bauxite Mining Company.' *Mining Top News*, 2006 (accessed November 23, 2009).
181. *Opportunities for Trade and Investment between Latin America and Asia-Pacific* (Santiago: Economic Commission for Latin America and the Caribbean, 2008), 61.
182. *Olaf De Groot and Miguel Perez Ludena, Foreign Direct Investment in the Caribbean: Trends, Determinants and Policies, Studies and Perspectives Series No. 35* (Santiago: United Nations Economic Commission for Latin America and the Caribbean, February 2014), 16–18 and 46.
183. Lisa E. Sachs and Karl P. Sauvant, 'BITs, DTTs and FDI Flows. An Overview,' in *The Effects of Treaties on Foreign Direct Investment: Bilateral Investment Treaties, Double Taxation Treaties, and Investment Flows*, ed. Karl P. Sauvant and Lisa E. Sachs (Oxford: Oxford University Press, 2009), xxvii–lxii.
184. J.F. Hornbeck, *CARICOM: Challenges and Opportunities for Caribbean Economic Integration* (Washington, DC: Congressional Research Service, January 7, 2008), 18.
185. Y. Yang, 'China's Integration into the World Economy: Implications for Developing Countries' (IMF Working Paper WP/03/245, Washington, DC, International Monetary Fund, 2003), 6.
186. 'Foreign Direct Investment in Latin America and the Caribbean Santiago: Economic Commission for Latin America and the Caribbean,' Briefing Note 2008, 29.
187. A. Persaud, 'Caribbean Countries Fishing for Investors at China Trade Fair-Guyana Misses First Day,' *Stabroek News*, September, 2003.
188. Caribbean Net News, 'China extends US$118 million in aid to Jamaica.' http://www.caribbeannetnews.com (accessed May 5, 2010).
189. Congressional Research Service, 2008.

190. David Zweig and Bi Jianhai, *Foreign Affairs* 84, no. 5 (September-October 2005): 25–38 and John Ghazvinian, *Untapped: The Scramble for African Oil* (New York: Harvest Books, 2008).
191. International Energy Agency, 2009. 'IEA Raises Oil Demand Outlook on China Consumption.' http://www.marketwatch.com/story/iea-raises-oil-demand-forecast-2009-08-12 (accessed June 2, 2010).
192. Stephanie Hanson, 'China, Africa and Oil, Backgrounder,' Council on Foreign Relations, June 6, 2008.
193. China Aluminum Network 2008, 'China to Build Aluminum Smelter in Trinidad.' http://www.alu.com.cn/enNews/NewsInfo_1755.html.
194. Jamil Anderlini, 'Lender with a Global Reach,' *Financial Times*, May 23, 2011.
195. Stephanie Hanson, 'China, Africa and Oil, Backgrounder,' Council on Foreign Relations, June 6, 2008.
196. The beneficiary countries of the Caribbean Basin Economic Recovery Act that are not parties to the Central America–Dominican Republic–United States Free Trade Agreement (CAFTA–DR) are Antigua and Barbuda, Aruba, The Bahamas, Barbados, Belize, the British Virgin Islands, Dominica, Grenada, Guyana, Haiti, Jamaica, Montserrat, Netherlands Antilles, Panama, St Kitts and Nevis, St Lucia, St Vincent and the Grenadines, and Trinidad and Tobago.
197. The Caribbean–Canada Trade Agreement is a Canadian government programme established in 1986 to provide duty-free access to the Canadian market for all products except the following items: textiles and apparel, footwear, luggage and handbags, leather garments, lubricating oils and methanol. The beneficiary countries are Anguilla, Antigua and Barbuda, The Bahamas, Bermuda, Barbados, Belize, the British Virgin Islands, the Cayman Islands, The Commonwealth of Dominica, Grenada, Guyana, Jamaica, Montserrat, St Kitts and Nevis, St Lucia, St Vincent and the Grenadines, Trinidad and Tobago, and the Turks and Caicos Islands.
198. The CAFTA-DR agreement is a free trade agreement between the US and five Central American countries (Costa Rica, El Salvador, Guatemala, Honduras, and
199. Richard L. Bernal, *Globalization: Everything but Alms: The EPA and Economic Development* (Kingston: Grace Kennedy Foundation, 2008).
200. 'Major Chinese Manufacturer of Biomedical Equipment Signals Intention to Invest in Jamaica.' Go-Jamaica Press Release, JAMPRO, December 2012.
201. M. Whitfield, 'China is Fnancing $3billion Resort in The Bahamas,' *Miami Herald*, February 23, 2011.
202. 'Dominican Tourism Project financed by China.' February 20, 2011. http://ambercoastrealty.com/tourism-investment-for-dominican-republic/ (accessed March 17, 2011).
203. *MOFCOM, 2009 Statistical Bulletin of China's Outward Foreign Direct Investment* (Beijing: MOFCOM, 2010), 116.
204. Martin Jacques, *When China Rules the World: The End of the Western World and the Birth of a New Global Order* (New York: Penguin Press, 2009), 182.
205. G. Bowley, 'Cash Helped China Win Costa Rica's Recognition,' *New York Times*, September 12, 2008, A8.
206. Wolfgang Arlt, *China as a New Tourism Source Market for Jamaica* (Heide, Germany: China Outbound Tourism Research Institute, 2008).
207. Kishore Mahbubani, *The New Asian Hemisphere: The Irresistible Shift of Global Power to the East* (New York: Public Affairs, 2008), 57.

208. *Chinese Outbound Tourism Market* (Madrid: World Tourism Organization, 2006).
209. *Profile of Chinese Arrivals in Jamaica* (Kingston: Jamaica Tourist Board, 2006).
210. J. Archibald, 'Chinese Tourists Viable Option for Barbados,' *Barbados Advocate*, May 3, 2010, 5 and Wolfgang Arlt, *China as a New Tourism Source Market for Jamaica* (Heide, Germany: China Outbound Tourism Research Institute, 2008)
211. Wolfgang Arlt, *China's Outbound Tourism* (London: Routledge, 2006).
212. Elizabeth C. Economy, *The River Runs Black: The Environmental Challenge to China's Future* (Ithaca: Cornell University Press, 2005) and Judith Shapiro, *China's Environmental Challenges* (London: Polity Press, 2012).
213. 'Influx of Chinese Workers Irks Local Unions,' *Inter Press Service*. http://www.ipsnews.net/2007/07/caribbean-influx-of-chinese-workers-irks-local-unions/ July 27, 2007.
214. Evan Ellis, 'China, S.A. as a Local Company in Latin America, Regional Insights, No. 1' (William J. Perry Center for Hemispheric Studies, 2013), 3.
215. Denis Scott Chabrol, 'Chinese Must Employ, Teach Guyanese-private Sector Arm,' March 4, 2013. https://guyaneseonline.files.wordpress.com/2013/03/chinese-businesses-must-employ-and-tech-guyanese-gcbc.pdf.
216. 'China's Bahamas Project Hits Hurdles: Model for Overseas Construction Faces Delays, Stirs Local Resentment,' *Wall Street Journal*, September 30, 2014. http://www.wsj.com/articles/chinas-bahamas-project-hits-hurdles-1412092767.
217. 'Are Chinese Convicts Working on Marriott? ...Brassington Offers "no comment,"' *Kaieteur News*, February 26, 2013.
218. Howard W. French, *China's Second Continent: How a Million Migrants are Building a New Empire in Africa* (New York: Alfred A. Knopf, 2014).
219. 'Intended Builder of Amila Project Being Probed in China for Shoddy Work,' *Stabroek News*, January 26, 2016.
220. Ibid.
221. 'Protests Continue against the All-Chinese Workforce in the Construction of the Marriott Hotel,' February 20, 2013. http://www.capitolnewsgy.com/2013/02/20/protests-continue-against-the-all-chinese-workforce-in-the-construction-of-the-marriott-hotel-20th-feb-2013/.
222. 'Govt. Not Worried Chinese Firm May Do Substandard Work on Marriott,' *Kaieteur News*, September 15, 2014.
223. Ibid.
224. 'NAPA Still World Class: Chinese Builder Defends Performing Arts Academy,' *Daily Express*, September 4, 2014.
225. 'Lifting the Curtain on NAPA's Problems,' *Daily Express*, April 10, 2014.
226. Ibid.
227. 'HDC to Demolish Two $26m Housing Projects,' The *Guardian*, May 29, 2012.
228. Rebecca Ray, Kevin P. Gallagher, Andres Lopez and Cynthia Sanborn, *China in Latin America: Lessons for South-South Cooperation and Sustainable Development* (Boston University, Centro de Investigacion para la Transformation, Tufts University and Universidad del Pacifico, 2015).
229. Audrey Alejandro, Daniel Compagnon, 'China's External Environmental Policy: Understanding China's Environmental Impact in Africa and How It Is Addressed,' *Environmental Practice* 15, no. 3 (2013): 220–27.
230. Rebecca Ray, Kevin P. Gallagher, Andres Lopez and Cynthia Sanborn, *China in Latin America*, 12.
231. David Shinn, 'The Environmental Impact of China's Investment in Africa,' *International Policy Digest*, April 8, 2015. http://intpolicydigest.org/2015/04/08/the-environmental-impact-of-china-s-investment-in-africa/.

232. 'Chinese Contractor Has to Adhere to The Rules-PM,' The *Gleaner*, December 6, 2012.
233. The Financial Times in an editorial suggested that the political leadership in China said 'that it needs fast growth more than it needs clean air, clean soil and clean rivers.' See 'Time China Got Serious on Pollution,' *Financial Times*, March 4, 2014, 10.
234. Elizabeth C. Economy and Michael Levi, *By All Means Necessary: How China's Resource Quest is Changing the World*, reprint ed. (Oxford University Press, 2015), 8.
235. 'Bai Shan Lin Came to Guyana Specifically for Large-scale Logging,' August 10, 2014. http://guyana.hoop.la/topic/bai-shan-lin-came-to-guyana-specifically-for-large-scale-logging.
236. 'Killing our Forest Giants....the PPP and Bai Shan Ling.' http://guyana.hoop.la/printer-friendly-topic/killing-our-forest-giants-the-ppp-and-bai-shan-ling
237. R. Evan Ellis, 'Suriname and the Chinese: Timber, Migration, and Less-Told Stories of Globalization,' *SAIS Review* 32, no. 2 (Summer–Fall 2012): 91 and 'Suriname's Palm-oil Sector to be Rehabilitated.' http://agritrade.cta.int/Agriculture/Commodities/Oil-crops/Suriname-s-palm-oil-sector-to-be-rehabilitated.
238. 'Chinese Investment Company Commits 116 million USD to Developing Suriname Palm oil Industry.' china.aiddata.org/projects/36696?iframey.
239. Michael Buckley, *Meltdown in Tibet: China's Reckless Destruction of Ecosystems from the Highlands of Tibet to the Deltas of Asia* (New York: Palgrave Macmillan, 2014). For a balanced view see Elizabeth C. Economy and Michael Levi, *All Means Necessary: How China's Resource Quest is Changing the World* (New York: Oxford University Press, 2014) and Dambisa Moyo, *Winner Take All: China's Race for Resources and What It Means for the World* (New York: Basic Books, 2012).
240. Wendy Townsend, 'Jamaica Selling Out its Paradise.' http://edition.cnn.com/2014/07/02/opinion/townsend-jamaica-iguana/ (accessed December 11, 2014).
241. 'Saving Goat Islands, Jamaica,' http://voices.nationalgeographic.com/2014/04/22/saving-goat-islands-jamaica/. Accessed December 11, 2014. 'Recent Developments in Proposed Goat Islands Project Worrying – JET,' *Jamaica Gleaner* August 8, 2014. http://jamaica-gleaner.com/latest/article.php?id=54733 (accessed December 11, 2014).
242. 'China has become an important ally in Chile's goal of diversifying its energy matrix away from fossil fuels. China's over-production of solar PV panels came at just the right time for Chile, which was looking for new sources of low-emissions electricity.' See Nicola Borregaard, Annie Dufey, Maria Teresa Ruiz-Tagle and Santiago Sinclair, 'Chinese Incidence on the Chilean Solar Power Sector, Working Group Discussion Paper 2015-4, Global Economic Governance Initiative' (Boston: Boston University, April, 2015).
243. Interview of Dr Omar Davies, formerly Jamaica's Minister of Transport, Works and Housing, March 16, 2016.
244. J. Wang, 'What Drives China's Growing Role in Africa?' (IMF Working Paper No. 07/211, International Monetary Fund, Washington, DC, 2007).
245. Devlin, Estevadeordal and Rodriguez-Clare, 2005; Loser, 2006; Jenkins, Peters & Moreira. 2008, 235–253; Lederman, Olarreaga and Perry, 2009, 5.
246. A. Cesa-Bianchi, M, Pesaran, A. Rebucci and T. Xu, 'China's Emergence in the World and Business Cycles in Latin America' (IDB Working Papers Series No. IDB-WP-266, Inter-American Development Bank, Washington, DC: September 2011).
247. Robert Devlin, Antoni Estevadeordal and Andrés Rodriguez-Clare, eds., *The Emergence of China: Opportunities and Challenges for Latin America and the Caribbean* (Washington, DC: Inter-American Development Bank, 2005); Loser, 2006; Jenkins, Peters & Moreira, 2008, 235–253; Lederman, Olarreaga & Perry, 2009, 5.

248. Cynthia J. Arnson and Jeffrey Davidow, *China, Latin America and the United States. The New Triangle* (Washington, DC, Woodrow Wilson International Center for Scholars, 2011), 4–5.
249. 'China, Brazil Secure $10-Billion Oil Deal.' http://en.ec.com.cn/article/newsroom/newsroomtrade/200905/798171_1.html (accessed May 13, 2010).
250. Bloomberg, 'China Lends Venezuela $20 Billion, Secures Oil Supply.' http://www.bloomberg.com/apps/news?pid=20601110&sid=atNhS5A6tTY4 (accessed May 13, 2010).

Chapter 3

1. Clyde Prestowitz, *Three Billion New Capitalists: The Great in Wealth to the East* (New York: Basic Books, 2006).
2. Ian Boyne, 'Why We Should Fear China,' *Sunday Gleaner*, November 11, 2007.
3. 3rd China–Caribbean Economic and Trade Cooperation Forum. http://cncforumenglish.mofcom.gov.cn/.
4. Revised Treaty Establishing the Caribbean Community, including the Caribbean Single Market and Economy, Article 6, 8.
5. 'Chinese President Says His Visit to Trinidad and Tobago is to Inject Vitality into Bilateral Ties.' english.sina.com/china/2013/0531/595465.html.
6. Draws on Robert G. Sutter, *Chinese Foreign Relations: Power and Policy since the Cold War*, 3rd ed. (Lanham: Rowman & Littlefield Publishers, 2012), 1–37 and Stuart Harris, *China's Foreign Policy* (London: Polity Press, 2014).
7. Section on 'Going Global' from the Eleventh Five-Year Plan (2006–2010) (National People's Congress, 2006). http://news.sina.com.cn/c/2006-03-16/16158457479s.shtml. Translation by IISD Chinese Outward Investment: An emerging Policy Framework 10 Chapter 37, Section 1.
8. Milton W. Meyer, *China: A Concise History*, 2nd ed. (Lanham: Rowman & Littlefield Publishers, 1994), 154.
9. Ibid., 11.
10. Juan Gabriel Tokatlian, 'A View from Latin America,' in *China's Expansion into the Western Hemisphere: Implications for Latin America and the United States*, ed. Riordan Roett and Guadalupe Paz, 65 (Washington, DC: Brookings Institution Press, 2008).
11. 'St. Kitts-Nevis Prime Minister Harris Uses Inaugural UN Address to Make Pitch for Taiwan,' *Times Caribbean Online*.
12. Bilateral Exchanges, Ministry of Commerce of the People's Republic of China. http://english.mofcom.gov.cn/.
13. 'Easy Money: The Caribbean and Taiwan,' The *Economis*t, April 7, 2004.
14. David Zweig and Bi Jianhai, 'China's Global Hunt for Energy,' *Foreign Affairs* 84, no. 5 (September/October 2005): 25–38. This is particularly the case in Africa. See John Ghazvinian, *Untapped: The Scramble for Africa's Oil* (New York: Harcourt, 2008), chapter 7.
15. 'China's Xi in Trinidad to Talk Energy, Bolster Ties,' The *Wall Street Journal* Online. http://www.wsj.com/articles/SB10001424127887324412604578519283382646360.
16. 'Taiwan to Search for Oil in Caribbean Sea,' *Jamaica Observer*, September 26, 2009.
17. *The Oceans Economy: Opportunities and Challenges for Small Island Developing States* (New York and Geneva: United Nations, 2014), 7.
18. Edward Tse, *The China Strategy: Harnessing the Power of the World's Fastest Growing Economy* (New York: Basic Books, 2010), 61–71.

19. Hyun-Hoon Lee, Donghyun Park, and Jing Wang, 'Different Types of Firms, Products, and Directions of Trade: The Case of the People's Republic of China, Asian Development Bank' (Working Paper Series on Regional Economic Integration No. 101, August 2012).
20. Richard L. Bernal, *Globalization. Everything But Alms: The EPA and Economic Development* (Kingston: Grace Kennedy Foundation, 2008).
21. This shift towards increased private sector involvement relative to official engagement has happened in other regions, for example, Africa. See Jian-Ye Wang, 'What Drives China's Growing Role in Africa' (IMF Working Paper No. 07/211, International Monetary Fund, Washington, DC, October 2007).
22. R. Foot, 'Chinese Strategies in a US-hegemonic Global Order: Accommodating and Hedging,' *International Affairs* 82, no. 1 (January 2006): 7–94.
23. David P. Calleo, *Follies of Power: America's Unipolar Fantasy* (Cambridge: Cambridge University Press, 2009), 50.
24. Elizabeth C. Economy and Adam Segal, 'The G-2 Mirage: Why the United States and China Are Not Ready to Upgrade Ties,' *Foreign Affairs* 88, no. 3 (May/June 2009): 2–6.
25. Steven W. Mosher, *Hegemon: China's Plan to Dominate Asia and the World* (New York: Encounter Books, 2006) and Bill Gertz, *The China Threat: How the People's Republic Targets America* (Darby, Penn.: Diane Publihing Company, 2002).
26. The long decline of China is traced in Will Hutton, *The Writing on the Wall: Why We Must Embrace China as a Partner or Face It as an Enemy* (New York: Free Press, 2006), chapter 2.
27. Angus Madison, *Chinese Economic Performance in the Long Run* (Paris: OECD, 1998).
28. *The Emergence of China: Opportunities and Challenges for Latin America and the Caribbean* (Washington, DC: Inter-American Development Bank, 2005), 125–40.
29. Fred Bergsten, 'The Asian Monetary Crisis: Proposed Remedies,' Testimony to the US House Representatives, Committee on Banking and Financial Services, November 13, 1997 and 'When China and India Go down Together,' The *Economist* 345, no. 22 (1997): 78–79.
30. This will have to be a priority for Chinese policy. Shahid Yusuf and Kaoru Nabeshima, *China's Development Priorities* (Washington, DC: World Bank, 2006), 78–79.
31. Cynthia A. Watson, 'U. S. Responses to China's Growing Interests in Latin America: Dawning Recognition of a Changing Hemisphere,' in *Enter the Dragon? China's Presence in Latin America* (Washington, DC: Woodrow Wilson International Center for Scholars, February, 2007).
32. Since January 2007 China currently has 2,146 peacekeepers deployed in ten missions mainly in Africa with the heaviest concentration of peacekeeping troops in Liberia where there are 563. See also Bill Gill and Chin-Hao Huang, 'China's Expanding Peacekeeping Role: Its Significance and the Policy Implications,' Stockholm International Peace Research Institute, Policy Brief, February, 2009.
33. The 'Peaceful Rise' school of thought has given way more assertive approaches, including an end to what some view as appeasement on the issue of Taiwan. See Mark Leonard, *What Does China Think?* (London: Fourth Estate, 2008), 88–90.
34. Jiang Shixue, 'The Chinese Foreign Policy Perspective,' in *China's Expansion into the Western Hemisphere: Implications for Latin America and the United States*, ed. Riordan Roett and Guadalupe Paz, 32 (Washington, DC: Brookings Institution Press, 2008).
35. The possibility of a US–China military conflict is still felt by many to be a distinct possibility. See Steve Tsang, *If China Attacks Taiwan: Military Strategy, Politics and Economics* (London: Routledge, 2006) and Ted Galen Carpenter, *America's Coming War with China: A Collision Course over Taiwan* (London: Palgrave Macmillan, 2006).

36. Richard C. Bush and Michael E. O'Hanlon, *A War Like No Other: The Truth about China's Challenge to America* (New York: Wiley, 2007).
37. Richard L. Bernal. 'China and Small Island Developing States,' forthcoming in *The China Monitor* (2012).
38. Richard L. Bernal, 'US-Caribbean Relations at the Dawn of the Twenty-First Century,' in, *The United States and Caribbean Strategies: Three Assessments, CSIS, Policy Papers on the Americas*, Vol. XIII, Study 4, ed. Richard L. Bernal, Anthony T. Bryan and Georges A. Fauriol (Washington, DC: Center for Strategic and International Studies, April 2001), 3–25; and Connie Veillette, Marl P. Sullivan, Clare Ribando Seelke and Coleen W. Cook, *U.S. Assistance to Latin America and the Caribbean: FY2006-FY2008 CRS Report to Congress* (Washington, DC: Congressional Research Service, December 28, 2007).
39. Timothy Harris, 'The Dynamics of International Diplomacy: The Case of China and Taiwan in the Caribbean, 1971–2005,' *Journal of Caribbean International Relations*, no. 2 (October 2006): 122–37. See page 136.
40. During the 1970s, some governments saw closer economic relations with socialist countries as an integral part of state-centred development strategies and the diversification of external relations, e.g., Guyana and Jamaica. See Richard L. Bernal, 'Restructuring Jamaica's Economic Relations with Socialist Countries, 1974–80,' *Development and Change* 17, no. 4 (October 1986): 607–634.
41. CIA Handbook 2009. https://www.cia.gov/library/publications/the-world-factbook.
42. 'China Statistical Yearbook 2006'. http://www.stats.gov.cn/tjsj/ndsj/2006/indexeh.htm. (accessed November 26, 2007).
43. Michael Glosny, China's Foreign Aid Policy: Lifting States out of Poverty or Leaving Them to the Dictators? (Washington, DC: Center for Strategic for International Studies, 2006).
44. Lan Xue, 'China's Foreign Aid Policy and Architecture,' IDS Bulletin 45, no. 4 (July 2014): 36–45. See page 38.
45. Ratna Sahay, 'Stabilization, Debt, and Fiscal Policy in the Caribbean' (IMF Working Paper 05/26, Monetary Fund, Washington, DC, 2005).
46. Kevin P. Gallagher, Amos Irwin and Katherine Koleski, *The New Banks in Town: Chinese Finance in Latin America* (Washington, DC: Inter-American Dialogue, 2012).
47. Ibid.
48. Tied aid has a long history. See Teresa Hayter, *Aid as Imperialism* (Harmondsworth: Penguin Books, 1971).
49. The Tied Aid 'Round Trip' – Oxfam America. http://www.oxfamamerica.org/static/oa3/files/aidnow-tiedaidroundtrip.pdf.
50. Catrinus Jepma, *The Tying of Aid* (Paris: Organization for Economic Co-operation and Development, 1991).
51. Full Text: China's Foreign Aid news.xinhuanet.com › Home › China. English.news.cn 2011-04-21.
52. 'China's Information Office of the State Council' (White Paper on China's Foreign Aid, Appendix I). http://english.gov.cn/official/2011-04/21/content_1849913_10.htm.
53. This critical point is made in Henry Kissinger, *On China* (New York: Penguin, 2011), 2.
54. Larry Rohter, 'Taiwan and Beijing Duel for Recognition in Central America,' *New York Times*, August 5, 1997.
55. See Sara Bongiorni, *A Year Without 'Made in China': One Family's True Life Adventure in the Global Economy* (New York: Wiley, 2007).
56. Robert Devlin, Antoni Estevadeordal and Andres Rodriguez-Clare, eds., *The Emergence of China: Opportunities and Challenges for Latin America and the Caribbean*

(Washington, DC: Inter-American Development Bank/Cambridge: Harvard University, 2006), 83.

57. 'Haier Service Centre Opens in Guyana,' *Guyana Times International*, February 24, 2012.
58. 'The Coffee Industry Board (CIF) Targets China for New Coffee Markets,' *Sunday Gleaner*, November 22, 2009.
59. Matthew Crabbe, *Myth-Busting China's Numbers: Understanding and Using China's Statistics* (New York: Palgrave Macmillan, 2014), 104.
60. Ibid., 105.
61. David Katz, 'War in a Tokyo: The Curious World of Japan's Reggae Scene.' http://www.factmag.com/.../war-ina-tokyo-the-curious-world-of-japans-re.
62. UN World Tourism Organization.
63. Kishore Mahbubani, *The New Asian Hemisphere: The Irresistible Shift of Global Power to the East* (New York: Public Affairs, 2008), 57.
64. Martin Jacques, *When China Rules the World: The End of the Western World and the Birth of a New Global World*, 2nd ed. (New York: Penguin Books, 2012), 512.
65. Michael J. Silverstein, Abneek Singh, Carol Liao and David Micheal, *The $10 Trillion Prize: Captivating the Newly Affluent in China and India* (Boston: Harvard Business Press, 2012), 45.
66. *Chinese Outbound Tourism Market* (UN World Tourism Organization, 2006).
67. 'China Signs MOU to Establish Air Link with Ja,' *Jamaica Observer*, June 17, 2015, 3.
68. Cuba–China Link Could Boost Tourism – World Travel Online.
69. news.travel168.net/20150123/35620.html, January 23, 2015.
70. C. Fred Bergsten, Bates Gill, Nicholas R. Lardy and Derek Mitchell, *China: The Balance Sheet: What the World Needs to Know Now about the Emerging Superpower* (New York: Public Affairs, 2006), 4.
71. 'Federation of International Trade Agencies (FITA) China Business Guide.' http://www.fita.org (accessed February 7, 2007).
72. 'China to build aluminum smelter in Trinidad', China Aluminium Network, http://www.alu.com.cn/enNews/NewsInfo_1755.html (accessed June 27, 2008).
73. David Renwick, 'How Ignorance Killed the Smelter,' *Trinidad Express*, September 22, 2010.
74. Edmond Campbell, 'Chinese Eye Air J,' The *Gleaner*, March 28, 2008, 1.
75. 'Jamaica and China Pursuing Stronger Business Partnership,' *Caribbean Net News*, August 18, 2009.
76. Lauren A. E. Schuker, 'Courting the Chinese,' *Wall Street Journal*, June 21, 2012.
77. Robert D. Kaplan, 'The Geography of Chinese Power,' *Foreign Affairs* 89, no. 3 (May/June 2010), 22–41.
78. Timothy Harris, 'The Dynamic of International Diplomacy: The Case of China and Taiwan in the Caribbean, 1971 to 2005,' *Journal of Caribbean International Relations*, no. 2 (October 2006): 122–37. See page 130.
79. 'Emmanuel confirmed as Saint Lucia's first Ambassador to Taiwan.' http://www.stlucianewsonline.com/saint-lucias-first-ambassador-to-taiwan-will-soon-leave-for-taipei/#sthash.WY4glRFC.dpuf.
80. 'China vs. Taiwan: Battle for Influence in the Caribbean.' http://www.coha.org/china-vs-taiwan-battle-for-influence-in-the-caribbean/ (accessed March 13, 2012).
81. 'St Kitts and Nevis to Speak up for Taiwan at UN,' The *China Post*, August 21, 2015. http:/www.chinapost.com.tw/taiwan/intl-community/2015/08/21/443824/St-Kitts.htm.%20%20.

Chapter 4

1. Jeffrey A. Bader, Obama and China's Rise: An Insider's Account of America's Asia Strategy (Washington, DC: Brookings Institution, 2012), 18–20.
2. The concern has been raised that the Caribbean is so fixated with relations with China that is has neglected relations with India. See 'Embrace China, but Let's Not Forget Old Friend India,' *Jamaica Observer*, Editorial, July 18, 2012.
3. For a critique of this view which he labels the 'soothing scenario', see James Mann, *The China Fantasy: How Our Leaders Explain Away Chinese Repression* (New York: Viking Penguin, 2007).
4. James Mann, *The China Fantasy: Why Capitalism Will Not Bring Democracy to China* (New York: Penguin, 2008).
5. Minxin Pei, *China's Trapped Transition: The Limits of Developmental Autocracy* (Cambridge: Harvard University Press, 2008).
6. While it is dated, it is typical of a certain alarmist mindset. See Gordon G. Chang, *The Coming Collapse of China* (New York: Random House, 2001).
7. Nicholas R. Lardy, *Sustaining China's Economic Growth: After the Global Financial Crisis* (Washington, DC: Peterson Institute for International Economics, 2012).
8. Justin Yifu Lin, *Demystifying the Chinese Economy* (Cambridge: Cambridge University Press, 2012), 16.
9. Kemal Dervis and Karim Foda, 'Emerging Asia and Rebalancing the World Economy,' in *Asia and Policymaking for the Global Economy*, ed. Kemal Dervis, Masahiro Kawai and Domenico Lombardi, 19–56 (Tokyo: Asian Development Bank Institute and Washington, DC: Brookings Institution Press, 2011).
10. David Shambaugh, 'The New Strategic Triangle: US and European Reactions to China's Rise,' *Washington Quarterly* 28, no. 3 (2005): 7–25.
11. 'The Chinese in Africa: Trying to Pull it Together,' *The Economist*, April 23, 2011, 73–75.
12. Richard Dowden, *Africa: Altered States, Ordinary Miracles* (New York: Public Affairs, 2009), 485.
13. Ibid., 484.
14. 'US ignoring region-PM,' *Trinidad Guardian*, September 6, 2006, 1.
15. 'Manning Critizes USG for Ignoring Caribbean.' http://dazzlepod.com/cable/06PORTOFSPAIN1040/ibbean http://dazzlepod.co.
16. Sir Ronald Sanders, 'Getting U.S. Attention in the Caribbean: Must It Be Chaos?' *Jamaica Observer*, September 20, 2009.
17. *Caribbean Insight* 33, no. 12 (March 26, 2010). See also 'PM Spencer pledges support for China,' March 17, 2012. http://www.caribarena.com/antigua/news/latest/100012-pm-spencer-pledges-support-for-china.html (accessed August 7, 2012).
18. Don Bohning, 'US Relations with Caribbean under Strain,' *Miami Herald*, October 27, 1998.
19. Ross Terrill, *The New Chinese Empire and What It Means for the United States* (New York: Basic Books, 2004) and Richard Bernstein and Ross H. Munro, *The Coming Conflict with China* (New York: Vintage, 1998).
20. Fareed Zakaria, 'The Rise of a Fierce Yet Fragile Superpower,' *Newsweek*, December 31, 2007/January 7, 2008, 12–13.
21. Wang Jisi, 'China's Search for Stability with America,' *Foreign Affairs* 84, no. 5 (September/October 2005): 39–48.
22. G. John Ikenberry, 'The Rise of China and the Future of the West,' *Foreign Affairs* 87, no. 2 (January/February 2008): 23–37.

23. Michael Elliott, 'The Chinese Century,' *Time Magazine*, November 11, 2007.
24. China's presence in Latin America is discussed in Cynthia Arnson, Mark Mohr and Riordan Roett, eds., *Enter the Dragon? China's Presence in Latin America* (Washington, DC: Woodrow Wilson Center for International Scholars, 2008).
25. 'China Overtakes Japan as Third Largest Exporter,' *Financial Times*, April 16, 2005.
26. James Kynge, *China Shakes the World: A Titan's Rise and Troubled Future and the Challenge for America* (New York: Mariner Books, 2007) and Ted C. Fishman, *China, Inc. How the Rise of the Next Superpower Challenges America and the World* (New York Scribner, 2006).
27. C. Fred Bergsten, Bates Gill, Nicholas R. Lardy and Derek Mitchell, *China: The Balance Sheet: What the World Needs to Know Now about the Emerging Superpower* (New York: Public Affairs, 2006) page 100.
28. John Gapper, 'Don't Boot out Tomorrow's Nobels,' *Financial Times*, October 13, 2011, 11.
29. James McGregor, *One Billion Customers: Lessons from the Front Lines of Doing Business in China* (New York: Free Press, 2007).
30. Stephen Leeb and Gregory Dorset, *Red Alert: How China's Growing Prosperity Threatens the American Way of Life* (New York: Business Plus, 2011).
31. Moises Naim, *Illicit: How Smugglers, Traffickers and Copycats are Hijacking the Global Economy* (New York: Doubleday Publishers, 2005), 119–30.
32. These are set out in *The Emergence of China: Opportunities and Challenges for Latin America for Latin America and the Caribbean* (Washington, DC: Inter-American Development Bank, 2005), 102.
33. Peter W. Navarro and Gregg Autry, *Death by China: Confronting the Dragon: A Global Call to Action* (New York: Pearson Prentice Hall, 2011).
34. These internal problems and their likely impact on China are discussed in Duncan Hewitt, *China: Getting Rich First* (New York: Pegasus Books, 2008).
35. Susan L. Shirk, *China: Fragile Superpower: How China's Internal Politics Could Derail Its Peaceful Rise* (Oxford: Oxford University Press, 2007).
36. Nicholas Eberstadt. 'Will China (continue) to Rise,' in *The Rise of China: Essays on the Future of Competition*, ed. Gary J. Schmitt, 154 (New York: Encounter Books, 2009).
37. Richard L. Bernal, *Globalization, Trade and Economic Development: A Study of the CARIFORM-EU Economic Partnership Agreement* (New York: Palgrave Macmillan, 2013).
38. Helen Morgan, 'Policy, Politics and Power: The Future for EU Leadership on Globaldev,' October 28, 2015. European Centre for Development Policy Management Weekly Newsletter, October 30, 2015.
39. David Shambaugh, 'The New Strategic Triangle: US and European Reactions to China's Rise,' *Washington Quarterly* 28, no. 3 (2005): 7–25.
40. André Wright, 'We Jamaicans Can't Blame our Entire Malaise on the Evil White Bogeyman,' *The Guardian*, October 2, 2015.
41. China Global Investment Tracker, American Enterprise Institute. https://www.aei.org/china-global-investment-tracker.
42. The UK's deals worth billions with China: what do they really mean? http://www.theguardian.com (accessed October 24, 2015).
43. Nina Hachigian and Mona Sutphen, *The Next American Century: How the US Can Thrive as Other Powers Rise* (New York: Simon & Schuster, 2008).
44. Kathrin Hille, 'China Seeks Reform of UN Peacekeeping,' *Financial Times*, 18 January, 2009.

45. Aron Viner, *The Emerging Power of Japanese Money* (Homewood: Dow-Jones-Irwin, 1988) and Clyde V. Prestowitz, Jr., *Trading Places: How We Allowed Japan to Take the Lead* (New York: Basic Books, 1988).
46. William H. Overholt, *Asia, America and the Transformation of Geopolitics* (Cambridge: Cambridge University Press, 2008), 79.
47. Bill Emmott, *Rivals: How the Power Struggle between China, India and Japan will Shape the Next Decade* (New York: Harcourt Books, 2008), 96–134.
48. 'Japan Not Leaving it All to China in the Caribbean,' *Jamaica Observer*, Editorial, July 30, 2014.
49. High Commission of India, Port of Spain, Trinidad and ... http://www.hcipos.in/eoi.php?id=Trade.
50. Hu Shauha, 'Small State Foreign Policy: The Diplomatic Recognition of Taiwan,' China: An International Journal 13, no. 2 (August 2015): 1–23.
51. Timothy Harris, 'The Dynamic of International Diplomacy: The Case of China and Taiwan in the Caribbean, 1971 to 2005,' *Journal of Caribbean International Relations*, No. 2 (October 2006): 122–37. See page 133.
52. Prime Minister Dr. Kenny D. Anthony - Address to the Nation on *relations* with China and Taiwan. http://www.stlucia.gov.lc/.../prime-minister-dr-kenny-d-anthony-address-..(accessed *September 14, 2012).*Cached
53. 'St. Lucia Torn between Two Lovers – China and Japan,' *Jamaica Observer*, September 16, 2012.
54. Prime Minister Dr. Kenny D. Anthony - Address to the Nation on *relations* with China and Taiwan. http://www.stlucia.gov.lc/.../prime-minister-dr-kenny-d-anthony-address-..(accessed September 14, 2012).
55. 'Taiwan restructures Grenada debt at 50 percent reduction,' *Caribbean News Now*, January 8, 2015. http://www.caribbeannewsnow.com/topstory-Taiwan-restructures-Grenada-debt-at-50-percent-reduction-24287.html.
56. Revised Treaty Establishing the Caribbean Community including the Caricom Single Market and Economy, Article 6, 8.
57. A. Collinder, 'The Coffee Industry Board (CIB) Targets China for New Coffee Markets,' *Jamaica Gleaner*, November 22, 2009, 10.
58. Edward Tse, *The China Strategy: Harnessing the Power of the World's Fastest Growing Economy* (New York: Basic Books, 2010), 52–54.
59. Globally dispersed transnational Chinese business networks are active in trade with China throughout the world. See Murray Weidenbaum and Samuel Hughes, *The Bamboo Network* (New York: Free Press, 1996).
60. Michael J. Silverstein, Abheek Singhi, Carol Liao and David Michael, *The $10 Trillion Prize: Captivating the Newly Affluent in China and India* (Boston: Harvard Business Press, 2012), 45.
61. Ibid., and Elizabeth Becker, *Overbooked: The Exploding Business of Travel and Tourism* (New York: Simon& Schuster, 2013), 309.
62. Sir Roland Sanders, 'Get a Slice of the Chinese Tourism Cake,' *Caribbean Net News*, March 20, 2006; 'Barbados: Caribbean Urged to Pursue Chinese Tourists,' *The Voice*, August 17, 2009; and Dominican Rep. Has What Chinese Tourists Look for ... http://www.dominicantoday.com/.../Dominican-Rep-has-wha.Dominican Today June 19, 2015.
63. 'Jamaica: Cruise Ship Brings "Record" of Chinese Tourists,' http:// www.philstar.com/.../jamaica-cruise-ship-brings-recor...The Philippine Star April 23, 2015.

64. 'Barbados Could Benefit from Chinese Tourists, http://www.caribbeannewsnow.com/headline-Barbados-could-benefit-from-Ch...Feb 6, 2014.
65. Elizabeth Becker, *Overbooked: The Exploding Business of Travel and Tourism* (New York: Simon & Schuster, 2013), 312–41.
66. Wolfgang Arlt, *China as a New Tourism Source Market for Jamaica* (China Outbound Tourism Research Institute, 2008).
67. The newness and complexity of outbound Chinese tourism is presented in Wolfgang Arlt, *China's Outbound Tourism* (London: Routledge, 2006).
68. There were 976 Chinese tourist in Jamaica in 2006 of total arrivals of 1,678, 905 in that year, with 55 per cent staying in private homes. See *Profile of Chinese Arrivals in Jamaica* (Kingston: Jamaica Tourist Board, March 2006).
69. 'Brand Jamaica Gets Big Boost in Beijing, China,' *Jamaica Observer*, September 1, 2015, 1.
70. Cuba Briefing, Caribbean Council, Issue number 839, September 14, 2015 and Cuba Briefing, number 840, September 21, 2015.
71. Edward Tse, *The China Strategy: Harnessing the Power of the World's Fastest Growing Economy* (New York: Basic Books, 2010), 61–71.
72. Hyun-Hoon Lee, Donghyun Park and Jing Wang, 'Different Types of Firms, Products, and Directions of Trade: The Case of the People's Republic of China' (Asian Development Bank Working Paper Series on Regional Economic Integration No. 101 August 2012).
73. The transformation of China's role as a source of aid is analysed in Gregory T. Chin, 'China as a "Net donor": Tracking Dollars and Sense,' *Cambridge Review of International Affairs* 25, no. 4 (December 2012): 579–603.
74. Ratna Sahay, 'Stabilization, Debt, and Fiscal Policy in the Caribbean' (IMF Working Paper WP05/26, International Monetary Fund, Washington, 2005).
75. Kevin Greenidge, Roland Craigwell, Chrystol Thomas and Lisa Drakes, 'Threshold Effects of Sovereign Debt: Evidence from the Caribbean' (IMF Working Paper WP/12/157, International Monetary Fund, Washington, June, 2012).
76. Richard L. Bernal, 'Dragon in the Caribbean. China–CARICOM Economic Relations,' *Round Table* 99, no. 408 (June 2010): 281–302.
77. Kevin P. Gallagher and Roberto Porzecanski, *Dragon in the Room: China and the Future of Latin American Industrialization* (Stanford: Stanford University Press, 2010), 11–38.
78. Ibid., 39–82.
79. Jorge Alberto Lopez A., Oscar Rodil M. And Saul Valdez G., 'The impact of China's Iincursion into the North American Free Trade Agreement (NAFTA) Intra-industry Trade,' *CAPAL Review*, no. 114 (December 2014): 83–100. See pages 98–99.
80. Kevin P. Gallagher and Roberto Porzecanski, *Dragon in the Room*, 83–97.
81. For example, Kenneth Rapoza, 'The Foreign Companies That are Buying up America,' Forbes Magazine, June 27, 2013. http://www.forbes.com/sites/kenrapoza/2013/06/27/the-foreign-companies-that-are-buying-up-america.
82. Diane Francis, 'Why are We Allowing China to bBuy American Companies?' *New York Post*, December 15, 2013, 1.
83. Richard L. Bernal, 'Foreign Investment and Development in Jamaica,' *Inter-American Economic Affairs* 38, no. 2 (Autumn 1984): 3–21.
84. 'Influx of Chinese Workers Irks Local Unions,' http://www.ipsnews.net/.../caribbean-influx-of-chinese-workers-irks-local-union (accessed July 27, 2007).
85. Evan Ellis, China, 'S.A. as a Local Company in Latin America,' *Regional Insights*, No. 1 (William J. Perry Center for Hemispheric Studies, 2013): 203.

86. Denis Scott Chabrol, Chinese Must Employ, Teach Guyanese Private Sector Arm, 4 March 4, 2013. http://www.demerarawaves.com/.../chinese-businesses-must-employ-teach- ...
87. This comment is based on the author's site visit in March 2015.
88. Carolyn Cooper, 'Selling Jamaica to "Mr. Chin,"' *Jamaica Observer*, 5July 5, 2015, 6.
89. Paula Williams Madison, *Finding Samuel Lowe: China, Jamaica, Harlem* (New York: Amistad, 2015), 193.
90. 'Cops Link Chinese to Organised Crime,' *Trinidad & Tobago Guardian*, July 18, 2015.
91. H.G. Helps, 'Chinese under Siege – Criminals, Cops Extort, Rob Businessmen at Will,' *Jamaica Observer*, July 14, 2013.
92. There were anti-Chinese riots nearly 100 years ago. See Howard Johnson, 'The Anti-Chinese Riots Of 1918 in Jamaica,' *Caribbean Quarterly* 28, no. 3 (1982): 19–32.
93. Adrian H. Ahearn, 'The Mexico–China–US Triangle: An Ethnographic Perspective,' in *China and the New Triangular Relationships in the Americas: China and Future of US–Mexico Relations*, ed. Enrique Dussel Peters, Adrian H. Ahearn and Harley Shaiken, 59–65 (Miami: Center for Latin American Studies and Mexico City: Centro de Estudios China-Mexico, Universidad Nacional Autonomía de Mexico, 2013).
94. Ariel C. Armony and Nicolás Velásquez, 'Anti-Chinese Sentiment in Latin America: An Analysis,' in *Beyond Raw Materials: Who are the Actors in the Latin America and Caribbean-China Relationship?*, ed. Enrique Dussel Peters and Ariel C. Armony, 17–49 (Buenos Aires: Nueva Sociedad, Buenos Aires: Friedrich-Ebert- Stiftung, México DF: Red Académica de América Latina y el Caribe sobre China and Pittsburgh: University of Pittsburgh, Center of Latin American Studies, 2015).
95. Chris Alden, *China in Africa* (London: Zed Books, 2007), 47–56.
96. 'Influx of Chinese Business Causing Concern Regionally,' *Antigua Observer*, January 30, 2012. http:// www.antiguaobserver.com/?p=70544 (accessed September 13, 2012).
97. Simon Romero, 'With Aid and Migrants, China Expands Its Presence in a South American Nation,' *New York Times*, April 11, 2011.
98. R. Evan Ellis, 'Suriname and the Chinese: Timber, Migration, and the Less-Told Stories of Globalization,' *SAIS Review* XXXII, no. 2 (Summer-Fall 2012): 85–97.
99. Ibid., 91.
100. Patricia Rey Mallén, 'China's Stake In Suriname: Why Is Beijing Interested in This Small South American Country?' *International Business Times*, June 1, 2013. China's Stake In Suriname - International Business Times. http://www.ibtimes.com/chinas-stake-suriname-wh...(accessed September 10, 2015).
101. H. Even Ellis, *China on the Ground in Latin America: Challenges for the Chinese and Impacts on the Region* (New York: Palgrave Macmillan, 2014), 188–93.
102. Brent Dean, 'U.S. Fears Baha Mar Chinese Migration,' *The Freeport News*, June 14, 2011. http://freeport.nassauguardian.net/national_local/65829088305882.php (accessed July 5, 2012).
103. 'Roulette Machines, We Linked to Laundering,' *Trinidad and Tobago Guardian*, October 5, 2014, 1.
104. Jason Chow, 'Cash-Strapped Nations Race to Attract Chinese Immigrants: Best Deals Come From Countries in Caribbean and Southern Europe,' *Wall Street Journal*, July 30, 2013.
105. Peter Wise, 'Investment or plan B Escape Route? Why Europe Attracts the Super-rich,' *Financial Times*, October 9, 2014, 4.

106. Lazaro Zamora and Theresa Cardinal Brown, *EB-5 Program: Successes, Challenges, and Opportunities for States and Localities* (Washington, DC: Bipartisan Policy Center, September, 2015), 4.
107. Kim Gittleson, 'Where is the Cheapest Place to Buy Citizenship?' June 4, 2014. http://www.bbc.com/news/business-27674135 (accessed November 27, 2015).
108. Donald J. Harris, 'Jamaica's Debt-Propelled Economy: A Failed Economic Strategy and Its Aftermath' (SALISES Working Paper Series No.1, University of the West Indies, 2010).
109. Richard L. Bernal, 'The Vicious Circle of Foreign Indebtedness: The Case of Jamaica,' in *External Debt and Development Strategy in Latin America*, ed. Antonio Jorge, Jorge SalazarCarrillo and Frank DiazPou, 111–28 (New York: Pergamon Press, 1985).
110. Richard L. Bernal, 'The Debt-Development Dilemma of Small Island Developing States: Review Article,' Social and Economic Studies 64, no. 2 (June 2015): 229–43.
111. Inder Ruprah, Karl Melgarejo and Ricardo Sierra, *Is There a Caribbean Sclerosis?* (Washington, DC: Inter-American Development Bank, 2014).
112. Compton Bourne, 'Financing for Development Challenges in Caribbean SIDS: A Case for Review of Eligibility Criteria for Access to Concessional Financing,' Report Prepared for the United Nations Development Programme, June, 2015.
113. Michele Robinson, 'Does Debt Restructuring Work? An Assessment of Remedial Actions,' in *Debt and Development in Small Island Developing States*, ed. Damien King and David Tennant, 207–18. See 214 (New York: Palgrave Macmillan, 2014) and IMF's World Economic Outlook Statistic 2015.
114. Full text: China's Policy Paper on Latin America and the Caribbean... news.xinhuanet.com/english/2008-11/05/content_10308117.htm.
115. 'CARICOM Wants to Use China's US$3 billion for Debt Restructuring,' January 11, 2015. http://cms2.caricom.org/media-center/communications/news-from-the-community/caricom-wants-to-use-chinas-us3-billion-for-debt-restructuring/P50.
116. Ken Davis, 'Inward FDI from China and its policy context,' Columbia FDI Profiles, Vale Columbia Center on Sustainable International Investment, October 18, 2010, 5.
117. *Doing Business 2014* (Washington, DC: World Bank/International Finance Corporation, 2013), and *Doing Business 2008* (Washington, DC: World Bank/International Finance Corporation, 2007).
118. *The Global Competitiveness Report 2015–16* (Geneva: World Economic Forum, 2013).
119. Inder Ruprah, Karl Melgarejo and Ricardo Sierra, *Is There a Caribbean Sclerosis? Stagnating Economic Growth in the Caribbean* (Washington, DC: Inter-American Development Bank, 2014), 27.
120. These are set out in Richard L. Bernal, *Globalization, Trade and Economic Development. The CARIFORUM–EU Economic Partnership Agreement* (New York: Palgrave MacMillan, 2013), 186–98.
121. The membership of the Caribbean Association of Investment Promotion Agencies comprises 19 investment promotion agencies within the region, including representation from the Dutch and British Overseas Countries and Territories. The member countries include: Antigua and Barbuda, The Bahamas, Barbados, Belize, the Cayman Islands, Curacao, Dominica, Dominican Republic, Grenada, Guyana, Haiti, Jamaica, St Kitts and Nevis, Montserrat, St Lucia, St Vincent and the Grenadines, Suriname, Trinidad and Tobago, and the Turks and Caicos Islands.
122. 'China extends US$118 million in aid to Jamaica,' *Caribbean Net News*. http://www.caribbeannetnews.com (accessed May 5, 2010).

123. Joel Backaler, *China Goes West: Everything You Need to Know About Chinese Companies Going Global* (New York: Palgrave Macmillan, 2014), 10–11.
124. J. Child and S. Rodriguez, 'The internationalization of Chinese firms: A Case for Theoretical Extension,' *Management and Organization Review* 1, no. 3 (2005): 381–410.
125. For example, the sale of bauxite to the Soviet Union from the late 1970s. See Carlton E. Davis, *Jamaica in the World Aluminum Industry Vol. II, 1974–1988: Bauxite Levy Negotiations* (Kingston: Jamaica Bauxite Institute, 1995), 315.
126. Adam Hersh, 'Chinese State-Owned and State-Controlled Enterprises,' Testimony before the US–China Economic and Security Review Commission, February 15, 2012. http://www.americanprogressaction.org/issues/economy/report/2012/02/15/11069/chinese-state-owned-and-state-controlled-enterprises.
127. David Shambaugh, *China Goes Global: The Partial Power* (Oxford: Oxford University Press, 2013), 180.
128. Martin Jacques, *When China Rules the World: The End of the Western World and the Birth of a New Global Order* (New York: Penguin, 2009), 182.
129. MOFCOM, 2009 Statistical Bulletin of China's Outward Foreign Direct Investment (Beijing, 2010), 116.
130. Thilo Hanemen, 'Changing Patterns of Chinese FDI. Drivers and Implications,' Stanford Center for International Development, December 6, 2011.
131. Ken Davies, 'Outward FDI from China and its Policy, 2012,' Columbia FDI Profiles, Vale Columbia Center on Sustainable International Investment, June 7, 2012, 14–15.
132. China Harbour Engineering Company Ltd. > About CHEC ...www.chec.bj.cn › Home › About CHEC › Corporate Overview.
133. China Communications Construction Company Ltd.-Home Page en.ccccltd.cn/.
134. These concerns prompted the Prime Minister of Jamaica to give a public assurance that all regulations would be observed in a road construction project being executed by a Chinese company, China Harbour Engineering Company, which has satisfactorily completed several projects in Jamaica. See 'Chinese Contractor Has to Adhere to The Rules-PM,' The *Gleaner*, December 6, 2012.
135. The *Financial Times* in an editorial suggested that the political leadership in China implied 'that it needs fast growth more than it needs clean air, clean soil and clean rivers.' See 'Time China Got Serious on Pollution,' *Financial Times*, March 4, 2014, 10.
136. Mallory Micetich, 'New NAM Ad Highlights China Pollution Offsetting Environmental Improvements by the United States,' September 9, 2015. http://www.nam.org/Newsroom/Press-Releases/2015/09/New-NAM-Ad-Highlights-China-Pollution-Offsetting-Environmental-Improvements-by-the-United-States/#sthash.v97WNPl3.dpuf.
137. Julie Hirschfield Davis and Corral Davenport, 'China to Announce Cap-and-Trade Program to Limit Emissions,' *New York Times*, September 24, 2015, 1.
138. Joshua D. Margolis and James P. Walsh, 'Misery Loves Companies: Rethinking Social Initiatives by Business,' *Administrative Science Quarterly* 48, no. 2 (June 2003): 268–305.
139. Adam B. Jaffe, S. R. Peterson, P. R. Portney, and R. N. Stavins, 'Environmental Regulation and the Competitiveness of US Manufacturing: What Does the Evidence Tell Us?' *Journal of Economic Literature* 33, Issue1 (March 1995): 132–63.
140. Silvia Albrizio, Tomasz Koźluk and Vera Zipperer, 'Empirical Evidence on the Effects of Environmental Policy Stringency on Productivity Growth' (OECD Economics Department Working Papers No. 1179, 2014).

141. Michael E. Porter, and Claas van der Linde, 'Toward a New Conception of the Environment-competitiveness Relationship', *The Journal of Economic Perspectives* 9, no. 4 (Autumn 1995): 97–118.
142. Francesco Testa, Fabio Iraldo and Marco Frey, "The Effect of Environmental Regulation on Firms' Competitive Performance: The Case of the Building and Construction Sector in Some EU Regions,' *Journal of Environmental Management* 92, Issue 9 (September 2011): 2,136–144.
143. Rebecca Ray, Kevin P. Gallagher, Andres Lopez and Cynthia Sanborn, *China in Latin America: Lessons for South-South Cooperation and Sustainable Development* (Boston University, Centro de Investigacion para la Transformation, Tufts University and Universidad del Pacifico, 2015).
144. Rebecca Ray, Kevin P. Gallagher, Andres Lopez and Cynthia Sanborn, *China in Latin America: Lessons for South-South Cooperation and Sustainable Development* (Global Economic Governance Initiative, Boston University; Center for Transformation Research; and Research Center of the University of the Pacific and Global Development and Environment Institute, Tufts University, 2015), 12.
145. 'China has become an important ally in Chile's goal of diversifying its energy matrix away from fossil fuels. China's over-production of solar PV panels came at just the right time for Chile, which was looking for new sources of low-emissions electricity.' See Nicola Borregaard, Annie Dufey, Maria Teresa Ruiz-Tagle and Santiago Sinclair, 'Chinese Incidence on the Chilean Solar Power Sector' (Working Group Discussion Paper 2015-4, Global Economic Governance Initiative, Boston University, Boston, April 2015).
146. Ucille Cambridge, 'T&T to Open Embassy in China: Focus on Trade, Cultural, Educational Exchanges,' *Trinidad Guardian*, May 15, 2013.
147. Karyl Walker, 'Free Passage-Gov't Waives Visas for Chinese Nationals,' *Jamaica Observer*, March 2014.
148. This prompted the speculation that in a Jamaica with almost 20 per cent unemployment 'the number of work permits to Chinese increasing and the waiving of visitor visas, it is not difficult to understand that the average worker could feel threatened by the 87 million unemployed Chinese.' See Orville Taylor, 'Chinese in Jamaica: Xenophobia or Justified Concern?' The *Gleaner*, March 9, 2014.
149. Stephanie Hanson, 'China, Africa and Oil, Backgrounder,' Council on Foreign Relations, June 6, 2008.
150. 'Cornering Foreign Fields: The Chinese and Arabs are Buying Poor Countries' Farms on a Colossal Scale,' The *Economist*, May 21, 2009.
151. Marie Olsson, 'Chinese "Land Grabs" in Africa – The Reality behind the News,' Swedish International Agricultural Network Initiative (SIANI), Policy Brief, May 4, 2012.
152. The beneficiary countries of the Caribbean Basin Economic Recovery Act that are not parties to the Central America–Dominican Republic–United States Free Trade Agreement (CAFTA–DR) are Antigua and Barbuda, Aruba, The Bahamas, Barbados, Belize, the British Virgin Islands, Dominica, Grenada, Guyana, Haiti, Jamaica, Montserrat, Netherlands Antilles, Panama, St Kitts and Nevis, St Lucia, St Vincent and the Grenadines, and Trinidad and Tobago.
153. The Caribbean–Canada Trade Agreement is a Canadian government programme established in 1986 to provide duty-free access to the Canadian market for all products except the following items: textiles and apparel, footwear, luggage and handbags,

leather garments, lubricating oils and methanol. The beneficiary countries are Anguilla, Antigua and Barbuda, The Bahamas, Bermuda, Barbados, Belize, The British Virgin Islands, The Cayman Islands, The Commonwealth of Dominica, Grenada, Guyana, Jamaica, Montserrat, St Kitts and Nevis, St Lucia, St Vincent and the Grenadines, Trinidad and Tobago, and The Turks and Caicos Islands.

154. The CAFTA–DR agreement is a free trade agreement between the US and five Central American countries (Costa Rica, El Salvador, Guatemala, Honduras, and Nicaragua) and the Dominican Republic.
155. Richard L. Bernal, *Globalization, Trade and Economic Development: A Study of the CARIFORUM–EU Economic Partnership Agreement* (New York: Palgrave MacMillan, December, 2013).
156. Major Chinese manufacturer of biomedical equipment signals intention to invest in Jamaica. - Firstlook - Go-Jamaica, Press Release JAMPRO, December 2012.
157. Julia Jhinkoo, 'Highlighting the China-Caribbean Relationship,' *Caribbean Centre for Money and Finance Newsletter* 6, no. 10 (October 2013): 1–3.
158. Avoiding non-tariff barriers has been identified as one of the motives for FDI. See John Wong and Sara Chan, 'China's Outward Direct Investment: Expanding Worldwide,' *China: An International Journal* 1, no. 2 (September 2003): 273–301.
159. 'China's Foreign Ports: The New Masters and Commanders,' The *Economist*, June 8, 2013.
160. *Foreign Direct Investment in Latin America and the Caribbean 2011* (Santiago: Economic Commission for Latin America and the Caribbean, 2012), 37.
161. 'Dominican Tourism Project financed by China,' February 20, 2011. http://ambercoastrealty.com/tourism-investment-for-dominican-republic/ (accessed March 17, 2011).
162. Michael J. Silverstein, Abheek Singhi, Carol Liao and David Michael, *The $10 Trillion Prize: Captivating the Newly Affluent in China and India* (Boston: Harvard Business Press, 2012), 45.
163. Ibid.
164. *The People's Republic of China and Latin America and the Caribbean: Dialogue and Cooperation for the New Challenges of the Global Economy* (Santiago, Chile: Economic Commission for Latin America and the Caribbean, October, 2012), 24.
165. China Aluminum Network (2008). 'China to build aluminum smelter in Trinidad.' http://www.alu.com.cn/enNews/NewsInfo_1755.html.
166. 'The Rise of China and its Energy Implications,' Executive Summary, James A. Baker III Institute for Public Policy, Rice University, December 2, 2011, 7.
167. 'China to Build Aluminum Smelter in Trinidad,' China Aluminum Network, http://www.alu.com.cn/enNews/NewsInfo_1755.html (accessed June 27, 2008).
168. David Renwick, 'How Ignorance Killed the Smelter,' *Trinidad Express*, September 22, 2010.
169. Edmond Campbell, 'Chinese Eye Air J,' *Jamaica Gleaner*, March 28, 2008, 1.
170. 'Jamaica and China Pursuing Stronger Business Partnership,' *Caribbean Net News*, August 18, 2009.
171. Lauren A. E. Schuker, 'Courting the Chinese,' *Wall Street Journal*, June 21, 2012.
172. Joel Backaler, *China Goes West: Everything You Need to Know about Chinese Companies Going Global* (New York: Palgrave Macmillan, 2014), 87–89 and 107–109.
173. 'Shuanghui Hopes $7bn Deal will Ally Produce Fears,' The *Financial Times*, May 30, 2013, 14.

174. 'China Pushes Firms to Shop for Famous Global Brands,' *Reuters*, Mar 7, 2011. http://www.reuters.com/.../us-china-overseas-deals-idUSTRE72626G20...
175. Rare earth elements or rare earth metals are 17 chemical elements specifically the 15 lanthanides, scandium and yttrium. See David McFadden, 'Jamaica Breaks Ground on Rare-earth Project,' *Miami Herald*, February 13, 2013.
176. Draws on Robert G. Sutter, *Chinese Foreign Relations: Power and Policy since the Cold War*, 3rd ed. (Lanham: Rowman & Littlefield Publishers, 2012), 1–37.
177. Section on 'Going Global' from the Eleventh Five-Year Plan (2006–2010) (National People's Congress, 2006). http://news.sina.com.cn/c/2006-03-16/16158457479s.shtml. Translation by IISD Chinese Outward Investment: An emerging Policy Framework 10 Chapter 37, Section 1.
178. Milton W. Meyer, *China: A Concise History* (Lanham: Rowman & Littlefield Publishers, second edition, revised, 1994), 11.
179. China's Policy Paper on Latin America and the Caribbean, 2008.
180. David C. Unger, *The Emergency State: America's Pursuit of Absolute Security at Al Costs* (New York: Penguin Press, 2012).
181. James Ledbetter, *The Unwarranted Influence: Dwight D. Eisenhower and the Military-Industrial Complex* (New Haven: Yale University Press, 2011).
182. For an example of this kind of thinking see Bill Gertz, *The China Threat: How the People's Republic Targets America* (Washington, DC: Regency Publishing Inc., 2000) and Peter W. Navarro and Greg Autry, *Death by China: Confronting the Dragon – A Global Call to Action* (New Jersey: Pearson FT Press, 2011).
183. Aaron L. Friedberg, *A Contest for Supremacy: China, America and the Struggle for Mastery in Asia* (New York: W.W. Norton & Company, 2011).
184. *US–China Security Perceptions Survey: Findings and Implications* (Washington, DC: Carnegie Endowment for International Peace, 2013), 25.
185. Umberto Eco, *Inventing the Enemy* (New York: Houghton, Mifflin Harcourt, 2012), 2.
186. Ibid., 3.
187. Chris Alden, *China in Africa: Partner, Competitor or Hegemon?* (London: Zed Books, 2007), Robert I. Rotberg, *China into Africa: Trade, Aid and Influence* (Washington, DC: Brookings Institution Press, 2008) and Deborah Brautigam, *The Dragon's Gift: The Real Story of China in Africa* (New York: Oxford University Press, 2011).
188. China's presence in Latin America is discussed in Riordan Roett and Guadelupe Paz, eds., *China's Expansion into the Western Hemisphere: Implications for Latin America and the United States* (Washington, DC: Brookings Institution, 2008) and Cynthia Arnson, Mark Mohr and Riordan Roett, eds., *Enter The Dragon? China's Presence in Latin America* (Washington, DC: Woodrow Wilson Center for International Scholars, 2008).
189. 'China Overtakes Japan as Third Largest Exporter,' *Financial Times*, April 16, 2005.
190. This shift towards increased private sector involvement relative to official engagement has happened in other regions, for example, Africa. See Jian-Ye Wang, 'What Drives China's Growing Role in Africa' (IMF Working Paper No. 07/211, International Monetary Fund, Washington, DC, October 2007).
191. Rachel Will, 'China's Stadium Diplomacy,' *World Policy Journal* 29, no. 2 (Summer 2012): 36–43.
192. *Jamaica Gleaner*, 'PLCA Scores with $22m China Harbour Deal,' September 9, 2012.
193. Robert Kagan, 'Ambition and Anxiety: America's Competition with China,' in *The Rise of China: Essays on the Future Competition*, ed. Gary J. Schmitt, 2 (New York: Encounter Books, 2009).

194. Edward Tse, *The China Strategy: Harnessing the Power of the World's Fastest Growing Economy* (New York: Basic Books, 2010), 61–71.
195. Hyun-Hoon Lee, Donghyun Park, and Jing Wang, 'Different Types of Firms, Products, and Directions of Trade: The Case of the People's Republic of China' (Asian Development Bank Working Paper Series on Regional Economic Integration No. 101 August 2012).
196. Richard L. Bernal, Globalization, *Trade and Economic Development: A Study of the CARIFORUM-EU Economic Partnership Agreement* (New York: Palgrave MacMillan, December, 2013).
197. John H. Dunning, *International Production and the Multinational Enterprise* (London: Allen & Unwin, 1981).
198. Mary-Françoise Renard, 'China's Trade and FDI in Africa' (African Development Bank Working Paper No. 126, May 2011).
199. William Wallis, 'China Shoemaker Thinks on Its Feet in Ethiopian Expansion,' *Financial Times*, June 4, 2013, 1.
200. Luke Hurst, 'Comparative Analysis of the Determinants of China's State-owned Outward Direct Investment in OECD and Non-OECD Countries,' *China & World Economy* 19, no. 4 (2011): 74–91.
201. Enrique Dussel Peters, 'Chinese FDI in Latin America: Does Ownership Matter? Working Group on Development and Environment in the Americas' (Discussion Paper No. 33, November 2012).
202. *Cuba: The Great Disruption for the Good of the Caribbean* (Bridgetown: Caribbean Hotel and Tourism Association, June 18, 2015).
203. 'Air China Opens First Direct Route between Beijing and Havana.' http://oncubamagazine.com/economy-business/air-china-opens-first-direct-route-between-beijing-and-havana/.
204. It has been suggested that that membership in the international financial institutions would be advantageous for Cuba. See Pavel Vidal and Scott Brown, *Cuba's Economic Reintegration: Begin with the International Financial Institutions* (Washington, DC: Atlantic Council, July 2015).
205. Richard Feinberg, *Soft Landing in Cuba? Emerging Entrepreneurs and Middle Classes* (Washington, DC: Brookings Institution, November 2013).
206. Natallie Rochester King, *Implications for Jamaica of United States Policy Changes toward Cuba* (Kingston: Caribbean Policy Research Institute, forthcoming 2015).
207. Thomas Friedman, *The Lexus and the Olive Tree: Understanding Globalization* (New York: Farrar, Straus & Giroux, 1999), 196.
208. Ucille Cambridge, 'T&T to Open Embassy in China: Focus on Trade, Cultural, Educational Exchanges,' *Trinidad Guardian*, May 15, 2013.
209. Henry Kissinger, *On China* (New York: Penguin Press, 2011), 5–32.
210. Sun Tzu, *The Art of War* (New York: Barnes & Noble, 2004).
211. *Selected Readings from the Works of Mao Tse-Tung* (Peking: Foreign Language Press, 1971), 85–133. On Mao's thought see Stuart R. Schram, *The Political Thought of Mao Tse-Tung* (Harmondsworth: Penguin, 1969).
212. Robert Bickers, *The Scramble for China: Foreign Devils in the Qing Empire* (New York: Penguin, 2011).
213. Orville Schell and John Delury, *Wealth and Power: China's Long March to the Twenty-First Century* (New York: Random House, 2013).
214. Margaret Macmillan, *Nixon and Mao: The Week that Changed the World* (New York: Random House, 2007) Henry Kissinger, *On China* (New York: Penguin Press, 2011).

215. Jacques Barzun, 'The Man in the American Mask,' *Foreign Affairs* 43, no. 3 (April 1965).
216. An exception is Mark Leonard, *What Does China Think?* (London: Fourth Estate, 2008).
217. Hu Angang, 'China in 2020: A New Type of Superpower' (Brookings Institution, Washington, DC, 2012).
218. Christopher R. Hughes, 'In Case You Missed It: China Dreams,' The *China Beat*, April 5, 2010.
219. Kevin P. Gallagher and Roberto Porzecanski, *Dragon in the Room: China and the Future of Latin American Industrialization* (Stanford: Stanford University Press, 2010), 11–38.
220. Ibid., 39–82.
221. Ibid., 83–97.
222. *MOFCOM, 2009 Statistical Bulletin of China's Outward Foreign Direct Investment* (Beijing, 2010), 12.
223. Enrique Dussel Peters, 'Chinese FDI in Latin America: Does Ownership Matter? Working Group on Development and Environment in the Americas' (Discussion Paper No. 33, November 2012), 1.
224. Michael F. Martin, *China's Sovereign Wealth Fund* (Washington, DC: Congressional Research Service, January 22, 2008).
225. *China: Description of Selected Government Practices and Policies Affecting Decision Making in the Economy, USITC Investigation 332–492* (Washington: United States International Trade Commission, 2007).
226. Randall Morck, Bernard Yeung, and Minyuan Zhao, 2008, 'Perspectives on China's Outward Foreign Direct Investment,' *Journal of International Business Studies* 39, no. 3: 337–50.
227. This Ministry is responsible for supervising all firms with foreign investments over $10,000.
228. B. Gill, B. and J. Reilly, 'The Tenuous Hold of China Inc. in Africa,' *Washington Quarterly* 30, no. 3 (Summer 2007): 37–52.
229. Henry Sanderson and Michael Forsythe, *China's Superbank: Debt, Oil and Influence-How China Development Bank is Rewriting the Rules of Finance* (Singapore: John Wiley & Sons, 2013), chapters 3 and 4.
230. Nargiza Salidjanova, 'Going Out: An Overview of China's Outward Foreign Direct Investment,' USCC Staff Research Report, US–China Economic and Security Commission, March 30, 2011.
231. Moses N. Kiggundu, 'A Profile of China's Outward Foreign Direct Investment to Africa,' Proceedings of the *American Society of Business and Behavioral Sciences* 15, no. 1 (2008): 130–44. http://www.docin.com (accessed February 2013).
232. Nargiza Salidjanova, 'Going Out: An Overview of China's Outward Foreign Direct Investment,' USCC Staff Research Report, US–China Economic and Security Commission, March 30, 2011.
233. Enrique Dussel Peters, 'Chinese FDI in Latin America: Does Ownership Matter? Working Group on Development and Environment in the Americas' (Discussion Paper No. 33, November 2012).
234. For example, the sale of bauxite to the Soviet Union from the late 1970s. See Carlton E. Davis, *Jamaica in the World Aluminium Industry, Vol. II, 1974-1988, Bauxite Levy Negotiations* (Kingston: Jamaica Bauxite Institute, 1995), 315.
235. Adam Hersh, 'Chinese State-Owned and State-Controlled Enterprises,' Testimony before the US–China Economic and Security Review Commission, February 15, 2012. http://www.americanprogressaction.org/issues/economy/report/2012/02/15/11069/chinese-state-owned-and-state-controlled-enterprises.

236. David Shambaugh, *China Goes Global: The Partial Power* (Oxford: Oxford University Press, 2013), 180.
237. Martin Jacques, *When China Rules the World: The End of the Western World and the Birth of a New Global Order* (New York: Penguin, 2009), 182.
238. *MOFCOM, 2009 Statistical Bulletin of China's Outward Foreign Direct Investment* (Beijing, 2010), 116.
239. Thilo Hanemen, 'Changing Patterns of Chinese FDI. Drivers and Implications,' Stanford Center for International Development, December 6, 2011.
240. Ruth Rama and John Wilkinson, 'Asian Agribusiness Investments in Latin America, with Case Studies from Brazil,' in *The Changing Nature of Asian-Latin America Economic Relations*, ed. German King, Jose Carlos Mattos, Nanno Mulder and Osvaldo Rosale, 41 (Santiago: Economic Commission for Latin America and the Caribbean, December, 2012).
241. Hong Song, 'Chinese Private Direct Investment and Overseas Chinese Network in Africa,' *China & World Economy* 19, Issue 4 (August–September 2011): 109–126.
242. Peter F. Drucker, *Managing in a Time of Great Change* (New York: Truman Talley Books/ Dutton, 1995), 205.
243. John Kao, 'The Worldwide Web of Chinese Business,' *Harvard Business Review*, (March/ April 1993): 24–35.
244. Murray Weidenbaum and Samuel Hughes, *The Bamboo Network* (New York: Free Press, 1996).
245. Wai-keung Chung, 'Western Corporate Forms and the Social Origins of Chinese Diaspora Entrepreneurial Networks,' in *Diaspora Entrepreneurial Networks: Four Centuries of History*, ed. Ina Baghdiantz McCabe, Gelina Harlaftis and Joanna Pepelasis Minoglou, 287–311 (Oxford: Berg, 2005).
246. Franciso Haro Navejas, 'China's Relations with Central America and the Caribbean States: Reshaping the Region,' in *From the Great Wall to the New World: Volume 11: China and Latin America in the 21st Century*, ed. Julia C. Strauss and Ariel C. Armony (Cambridge: Cambridge University Press, 2010).
247. Paul B. Tjon Sie Fat, *Chinese New Migrants in Suriname: The Inevitability of Ethnic Performing* (Amsterdam: Amsterdam University Press, 2009).
248. R. Evan Ellis, 'Suriname and the Chinese: Timber, Migration, and Less-Told Stories of Globalization,' *SAIS Review* 32, no. 2 (Summer-Fall 2012): 85–97. See page 88.
249. Paula Williams Madison, *Finding Samuel Lowe: China, Jamaica, Harlem* (New York: Amistad, 2015).
250. James E. Rauch and Vitor Trindade, 'Ethnic Chinese Networks in International Trade,' *The Review of Economics and Statistics* 84, no. 1(February 2002): 116–30.
251. Social networks engender trust that facilitates contractual arrangements that promote trade. See James E. Rauch, 'Business and Social Networks in International Trade,' *Journal of Economic Literature* 39 (December 2001): 1,177–203.
252. 'Chinese Firm Bids for Stake in Jamalco,' *Jamaica Gleaner*, March 26, 2010.
253. 'Caribbean, Chinese Talk Business in New York,' *Jamaica Gleaner*, June 12, 2013.
254. Chris Alden, *China in Africa* (London: Zed Books, 2007), 47–56.
255. 'Influx of Chinese business causing concern regionally,' January 30, 2012. http://www.antiguaobserver.com/?p=70544 (accessed September 13, 2012).
256. R. Evan Ellis, *Suriname and the Chinese: Timber, Migration, and the Less-Told Stories of Globalization* (forthcoming).
257. Simon Romero, 'With Aid and Migrants, China Expands Its Presence in a South American Nation,' *New York Times*, April 11, 2011.

258. Brent Dean, 'U.S. Fears Baha Mar Chinese Migration,' The *Freeport News*, June 14, 2011. http://freeport.nassauguardian.net/national_local/65829088305882.php (accessed July 5, 2012).
259. http://fortune.com/global500/
260. David Shambaugh, *China Goes Global: The Partial Power* (Oxford: Oxford University Press, 2013), 177.
261. Jamil Anderlini, 'Lender with a Global Reach,' *Financial Times*, May 23, 2011.
262. R. Evan Ellis, 'Learning the Ropes,' *Americas Quarterly* 6, no. 4 (Fall 2012): 28–34.
263. Karl Sauvant, 'New Kid on the Block Learning the Rules,' *East Asian Forum Quarterly* 4, no. 2 (April-June 2012): 11–12.
264. There is no intention to survey this literature but merely to indicate some of the sources which set out the pros and cons of FDI and cite them from different dates to indicate that the debate has continued. For a succinct overview see Gerald Meier, *Leading Issues in Economic Development*, 2n ed. (Oxford University Press, 1970), 296–308; Theodore H. Moran, *Foreign Direct Investment and Development* (Washington, DC: Institute for International Economics, 1998), particularly chapter 1; Prakash Loungani and Assaf Razin, 'How Beneficial Is Foreign Direct Investment for Developing Countries?' *Finance and Development* 38, no. 2 (June 2001): 1–7; Theodore H. Moran, *Foreign Direct Investment and Development: Launching a Second Generation of Policy Research* (Washington, DC: Peterson Institute for International Economics, 2011); and Thomas Farole and Deborah Winkler, 'Does FDI Work for Africa? Assessing Local Spillovers in a World of Global Value Chains,' World Bank, Economic Premise, No. 135, February 2014.
265. Discussions of FDI in the Caribbean include W. Arthur Lewis, 'The Industrialisation of the British West Indies,' *Caribbean Economic Review* II, no. 1 (May 1950); Edwin Carrington, 'Industrialization By Invitation In Trinidad Since 1950,' *New World Quarterly* 4, no. 2 (1968); Norman Girvan, *Foreign Capital and Economic Underdevelopment in Jamaica* (Mona, Jamaica: Institute of Social and Economic Research, University of the West Indies, 1971); Richard L. Bernal, 'Foreign Capital and Development in Jamaica,' *InterAmerican Economic Affairs* 38, no. 2 (Autumn 1984): 321; and Ramesh F. Ramsaran, *U.S. Investment in Latin America and the Caribbean* (New York: Palgrave Macmillan, 1985).
266. *Foreign Direct Investment for Development. Maximizing Benefits, Minimizing Costs* (Paris: Organization For Economic Co-operation and Development, 2002).
267. Thomas Farole and Debra Winkler, eds., *Making Foreign Direct Investment Work for Sub-Saharan Africa: Local Spillovers and Competiveness in Global Value Chains* (Washington, DC: World Bank, 2014).
268. Albert O. Hirschman, *The Strategy of Economic Development* (New Haven: Yale University Press, 1958).
269. E. Borensztein, J. W. Lee and J. DeGregorio, 'How Does Foreign Investment Affect Growth' (Working Paper No. 5057, National Bureau of Economic Research, 1995).
270. Hollis Chenery and Alan Strout, 'Foreign assistance and Economic Development,' *American Economic Review* 56, no. 4 (1966): 679–733.
271. Richard L. Bernal, 'Foreign Investment and Development in Jamaica,' *Inter American Economic Affairs* 38, no. 2 (Autumn 1984): 3–21.
272. The costs and benefits of FDI by multinational corporations is succinctly summarized in E. Wayne Nfziger, *Economic Development*, 4th ed. (Cambridge: Cambridge University Press, 2006), 537–38.
273. Peter Nolan, *Is China Buying the World?* (Cambridge: Polity Press, 2012).

274. *Foreign Direct Investment in LDCs: Lessons Learned from the Decade 2001–2010 and then Way Forward* (Geneva: United Nations conference on Trade and Development, 2011), 12.
275. Dambisa Moyo, *Winner Take All: China's Race for Resources and What it Means for the Rest of the World* (Toronto: Harper Collins, 2012), 167.
276. These concerns prompted the Prime Minister of Jamaica to give a public assurance that all regulations would be observed in a road construction project being executed by a Chinese company, China Harbour Engineering Company, which has satisfactorily completed several projects in Jamaica. See 'Chinese Contractor Has to Adhere to the Rules – PM,' The *Gleaner*, December 6, 2012.
277. Lisa E. Sachs and Karl P. Sauvant, 'BITs, DTTs and FDI Flows: An Overview,' in *The Effects of Treaties on Foreign Direct Investment: Bilateral Investment Treaties, Double Taxation Treaties, and Investment Flows*, ed. Karl P. Sauvant and Lisa E. Sachs, xxvii–lxii (Oxford: Oxford University Press, 2009).
278. J. F. Hornbeck, *CARICOM: Challenges and Opportunities for Caribbean Economic Integration* (Washington, DC: Congressional Research Service, January 7, 2008), 18.
279. On Cuba's policy on FDI, see Richard Feinberg, *The New Cuban Economy: What Roles for Foreign Investment?* (Washington, DC: Brookings Institution, 2012).
280. 'Cuba Passes Law to Attract Foreign Investors – Americas.' March 30, 2014. http://www.aljazeera.com/news/americas/2014/03/cuba-passes-law-attract-foreign-investors-2014329174342904833.html.
281. A. Persaud, 'Caribbean Countries Fishing for Investors at China Trade Fair – Guyana Misses First Day,' *Stabroek News*, September 2003.
282. 'China Extends US$118 Million in Aid to Jamaica,' *Caribbean Net News*. http://www.caribbeannetnews.com (accessed May 5, 2010).

Epilogue

1. Lionel Vairon, *China Threat?: The Challenges, Myths, and Realities of China's Rise* (New York: CN Times Books, 2013).
2. Edward S. Steinfeld, *Playing Our Game: Why China's Rise Doesn't Threaten the West* (New York: Oxford University Press, 2010).
3. Kevin Gallagher, *The China Triangle: Latin America's China Boom and the Fate of the Washington Consensus* (New York: Oxford University Press, 2016), 100–08.
4. Stefan Halper, *The Beijing Consensus: How China's Authoritarian Model Will Dominate the Twenty-First Century* (New York: Basic Books, 2010).
5. Zachary Karabell, 'China's Money Can Make Us Safer,' *Washington Post*, April 3, 2016, B1and B3.
6. William Mauldin, 'Rising Chinese Investment Drawing Scrutiny,' *Wall Street Journal*, April 13, 2016, A2.
7. Anne Steele, 'Starwood Takes Sweetened Offer,' *Wall Street Journal*, March 22, 2016, B1–B2.
8. Steve Johnson, 'Chinese Tourists Fuel Global Travel Boom,' *Financial Times*, March 22, 2016, 3.
9. Ibid.
10. 'Barbados and China Sign Two Treaties", March 23, 2016, http://www.nationnews.com/nationnews/news/79301/barbados-china-sign-treaties#sthash.CNmDsBxN.dpuf.
11. 'Embezzlers on the Run Hauled in from Caribbean islands,' February 6, 2016, http://www.thestandard.com.hk/breaking-news.php?id=71114.

12. 'China Communications to Build Regional Headquarters in Kingston,' *Jamaica Observer,* March 27, 2016, 1.
13. 'UWI Goes Global, Establishing New Institute with China,' http://sta.uwi.edu/news/releases/release.asp?id=1527.
14. Mark S. Ferrara, *Palace of Ashes: China and the Decline of American Higher Education* (Baltimore: Johns Hopkins University Press, 2015).
15. Frank Frankopan, *The Silk Roads: A History of the World* (New York: Knopf, 2016), xv.
16. 'Chinese investment is welcomed with caution,' *Financial Times,* March 28, 2016, 8.
17. 'China's Transition to Slower but Better Growth,' IMF Survey, August 14, 2015.
18. Kevin Gallagher, *The China Triangle,* 61.
19. Demetri Sevastopulo, 'Beijing Steps up South China Sea Reef Building Despite US Protests,' *Financial Times,* 16/17 January 16/17, 2016, 1.
20. Mao in a 1957 speech said: 'We are not afraid of atomic warfare. Why? Because China has 600 million people. Even if 200 million people were killed by atomic weapons, 400 million people would still survive. Even if 400 million people were killed, 200 million would still survive. Even if 200 million survived, China would still constitute a big country of the world.'
21. Chico Harlan, 'China's Slowdown Threatens One of the World's Great Success Stories.' *Washington Post,* February 7, 2016, G1–G5.
22. Thomas L. Freidman, *The Lexus and the Olive Tree: Understanding Globalization* (New York: Farrar, Straus and Giroux, 1999), 195.
23. Stockholm International Peace Research Institute, SIPRI Military Expenditure Database, April 2016. Data are for 2015.
24. David Shambaugh, *China's Future* (Cambridge: Polity Press, 2016).
25. Sun Tzu, *The Art of War* (New York: Metro Books, 2001), 178.
26. "China to fund construction of new hospital in Dominica", *Jamaica Observer,* August 10, 2016.
27. "Chinese company buys Alpart for US$299m", *Jamaica Observer,* July 19, 2016.
28. "Chinese Firm To Establish US$2 Billion Industrial Zone Near Alpart", *Gleaner,* July 28, 2016.
29. Donald Mills, *Journeys and Missions at Home and Abroad* (Kingston: Arawak Publishers, 2009); Rudy Insanally, *Multilateral Diplomacy for Small States: The Art of Letting Others Have Your Way* (Georgetown: Guyenterprise Advertising Agency, 2012); and Rudy Insanally, *Dancing between the Raindrops: A Dispatch from a Small State Diplomat* (N.A., 2015).
30. Richard L. Bernal, *The Influence of Small States on Superpowers: Jamaica and the US Foreign Policy* (Lanham: Lexington Publishers, 2015).

Bibliography

BOOKS AND JOURNAL ARTICLES

Abdenur, Adriana Erthal. 'China and the BRICS Development Bank: Legitimacy and Multilateralism in South–South Cooperation.' *IDS Bulletin* 45, no. 4 (July 2014): 85–101.

Abrami, Regina M., William C. Kerby and F. Warren McFarlan. *Can China Lead? Reaching the Limts of Power and Growth*. Cambridge: Harvard Business School Publishing Corporation, 2014.

Abramovitz, Morton, and Stephen Bosworth. 'America Confronts the Asian Century,' *Current History* (April 2006): 147–52.

Ahearn, Adrian H. 'The Mexico–China–U.S. Triangle: An Ethnographic Perspective.' In *China and the New Triangular Relationships in the Americas: China and Future of US–Mexico Relations*, edited by Enrique Dussel Peters, Adrian H. Ahearn and Harley Shaiken, 59–65. Miami: Center for Latin American Studies and Mexico City: Centro de Estudios China-Mexico, Universidad Nacional Autonomía de Mexico, 2013.

Ahmed, Liaquat. *Lords of Finance: The Bankers Who Broke the World*. New York: Penguin Press, 2009.

Albright, Madeleine. *Memo to the President Elect: How We Can Restore America's Reputation and Leadership*. New York: Harper, 2008.

Alden, Chris. *China in Africa: Partner, Competitor or Hegemon?* London: Zed Books, 2007.

Alejandro, Audrey, and Daniel Compagnon. 'China's External Environmental Policy: Understanding China's Environmental Impact in Africa and How It Is Addressed.' Environmental Practice 15, no. 3 (2013): 220–27.

Amsden, Alice H. *Asia's Next Giant: South Korea and Late Industrialization*. Oxford: Oxford University Press, 1992.

Amin, Samir. *Eurocentricism*. 2nd ed. New York: Monthly Review Press 2009.

Amyx, Jennifer. *Japan's Financial Crisis: Institutional Rigidity and Reluctant Change*. Princeton: Princeton University Press, 2006.

Anderson, Patricia, and Michael Witter. 'Crisis, Adjustment and Social Change: A Case Study of Jamaica.' In *Consequences of Structural Adjustment: A Review of the Jamaican Experience*, edited by Elsie Le Franc, 1–55. Kingston: Canoe Press, 1994.

Angang, Hu. *China in 2020: A New Type of Superpower*. Washington, DC: Brookings Institution, 2012.

Arlt, Wolfgang. *China's Outbound Tourism*. London: Routledge, 2006.

Armony, Ariel C., and Nicolás Velásquez. 'Anti-Chinese Sentiment in Latin America: An Analysis.' *In Beyond Raw Materials Who are the Actors in the Latin America and Caribbean-China Relationship?* Edited by Enrique Dussel Peters and Ariel C. Armony, 17–49. Buenos Aires: Nueva Sociedad, Buenos Aires: Friedrich-Ebert-Stiftung; México DF: Red Académica de América Latina y el Caribe sobre China and Pittsburgh: University of Pittsburgh, Center of Latin American Studies, 2015.

Arnson, Cynthia J., and Jeffrey Davidow. *China, Latin America and the United States: The New Triangle*. Washington, DC: Woodrow Wilson International Center for Scholars, 2011.

Arnson, Cynthia J., and Jorge Heine with Christine Zaino, eds. *Reaching Across the Pacific: Latin America and Asia in the new Century*. Washington, DC: Woodrow Wilson Center for International Scholars, 2014.

———. *Latin America and the Caribbean and China: Towards a New Era in Economic Cooperation*. Santiago: United Nations Economic Commission for Latin America and the Caribbean, 2015.

Arnson, Cynthia, Mark Mohr and Riordan Roett, eds. *Enter The Dragon? China's Presence in Latin America*. Washington, DC: Woodrow Wilson Center for International Scholars, 2008.

Austin, Greg, and Franz-Stefan Gady. *Cyber Détente between the United States and China: Shaping the Agenda*. Washington, DC: East-West Institute, 2012.

Avramovic, Dragoslav. 'Financial Co-operation among Developing Countries: Issues and Opportunities.' In *The Rich and the Poor: Development, Negotiations and Cooperation – An Assessment*, edited by Altaf Gauhar, 205–225. London: Third World Foundation, 1983.

Ayres, Robert L. *Banking on the Poor:The World Bank and World Poverty*. Cambridge: MIT Press, 1983.

Babb, Sarah. *Behind the Development Banks: Washington Politics, World Poverty and the Wealth of Nations*. Chicago: University of Chicago Press, 2009.

Babbin, Jed. *Showdown: Why China Wants War With the United States*. Regnery Publishing, 2006.

Bacevich, Andrew. *The Limits of Power: The End of American Exceptionalism*. New York: Metropolitan Books, 2008.

Backaler, Joel. *China Goes West: Everything You Need to Know about Chinese Companies Going Global*. New York: Palgrave Macmillan, 2014.

Bader, Jeffrey A. *Obama and China's Rise: An Insider's Account of America's Asia Strategy*. Washington, DC: Brookings Institution, 2012.

Barbera, Robert J. *The Cost of Capitalism: Understanding Market Mayhem and Stabilizing our Economic Future*. New York: McGraw Hill, 2009.

Barr, Michael. *Who's Afraid of China? The Challenge of Chinese Soft Power*. London: Zed Books, 2011.

Barzun, Jacques. 'The Man in the American Mask,' *Foreign Affairs* 43, no. 3 (April 1965): 426–35.

Basdeo, Sahadeo, and Graeme Mount. *The Foreign Relations of Trinidad and Tobago: The Case of a Small State in the Global Arena*. Port of Spain: Lexicon Trinidad Ltd., 2001.

Becker, Elizabeth. *Overbooked: The Exploding Business of Travel and Tourism*. New York: Simon & Schuster, 2013.

Bergsten, Fred. 'When China and India Go Down Together.' *Economist* 345, no. 22 (1997): 78–79.

Bergsten, C. Fred, et al. *China: The Balance Sheet –What the World Needs to Know Now about the Emerging Superpower*. New York: Public Affairs, 2006.

———. *China's Rise: Challenges and Opportunities*. Washington, DC: Peterson Institute for International Economics and the Center for Strategic and International Studies, 2008.

Bergsten, Fred, and Joseph Gagnon. 'Time for a Fightback in the Currency Wars.' *Financial Times*, September 4, 2012.

Bergsten, Fred, and Marcus Noland. *Reconciling Differences? United States–Japan Economic Conflict*. Washington, DC: Institute for International Economics, 1993.

Bernal, Richard L. 'China and Small Island Developing States.' *Africa–East Asian Affairs, The China Monitor*, Issue 1 (August 2012): 3–30.

———. 'China's Growing Economic Presence in the Caribbean.' *The World Economy* 38, Issue 9 (September 2015): 1,409–37.

———. 'The Debt-Development Dilemma of Small Island Developing States. Review Article.' *Social and Economic Studies* 64, no. 2 (June 2015): 229–43.

———. 'Dragon in the Caribbean: China–CARICOM Economic Relations.' *Round Table* 99, no. 408 (2010): 1–22; 281–302.

———. 'Foreign Capital and Development in Jamaica.' *InterAmerican Economic Affairs* 38, no. 2 (Autumn 1984): 3–21.

———. 'Foreign Investment and Development in Jamaica.' *Inter-American Economic Affairs* 38, no. 2 (Autumn 1984): 3–21.

———. *Globalization: Everything but Alms: The EPA and Economic Development.* Kingston: Grace Kennedy Foundation, 2008.

———. *Globalization, Trade and Economic Development: A Study of the CARIFORUM-EU Economic Partnership Agreement.* New York: Palgrave MacMillan, 2013.

———. *The Influence of Small States on Superpowers: Jamaica and U.S. Foreign Policy.* Lanham: Lexington Publishers, 2015.

———. 'Restructuring Jamaica's Economic Relations with Socialist Countries, 1974–1980.' *Development and Change* 17, no. 4 (October 1986): 607–34.

———. 'The Unimportance of the English Speaking Caribbean in US Foreign Policy as told by Presidents and Secretaries of State.' *Caribbean Journal of International Relations & Diplomacy* 1, no.1 (February 2013): 132–50.

———. 'The Vicious Circle of Foreign Indebtedness: The Case of Jamaica.' In *External Debt and Development Strategy in Latin America*, edited by Antonio Jorge, Jorge SalazarCarrillo and Frank DiazPou, 111–28. New York: Pergamon Press, 1985.

Bergsten, C. Fred, Charles Freeman, Nicholas R. Lardy and Derek J. *Mitchell. China's Rise: Challenges and Opportunities.* Washington, DC: Peterson Institute for International Economics and the Center for Strategic and International Studies, 2008.

Bernstein, Richard, and Ross H. Munro. *The Coming Conflict with China.* New York: Vintage, 1998.

Bértola, Luis, and José Antonio Ocampo. *The Economic Development of Latin America since Independence.* New York: Oxford University Press, 2012.

Bhalla, Surjit S. *Devaluing to Prosperity: Misaligned Currencies and Their Growth Consequences.* Washington, DC: Institute for International Economics, 2012.

Bhattasali, Deepak, *Li* Shantong and Will *Martin*. 'China's Accession to the World Trade Organization, Policy Reform, and Poverty Reduction: An Introduction.' *World Bank Economic Review* 10, issue 1 (2004): 1–2.

Bickers, Robert. *The Scramble for China: Foreign Devils in the Qing Empire.* New York: Penguin Global, 2011.

Bijian, Zheng. 'China's Peaceful Rise to Great Power Status.' *Foreign Affairs* 84, no. 5 (September– October 2005): 18–24; see 22.

Birdsall, Nancy. 'The World Bank: Toward a Global Club.' In *Global Governance Reform. Breaking the Stalemate,* edited by Colin I. Bradford and Johannes F. Linn, 50–59. See 57. Washington, DC: Brookings Institution, 2007.

Block, Fred. *The Origins of International Economic Disorder: A Study of United States International Monetary Policy from World War II to the Present.* Berkeley: University of California Press, 1978.

Blyth, Mark. *Austerity: The History of a Dangerous* Idea. Oxford: Oxford University Press, 2015.

Bongiorni, Sara. *A Year without 'Made in China': One Family's True Life Adventure in the Global Economy.* New York: Wiley, 2007.

Blaut, J. M. *Eight Eurocentric Historians.* London: Guildford Press, 2000.

James Bradley, *The Imperial Cruise: A Secret History of Empire and War.* Back Bay Books, 2010.

Broadman, H. G. *Africa's Silk Road: China and India's New Economic Frontier.* Washington, DC: World Bank, 2007.

Brautigam, Deborah. *The Dragon's Gift: The Real Story of China in Africa*. New York: Oxford University Press, 2011.

Brown, Gordon. *Beyond the Crash: Overcoming the First Crisis of Globalization*. New York: Free Press, 2010.

Bremmer, Ian. *Superpower: Three Choices, for America's Role in the World*. New York: Portfolio/ Penguin, 2015.

Brezezinski, Zbigniew. *Strategic Vision: America and the Crisis of Global Power*. New York: Basic Books, 2012.

The BRICS Report: A Study of Brazil, Russia, India, China and South Africa with Special Focus on Synergies and Complementarities. New Delhi: Oxford University Press, 2012.

Buckley, Michael. *Meltdown in Tibet: China's Reckless Destruction of Ecosystems from the Highlands of Tibet to the Deltas of Asia*. New York: Palgrave Macmillan, 2014.

Budhoo, Davison L. *Enough Is Enough: Dear Mr. Camdessus-Open Letter of Resignation to the Managing Director of the International*. Apex Press, 1990.

Bush, Richard C., and Michael E. O'Hanlon. *A War Like No Other: The Truth About China's Challenge to America*. New York: Wiley, 2007.

Christopher Caldwell. *Reflections on the Revolution in Europe: Immigration, Islam and the West*. New York: Anchor, 2010.

Calleo, David P. *Beyond American Hegemony: The Future of the Western Alliance*. New York: Basic Books, 1987.

Follies of Power: America's Unipolar Fantasy. Cambridge: Cambridge University Press, 2009.

Calleo, David P., and Benjamin M. Rowland. *America and the World Political Economy*. Bloomington: Indiana University Press, 1973.

Cardoso, Fernando Henrique, and Enzo Faletto. *Dependence and Development in Latin America*. Berkeley: University of California, 1979.

CARICOM. *Our Caribbean Community. An Introduction*. Kingston: Ian Randle Publishers, 2005.

Carpenter, Ted Galen. *America's Coming War with China: A Collision Course over Taiwan*. New York: Palgrave Macmillan, 2006.

Carrington, Edwin. 'Industrialization By Invitation In Trinidad Since 1950.' *New World Quarterly* 4, no. 2 (1968).

CELAC. *Exploring Opportunities for Cooperation on Trade and Investment*. Santiago: United Nations Economic Commission for Latin America and the Caribbean, January, 2015, 6.

The Challenge to the South: The Report of the South Commission. Oxford: Oxford University Press, 1990.

Chance, Giles. *China and the Credit Crisis: The Emergence of a New World Order*. Singapore: John Wiley & Sons, 2010.

Chang, Gordon G. *The Coming Collapse of China*. New York: Random House, 2001.

Chang, Ha-Joon. *Kicking Away the Ladder*. London: Anthem Press, 2002.

Chaze, Aaron. *An Investor's Guide to the Next Economic Superpower*. New York: Wiley, 2006.

Chelleney, Brahma. *Asia Juggernaut: The Rise of China, India, and Japan*. New York: HarperCollins Publishers, 2010.

Chen, Ray. *The Shopkeepers*. Kingston: Periwinkle Publishers, 2004.

Chenery, Hollis B., and M. Syrquin. *Patterns of Development, 1950–1970*. London: Oxford University Press, 1975.

Child, J., and S. Rodriguez. 'The Internationalization of Chinese firms: A Case for Theoretical Extension.' *Management and Organization Review* 1, no. 3 (2005): 381–410.

Chin, Gregory T. 'China as a "Net Donor": Tracking Dollars and Sense,' *Cambridge Review of International Affairs* vol. 25, no. 4 (December 2012): 579–603.

Christensen, Thomas J. *The China Challenge: Shaping the Choices of a Rising Power.* New York: W. W. Norton & Company, 2015.

Chua, Amy. *Day of Empire: How Hyperpowers Rise to Global Dominance and Why They Fall.* New York: Random House, 2007.

Chung, Wai-keung. 'Western Corporate Forms and the Social Origins of Chinese Diaspora Entrepreneurial Networks.' In *Diaspora Entrepreneurial Networks: Four Centuries of History*, ed. Ina Baghdiantz McCabe, Gelina Harlaftis and Joanna Pepelasis Minoglou, 287–311. Oxford: Berg, 2005.

Clarke, Richard A., and Robert K. Knake. *Cyber War: The Next Threat to National Security and What to Do about It.* New York: HarperCollins, 2010.

Cleveland, Harold Van B. 'The International Monetary System in the Interwar Period.' In *Balance of Power or Hegemony: The Interwar Monetary System*, edited by Benjamin M. Rowland, 3–59. New York: The Lehrman Institute/ New York University Press, 1976.

Clinton, Hilary. 'America's Pacific Century,' *Foreign Affairs*, November 2011. http://www.foreignpolicy.com/node/1002667 .

Cohen, Benjamin J. *The Geography of Money.* Ithaca: Cornell University Press, 1998.

———. *Global Monetary Governance.* New York: Routledge, 2009.

Cohen, Paul. *Discovering History in China: American Historical Writing on the Recent Chinese Past.* New York: Columbia University Press, 2010.

Cohen, Stephen P. *India Emerging Power.* Washington, DC: Brookings Institution, 2001.

Cornia, Giovanni Andrea, Richard Jolly and Frances Stewart. *Adjustment with a Human Face: Protecting the Vulnerable and Promoting Growth.* Oxford: Oxford University Press, 1987.

Crabbe, Matthew. *Myth-Busting China's Numbers: Understanding and Using China's Statistics.* New York: Palgrave Macmillan, 2014.

Culpeper, Roy. *The Multilateral Development Banks.* Vol.5 Titans or Behemoths? Blouder: Lynne Reinner Publishers, 1997.

Danaher, Kevin, ed. *50 Years is Enough: The Case Against the World Bank and the International Monetary Fund.* Boston: South end Press, 1994.

Davis, Carlton E. *Jamaica in the World Aluminium Industry, Vol. II, 1974–1988, Bauxite Levy Negotiations.* Kingston: Jamaica Bauxite Institute, 1995.

Davis, Julie Hirschfield, and Corral Davenport. 'China to Announce Cap-and-Trade Program to Limit Emissions.' *New York Times*, September 24, 2015, 1.

deBurgh, Hugo. *China: Friend or Foe?* London: Icon Group International, 2007.

de Cecco, Marcello. *Money and Empire: The International Gold Standard, 1890–1914.* Oxford: Basil Blackwell, 1974.

Demas, William. *The Economics of Development in Small Countries with Special Reference to the Caribbean.* Montreal: McGill University Press, 1965.

Dervis, Kemal, and Karim Foda. 'Emerging Asia and Rebalancing the World Economy.' In *Asia and Policymaking for the Global Economy*, ed. Kemal Dervis, Masahiro Kawai and Domenico Lombardi, 19–56. Tokyo: Asian Development Bank Institute, and Washington, DC: Brookings Institution Press, 2011.

Devlin, Robert, Antoni Estevadeordal and Andres Rodriguez-Clare, eds. *The Emergence of China: Opportunities and Challenges for Latin America and the Caribbean.* Washington, DC: Inter-American Development Bank/Cambridge: Harvard University, 2006.

Ding, Shen. *The Dragon's Hidden Wings.* Lanham, MD: Lexington Books, 2008.

Dobbs, Lou. *Exporting America: Why Corporate Greed is Shipping American Jobs Overseas.* New York: Warner Business Books, 2004.

Dos Santos, Theotonio. 'The Structure of Dependence.' *American Economic Review* 60, no. 2 (May 1970): 231–36.

Dowden, Richard. *Africa: Altered States, Ordinary Miracles*. New York: Public Affairs, 2009.
Drucker, Peter F. *Managing in a Time of Great Change*. New York: Truman Talley Books/ Dutton, 1995.
Dunning, John H. *International Production and the Multinational Enterprise*. London: Allen & Unwin, 1981.
Eberstadt, Nicholas. 'Will China (Continue) to Rise?' In *The Rise of China: Essays on the Future of Competition*, ed. Gary J. Schmitt. New York: Encounter Books, 2009.
Eco, Umberto. *Inventing the Enemy*. New York: Houghton, Mifflin Harcourt, 2012.
Economy, Elizabeth C., and Adam Segal. 'The G-2 Mirage: Why the United States and China Are Not Ready to Upgrade Ties.' *Foreign Affairs* 88, no. 3 (May/June 2009): 2–6.
Economy, Elizabeth C. T*he River Runs Black: The Environmental Challenge to China's Future*. Ithaca: Cornell University Press, 2005.
Economy, Elizabeth C., and Michael Levi. Al*l Means Necessary: How China's Resource Quest is Changing the World*. New York: Oxford University Press, 2014.
Ellis, R. Evan. *China–Latin America Military Engagement: Good Will, Good Business and, Strategic Position*. Carlisle Barracks, PA: Strategic Studies Institute, 2011.
———. *China in Latin America: The Whats and Wherefores*. Boulder: Lynne Rienner, 2009.
———. *China on the Ground in Latin America: Challenges for the Chinese and Impacts on the Region*. New York: Palgrave Macmillan, 2014.
———. 'Learning the Ropes,' *Americas Quarterly* vol. 6, no. 4 (Fall 2012): 28–34.
———. 'Suriname and the Chinese: Timber, Migration, and Less-Told Stories of Globalization,' *SAIS Review* 32, no. 2 (Summer–Fall 2012).
Emmott, Bill. *Rivals: How the Power Struggle between China, India and Japan will Shape Our Next Decade*. Orlando: Harcourt, 2008.
Erickson, Dan P., and Janice Chen. 'China, Taiwan, and the Battle for Latin America.' *Fletcher Forum of World Affairs* 31, no. 2 (2007): 69–89.
Fallows, James. *Looking at the Sun: The Rise of a New East Asian Economic and Political System*. New York: Pantheon Books, 1994.
Farnsworth, Eric. 'Memo to Washington: China's Growing Presence in Latin America.' *Americas Quarterly* (Winter 2012).
———. 'The New Mercantilism: China's Emerging Role in the Americas.' *Current History* (February 2011): 56–61.
Fat, Paul B. Tjon Sie. *Chinese New Migrants in Suriname: The Inevitability of Ethnic Performing*. Amsterdam: Amsterdam University Press, 2009.
Fenby, Jonathan. *Will China Dominate the 21st Century*? London: Polity Press, 2014.
Ferrara, Mark S. *Palace of Ashes: China and the Decline of American Higher Education*. Baltimore: Johns Hopkins University Press, 2015.
Ferguson, Niall. *The Ascent of Money: A Financial History of the World*. New York: Penguin Books, 2008.
———. 'A World without Power.' *Foreign Policy* (July/August 2004): 32–39.
———. *Colossus: The Price of America's Empire*. New York: Penguin Press, 2004.
Ferguson, Tyrone. *Structural Adjustment and Governance: The Case of Guyana*. Georgetown: Public Affairs Consulting Enterprise, 1995.
Fishman, Charles. *The Wal-Mart Effect: How the World's Most Powerful Company Really Works – and How It's Transforming the American Economy*. New York: Penguin Books, 2006.
Fishman, Ted C. *China, Inc: How the Rise of the Next Superpower Challenges America and the World*. New York: Scribner, 2006.
Foot, R. 'Chinese Strategies in a US-hegemonic Global Order: Accommodating and Hedging.' *International Affairs* 82, no. 1 (January 2006): 77–94.

Frank, Andre Gunder. *ReOrient: Global Economy in the Asian Age*. Berkeley: University of California Press, 1998.

Frankel, Francine R. 'Introduction.' In *The India–China Relationship: What the United States Needs to Know,* eds. Francine R. Frankel and Harry Harding, 13–24. New York: Columbia University Press, 2004.

Frankel, Jeffrey A. 'Is Japan Creating a Yen Bloc in East Asia and the Pacific?' In *Asia Pacific Regionalism: Readings in International Relations*, eds. Ross Garnaut and Peter Drydale, 227–49. Pymble, Australia: Harper Educational, 1994.

Frankopan, Frank. *The Silk Roads: A History of the World*. New York: Knopf, 2016.

French, Howard W. *China's Second Continent: How a Million Migrants are Building a New Empire in Africa*. New York: Alfred A. Knopf, 2014.

Friedberg, Aaron L. 'Bucking Beijing: An Alternative US China Policy.' *Foreign Affairs* 91, no. 5 (September–October 2012): 48–58.

———. *A Contest for Supremacy: China, America and the Struggle for Mastery in Asia*. New York: W.W. Norton & Company, 2011.

Friedman, Thomas L. *The Lexus and the Olive Tree: Understanding Globalization*. New York: Farrar, Straus & Giroux, 1999.

———. *The World is Flat: A Brief History*. New York: Farrer, Straus and Giroux, 2005.

Friedman, Thomas L., and Michael Mandelbaum. *That Used to Be Us: How America Fell Behind in the World It Invented and How We Can Come Back*. New York: Farrar, Straus and Giroux, 2011.

Fukuyama, Francis. *The End of History and the Last Man*. New York: Free Press, 1992.

Furtado, Celso. *Development and Underdevelopment*. Berkeley: University of California, 1974.

Galbraith, J.K. *A Short History of Financial Euphoria*. New York: Penguin Publishers, 1994.

Gallagher, Kevin. *The China Triangle: Latin America's China Boom and the Fate of the Washington Consensus*. New York: Oxford University Press, 2016.

Gallagher, Keven P., and Roberto Porzecanski. *The Dragon in the Room: China and the Future of Latin American Industrialization*. Stanford: Stanford University Press, 2010.

Gardner, Richard C. *Sterling-Dollar Diplomacy in Current Perspective: The Origins and the Prospects of Our International Economic Order*. New York: Columbia University Press, 1980.

Germain, Randal D. *The International Organization of Credit*. Cambridge: Cambridge University Press, 1998.

Gertz, Bill. *The China Threat: How the People's Republic Targets America*. Darby, PA: Diane Publishing Company, 2002.

Ghazvinian, John. *Untapped: The Scramble for Africa's Oil*. New York: Mariner Books, 2008.

Gill, Bates and James Reilly. 'The Tenuous Hold of China INC. in Africa.' *Washington Quarterly* 30, no. 3 (Summer 2007): 41.

Gilpin, Robert. *The Political Economy of International Relations*. Princeton: Princeton University Press, 1987.

Girvan, Norman. *Foreign Capital and Economic Underdevelopment in Jamaica*. Mona, Jamaica: Institute of Social and Economic Research, University of the West Indies, 1971.

Glaser, Charles L. 'A U.S.–China Grand Bargain? The Hard Choice between Military Competition and Accommodation.' *International Security* 39, Issue 4 (Spring 2015): 49–90.

Glosny, Michael. *China's Foreign Aid Policy: Lifting States out of Poverty or Leaving Them to the Dictators?* Washington, DC: Center for Strategic for International Studies, 2006.

Gnazales-Vincente, Ruben. 'The Political Economy of Sino-Peruvian Relations: A New Dependency.' *Journal of Current Chinese Affairs* 4, no. 1 (2012): 97–131.

Griesgraber, JoMarie, and Bernhard G. Gunter, eds. *Promoting Development: Effective Global Institutions for the Twenty-First Century*. London: Pluto Press, 1995.

Grimes, William W. *Unmaking the Japanese Miracle: Macroeconomic Politics, 1985–2000*. Ithaca: Cornell University Press, 2001.

Gross, Daniel. *Better, Stronger, Faster: The Myth of America's Decline and the Rise of a New Economy*. New York: Free Press, 2012.

Gupta, Anil K., and Haiyan Wang. *Getting China and India Right: Strategies for Leveraging the World's Fastest Growing Economies for Global Advantage*. San Francisco: Jossey-Bass, 2009.

Gupta, Indrani, Bishwanath Golder and Arup Mitra. 'The Case of India.' In *International Trade in Health Services: A Development Perspective*, eds. Simonetta Zirrrilli and Colette Kinnon, 213–36. Geneva: UNCTAD, 1998.

Gurtov, Mel. *Will This Be China's Century? A Skeptic's View*. Boulder and London: Lynne Rienner, 2013.

Hachigian, Nina, and Mona Sutphen. *The Next American Century: How the US Can Thrive as Other Powers Rise*. New York: Simon & Schuster, 2008.

Halper, Stefan. *The Beijing Consensus: How China's Authoritarian Model Will Dominant the Next Century*. New York: Basic Books, 2010.

Hanson, G.H., and R. Robertson. 'China and the Recent Evolution of Latin America's Manufacturing Exports.' In *China's and India's Challenge to Latin America: Opportunity or Threat*, eds. Daniel Lederman, Marcelo Olarreaga and Guillermo E. Perry, 145–78. Washington, DC: World Bank, 2009.

Harper, Stefan. *The Beijing Consensus: How China's Authoritarian Model Will Dominate the Twentieth Century*. New York: Basic Books, 2010.

Harris, Stuart. *China's Foreign Policy*. London: Polity Press, 2014.

Harris, Timothy. 'The Dynamics of International Diplomacy: The Case of China and Taiwan in the Caribbean, 1971–2005.' *Journal of Caribbean International Relations*, no. 2 (October 2006): 122–37.

Hayter, Teresa. *Aid as Imperialism*. Harmondsworth: Penguin Books, 1971.

Hewitt, Duncan. *China: Getting Rich First*. New York: Pegasus Books, 2008.

Hira, Ron, and Anil Hira. *Outsourcing America: What's behind Our National Crisis and How We Can Reclaim American Jobs*. New York: Amacom, 2005.

Hirschman, Albert O. *The Strategy of Economic Development*. New Haven: Yale University Press, 1958.

Hobsbawn, Eric with Antonio Polito. *On the Edge of the New Century*. New York: New Press, 2000.

Hodgson, Godfrey. *The Myth of American Exceptionalism*. New Haven: Yale University Press, 2009.

Hobson, John M. *The Eastern Origins of Western Civilization*. Cambridge: Cambridge University Press, 2004.

Holland, Stuart. *Towards a New Bretton Woods: Alternatives for the Global Economy*. London: Spokesman, 1994.

Huang, Yasheng. 'The Next Asian Miracle.' *Foreign Policy* 167 (July/August 2008): 32–40.

Huang, Yasheng, and Tarun Khanna. 'Can India Overtake China.' *Foreign Policy* 137 (July/August, 2003): 74–81.

Huntington, Samuel P. *The Clash of Civilizations and the Remaking of World Order*. New York: Simon & Schuster, 1996.

Hurst, Luke. 'Comparative Analysis of the Determinants of China's State-owned Outward Direct Investment in OECD and Non-OECD Countries,' *China & World Economy* 19, no. 4 (2011): 74–91.

Hutton, Will. *The Writing on the Wall: Why We Must Embrace China as a Partner or Face it as an Enemy*. New York: Free Press, 2006.

Ikenberry, G. John. 'The Rise of China and the Future of the West.' *Foreign Affairs* 87, no. 2 (January/February 2008): 22–37.

Insanally, Rudy. *Dancing between the Raindrops: A Dispatch from a Small State Diplomat: A Dispatch from a Small State Diplomat*. Unpublished, 2015.

———. *Multilateral Diplomacy for Small States: The Art of Letting Others Have Your Way*. Georgetown: Guyenterprise Advertising Agency, 2012.

Irvin, Neil. *The Alchemists: Three Central Bankers and a World on Fire*. New York: Penguin, 2014.

Ishihara, Shintaro. *The Japan That Can Say No: Why Japan will be First among Equals*. New York: Touchstone, 1992.

Jacques, Martin. *When China Rules the World: The End of the Western World and the Birth of a New Global Order*. New York: Penguin Books, 2009.

———. *When China Rules the World: The End of the Western World and the Birth of a New Global Order*. 2nd ed. New York: Penguin Books, 2012.

Jaffe, Adam B. , S. R. Peterson, P. R. Portney, and R. N. Stavins. 'Environmental Regulation and the Competitiveness of US Manufacturing: What Does the Evidence Tell Us?' *Journal of Economic Literature* 33, Issue 1 (March 1995): 132–63.

Jenkins, Rhys. 'The "China Effect" on Commodity Prices and Latin American Export Earnings.' *CEPAL Review*, no. 103 (April 2011): 73–87.

Jenkins, Rhys, Enrique Dussel Peters and Mauricio Mesquita Moreira. 'The Impact of China on Latin America and the Caribbean.' *World Development* 36, no. 2 (2008): 235–53.

———. 'Introduction.' In *China and Latin America Economic Relations in the Twenty-first Century*, edited by Rhys Jenkins and Enrique Dussel Peters, 1–20. Bonn and Mexiko City: Deutsches Institut für Entwicklungspolitik (DIE), Universidad Nacional Autónoma de México and Centro de Estudios China-México, 2009.

Jepma, Catrinus. *The Tying of Aid*. Paris: Organization for Economic Co-operation and Development, 1991.

Jinping, Xi. *The Governance of China*. Beijing: Foreign Languages Press, 2014.

Jisi, Wang. 'China's Search for Stability with America.' *Foreign Affairs* 84, no. 5 (September/October 2005): 39–48.

Joffe, Josef. *The Myth of America's Decline: Politics, Economics, and a Half Century of False Prophecies*. New York: Liveright Publishing, 2013.

Johnson, Chalmers. *MITI and the Japanese Miracle: The Growth of Industrial Policy 1925–1975*. Stanford: Stanford University Press, 1982.

———. *Nemesis: The Last Days of the American Empire*. New York: Metropolitan Books, 2006.

Johnson, Howard. 'The Anti Chinese Riots of 1918 in Jamaica.' *Caribbean Quarterly* 28, no. 3 (1982): 19–32.

Johnson, Kim. *Descendants of the Dragon: The Chinese in Trinidad 1808–2006*. Kingston: Ian Randle Publishers, 2006.

Jones, Bruce. *Still Ours to Lead: America. Rising Powers, and the Tension between Rivalry and Restraint*. Washington, DC: Brookings Institution, 2014.

Kagan, Robert. *Paradise and Power: America and Europe in the New World Order*. New York: Vintage, 2004.

———. *The Return of History and the End of Dreams*. New York: Alfred A. Knopf, 2008.

———. 'Ambition and Anxiety: America's Competition with China.' In *The Rise of China: Essays on the Future Competition*, ed. Gary J. Schmitt, 1–23. New York: Encounter Books, 2009.

———. *The World America Made*. New York: Knopf, 2012.

Kamdir, Mira. *Planet India: The Turbulent Rise of the Largest Democracy and the Future of Our World*. New York: Scribner, 2008.

Kao, John. 'The Worldwide Web of Chinese Business.' *Harvard Business Review* (March/April 1993): 24–35.

Kaplan, Robert D. *Asia's Cauldron: The South China Sea and the End of a Stable Pacific*. New York: Random house, 2014.

———. 'The Geography of Chinese Power.' *Foreign Affairs* 89, no. 3 (May/June 2010): 22–41.

———. *Monsoon: The Indian Ocean and the Future of American Power*. New York: Random House, 2010.

Karabell, Zachary. *Superfusion: How China and America Became One Economy and Why the World's Prosperity Depends on it*. New York: Simon & Schuster, 2009.

Kenen, Peter B. *Reform of the International Monetary Fund, CSR NO. 29*. New York: Council on Foreign Relations, May, 2007.

Kennedy, Paul. *The Rise and Fall of the Great Powers*. New York: Vintage Books, 1987.

Keohane, Robert O. *After Hegemony: Cooperation and Discord in the World Political Economy*. Princeton: Princeton University Press, 1984.

———. 'Hegemony and After: Knowns and Unknowns in the Debate over Decline.' *Foreign Affairs* 91, no. 4 (July/August 2012): 114–18.

———. 'The Theory of Hegemonic Stability and Changes in International Economic Regimes, 1967–1977.' In *Change in the International System*, edited by Ole R. Hoisti, Randolph M. Siverson and Alexander L. George, 131–62. Boulder: Westview Press, 1980.

Khanna, Parang. *The Second World: Empires and Influence in the New Global Order*. New York: Random House, 2008.

Kiernan, Victor G. *The Lords of Mankind*. Harmondsworth: Penguin, 1969.

Kiggundu, Moses N. 'A Profile of China's Outward Foreign Direct Investment to Africa,' Proceedings of the *American Society of Business and Behavioral Sciences* vol. 15, no. 1 (2008): 130–44.

Killick, Tony, ed. *The Quest for Economic Stabilisation: The IMF and the Third World*. London: Heinemann Educational Books, 1984.

Kindleberger, Charles. *The World in Depression, 1929–1939*. Berkeley: University of California, 1973.

King, Kenneth. *China's Aid and Soft Power in Africa*. African Issues, 2013.

King, Stephen D. *Losing Control: The Emerging Threats to Western Prosperity*. New Haven: Yale University Press, 2010.

Kissinger, Henry. *Diplomacy*. New York: Simon & Schuster, 1993.

———. *Does America Need A Foreign Policy? Towards Diplomacy for the 21st Century*. New York: Simon & Schuster, 2001.

———. *On China*. New York: Penguin Books, 2011.

Klare, Michael T. 'The New Geography of Conflict.' *Foreign Affairs* 80. no. 3 (May/June 2001): 49–61.

———. *Resource Wars: The New Landscape of Conflict*. New York: Henry Holt, 2002.

Kobayashi-Hilary, Mark. *Outsourcing to India: The Offshore Advantage*. 2nd ed. New York: Springer, 2005.

Krasner, Stephen D., and Michael C. Webb. 'Hegemonic Stability Theory: An Empirical Analysis.' *Review of International Studies* 15, no. 2 (1989): 183–98.

Krauthammer, Charles. 'The Unipolar Moment.' *Foreign Affairs* 70, no. 1, America and the World (1990/1991): 23–33.

Kristof, Nikolas D. and Sheryl WuDunn. *Thunder from the East: Portrait of a Rising Asia*. New York: Knopf, 2000.

Krugman, Paul. 'Taking on China.' *New York Times*, March 14, 2010.

Kubo, Fumiaki. 'Japan's Foreign and Security Policy toward the United States: Between Pacifism and the Logic of Alliance.' In *Japan's Vision for East Asia: Diplomacy Amid Geopolitical Changes*, edited by in Shihoko Goto, 18–30. Washington, DC: Wilson Center, 2014.

Kupchan, Charles A. No *One's World. The West, the Rising Rest, and the Coming Global Turn*. New York: Oxford University Press, 2012.

Kurlantzick, Joshua. *Charm Offensive: How China's Soft Power is Transforming the World*. New Haven: Yale University Press, 2008.

Kuznets, Simon. 'Economic Growth of Small National.' In *Economic Consequences of the Size of Nations*, ed. E.A.G. Robinson, 14–32. London: MacMillan, 1960.

Kynge, James. *China Shakes the World: A Titan's Rise and Troubled Future and the Challenge for America*. New York: Houghton Mifflin, 2006.

Lak, Daniel. *India Express: The Future of the New Superpower*. New York: Palgrave Macmillan, 2009.

Lai, Walton Look. *The Chinese in the West Indies 1806–1995: A Documentary History*. Kingston: The Press, University of the West Indies, 2000.

———. *Indentured Labour, Caribbean Sugar: Chinese and Indian Migrants to the British West Indies, 1838–1918*. Baltimore: Johns Hopkins University Press, 2004.

———. 'Origins of the Caribbean Chinese Community.' *Journal of Caribbean Studies* 14, no.1 (2000): 25–38.

Laqueur, Walter. *After the Fall: The End of the European Dream and the Decline of the Continent*. New York: Thomas Dunne Books, 2010.

Lardy, Nicholas R. *Sustaining China's Economic Growth: After the Global Financial Crisis*. Washington, DC. Peterson Institute for International Economics, 2012.

Latin American and Caribbean Cyber Security Trends. Washington, DC: Organization of American States, June 2014.

Ledbetter, James. *The Unwarranted Influence: Dwight D. Eisenhower and the Military-Industrial Complex*. New Haven: Yale University Press, 2011.

Lederman, Daniel, Marcelo Olarreaga and Guillermo E. Perry. 'Latin America's Response to China and India: Overview of the Research Findings and Policy Implications.' In *China's and India's Challenge to Latin America. Opportunity or Threat*, eds. Daniel Lederman, Marcelo Olarreaga and Guillermo E. Perry, 3–38; 101–120. Washington, DC: World Bank, 2009.

Leeb, Stephen, and Gregory Dorset. *Red Alert: How China's Growing Prosperity Threatens the American Way of Life*. New York: Business Plus, 2011.

Leonard, Mark. *What Does China Think?* London: Fourth Estate, 2008.

———. *Why Europe Will Run the 21st Century*. New York: Public Affairs, 2006.

Lever-Tracy, Constance, David Fu-Keune Ip and Noel Tracy. *The Chinese Diaspora and Mainland China: An Emerging Economic Synergy*. Houndmills: Macmillan Press, 1996.

Levy, Jacqueline. 'The Economic Role of the Chinese in Jamaica, The Grocery Retail Trade.' *Jamaican Historical Review*, no. 5 (1986): 31–49.

Lewis, W. Arthur. 'The Industrialisation of the British West Indies.' *Caribbean Economic Review* II, no. 1 (May 1950).

Liang, Qiao, and Wang Xiangsui. *Unrestricted Warfare: China's Master Plan to Destroy America*. Los Angeles: Pan American Publishing Company, 2002.

Lieberthal, Kenneth, and Peter W. Singer. *Cybersecurity and U.S.–China Relations*. Washington, DC: Brookings Institution, 2012.

Lin, Justin Yifu. *Demystifying the Chinese Economy*. Cambridge: Cambridge University Press, 2012.

Lincoln, Edward J. *Japan's New Global Role*. Washington, DC: Brookings Institution, 1993.

Lipset, Seymour Martin. *American Exceptionalism: A Double-Edged Sword*. New York: W.W. Norton, 1997.

Liu, Yu, and Dingding Chen. 'Why China Will Democratize,' *The Washington Quarterly* vol. 35, no.1 (Winter 2012): 41–63.

Look Lai, Walton. *Indentured Labour, Caribbean Sugar: Chinese and Indian Migrants to the British West Indies, 1838–1918*. Baltimore: Johns Hopkins University Press, 2004.

———. *The Chinese in the West Indies 1806–1995: A Documentary History*. Kingston: The Press, University of the West Indies, 2000.

Lopez, Jorge A. Alberto, Oscar M. Rodil and Saul G. Valdez. 'The Impact of China's Incursion into the North American Free Trade Agreement (NAFTA) Intra-industry Trade.' *CAPAL Review*, no. 114 (December 2014): 83–100.

Loser, Claudio M. *The Growing Economic Presence of China in Latin America*. Miami: Center for Hemispheric Policy, University of Miami, 2006.

Loungani, Prakash, and Assaf Razin. 'How Beneficial Is Foreign Direct Investment for Developing Countries?' *Finance and Development* 38, no. 2 (June 2001): 1–7.

Luce, Edward. *In Spite of the Gods: The Strange Rise of Modern India*. New York: Doubleday, 2007.

———. *Time to Start Thinking: America in an Age of Decline*. New York: Atlantic Monthly Press, 2012.

Macmillan, Margaret. *Nixon and Mao: The Week that Changed the World*. New York: Random House, 2007.

Maddison, Angus. *Chinese Performance in the Long Run*. Paris: Organization for Economic Cooperation and Development, 1998.

Madison, Paula Williams. *Finding Samuel Lowe: China, Jamaica, Harlem*. New York: Amistad, 2015.

Mahbubani, Kishore. *India, China and Globalization: The Emerging Superpowers and the Future of Economic Development*. New York: Palgrave Macmillan, 2007.

———. *The New Asian Hemisphere: The Irresistible Shift of Global Power to the East*. New York: Public Affairs, 2008.

Mahtaney, Piya. *India, China and Globalization: The Emerging Superpowers and the Future of Economic Development*. London: Palgrave, 2007.

Mandelbaum, Michael. *The Road to Global Prosperity*. New York: Simon & Schuster, 2104.

Mann, James. *The China Fantasy: How Our Leaders Explain Away Chinese Repression*. New York: Viking, 2007.

———. *The China Fantasy: Why Capitalism Will Not Bring Democracy to China*. New York: Penguin Books, 2008.

Margolis, Joshua D., and James P. Walsh. 'Misery Loves Companies: Rethinking Social Initiatives by Business.' *Administrative Science Quarterly* 48, no. 2 (June 2003): 268–305.

Mayhew, Nicholas. *Sterling: The History of a Currency*. New York: John Wiley, 2000.

McGregor, James. *One Billion Customers: Lessons from the Front Lines of Doing Business in China*. New York: Free Press, 2007.

McKinnon, Ronald, and Kenichi Ohno. *Dollar and Yen: Resolving Economic Conflict between the United States and Japan*. Cambridge: MIT Press, 1997.

Meier, Gerald. *Leading Issues in Economic Development.* 2nd ed. Oxford University Press, 1970.

Meredith, Robyn, ed. *The Elephant and the Dragon: The Rise of India and China and What it Means for All of US.* New York: W.W. Norton, 2007.

Micetich, Mallory. 'New NAM Ad Highlights China Pollution Offsetting Environmental Improvements by the United States.' September 9, 2015. http://www.nam.org/Newsroom/Press-Releases/2015/09/New-NAM-Ad-Highlights-China-Pollution-Offsetting-Environmental-Improvements-by-the-United-States/#sthash.v97WNPl3.dpuf.

Michishita, Narushige, and Richard J. Samuels. 'Huggin and Hedging. Japanese Grand Strategy in the Twentith-First Century.' In *World Views of Aspiring Powers. Domestic Foreign Policy Debates in China, India, Iran, Japan and Russia,* edited by Henry R. Nau and and Deepa M. Ollapally, 146–80. Oxford: Oxford University Press, 2012.

Mills, Donald. *Journeys and Missions at Home and Abroad.* Kingston: Arawak Publishers, 2009.

Minisky, Hyman P. *Can It Happen Again?: Essays on Instability and Finance.* Routledge, 1982.

———. *Stabilizing an Unstable Economy.* New York: McGraw-Hill Educational, 2008.

Morck, Randall, Bernard Yeung, and Minyuan Zhao. 'Perspectives on China's Outward Foreign Direct Investment,' *Journal of International Business Studies* 39, no. 3 (2008): 337–50.

Moreira, Mauricio Mesquita. 'Fear of China: Is There a Future for Manufacturing in Latin America?' *World Development* 35, no.3:355–76.

Morrison, Wayne M. *China's Economic Rise: History, Trends, Challenges, and Implications for the United States.* Washington, DC: Congressional Research Service, March 4, 2013.

Mosher, Steven W. *Hegemon: China's Plan to Dominate Asia and the World.* New York: Encounter Books, 2006.

Mosley, Paul, Jane Harrigan and John Toye, eds. *Aid and Power: The World Bank and Policy-based Lending.* Vol 1. London: Routledge, 19991.

Moyo, Dambisa. *Winner Take All: China's Race for Resources and What It Means for the Rest of the World.* New York: HarperCollins, 2012.

Meyer, Milton W. *China: A Concise History.* 2nd ed. Lanham: Rowman & Littlefield Publishers, 1994.

Naim, Moises. 'Does the Obama Administration have a foreign policy for Latin America?' *Americas Quarterly* (Winter 2011).

———. *Illicit; How Smugglers, Traffickers and Copycats are Hijacking the Global Economy.* New York: Doubleday Publishers, 2005.

Naipaul, V.S. *India: An Area of Darkness.* London: André Deutsch, 1964.

———. *India. A Wounded Civilization.* New York: Alfred A. Knopf, 1977.

———. *India. A Million Mutinies Now.* New York: Viking, 1991.

Nath, Kamal. *India's Century.* New York: McGraw Hill, 2008.

Nathan, Andrew J., and Andrew Scobell. 'How China Sees America.' *Foreign Affairs* 91, no. 5 (September–October 2012): 32–47.

Nau, Henry R. *The Myth of America's Decline.* Oxford: Oxford University Press, 1990.

Navarro, Peter W., and Gregg Autry. *Death by China: Confronting the Dragon – A Global Call to Action.* New York: Pearson Prentice Hall, 2011.

Navejas, Francisco Haro. 'China's Relations With Central America and the Caribbean States: Reshaping the Region.' In *From the Great Wall to the New World: Volume 11: China and Latin America in the 21st Century,* edited by Julia C. Strauss and Ariel C. Armony. Cambridge: Cambridge University Press, 2010.

Nayar, Baldev Raj and T.V. Paul. *India in the World Order: Searching for Major-Power Status*. Cambridge: Cambridge University Press, 2003.

Needham, Joseph. *Science and Civilisation in China*. 24 Volumes. Cambridge: Cambridge University Press, 1954–2004.

Nilekani, Nandan. *Imagining India: The Idea of a Renewed Nation*. London: Penguin Books, 2009.

Nolan, Peter. *Is China Buying the World?* Cambridge: Polity Press, 2012.

Nye, Joseph S. *The Paradox of American Power: Why the World's Only Superpower Can't Go it Alone*. Oxford: Oxford University Press, 2002.

———. *Soft Power: The Means to Success in World Politics*. New York: Public Affairs, 2004.

———. *The Future of Power*. New York: Public Affairs, 2011.

———. 'China's Soft Power.' *Wall Street Journal*, May 8, 2012.

Overholt, William H. *Asia, America and the Transformation of Geopolitics*. Cambridge: Cambridge University Press, 2008.

Palan, Ronen. *Richard Murphy and Christian Chavagneux, Tax Havens: How Globalization Really Works*. Ithaca: Cornell University Press, 2010.

Payer, Cheryl. The Debt Trap: The IMF and the Third World. New York: Monthly Review Press, 1975.

———. *The World Bank: A Critical Analysis*. New York: Monthly Review Press, 1982.

Pearce, Fred. *The Land Grabbers: The New Fight over Who Owns the Earth*. Boston: Beacon Press, 2012.

Pei, Minxin. *China's Trapped Transition: The Limits of Developmental Autocracy*. Cambridge: Harvard University Press, 2008.

———. 'Asia Rise.' *Foreign Policy* 173 (July/August 2009): 32–36.

Perkovich, George. 'Is India a Major Power?' *Washington Quarterly* (Winter 2003–2004): 129–43.

Phillips, David A. *Reforming the World Bank: Twenty Years of Trial and Error*. Cambridge: Cambridge University Press, 2009.

Phillips, N. 2007. Consequences of an Emerging China: Is Development Space Disappearing for Latin America and the Caribbean? Working Paper No. 14. Centre for International Governance Innovation, January 2007.

Pillsbury, Michael. *The Hundred-Year Marathon: China's Secret Strategy to Replace America as the Global Superpower.* New York: Henry Holt and Co., 2015.

Pincus, Jonathan R., and Jeffrey A. Winters, eds. *Reinventing the World Bank*. Ithaca: Cornell University Press, 2002.

Pomeranz, Kenneth. *The Great Divergence: China, Europe and the Making of the Modern World Economy*. Princeton: Princeton University Press, 2000.

Porter, Michael E., and Claas van der Linde. 'Toward a New Conception of the Environment-competitiveness Relationship.' *The Journal of Economic Perspectives* 9, no. 4 (Autumn 1995): 97–118.

Powell III, Adam Clayton . 'Many Voices: Is Anyone Listening?' In *America's Dialogue with the World*, edited by William P. Kiehl, 115–28. Washington, DC: Public Diplomacy Council, 2006.

Prasad, Eswar. *The Dollar Trap: How the U.S. Dollar Tightened Its Grip on Global Finance*. Princeton: Princeton university Press, 2014.

Prasad, Eswar, and Lei Ye, *The Renminbi's Role in the Global Monetary System*. Washington, DC: Brookings Institution, 2012.

Prebisch, Raul. 'Commercial Policy in the Underdeveloped Countries.' *American Economic Review* 49, no. 2 (May 1959): 251–73.

———. *The Economic Development of Latin America and Its Principal Problems.* New York: United Nations Economic Commission for Latin America, 1950.

Prestowitz, Clyde. *Three Billion New Capitalists: The Great in Wealth to the East.* New York: Basic Books, 2006.

Prestowitz Jr., Clyde V. *Trading Places: How We Allowed Japan to Take the Lead.* New York: Basic Books, 1988.

Prud'homme, Alex. *The Ripple Effect: The Fate of Freshwater in the Twenty-First Century.* New York: Scribner, 2011.

Rama, Ruth, and John Wilkinson. 'Asian Agribusiness Investments in Latin America, with Case Studies from Brazil,' in *The Changing Nature of Asian-Latin America Economic Relations,* edited by. German King et al. Santiago: Economic Commission for Latin America and the Caribbean, December, 2012.

Ramsaran, Ramesh F. *US Investment in Latin America and the Caribbean.* New York: Palgrave Macmillan, 1985.

Ratner, Ely. 'Rebalancing to Asia with an Insecure China,' *The Washington Quarterly* 36, no.2 (Spring 2013): 21–38.

Rauch, James E. 'Business and Social Networks in International Trade.' *Journal of Economic Literature* 39 (December 2001): 1,177–1,203.

Rauch, James E. and Vitor Trindade. 'Ethnic Chinese Networks in International Trade.' *Review of Economics and Statistics* 84, no. 1(February 2002): 116–30.

Ray, Rebecca, Kevin P. Gallagher, Andres Lopez and Cynthia Sanborn. *China in Latin America: Lessons for South-South Cooperation and Sustainable Development.* Boston University, Centro de Investigacion para la Transformation, Tufts University and Universidad del Pacifico, 2015.

Rees-Mogg, William. 'This is the Chinese Century.' The *Times,* January 3, 2005.

Reducing Transatlantic Barriers to Trade and Investment: An Economic Assessment Final Project Report. London: Centre for Economic Policy Research, March 2013.

Reid, T.R. *The United States of Europe: The New Superpower and the End of American Supremacy.* New York: Penguin Books, 2005.

Reinhart, Carmen M., and Kenneth S. Rogoff. *This Time is Different: Eight Centuries of Financial Folly.* Princeton: Princeton University Press, 2009.

'Restructuring Jamaica's Economic Relations with Socialist Countries, 1974–1980.' *Development and Change* 17, no. 4 (October 1986): 607–34.

Robinson, Michele. 'Does Debt Restructuring Work? An Assessment of Remedial Actions.' In *Debt and Development in Small Island Developing States,* edited by Damien King and David Tennant, 207–18. New York: Palgrave Macmillan, 2014.

Roett, Riordan and Guadelupe Paz, eds. *China's Expansion into the Western Hemisphere: Implications for Latin America and the United States.* Washington, DC: Brookings Institution, 2008.

Romero, Simon. 'With Aid and Migrants, China Expands its Presence in a South American Nation.' *New York Times,* April 11, 2011.

Rosales, Osvaldo and Mikio Kuwayama. 'Latin America Meets China and India: Prospects and Challenges for Trade and Investment.' *CEPAL Review,* no. 93 (December 2007): 81–103.

———. *China and Latin America and the Caribbean: Building a Strategic Economic and Trade Relationship.* Santiago: Economic Commission for Latin America and the Caribbean, April, 2012.

Rosen, Daniel H., and Zhi Wang. *The Implications of China–Taiwan Economic Relations.* Washington, DC: Institute for International Economics, 2011.

Ross, Robert S., and Zhu Feng. 'Introduction.' In *China's Ascent: Power, Security, and the Future of International Politics*, edited by Robert S. Ross and Zhu Feng, 1–10. Ithaca: Cornell University Press, 2008.

Rotberg, Robert I. *China into Africa: Trade, Aid and Influence*. Washington, DC: Brookings Institution Press, 2008.

Rowland, Benjamin M. 'Preparing the American Ascendancy: The Transfer of Economic Power from Britain to the United States, 1933–1944.' In *Balance of Power or Hegemony: The Interwar Monetary System*, edited by Benjamin m. Rowland. New York: The Lehrman Institute/New York University Press, 1976.

Rubin, Robert E. and Jacob Weisberg. *In an Uncertain World*. New York: Random House, 2003.

Sachs, Jeffrey. 'Welcome to the Asian Century by 2050, China and Maybe India Will Overtake the US Economy in Size.' *Fortune*, January 12, 2004.

Sachs, Lisa E. and Karl P. Sauvant. 'BITs, DTTs and FDI Flows: An Overview.' In *The Effects of Treaties on Foreign Direct Investment: Bilateral Investment Treaties, Double Taxation Treaties, and Investment Flows*, edited by Karl P. Sauvant and Lisa E. Sachs, xxvii–lxii. Oxford: Oxford University Press, 2009.

Said, Edward. *Orientalism*. New York: Vintage Books, 1979.

Sanders, Ronald. 'Get a Slice of the Chinese Tourism Cake.' *Caribbean Net News*, March 20, 2006.

———. 'China's Presence in Dominica.' http://www.sirronaldsanders.com/viewarticle.aspx?ID=232. Accessed April 28, 2011.

Sanderson, Henry, and Michael Forsythe. *China's Superbank: Debt, Oil and Influence – How China Development Bank Is Rewriting the Rules of Finance*. Singapore: John Wiley & Sons, 2013.

Sanger, David E. *The Inheritance: The World Obama Confronts and the Challenges to American Power*. New York: Harmony Books, 2009.

Sanyal, Sanjeev. *The Indian Renaissance: India's Rise after a Thousand Years of Decline*. New York/New Delhi: Penguin Books, 2008.

Sauvant, Karl. 'New Kid on the Block Learning the Rules,' *East Asian Forum Quarterly* vol.4, no.2 (April–June 2012): 11–12.

Schell, Orville, and John Delury. *Wealth and Power: China's Long March to the Twenty-First Century*. New York: Random House, 2013.

Schram, Stuart R. *The Political thought of Mao Tse-Tung*. Harmondsworth: Penguin, 1969.

Schui, Florian. *Austerity: The Great Failure*. New Haven: Yale University Press, 2014.

Selected Readings from the Works of Mao Tse-Tung. Peking: Foreign Language Press, 1971.

Shambaugh, David. *China Goes Global: The Partial Power*. Oxford: Oxford University Press, 2013.

———. *China's Future*. Cambridge: Polity Press, 2016.

———. 'The New Strategic Triangle: US and European Reactions to China's Rise.' *Washington Quarterly* 28, no. 3 (2005): 7–25.

Sharman, J.C. 'Chinese Capital Flows and Offshore Financial Centers,' *The Pacific Review* vol. 25, no. 3 (2012): 317–37.

Shapiro, Judith. *China's Environmental Challenges*. London: Polity Press, 2012.

Shauha, Hu. 'Small State Foreign Policy: The Diplomatic Recognition of Taiwan.' *China: An International Journal* 13, no. 2 (August 2015): 1–23.

Shingling, Sun. 'Economic Relations across the Taiwan Straits and Beijing's Polciy Adjustment.' In *Cross-Taiwan Straits Relations since 1979: Policy Adjustments and Institutional Change across the Straits*, edited by Kevin G. Cai, 51–86. Singapore: World Scientif Publishing Co., 2011.

Shirk, Susan L. 'One-Sided Rivalry: China's Perceptions and Policies towards India.' In *The India-China Relationship*, eds. Francine R. Frankel and Harry Harding, 75–102. New York: Columbia University Press, 2004.

———. *China: Fragile Superpower: How China's Internal Politics Could Derail Its Peaceful Rise*. Oxford: Oxford University Press, 2007.

Shixue, Jiang. 'The Chinese Foreign Policy Perspective.' In *China's Expansion into the Western Hemisphere: Implications for Latin America and the United States*, ed. Riordan Roett and Guadalupe Paz, 111–47. Washington, DC: Brookings Institution Press, 2008.

Sieff, Martin. *Shifting Superpowers: The New and Emerging Relationship between the United States, China and India*. Washington, DC: Cato Institute, 2009.

Silverstein, Michael J., et al. *The $10 Trillion Prize: Captivating the Newly Affluent in China and India*. Boston: Harvard Business Press, 2012.

Skidelsky, Robert J. 'Retreat from Leadership: The Evolution of British Economic Policy, 1870–1940.' In *Balance of Power or Hegemony: The Interwar Monetary System*, edited by Benjamin m. Rowland, 147–92. See pages 15—51. New York: The Lehrman Institute/ New York University Press, 1976.

Slaughter, Anne-Marie. 'America's Edge: Power in the Networked Century.' *Foreign Affairs*, 88, no. 1 (January–February 2009): 94–113.

Sobhan, Farooq. 'Opportunities for South-South Cooperation.' In *Crisis & Response: The Challenge of South-South Economic Cooperation*, edited by oordin Sopiee, B A Hamzah and Leong Choon Heng, 63. Institute of Strategic and International Studies Malaysia, 1988.

Song, Hong. 'Chinese Private Direct Investment and Overseas Chinese Network in Africa,' *China & World Economy* vol. 19, Issue 4 (August–September 2011): 109–26.

Steil, Benn. *The Battle of Bretton Woods: John Maynard Keynes, Harry Dexter White, and the Making of the New World Order*. Princeton: Princeton University Press, 2014.

Steinfeld, Edward S. *Playing Our Game: Why China's Rise Doesn't Threaten the West*. New York: Oxford University Press, 2010.

Stigilitz, Joseph E. *Globalization and Its Discontents*. New York: W.W. Norton & Company, 2002.

———. 'Is There a Post-Washington Consensus Consensus?' In *The Washington Consensus Reconsidered: Towards a New Global Governance*, edited by Narcis Serra and Joseph E. Stiglitz. Oxford: Oxford University Press, 2008.

Strange, Susan. Mad Money: When Markets Outgrow Governments. Ann Arbor: University of Michigan Press, 1998.

———. The Retreat of the State: The Diffusion of Power in the World Economy. London: Cambridge University Press, 1996.

———. *Sterling and British Policy: A Political Study of an International Currency in Decline*. London: Oxford University Press, 1971.

Streeten, Paul. 'The Special Problems of Small Countries.' *World Development* 21, no. 2 (1993): 197–202.

Streifel, Shane. *Impact of China and India on Global Commodity Markets: Focus on Metals and Minerals and Petroleum*. Washington, DC: World Bank Development Group, 2006.

Stuckler, David. *The Body Economic: Why Austerity Kills*. New York: Basic Books, 2013.

Studwell, Joe. *Impact of China and India on Global Commodity Markets on Earth*. New York: Grove Press, 2003.

Sue-A-Quan, Trev. *Cane Reapers: Chinese Indentured Immigrants in Guyana*. Parksville: Riftswood Publishers, 1999.

Sun, Yun. 'China's Aid to Africa: Monster or Messiah?' *Brookings East Asia Commentary* No. 75 (February 2014): 1.

Sutter, Robert G. *Chinese Foreign Relations: Power and Policy since the Cold War*. Lanham: Rowman & Littlefield Publishers, Third Edition, 2012.

———. *US–Chinese Relations: Perilous Past, Pragmatic Future*. London: Rowman & Littlefield Publishers, 2010.

Summers, Tim. *China's Global Personality: Asia Programme Research Paper*. London: Chatham House, June, 2014.

Sunkel, Osvaldo. 'The Centre-Periphery Model.' *Social and Economic Studies* 22, no. 1 (March 1973): 132–76.

———. 'National Development Policy and External Dependence in Latin America.' *The Journal of Development Studies* 6, no. 1 (October 1969).

Sweig, David and Bi Jianhai. 'China's Global Hunt for Energy.' *Foreign Affairs* 84, no. 5 (2005): 25–38.

Temin, Peter, and David Vines. *The Leaderless Economy: Why the World Economic System Fell Apart and How to Fix It*. Princeton: Princeton University Press, 2013.

Terrill, Ross. *The New Chinese Empire and What it Means for the United States*. New York: Basic Books, 2004.

Testa, Francesco, Fabio Iraldo and Marco Frey. 'The Effect of Environmental Regulation on Firms' Competitive Performance: The Case of the Building and Construction Sector in Some EU Regions.' *Journal of Environmental Management* 92, Issue 9 (September 2011): 2,136–144.

Thorp, Rosemary. *Progress, Poverty and Exclusion*. Washington, DC: Inter-American Development Bank, 1998.

Timperlake, Edward. *Red Dragon Rising: Communist China's Military Threat to America*. Washington, DC: Regnery Publishing, 2002.

Tokatlian, Juan Gabriel. 'A View from Latin America.' In *China's Expansion into the Western Hemisphere: Implications for Latin America and the United States*, ed. Riordan Roett and Guadalupe Paz, 148–69. Washington, DC: Brookings Institution Press, 2008.

Truman, Edwin M. 'Overview on IMF Reform.' In *Reforming the IMF for the 21st Century*, edited by in Edwin M. Truman. Washington, DC: Institute for International Economics, 2006.

Tsang, Steve. *If China Attacks Taiwan: Military Strategy, Politics and Economics*. London: Routledge, 2006.

Tse, Edward. *The China Strategy: Harnessing the Power of the World's Fastest Growing Economy*. New York: Basic Books, 2010.

Tzu, Sun. *The Art of War*. New York: Barnes & Noble, 2004.

Unger, David C. *The Emergency State: America's Pursuit of Absolute Security at All Costs*. New York: Penguin Press, 2012.

Vairon, Lionel. *China Threat? The Challenges, Myths, and Realities of China's Rise*. New York: CN Times Books, 2013.

Vernon, Raymond. *In the Hurricane's Eye: The Troubled Prospects of Multinational Enterprises*. Cambridge: Harvard University Press, 1998.

Viner, Aron. *The Emerging Power of Japanese Money*. Homewood: Dow Jones-Irwin, 1988.

Vines, Alex. 'The Scramble for Resources: African Case Studies.' *South African Journal of International Affairs* 13, Issue 1(2006): 63–75.

Vleck, William. *Offshore Finance and Small States: Sovereignty, Size and Money*. New York: Palgrave Macmillan, 2008.

Vogel, Ezra. *Japan as Number One: Lessons for America*. New York: Harper Colophon, 1979.

Wallerstein, Immanuel. 'The Incredible Shrinking Eagle: The End of Pax Americana.' *Foreign Policy*, no. 131 (July–August, 2002): 60–69.

———. 'The Eagle Has Crash Landed.' *Foreign Policy*, no. 131 (July–August 2002): 60–68.

Walter, Andrew. *World Power and World Money*. London: Harvester Wheatsheaf, 1993.

Watkins, Ralph. 'Meeting the China Challege to Manufacturing in Mexico.' In *China and the New Triangular Relationships in the Americas. China and the Future of US–Mexico Relations*, edited by Enrique Dussel Peters, Adrian H. Hearn and Harley Skaiken, 37–55. Miami: Center for Latiin American Studies, University of Miami, 2013.

Watson, Cynthia A. 'US Responses to China's Growing Interests in Latin America: Dawning Recognition of a Changing Hemisphere.' In *Enter the Dragon? China's Presence in Latin America*, ed. Cynthia Arnson, Mark Mohr and Riordan Roett, 65–69. Washington, DC: Woodrow Wilson International Center for Scholars, February, 2007.

Weidenbaum, Murray and Samuel Hughes. *The Bamboo Network*. New York: Free Press, 1996.

Will, Rachel. 'China's Stadium Diplomacy.' *World Policy Journal* 29, no. 2 (Summer 2012): 36–43.

Williams, Brad and Purnendra Jain. 'Japan: Descending Asian Giant?' In *Japan in Decline: Fact or Fiction?*, eds. Purnendra Jain and Brad Williams, xii–xxiii. Folkstone: Global Oriental, 2011.

Williamson, John. 'What Washington Means by Policy Reform.' In *Latin American Readjustment: How Much has Happened*, edited by John Williamson. Washington: Institute for International Economics, 1989.

Wilson, Andrew R. *The Chinese in the Caribbean*. Princeton: Marcus Wiener Publishers, 2004.

Winchester, Simon. *The Man Who Loved China: The Fantastic Story of the Eccentric Scientist Who Unlocked the Mysteries of the Middle Kingdom*. New York: HarperCollins Publishers, 2008.

Winters, L. Alan and Shahid Yusuf. *Dancing with Giants: China, India and the Global Economy*. Washington, DC: World Bank and Institute of Policy Studies, 2007.

Wise, Carol, and Cintia Quiliconi. 'China's Surge in Latin American Markets: Policy Challeges and Responses.' *Politics & Policy* 35, no. 3 (2007): 410–38.

Wohlforth, William. 'The Stability of a Unipolar World.' *International Security* 24, no. 1 (Summer 1999): 5–41. See page 23

Wolf Jr, Charles, Xiao Wang and Eric Warner, *China's Foreign Aid and Government sponsored Investment Activities: Scale, Content, Destinations and Implications*. Santa Maria: Rand Corporation, 2013.

Woods, Ngaire. *The Globalizers: The IMF, the World Bank and Their Borrowers*. Ithaca: Cornell University Press, 2006.

World Economic Forum. *The Global Competitiveness Report 2015–16*. Geneva: World Economic Forum, 2015.

Wright, Richard. *The Colour Curtin: The Bandung Conference*. London: Dobson, 1955.

Xue, Lan. 'China's Foreign Aid Policy and Architecture.' *IDS Bulletin* 45, no. 4 (July 2014): 36–45.

Yusuf, Shahid and Kaoru Nabeshima. *China's Development Priorities*. Washington, DC: World Bank, 2006.

Yusuf, S., K. Nabeshima and D.W. Perkins. 'China and India Reshape Global Industrial Geography.' In *Dancing with the Giants: China, India and the Global Economy*, ed. L. Alan Winter and Shahid Yusuf, 35–66. Washington, DC: World Bank and Institute of Policy Studies, 2007.

Zakaria, Fareed. *The Post-American World*. New York: W.W. Norton, 2008.

———. *The Post-American World*. 2nd ed. New York: W.W. Norton & Company, 2011.

Zamora, Lazaro, and Theresa Cardinal Brown. *EB-5 Program: Successes, Challenges, and Opportunities for States and Localities*. Washington, DC: Bipartisan Policy Center, September, 2015.

Zweig, David and Bi Jianhai. 'China's Global Hunt for Energy.' *Foreign Affairs* 84, no. 5 (September/October 2005): 25–38.

TESTIMONIES

Bergsten, Fred. 'The Asian Monetary Crisis: Proposed Remedies.' Testimony to the US House Representatives, Committee on Banking and Financial Services, November 13, 1997.

Hersh, Adam. 'Chinese State-Owned and State-Controlled Enterprises,' Testimony before the US–China Economic and Security Review Commission, February 15, 2012. http://www.americanprogressaction.org/issues/economy/report/2012/02/15/11069/chinese-state-owned-and-state-controlled-enterprises/.

REPORTS

Arlt, Wolfgang. 'China as a New Tourism Source Market for Jamaica.' China Outbound Tourism Research Institute, 2008.

Austin, Greg, and Franz-Stefan Gady. 'Cyber Détente Between the United States and China: Shaping the Agenda.' East-West Institute, Washington, DC, 2012.

Bourne, Compton. 'Financing for Development Challenges in Caribbean SIDS: A Case for Review of Eligibility Criteria for Access to Concessional Financing.' Report Prepared for the United Nations Development Programme, June 2015.

Castaneda, Sebastian. 'China's Policy Paper on Latin America and the Caribbean.' Council on Hemispheric Affairs, Washington, DC, July 29, 2009.

'China and Cyber-Security: Political, Economic, and Strategic Dimensions.' Report from Workshops held at the University of California, San Diego April 2012, 1.

The Commonwealth. 'A Future for Small States: Overcoming Vulnerability'. Commonwealth Secretariat, London, 1997.

The Commonwealth. 'Vulnerability: Small States in the Global Society.' Commonwealth Secretariat, London, 1985.

Davis, Ken. 'Inward FDI from China and Its Policy Context.' Columbia FDI Profiles, Vale Columbia Center on Sustainable International Investment, October 18, 2010, 5.

Economic Commission for Latin America and the Caribbean. 'A Regional Integration Fund of the Free Trade Area of the Americas.' *ECLAC*, LC/R 1738, July 10, 1997.

Ellis, Evan. 'China, S.A. as a Local Company in Latin America, Regional Insights, No. 1.' William J. Perry Center for Hemispheric Studies, 2013.

Erikson, Daniel. 'China in the Caribbean: The New Big Brother.' The Jamestown Foundation, Washington, DC, December 16, 2009.

Farole, Thomas, and Deborah Winkler. 'Does FDI Work for Africa? Assessing Local Spillovers in a World of Global Value Chains.' World Bank, Economic Premise, No. 135, February, 2014.

———. 'Making Foreign Direct Investment Work for Sub-Saharan Africa. Local Spillovers and Competiveness in Global Value Chains.' Washington, DC: World Bank, Washington, DC, 2014.

Feinberg, Richard. 'The New Cuban Economy: What Roles for Foreign Investment?' Brookings Institution, Washington, DC, 2012.

———. 'Soft Landing in Cuba? Emerging Entrepreneurs and Middle Classes.' Brookings Institution, Washington, DC, November, 2013.

'Foreign Direct Investment for Development. Maximizing Benefits, Minimizing Costs.' Organization for Economic Co-operation and Development, Paris, 2002.

Gallagher, Kevin P., Amos Irwin and Katherine Koleski. 'The New Banks in Town: Chinese Finance in Latin America.': Inter-American Dialogue, Washington, DC, 2012.

Hanson, Stephanie. US Council on Foreign Relations. 'China, Africa and Oil, Backgrounder,' June 6, 2008.

Hornbeck, J.F. 'CARICOM: Challenges and Opportunities for Caribbean Economic Integration.' Congressional Research Service, Washington, DC, January 7, 2008.

IADB. 'The Emergence of China: Opportunities and Challenges for Latin America and the Caribbean.' Inter-American Development Bank, Washington, DC, 2005.

IMF. 'World Economic Outlook, April 2015.' International Monetary Fund, Washington, DC, 2015.

King, Natallie Rochester. 'Implications for Jamaica of United States Policy Changes toward Cuba.' Caribbean Policy Research Institute, Kingston, forthcoming.

Lawrence, Susan V., and Thomas Lum. 'US–China Relations: Policy Issues.' Congressional Research Service, Washington, DC, March 2011.

Loser, Claudio M. 'The Growing Economic Presence of China in Latin America.' Center for Hemispheric Policy, University of Miami, Miami, 2006.

Lum, Thomas, et al. 'China's Foreign Aid Activities in Latin America and Southeast Asia.' Congressional Research Service, Washington, DC, 2009.

———. Foreign Affairs, Defense, and Trade Division. 'Comparing Global Influence: China's and US Diplomacy, Foreign Aid, Trade, and Investment in the Developing World.' Congressional Research Service, Washington, DC, August 15, 2008.

Martin, Michael F. 'China's Sovereign Wealth Fund.' Congressional Research Service, Washington, DC, January 22, 2008.

'The Military and Security Developments Involving the People's Republic of China.' Annual Report to Congress, 2013, Department of Defence, Washington, DC, 2013.

MOFCOM. 'Statistical Bulletin of China's Outward Foreign Direct Investment.' Beijing, various years.

Moran, Theodore H. 'Foreign Direct Investment and Development.' Institute for International Economics, Washington, DC, 1990.

Morrison, Wayne M. 'China's Economic Rise: History, Trends, Challenges, and Implications for the United States.' Congressional Research Service, Washington, DC, March 4, 2013.

Ruprah, Inder, Karl Melgarejo and Ricardo Sierra. 'Is There a Caribbean Sclerosis?' Inter-American Development Bank, Washington, DC, 2014.

Salidjanova, Nargiza. 'Going out: An Overview of China's Outward Foreign Direct Investment.' USCC Staff Research Report, US–China Economic and Security Review Commission, March 30, 2011.

'Stockholm International Peace Research Institute.' SIPRI Military Expenditure Database, April 2016. Data are for 2015.

UN. 'Latin America and the Caribbean and China: Towards a New Era in Economic Cooperation.' United Nations Economic Commission of Latin America and the Caribbean, Santiago, May, 2015.

———. 'The Oceans Economy: Opportunities and Challenges for Small Island Developing States.' United Nations, New York and Geneva, 2014.

UN World Tourism Organization. 'Chinese Outbound Tourism Market.' UN World Tourism Organization, Geneva, 2006.

United Nations Economic Commission of Latin America and the Caribbean. 'The Changing Nature of Asian-Latin America Economic Relations.' United Nations Economic Commission of Latin America and the Caribbean, Santiago, 2012.

University of California. 'China and Cyber-Security: Political, Economic, and Strategic Dimensions.' Report from Workshops held at the University of California, San Diego, April 2012.

US Congress. Congressional Budget Office. 'The Budget and Economic Outlook: An Update 2009.': The Congress of the United States, Washington, DC, 2009.

'US–China Security Perceptions Survey: Findings and Implications.' Carnegie Endowment for International Peace, Washington, DC, 2013, 25.

US Department of Treasury. 'Major Foreign Holders of Treasury Securities.' Department of the Treasury/Federal Reserve Board, Washington, DC, November 17, 2009.

US International Trade Commission. 'Caribbean Region: Review of Economic Growth and Development.' US International Trade Commission Publication 4000, Washington, DC, 2008.

———. 'China: Description of Selected Government Practices and Policies Affecting Decision Making in the Economy, USITC Investigation 332–492.' United States International Trade Commission, Washington, DC, 2007.

Veillette, Connie et al. Foreign Affairs, Defense, and Trade Division. 'US Assistance to Latin America and the Caribbean: FY2006-FY2008.' CRS Report to Congress, Congressional Research Service, Washington, DC, December 28, 2007.

Vidal, Pavel, and Scott Brown. 'Cuba's Economic Reintegration Begins with the International Financial Institutions.' Atlantic Council, Washington, DC, July 2015.

World Economic Forum. 'The Global Competitiveness Report 2010–2011.' World Economic Forum, Geneva, 2010.

ABSTRACTS, MONOGRAPHS, WORKING PAPERS, BRIEFING NOTES, POLICY BRIEFS, PRESENTATIONS AND DISCUSSION PAPERS

Albrizio, Silvia, Tomasz Kozluk and Vera Zipperer. 'Empirical Evidence on the Effects of Environmental Policy Stringency on Productivity Growth.' OECD Economics Department Working Papers No. 1179, 2014.

Arora, Vivek, and Athanasios Vamvakidis, 'China's Economic Growth: International Spillovers.' IMF Working Papers WP/10/165. Washington, DC, International Monetary Fund, 2010.

Bernal, Richard L. 'China's Rising Investment Profile in the Caribbean.' Economics Brief, Inter-American Dialogue, October, 2013

———. 'The Integration of Small Economies in the Free Trade Area of the Americas, CSIS.' Policy Paper on the Americas, Vol. IX, Study No.1. Center for Strategic and International Studies, Washington, DC, February 2, 1998.

———. 'US–Caribbean Relations at the Dawn of the Twenty-First Century.' In *The United States and Caribbean Strategies:Three Assessments*, ed. Richard L. Bernal, Anthony T. Bryan and Georges A. Fauriol. CSIS, Policy Papers on the Americas, Vol. XIII, Study 4, 3–25. Center for Strategic and International Studies, Washington, DC, April 2001.

Birdsall, Nancy Augusto de la Torre, and Felipe Valencia Caicedo. 'The Washington Consensus: Assessing a Damaged Brand.' Working Paper No. 213. Center for Global Development, Washington, DC, 2010.

Borregaard, Nicola, Annie Dufey, Maria Teresa Ruiz-Tagle and Santiago Sinclair. 'Chinese Incidence on the Chilean Solar Power Sector.' Working Group Discussion Paper 2015–4, Global Economic Governance Initiative, Boston University, Boston, April, 2015.

Cesa-Bianchi, A., et al. 'China's Emergence in the World and Business Cycles in Latin America.' IDB Working Papers Series No. IDB-WP-266. Inter-American Development Bank, Washington, DC, September 2011.

'China's Information Office of the State Council.' White Paper on China's Foreign Aid, Appendix I. http://english.gov.cn/official/2011-04/21/content_1849913_10.htm.

'China's Policy Paper on Latin America and the Caribbean, 2008.'

'Chinese foreign direct investment in Latin America and the Caribbean.' Working Document, Summit on the Global Agenda, World Economic Forum, Abu Dhabi, November 18–20, 2013, 7.

'Cuba Briefing.' Caribbean Council, Issue number 839, September 14, 2015.

'Cuba Briefing.' Caribbean Council, Isuue number 840, September 21, 2015.

'Cuba: The Great Disruption for the Good of the Caribbean.' Caribbean Hotel and Tourism Association, Bridgetown, Barbados, June 18, 2015.

Davis, Ken. 'Inward FDI from China and Its Policy Context.' Columbia FDI Profiles, Vale Columbia Center on Sustainable International Investment, October 18, 2010.

Ellis, R. Evan. 'The United States, Latin America and China: A "Triangular Relationship"'? Inter-American Dialogue Working Paper, May 2012.

Economic Commission for Latin America and the Caribbean. 'Foreign Direct Investment in Latin America and the Caribbean.' Briefing Note, Santiago, Economic Commission for Latin America and the Caribbean, 2008.

Eichengreen, Barry. 'Hegemonic Stability Theories of the International Monetary System, National Bureau of Economic Research.' Working Paper No. 2193, March 1987, 58.

'Foreign Direct Investment in LDCs: Lessons Learned from the Decade 2001–2010 and the Way Forward.' United Nations Conference on Trade and Development, Geneva, 2011, 12.

Gill, Bill, and Chin-Hao Huan. 'China's Expanding Peacekeeping Role: Its Significance and the Policy Implications.' Policy Brief, Stockholm International Peace Research Institute, February, 2009.

'Globalized, Resilient, Dynamic: The New Face of LAC.' IMF-World Bank Power Point Presentation. Washington, DC, October 6, 2010.

Greenidge, Kevin, et al. 'Threshold Effects of Sovereign Debt: Evidence from the Caribbean,' IMF Working Paper WP/12/157, June 2012. Washington, DC: International Monetary Fund.

Griffith-Jones, Stephany. 'A BRICS Development Bank: A Dream Coming True?' UNCTAD Discussion Paper No. 215, March 2014, 7.

Hanemen, Thilo. 'Changing Patterns of Chinese FDI: Drivers and Implications.' Stanford Center for International Development, December 6, 2011.

Harris, Donald J. 'Jamaica's Debt-Propelled Economy: A Failed Economic Strategy and Its Aftermath.' SALISES Working Paper Series No.1, University of the West Indies, 2010.

Hersh, Adam. 'Chinese State-Owned and State-Controlled Enterprises, Testimony before the U.S.-China Economic and Security Review Commission.' February 15, 2012. http://www.americanprogressaction.org/issues/economy/report/2012/02/15/11069/chinese-state-owned-and-state-controlled-enterprises/.

International Monetary Fund. 'St Kitts and Nevis – Second Review under the Stand-By Arrangement and the Financing Assurances Review, and Request for Waivers of Applicability.' Staff Report and Press Release, May 4 2012.

Kai Guo and Papa N'Diaye. 'Is China's Export-Oriented Growth Sustainable?' IMF Working Paper WP/09/172, International Monetary Fund, Washington, DC, 2009.

Lee, Hyun-Hoon, Donghyun Park and Jing Wang. 'Different Types of Firms, Products, and Directions of Trade: The Case of the People's Republic of China.' Asian Development Bank Working Paper Series on Regional Economic Integration No. 101, August 2012.

Lin, J.Y., and Y. Wang. 'China's Integration with the World: Development as a Process of Learning and Industrial Upgrading.' World Bank Research Working Paper No. 4799, World Bank, Washington, DC, 2008.

Meltzer, Joshua P. 'U.S.–China Joint Presidential Statement on Climate Change: The Road to Paris and

Mohan, Rakesh, and Muneesh Kapur. 'Emerging Powers and the Global Goverance: Whither the IMF?' IMF Working Paper WP/15/219, October, 2015, 4.

Moran, Theodore H. 'Foreign Direct Investment and Development: Launching a Second Generation of Policy Research.' Peterson Institute for International Economics, Washington, DC, 2011.

Moreira, Mauricio. 'Fear of China: Is there a Future for Manufacturing in Latin America?' INTAL-ITD Occasional Paper 36, April 2006.

Peters, Enrique Dussel. 'Chinese FDI in Latin America: Does Ownership Matter?' Working Group on Development and Environment in the Americas, Discussion Paper No. 33, November 2012.

Phillips, N. 'Consequences of an Emerging China: Is Development Space Disappearing for Latin America and the Caribbean?' Working Paper No. 14, Centre for International Governance Innovation, January 2007.

Renard, Mary-Françoise. 'China's Trade and FDI in Africa.' African Development Bank Working Paper No. 126, May 2011.

Rosales, Osvaldo, and Sebastian Herreros. 'Mega-regional trade negotiations: What is at stake for Latin America?' Inter-American Dialogue, Trade Policy Working Paper, January 2014, 4–5.

Rosen, Daniel H., and Thilo Hanemann. 'China's Changing Outbound Foreign Direct Investment Profile: Drivers and Policy Implications.' Policy Brief No. PBO9-14, Institute of International Economics, Washington, June 2009.

Rosnick, David. 'TTIP: Are 40 Cents a Day Big Gains?' Issue Brief, Centre for Economic Policy Research, Washington, DC, August 12, 2015.

Sahay, Ratna. 'Stabilization, Debt, and Fiscal Policy in the Caribbean.' IMF Working Paper 5/26, International Monetary Fund, Washington, DC, 2005.

Scissons, Derek. 'Chinese Outward Investment: Acceleration Features the US, The Heritage Foundation.' Issue Brief No. 3656, July 9, 2002.

Sutherland, D., and B. Matthews. 'Round Tripping or Capital Augmenting OFDI: Chinese Outward Investment and the Caribbean Tax Heavens.' Paper prepared for Leverhulme Centre for Research on Globalization and Economic Policy, University of Nottingham, Nottingham, 2009.

United Nations Development Programme. 'Achieving Debt Sustainability and the MDGs in Small Island Developing States.' Discussion Paper, United Nations Development Programme, October 20, 2010.

Wang, Jian-Ye. 'What Drives China's Growing Role in Africa.' IMF Working Paper No. 07/211.' International Monetary Fund, Washington, DC, October, 2007.

World Bank. 'Latin America and the Caribbean's Long-Term Growth: Made in China.' World Bank, Washington, DC, 2011.

Xiao, Geng. 'People's Republic of China's Round-Tripping FDI: Scale, Causes and Implications.' Asian Development Bank Discussion Paper No. 7, July 2, 2004.

Yang, Yongzheng. 'China's Integration into the World Economy: Implications for Developing Countries.' IMF Working Paper WP/03/245, 6. International Monetary Fund, Washington, DC, December 2003.

OTHER

Abramovitz, Morton, and Stephen Bosworth, 'America Confronts the Asian Century,' *Current History* (April 2006): 147–52.

'Address by the Most Hon. P.J. Patterson, Prime Minister of Jamaica at the China/Jamaica Business Seminar.' Shanghai, June 23, 2005. Jamaica Information Service. http://www.jis.gov.jm/address-by-the-most-honourable-..Jun 23, 2005.

Anderlini, Jamil, 'Lender with a Global Reach,' *Financial Times*, May 23, 2011.

Anderlini, Jamil, and Kiran Stacey. 'George Osborne Rejected Diplomatic Advice to Join China-led Bank.' *Financial Times*, March 26, 2015.

Anthony, Kenny, 'Address to the Nation on Relations with China and Taiwan,' http://www.stlucia.gov.lc/.../prime-minister-dr-kenny-d-anthony-address-... Accessed *September 14, 2012.*

'Air China Opens First Direct Route between Beijing and Havana.' http://oncubamagazine.com/economy-business/air-china-opens-first-direct-route-between-beijing-and-havana/.

'Apec Summit Backs Beijing Roadmap to Vast Asia-Pacific Free Trade Area.' The *Guardian*, November 11, 2014. http://www.theguardian.com/world/2014/nov/11/apec-summit-beijing-roadmap-asia-pacific-free-trade-area. Accessed July 6, 2015.

'Are Chinese Convicts Working on Marriott? ...Brassington Offers "no comment,"' *Kaieteur News*, February 26, 2013.

'Arrival of Chinese Construction Workers.' http:// www.gov.gd/egov/news/2010/mar10/17_03_10/item_3. Accessed May 3, 2010.

'Asia-Pacific Strategic Engagement Initiative-US Department of State.' http://www.state.gov. Press Release, July 2012.

Atlantic Monthly. 'Do We Need To Be No. 1?' April 1986, 100–108.

Banyan, 'Barack Obama in Asia: Glaring Omission.' http://www.economist.com/blogs/banyan/2010/11/barack_obama_asia?fsrc=scn/tw/te/bl/clephantroom. Accessed November 10, 2010.

Barbados Advocate. 'Chinese Tourists Viable Option for Barbados.' May 3, 2010.

Barbados Advocate. 'For a Win-Win China–Caribbean Cooperation.' December 1, 2010.

'Barbados and China Sign Two Treaties.' March 23, 2016, http://www.nationnews.com/nationnews/news/79301/barbados-china-sign-treaties#sthash.CNmDsBxN.dpuf

'Barbados: Caribbean Urged to Pursue Chinese Tourists,' *The Voice*, August 17, 2009.

'Barbados Could Benefit from Chinese Tourists.' *Caribbean News Now*, February 6, 2014. http://www.caribbeannewsnow.com/headline-Barbados-could-benefit-from-Chinese-tourists-19766.html.

'Bai Shan Lin Came to Guyana Specifically for Large-scale Logging.' August 10, 2014. http://guyana.hoop.la/topic/bai-shan-lin-came-to-guyana-specifically-for-large-scale-logging.

'Beijing Declaration of the First Ministerial Meeting of the CELAC, January 8–9, 2015.' http://www.chinacelacforum.org/chn/zywj/t1230938.htm. Accessed July 6, 2015.

Bernal, Richard L. 'The Growing Economic Presence of China in the Caribbean.' http://www.imf.org/external/np/seminars/eng/2010/carib/pdf/bernal2.pdf. Accessed January 2011.

'Best Global Universities for Engineering.' http://www.usnews.com/education/best-global-universities/engineering.

'Bilateral Exchanges, Ministry of Commerce of the People's Republic of China.' http://www.english.mofcom.gov/bilateralexchanges/bilateralexchanges.html.

Bloomberg. 'China Lends Venezuela $20 Billion, Secures Oil Supply.' http://www.bloomberg.com/apps/news?pid=20601110&sid=atNhS5A6tTY4. Accessed May 13, 2010.

Bohning, Don, 'US Relations with Caribbean under Strain,' *Miami Herald*, October 27, 1998.

'Brand Jamaica Gets Big Boost in Beijing, China.' *Jamaica Observer*, September 1, 2015, 1.

Bryan, Chad. 'Prime Minister Thanks China for Enjoyment Garden.' August 20, 2015. http://www.jis.gov.jm/prime-minister-thanks-china-for-e. Accessed August 21, 2015.

Business Week. 'Reshaping the World Economy.' August 22, 2005.

'Calculated from IMF, World Economic Outlook Database, April 2013.' http://www.imf.org/external/pubs/ft/weo/2013/01/weodata/weorept.aspx.

Cambridge, Ucille, 'T&T to Open Embassy in China: Focus on Trade, Cultural, Educational Exchanges,' *Trinidad Guardian*, 15 May 2013.

CANA News. 'Guyana-Migration-Opposition Condemns Plans to Grant Citizenship to Chinese Nationals,' December 6, 2010.

'Caribbean, Chinese Talk Business in New York,' *Jamaica Gleaner*, 12 June 2013.

Caribbean Media Corporation. 'China Donates $1m to Grenada,' *May 28, 2008*.

Caribbean Insight 33, no. 12 (26 March 2010).

Caribbean Net News. 'China Extends US$118 million in Aid to Jamaica.' May 5, 2010. http://www.caribbeannetnews.com.

Caribbean Net News, 'Antigua-Barbuda Receives Further Support from China.' March 19, 2010. http://www.caribbeannewsnow.com/caribnet/antigua/antigua.php?news_id=22133&start=40&category_id=4.

Caribbean Net News. 'Jamaica and China Pursuing Stronger Business Partnership.' August 18, 2009. http:// www.caribbeannetnews.com.

'CARICOM Wants to Use China's US$3 billion for Debt Restructuring.' January 11, 2015. http://cms2.caricom.org/media-center/communications/news-from-the-community/caricom-wants-to-use-chinas-us3-billion-for-debt-restructuring/P50.

Chabrol, Denis Scott, 'Chinese Must Employ, Teach Guyanese-private Sector Arm,' http://www.demerarawaves.com/.../chinese-businesses-must-employ-teach-....

China Aluminum Network. 'China to Build Aluminum Smelter in Trinidad.' http://www.alu.com.cn/enNews/NewsInfo_1755.html. Accessed June 27, 2008.

'China, Brazil Secure $10-Billion Oil Deal.' http://en.ec.com.cn/article/newsroom/newsroomtrade/200905/798171_1.html. Accessed May 13, 2010.

'China Briefing 2011.' http://www.china-briefing.com/news/2011/08/02/china-costa-rica-fta-comes-into-effect.html.

'China Communications to Build Regional Headquarters in Kingston.' *Jamaica Observer*, March 27, 2016, 1.

'The China Decade.' *Time Magazine*, August 31, 2015, 39–42. See page 40.

'China Extends US$118 Million in Aid to Jamaica,' *Caribbean Net News*, http:// www.caribbeannetnews.com.

'China Gloats as Europeans Rush to Join Asian Bank.' *Washington Post*. http://www.washingtonpost.com/.../china-gloats-as-europea...Accessed March 19, 2015.

'China Global Investment Tracker, American Enterprise Institute.' https://www.aei.org/china-global-investment-tracker/.

'China, Grenada Celebrate 10th Anniversary of Ties Resumption.' January 21, 2015. http://english.gov.cn/news/international_exchanges/2015/01/21/content_281475042278268.htm.

'China Harbour Engineering Company Ltd. > About CHEC,' http:// ...www.chec.bj.cn.

'China Offers Eight More Scholarships in Medicine.' http://www.kaieteurnewsonline.com/2011/07/07/china-offers-eight-more-scholarships-in-medicine/.

'China Overtakes Japan as Third Largest Exporter,' *Financial Times*, April 16, 2005.

'China Pledges More Support to Caribbean Region,' September 9, 2007. http://www.chinadaily.com.cn/china/2007-09/09/content_6091669.htm.

'China Signs MOU to Establish Air Link with Ja.' *Jamaica Observer*, June 17, 2015, 3.

'China Statistical Yearbook 2006.' http://www.stats.gov.cn/tjsj/ndsj/2006/indexeh.htm. Accessed November 26, 2007.

'China vs. Taiwan: Battle for Influence in the Caribbean.' March 13, 2012. http://www.coha.org/china-vs-taiwan-battle-for-influence-in-the-caribbean/.

'China's 2011 Outward Investment Growth Slows to 8.5 Percent,' http://www. reuters.com/.../china-economy-investment-idINL4E8JU2MW2012... Accessed March 19, 2013.

'China's Bahamas Project Hits Hurdles: Model for Overseas Construction Faces Delays, Stirs Local Resentment.' *Wall Street Journal*, September 30, 2014. http://www.wsj.com/articles/chinas-bahamas-project-hits-hurdles-1412092767.

'China's Policy Paper on Latin America and the Caribbean,' http://www.chinadaily.com.cn/china/2008-11/06/content_7179488.htm.

'China's Role in Jamaica: No Strings Attached.' *Jamaica Gleaner*, May 3, 2015, 1.

'China's Silk Road Fund Announced Its 1st Investment Project.' April 26, 2015. http://www.livetradingnews.com/chinas-silk-road-fund-announced-its-1st-investment-project-103415.htm#.Vava9_lVhBc. Accessed July 12, 2015.

'China's Transition to Slower but Better Growth,' *IMF Survey*, August 14, 2015.

'China's Xi in Trinidad to Talk Energy, Bolster Ties.' *Wall Street Journal*. http://www.wsj.com/.../SB10001424127887324412604578519283382646 36....

'China's Xi Offers Caribbean Nations $3 Billion in Loans – Bloomberg.' http:// www.bloomberg.com.

'Chinese Contractor Has to Adhere to The Rules-PM.' The *Gleaner*, December 6, 2012.

'Chinese Firm Bids for Stake in Jamalco,' *Jamaica Gleaner*, March 26, 2010.

'Chinese Investment Company Commits 116 million USD to Developing Suriname Palm oil Industry.' china.aiddata.org/projects/36696?iframey.

'Chinese Investment is Welcomed with Caution.' *Financial Times*, March 28, 2016, 8.

'Chinese Military Men Sanguine of Victory.' The *Daily Gleaner*, October 1, 1940.

'Chinese Premier's Speech at ECLAC.' http://www.china.org.cn/world/2012-06/27/content_25752050.htm.

'Chinese President Says His Visit to Trinidad and Tobago to Inject Vitality into Bilateral.' http:// tiesenglish.peopledaily.com.cn.

'Chinese Renminbi to Be Included in IMF's Special Drawing Right Basket.' IMF Survey, December 1, 2015. http://www.imf.org/external/pubs/ft/survey/so/2015/NEW120115A.htm.

'Chinese Vice President Winds up Official Visit to Jamaica.' February 15, 2009. http://news.xinhuanet.com/english/2009-02/15/content_10820595.htm.

Chow, Jason. 'Cash-Strapped Nations Race to Attract Chinese Immigrants: Best Deals Come From Countries in Caribbean and Southern Europe.' *Wall Street Journal*, July 30, 2013.

Chunyan, Zhang, Zhao Yinan and Chen Weihua. '46 Countries Apply to AIIB.' *China Daily*, April 1, 2015. http://usa.chinadaily.com.cn/world/2015-04/01/content_19965536.htm.

'CIA Handbook 2009.' https://www.cia.gov/library/publications/the-world-factbook.

Collinder, A. 'The Coffee Industry Board (CIB) Targets China for New Coffee Markets,' *Jamaica Gleaner*, November 22, 2009, 10.

'Confucius Institute - University of the West Indies.' http://www.mona.uwi.edu/.../confucius-institute-. University of the West Indies

'Confucius Institute at the University of Guyana Officially Inaugurated.' embassygy.chineseembassy.org/eng/.

'Congressional Research Service, 2008.'

Cooper, Carolyn. 'Selling Jamaica to "Mr. Chin."' *Jamaica Observer*, July 5, 2015, 6.

'Cops Link Chinese to Organised Crime.' *Trinidad and Tobago Guardian*, July 18, 2015.

'Cuba–China Link Could Boost Tourism.' *World Travel Online*. January 23, 2015. http://www.news.travel168.net/20150123/35620.html.

'Cuba Passes Law to Attract Foreign Investors – Americas.' *Aljazeera*, March 30, 2014. http://www.aljazeera.com/news/americas/2014/03/cuba-passes-law-attract-foreign-investors-2014329174342904833.html.

Davies, Omar. 'Interview.' March 16, 2016.

Dean, Brent 'US Fears Baha Mar Chinese Migration.' *The Freeport News*, June 14, 2011. http://freeport.nassauguardian.net/national_local/65829088305882.php. Accessed July 5, 2012.

Desai, Raj M., and James Raymond Vreeland. 'What the New Bank of BRICS is All About.' *Washington Post*, July 17, 2014.

'Dominica Signs Framework Agreement with China.' http://www.dominicacentral.com/general/community/dominica-signs-framework-agreement-with-china.html. Accessed May 13, 2010.

'Dominican Tourism Project Financed by China.' http://ambercoastrealty.com/tourism-investment-for-dominican-republic. Accessed February 20, 2011.

'Dominican Rep. Has What Chinese Tourists Look for ...' *Dominican Today*. http://www.dominicantoday.com/dr/tourism/2015/6/19/55438/Dominican-Rep-has-what-Chinese-tourists-look-for.

Donnan, Shawn. 'SDR Move Seen as Vote of Confidence in China's Leaders.' *Financial Times*, November 30, 2015.

Economist. 'The Chinese in Africa: Trying to Pull it Together.' April 23, 2011.

———. 'Easy Money: The Caribbean and Taiwan.' April 7, 2004.

———. 'Have Yuan, Will Travel.' September 1–7, 2012.

———. 'Land of Promise.' November 2009.

———. 'Pushing Back.' December 18, 2010.

———. 'When China and India Go down Together.' 345, no. 22 (1997).

Edmunds, Kevin. 'Guyana: Colonialism with Chinese Characteristics?' North American Congress on Latin America, June 26, 2013. https://nacla.org/.../guyana-c...

Eilperin, Juliet, and Kevin Sief. 'Obama Finds a Kenyan Audience Receptive to His Critique.' *Washington Post*, July 27, 20015, A5.

Elliott, Michael. 'The Chinese Century.' *Time Magazine*, November 11, 2007.

'Embezzlers on the Run Hauled in from Caribbean Islands.' February 6, 2016,
http://www.thestandard.com.hk/breaking-news.php?id=71114.

'Embrace China, but Let's Not Forget Old Friend India.' *Jamaica Observer*, Editorial, 18 July 2012.

'Emmanuel Confirmed as Saint Lucia's First Ambassador to Taiwan.' http://www.stlucianewsonline.com/saint-lucias-first-ambassador-to-taiwan-will-soon-leave-for-taipei/#sthash.WY4glRFC.dpuf.

'Federation of International Trade Agencies (FITA) China Business Guide.' http://www.fita.org. Accessed February 7, 2007.

'Fifth BRICS Summit Declaration and Action Plan, Paragraph 9.' http://www.brics5.co.za/fifth-brics-summit-declaration-and-action-plan/. Accessed April 1, 2015.

'Full text: China's Policy Paper on Latin America and the Caribbean...' http://news.xinhuanet.com/english/2008-11/05/content_10308117.htm.

Gapper, John. 'Don't Boot out Tomorrow's Nobels.' *Financial Times*, 13 October 2011, 11.

Grainger, Matt, and Kate Geary. 'The New Forests Company and its Uganda plantations, Oxfam Case Study.' *Oxfam International*, September 22, 2011. http://www.oxfamamerica.org/explore/research-publications/the-new-forests-company-and-its-uganda-plantations/. Accessed July 11, 2015.

Gillum, Jack. 'Senate: China Hacked U.S. Military Contractor Networks.' *Huffington Post*, November 17, 2014. http://www.huffingtonpost.com/news/china-hacking-us.

Gittleson, Kim. 'Where is the Cheapest Place to Buy Citizenship?' June 4, 2014. http://www.bbc.com/news/business-27674135 .Accessed November 27, 2015.

Global Post of Canada. 'Why is China Spending Billions in the Caribbean?' April 22, 2011.

'Going Global from the Eleventh Five-Year Plan (2006–2010).' National People's Congress, 2006. http://news.sina.com.cn/c/2006-03-16/16158457479s.shtml.

Goldman Sachs. 'India Rising Growth Potential.' 2007.

Government of the People's Republic of China. 'China's Policy Paper on Latin America and the Caribbean.' November 5, 2008. http://www.normangirvan.info/wp-content/uploads/2011/05/china-in-the-caribbean-2007-2011.pdf.

'Govt. Not Worried Chinese Firm May Do Substandard Work on Marriott.' *Kaieteur News*, September 15, 2014.

'Grenada–China Relation Is Stronger Than Ever.' January 22, 2015. http://on.grenadianbuzz.com/grenadainformer/2015/01/22/grenada-china-relation-is-stronger-than-ever/.

'Ground Breaking for Roseau to Portsmouth Road Rehabilitation Strengthens Dominica–China Relations.' http://www.dominica.gov.dm/cms/index.php?q=node/969. Accessed March 4, 2010.

Guardian. 'China Crashes Cafta's Party.' June 5, 2010.

Guyana Press. 'Guyana, China Engage in Multiple Agreements, from Health Care to Training.' http://www.guyanapress.com/archives/6009. Accessed March 31, 2011.

'Haier Service Centre Opens in Guyana.' *Guyana Times International*, February 24, 2012.

Harlan, Chico. 'China's Slowdown Threatens One of the World's Great Success Stories.' *Washington Post*, February 7, 2016, G1–G5.

Harlan, Chico, and Jia Lynn Yang. 'Japan Stokes Territorial Tensions with Purchase of Islands.' *Washington Post*, September 12, 2012, A11.

'HDC to Demolish Two $26m Housing Projects.' The *Guardian*, May 29, 2012.

Helps, H.G. 'Chinese under Siege – Criminals, Cops Extort, Rob Businessmen at Will.' *Jamaica Observer*, July 14, 2013.

Hille, Kathrin. 'China Seeks Reform of UN Peacekeeping.' *Financial Times*, January 18, 2009.

'High Commission of India, Port of Spain, Trinidad and ...' http://www.hcipos.in/eoi.php?id=Trade.

Hornby, Lucy. 'Beijing to Lend Venezuela $5b to boost Oil Production.' *Financial Times*, September 3, 2015, 3.

Hornby, Lucy, and Tom Michell. 'China Pledges No More "Sudden Changes" after IMF Decision on Currency.' *Financial Times*, December 2, 2015, 4.

Hughes, Christopher R. 'In Case You Missed It: China Dreams.' *The China Beat*, April 5, 2010.

'IMF's Executive Board Completes Review of SDR Basket, Includes Chinese Renminbi.' Press Release No. 15/540 November 30, 2015. http://www.imf.org/external/np/sec/pr/2015/pr15540.htm.

'IMF's World Economic Outlook Statistic 2015.' https://www.imf.org/external/pubs/ft/weo/2015/02/weodata/index.aspx.

'Intended Builder of Amila Project Being Probed in China for Shoddy Work.' *Stabroek News*, January 26, 2016.

'Influx of Chinese Workers Irks Local Unions.' http:/ / www.ipsnews.net/ ... / caribbean-influx-of-chinese-workers-irks-local-union, July 27, 2007.
'Influx of Chinese Business Causing Concern Regionally.' http://www.antiguaobserver.com/?p=70544. Accessed September 13, 2012.
International Energy Agency. 'IEA Raises Oil Demand Outlook on China Consumption.' August 12, 2009. http://www.marketwatch.com/story/iea-raises-oil-demand-forecast-2009-08-12. Accessed June 2, 2010.
Interview Errol Hewitt, November 12, 2015.
Ishamel, Odeen. 'China's Influence Growing in Latin America and the Caribbean.' July 1, 2009. http://archive.sharenews.com/opinion/2009/07/01/china%E2%80%99s-influence-growing-latin-america-caribbean.
'Jamaica: Cruise Ship Brings 'Record' of Chinese Tourists.' *The Philippine Star*, April 23, 2015. http://www.philstar.com/travel-and-tourism/2015/04/23/1447041/jamaica-cruise-ship-brings-record-chinese-tourists.
Jamaica Gleaner. 'China Cancels Debt Owed by Guyana.' July 13, 2007.
———. 'China–Caribbean Ties Offer Alternative Development Model.' February 20, 2011.
———. 'Chinese Eye Air J.' March 28, 2008.
———. 'Chinese Firm Bids for Stake in Jamalco.' March 26, 2010.
———. 'The Coffee Industry Board (CIB) Targets China for New Coffee Markets.' November 22, 2009.
———. 'Jamaica, China sign US$500m investment Pact.' February 5, 2010.
———. 'PLCA Scores with $22m China Harbour Deal.' September 9, 2012.
———. 'Why We Should Fear China.' November 11, 2007.
Jamaica Observer. 'Big Shipment of J'can Coffee off to China.' April 6, 2011.
———. 'China Harbour Engineering Company: Building a Better Jamaica.' September 2, 2011.
———. 'Embrace China, but Let's Not Forget Old Friend India.' July 18, 2012.
———. 'Govt Seals Sugar Deal with Complan: Chinese Company Investing US$156m in Industry.' August 16, 2011.
———. 'Jamaicans Begin Chinese odyssey.' September 12, 2010.
———. 'JDF Gets Military Aid from China.' August 23, 2011.
———. 'St Lucia Torn between Two Lovers – China and Japan.' September 16, 2012.
———. 'St Vincent Defends Diplomatic Ties with Taiwan.' May 4, 2011.
———. 'Taiwan to Search for Oil in Caribbean Sea.' September 26, 2009.
Inter Press Service, 'Caribbean: Influx of Chinese Workers Irks Local Unions.' http://ipsnews.net/news.asp?idnews=386912009. Accessed April 10, 2010.
'J$8b Sugar Divestment Agreements Signed between Government and Chinese Investors.' http://www.jis.gov.jm/news/opm-news/24875. Accessed August 2, 2010.
'Japan Not Leaving it All to China in the Caribbean.' *Jamaica Observer*, editorial, July 30, 2014.
'Jealous India Jostles with China for US Favour.' *Sydney Morning Herald*, November 28, 2009.
Jinfu, Du. 'China Statement to the Caribbean Development Bank BOG-40.' May 2010.
Katz, David. 'War in a Tokyo: The Curious World of Japan's Reggae Scene.' http://www.factmag.com/.../war-ina-tokyo-the-curious-world-of-japans-re.
'Killing our Forest Giants....the PPP and Bai Shan Ling.' http://guyana.hoop.la/printer-friendly-topic/killing-our-forest-giants-the-ppp-and-bai-shan-ling.
Johnson, Steve. 'Chinese Tourists Fuel Global Travel Boom.' *Financial Times*, March 22, 2016, 3.
'Lifting the Curtain on NAPA's Problems.' *Daily Express*, April 10, 2014.

'Mainland welcomes Taiwan's participation in AIIB - China ...' *China Daily*. http://www.chinadaily.com.cn/business/.../content_19967221.htm. Accessed April 1, 2015.

Mallén, Patricia Rey. 'China's Stake In Suriname: Why Is Beijing Interested In This Small South American Country?' *International Business Times*, June 1, 2013. http://www.ibtimes.com/chinas-stake-suriname-why-beijing-interested-small-south-american-country-1286359.

'Manning Critizes USG for Ignoring Caribbean.' http://dazzlepod.com/cable/06PORTOFSPAIN1040/ibbean http://dazzlepod.co.

Manson, Katrina. 'Beware Tribalism – It Will Tear You Apart, Obama Tells.' *Financial Times*, July 27, 2015, 4.

Mauldin, William. 'Rising Chinese Investment Drawing Scrutiny.' *Wall Street Journal*, April 13, 2016, A2.

McFadden, David. 'Jamaica Breaks Ground on Rare-earth Project.' *Miami Herald*, 13 February 2013.

Miami Herald. 'China is Financing $3billion Resort in the Bahamas.' February 23, 2011.

Mining Top News 2006. 'Bosai Mining Acquires South America Bauxite Mining Company.' November 23, 2009.

MOFCOM. '2009 Statistical Bulletin of China's Outward Foreign Direct Investment.' Beijing, 2010, 116.

Morgan, Helen. 'Policy, Politics and Power: The Future for EU Leadership on #globaldev.' October 28, 2015. European Centre for Development Policy Management Weekly Newsletter, October 30, 2015.

'NAPA Still World Class: Chinese Builder Defends Performing Arts Academy.' *Daily Express*, September 4, 2014.

'New Confucius Institute Location Officially Opens.' http://www.cob.edu.bs/.../Confucius Institute New Location College of The Bahamas.

Newsweek. 'Empire at Risk.' December 7, 2009.

———. 'The Rise of a Fierce yet Fragile Superpower.' December 31, 2007, January 7, 2008.

New York Times. 'A Chinese Century? Maybe it's the Next One.' August 19, 2007.

———. 'Asia Free Trade Raises Hopes and Fears about China.' January 1, 2010.

———. 'Cash Helped China Win Costa Rica's Recognition.' September 12, 2008.

———, 'Obama Courts Emergent India as Deeper Ally.' November 9, 2010.

———. 'Warning on Impact of China and India Oil Demand.' November 7, 2007.

———. 'With Aid and Migrants, China Expands Its Presence in a South American Nation.' April 10, 2011.

'Patterson Leaves for Asia Today.' *Jamaica Observer*, June 9, 2005. http://www.jamaicaobserver.com/news/82044_Patterson-leaves-for-Asia-today.

Persaud, A. 'Caribbean Countries Fishing for Investors at China Trade Fair – Guyana Misses First Day.' *Stabroek News*, September, 2003.

Pilling, David, and Josh Noble. 'Bernake blames Congress for China's AIIB.' *Financial Times*, June 3, 2015, 4.

'PM Spencer Pledges Support for China.' http://www.caribarena.com/antigua/news/latest/100012-pm-spencer-pledges-support-for-china.html. Accessed August 7, 2012.

Profile of Chinese Arrivals in Jamaica. Kingston: Jamaica Tourist Board, March, 2006.

'Protests Continue against the All-Chinese Workforce in the Construction of the Marriott Hotel,' February 20, 2013. http://www.capitolnewsgy.com/2013/02/20/protests-continue-against-the-all-chinese-workforce-in-the-construction-of-the-marriott-hotel-20th-feb-2013/.

'Recent Developments in Proposed Goat Islands Project Worrying – JET.' *Jamaica Gleaner* August, 8, 2014. http://jamaica-gleaner.com/latest/article.php?id=54733. Accessed December 11, 2014.

Rees-Mogg, William. 'This is the Chinese Century.' *The Times*, January 3, 2005.

'Remarks by President Obama and Prime Minister Abe of Japan in Joint Press Conference.' https://www.whitehouse.gov/.../remarks-president-obama-an...White House, Apr 28, 2015.

'Revised Treaty Establishing the Caribbean Community Including the Caricom Single Market and Economy,' Article 6, 8.

Rohter, Larry. 'Taiwan and Beijing Duel for Recognition in Central America.' *New York Times*, August 5, 1997.

Sahu, Prasanta. 'Brics Nations Broadly Agree on Capital Structure of Bank: Group Yet to Decide on Offering Stake in Joint Bank to Developed Countries.' *Wall Street Journal*, August 28, 2013.

Sanders, Sir Ronald. 'Getting US Attention in the Caribbean: Must It Be Chaos?' *Jamaica Observer*, September 20, 2009.

Sanger, David E. 'U.S. Blames China's Military Directly for Cyberattacks.' *New York Times*, May 6, 2013.

'Saving Goat Islands, Jamaica.' http://voices.nationalgeographic.com/2014/04/22/saving-goat-islands-jamaica/. Accessed December 11, 2014.

Scannell, Kara, and Gina Chon. 'Cyber Insecurity.' *Financial Times*, July 15, 2015, 8.

Schuker, Lauren A.E. 'Courting the Chinese.' *Wall Street Journal*, June 21, 2012.

The Second China–Caribbean Economic and Trade Cooperation Forum, Xaimen, 2007.

Secretary Clinton's Views of US Rebalancing of Relations with Asia Are Set out in Hilary Clinton, America's Pacific Century.' *Foreign Affairs*, November, 2011. http://www.foreignpolicy.com/node/1002667.

Sevastopulo, Demetri. 'Beijing Steps up South China Sea Reef Building Despite US Protests.' *Financial Times*, January 16/17, 2016, 1.

———. 'US Set to Tackle Chinese Hackers with Sanctions.' *Financial Times*, September 1, 2015, 4.

Shinn, David. 'The Environmental Impact of China's Investment in Africa.' *International Policy Digest*, April 8, 2015. http://intpolicydigest.org/2015/04/08/the-environmental-impact-of-china-s-investment-in-africa/.

'Shuanghui Hopes $7bn Deal Will Ally Produce Fears.' *Financial Times*, May 30, 2013, 14.

Silvera, Janet. 'Visas, Air Transport Hindering Chinese Tourists Coming to Jamaica.' *Daily Gleaner*, 24 April 2013.

'Sixth BRICS Summit – Fortaleza Declaration.' http://brics6.itamaraty.gov.br/.../214-sixth-brics-summit-fortaleza-declaration. Accessed March 23, 2015.

Smith, Geoffrey. 'China's Slowdown Pushes Commodity Prices to New Lows.' *Fortune*, July 24, 2015. http://fortune.com/2015/07/24/chinas-slowdown-pushes-commodity-prices-to-new-lows/.

Stabroek News. 'Amaila Hydro-Project Construction Agreement Signed in China.' September 12, 2012.

———. 'Caribbean Countries Fishing for Investors at China Trade Fair – Guyana Misses First Day.' September, 2003.

———.'First Batch of Sugar Rolls off Skeldon Factory.' May 5, 2010.

Steele, Anne. 'Starwood Takes Sweetened Offer.' *Wall Street Journal*, March 22, 2016, B1–B2.

'St Lucia Torn between Two Lovers – China and Japan.' *Jamaica Observer*, 16 September 2012.

'St Kitts and Nevis PM Defends Diplomatic Relations with Taiwan.' http://www.cuopm.com/newsitem_new.asp?articlenumber=1553. Accessed May 18, 2011.

'St Kitts-Nevis Prime Minister Harris Uses Inaugural UN Address to Make Pitch For Taiwan.' http://www.timescaribbeanonline.com/.../st-kitts-nevis-prime-minister-harris-uses-ina...Sep 27, 2015.

'St Kitts and Nevis to Speak up for Taiwan at UN.' The *China Post*, August 21, 2015. http://www.chinapost.com.tw/taiwan/intl-community/2015/08/21/443824/St-Kitts.htm.

Sun-Sentinel. 'Ready for China's Approach: Caribbean Wants to Enhance its Contacts.' January 30, 2005.

'Suriname's Palm-oil Sector to be Rehabilitated.' http://agritrade.cta.int/Agriculture/Commodities/Oil-crops/Suriname-s-palm-oil-sector-to-be-rehabilitated.

'Taiwan Restructures Grenada Debt at 50 Percent Reduction.' *Caribbean News Now*, January 8, 2015.

http://www.caribbeannewsnow.com/topstory-Taiwan-restructures-Grenada-debt-at-50-percent-reduction-24287.html.

'Ten to Study in China.' August 21, 2014. http://www.barbadostoday.bb/2014/08/21/ten-to-study-in-china/.

Thurow, Lester. 'A Chinese Century? Maybe It's the Next One.' *New York Times*, August 19, 2007.

'The Tied Aid "Round Trip.' *Oxfam America*. http://www.oxfamamerica.org/static/oa3/files/aidnow-tiedaidroundtrip.pdf.

'Third China–Caribbean Economic and Trade Cooperation Forum.' http://Cncforumenglish.mofcom.gov.cn.

'Time China Got Serious on pollution.' *Financial Times*, March 4, 2014, 10.

Time Magazine. 'The Chinese Century.' November 11, 2007.

Times. 'This is the Chinese Century.' January 3, 2005.

'Top Engineering Universities in the World.' http://www.usnews.com/education/best-global-universities/engineering.

Townsend, Wendy. 'Jamaica Selling out Its Paradise.' http://edition.cnn.com/2014/07/02/opinion/townsend-jamaica-iguana/. Accessed December 11, 2014.

Trinidad Express. *'China Moves to Deepen Ties.' January 31, 2011.*

———. 'China, T&T Agree to US$49m Asphalt Deal.' September 23, 2011.

——— 'How Ignorance Killed the Smelter.' September 22, 2010.

Trinidad Guardian, 'Chinese Labour Making T&T Mas.' February 10, 2011.

———. 'Foreign Invasion.' July 4, 2009.

Tsang, Wing Yin. 'Enterprise Development among Chinese Immigrants in Jamaica.' Doctoral Thesis, Economic Development Policy, The University of the West Indies, Jamaica, 2014, 135.

Tu, Lynn and W. Alex Sanchez. 'China vs. Taiwan: Battle for Influence in the Caribbean.' Council for Hemispheric Affairs, Tuesday, March 13, 2012, Research Memorandum 12.11.

'The UK's Deals Worth Billions with China: What Do They Really Mean?' http://www.theguardian.com, October 24, 2015.

US Department of State. 'Asia-Pacific Strategic Engagement Initiative-US Department of State,' http://www.state.gov> Press Release, July 2012.

'US–Korea Free Trade Agreement.' http://www.ustr.gov/trade-agreements/free-trade-agreements/korus-fta/.

'US$40 Million Loan from China to Finance Major Projects in Dominica's Capital City.' http://www.dominica.gov.dm/cms/index.php?q=node/969.

'US Ignoring Region – PM.' *Trinidad Guardian*, September 6, 2006, 1.

'UWI Goes Global, Establishing New Institute with China.' http://sta.uwi.edu/news/releases/release.asp?id=1527.

Voice. 'Barbados: Caribbean urged to Pursue Chinese Tourists.' August 18, 2009.

Wall Street Journal. 'Beijing Rebuffs Hopes of Bailout.' September 26, 2011.

———. 'Courting the Chinese Buyer.' June 21, 2012.

Wallis, William. 'China Shoemaker Thinks on Its Feet in Ethiopian Expansion.' *Financial Times*, June 4, 2013, 1.

Washington Post. 'A World with No oOne in Charge.' December 5, 2010.

———. 'As China Rises, So Does its Influence on the Hill.' January 9, 2010.

———. 'Clinton Addresses China Spat.' January 12, 2010.

———. 'Chinese Leaders Ordered Google Hack, US Was Told.' December 5, 2010.

———. 'A Power Shift in Asia.' September 25, 2011.

———. 'In Brazil, from Prisoner to President.' December 5, 2010.

———. 'Pakistan Has Nothing to Fear from India.' November 22, 2009.

———. 'Surgeries, Side Trips for India's Tourists.' October 21, 2004.

Wise, Peter. 'Investment or Plan B Escape Route? Why Europe Attracts the Super-rich.' *Financial Times*, October 9, 2014, 4.

Washington Times. 'China's Whampoa Ltd. Opens Port in Bahamas.' November 20, 2001.

Wolf, Martin. 'A Rebuff of China's AIIB Would be Folly.' *Financial Times*, March 2015.

Wright, André. 'We Jamaicans Can't Blame Our Entire Malaise on the Evil White Bogeyman.' The *Guardian*, October 2, 2015.

Wright, Robert, and Andy Sharman. 'Cyber Hack Leads to Mass Car Recall.' *Financial Times*, July 25–26, 2015.

Zakaria, Fareed. 'China is Not the World's Other Superpower.' *Washington Post*, 6 June 2013, A15.

———. 'The Rise of a Fierce Yet Fragile Superpower.' *Newsweek*, December 31, 2007/January 7, 2008, 12–13.

Zoellick, Robert. 'Shunning Beijing's Infrastructure Bank was a Mistake for the US.' *Financial Times*, June 7, 2015, 6.

Index

Africa: China relations, 38, 41, 59–61, 63, 83, 92; Chinese debt forgiveness in, 94; China's impact on, 13, 15–16
Agriculture: opportunities for Chinese investment in Caribbean, 58, 103,
Alumina: exports to China, 80, 40; Chinese interest in Jamaica's, 101–102, 112, 169, 185
Ancient civilization: India as an, 5, 11, 47, 50
Anthony, Prime Minister Kenny: and China, 146; and Taiwan, 146
Antigua and Barbuda: agreements between China and, 79; Chinese aid to, 93; Chinese delegations visiting, 118; diplomatic ties with China, 122; high level visits to China, 70;
Apparel industry: China's impact on Caribbean exports from the, 58, 89
Argentina: exports to China by, 58, 83
ASEAN–Australia–New Zealand Free Trade Agreement, 5
Asia: historic dominance of, 2, 3, 14–17; holdings of US securities by countries in, 53, 207; India and, 27; economic rise of, 11; global influence of, 11; intra-regional trade in, 4–5, 10; perceptions of, 17
Asian Century, 3, 11
Asia–Pacific Strategic Engagement Initiative (ASPEI): and regional stability, 20
Assets Supervision and Administration Commission (SASAC): and outward FDI from China, 98, 133

Bahamas, The: Chinese development assistance to, 93, 103 ; Chinese construction projects in, 100, 101, 103, 108 ; Chinese delegations visiting, 117–19, 121; diplomatic ties with China, 70, 78, 116, 121, 144, 147; Chinese investment in tourism in, 165, 166
Bank of China: investment in Caribbean tourism, 106, 133, 166
Barbados: agreements between China and, 103–104, 189, 194; Chinese construction projects in, 90, 91, 108; Chinese delegations to, 122–28; diplomatic ties with China, 78–79, 116, 121, 147; high level visits to China, 159
Belize: Chinese aid to, 92; diplomatic ties between Taiwan and, 69; opportunities for Chinese investment in, 93, 103
Bilateral investment treaties (BIT): between China and Caribbean governments, 103, 158; between the US and the Caribbean, 103
Bi-polar world: China and US dominance in a, 94
Bollywood: global appeal of, 49
Border disputes: Asian, 4; China–Pakistan, 4, 50
Bretton Woods: role of, 14
Britain: 19th century dominance of, 1, 11, 13
Brazil: Chinese loan to, 114; and shifts in global economic power, 2; trade between China and, 58, 83, 87, 88, 103
Blue Mountain Coffee: export to China, 85, 149
Bush, George W.: and China, 19

Capitalism: and democracy, 9, 15, 21, 136, 196
Caribbean: China's economic presence in the, 35, 78, 91–95, 114, 118, 121, 127; China's FDI in the, 77, 96–106, 150–52, 168, 186; and China's foreign policy, 69–75, 119–24, 141–42, 169–70; definition of, 65–66, 118–20; Chinese labourers in the, 67, 90; China's tourism market and the, 106–07, 131–32, 149–50; debt servicing in the, 93, 146, 150–52, 156–58; diplomatic ties with China, 65 ,77, 116–18; global economic crisis and the, 80, 85, 127, 130, 132, 139, 157; and Japan, 139, 142; market access to US, Canada and the EU, 135, 136, 137; trade with China, 79–89, 113, 129–31, 148–49
Caribbean Basin Economic Recovery Act: and China, 44, 105, 123, 165
Caribbean Canada Trade Agreement (CARIBCAN), 44, 105, 165

Caribbean–China relations, 77–79; and understanding of Chinese culture and ideology, 61, 202; and traditional partnerships, 68, 115–17; and US–Caribbean relations, 138
Caribbean Development Bank (CDB): China's shares in the, 94
Caribbean embassies: in China, 68, 72
Caribbean exports, 83, 88, 130; to China, 58, 80, 82–85, 130
Caribbean imports: from China, 79–81, 84, 86, 87, 113–14, 130, 148, 190, 192, 201
Caribbean investment: in China, 104
Caribbean natural resources: China and, 110, 191
Caribbean tourism: Chinese investment in, 101, 102–103, 105, 106, 165–66, 176, 193; and the Chinese travel market, 106–107, 131, 149–50
Caribbean–US relations, 103, 189
CARIFORUM–EU Economic Partnership Agreement, 44, 105, 123, 140, 165, 174
Cayman Islands, The: and Chinese round-tripping, 98
Central Bank of China: and Chinese acquisitions, 106
Century of Humiliation: China and the, 12, 45, 125, 179
Chang, Ray: and the China-Jamalco project, 184
Chile: exports to China, 58, 83, 87
Chimerica: and interdependence of US and China, 8, 29
China: Africa relations, 59–60; Caribbean relations, 70, 115–32, 134–35, 138, 192; democracy, 15, 21, 74, 116, 119, 136–37, 177–78, 196 ; development assistance from, 78, 79, 83, 86, 91–95, 113, 115, 118, 120, 126–28, 147, 152, 168, 172, 174, 190, 196, 201; economic dominance of, 11, 14, 27, 113, 170, ; and Europe, 55–56; foreign policy of, 69–75, 119–24, 141–42, 169–70; and the global economy, 12–13, 31; and Haiti, 20, 71–72, 78, 80–82, 83, 89, 94, 99, 125; in international affairs, 2, 11, 12, 15, 19, 22, 27, 31, 63, 79, 113, 119, 125, 140, 143, 169–70, 171, 173, 190, 194, 202; Latin America relations, 1, 13, 15, 16, 20, 35, 57–59, 62, 63, 69, 74, 77, 83, 84, 87–89, 91, 101, 103, 109, 113–14, 120, 125, 127, 139, 142, 152, 185; military power of, 10–11, 12, 15, 26, 29, 31, 44, 113, 116, 148, 179 ; and state dominance of economic activity, 28, 97, 160, 180, 181, 182; and the travel market, 107, 149, 176; and US debt, 9; and US securities, 52–53
China–ASEAN Free Trade Agreement, 5
China–Caribbean consultations, 117
China–Caribbean Economic and Trade Cooperation Forum (CCF), 68, 79, 117, 127, 147
China–Caribbean Joint Business Council (CCBC), 79, 117
China–Caribbean relationship: the expanded, 65–79, 95–96: and US–Caribbean relations, 138
China–Caribbean Trade Fair, 117
China Communications Construction Company (CCCC): and investment in the Caribbean, 90, 162
China Development Bank: and Africa, 181; and the DBJ, 86; and investment opportunities, 90, 105; loan to Brazil, 114, Ecuador, 114
China Harbour Engineering Company (CHEC): Caribbean projects, 77, 90, 108, 110, 162; and new Chinese investments, 194
China–India relations, 3–6, 11, 47–50, 63, 141, 144
China–Jamaica relations, 67–71, 74–76, 86
China–Japan relations, 4, 5
China Jiangsu: and Chinese workers in the Caribbean, 108, 109, 154
China National Offshore Oil Corp.: and investments in oil, 181
China National Petroleum Corp.: and investments in oil, 181
China National Technical Import and Export Corporation (CNTIC): projects in Guyana, 90
China–Taiwan rivalry, 65, 148, 201; and the Caribbean, 65, 79, 92, 113–14, 120, 124, 126, 146, 173, 174 190–91; and China's foreign policy, 15, 66, 66–69
China–US relations: 43, 53, 63, 192; and global stability, 172
Chinalco: and Chinese acquisitions, 106
Chinese aid. *See* Development assistance
Chinese Benevolent Society: seminars on the Chinese business environment, 184
Chinese Century; concept of the, 11, 12, 14, 143
Chinese Communist Party: and economic stability, 22
Chinese Diaspora: and Chinese foreign investment, 183
Chinese enterprises: framework for, 181

Chinese exports: to the Caribbean, 80, 122, 153
Chinese FDI: as a share of global FDI, 30, 96; in the Caribbean, 98–103, 123, 151, 152, 158–60, 164, 168, 174, 175, 186, 193, 196–97. *See also* Construction projects and Round-tripping
Chinese investments: in the Caribbean, 193; in LAC, 58, 77; opportunities for, 95, 105, 122, 164; state control of, 160. *See also* Chinese FDI and Construction projects
Chinese loans: to the Caribbean, 128. *See also* Chinese FDI and Round-tripping
Chinese Multimedia Language laboratory: at the UWI, Mona, 86
Chinese SOEs: and outward FDI, 96
Chinese workers: in the Caribbean, 90, 95, 106, 108, 154, 156, 166
Clinton, Former Secretary of State Hillary: and APSEI, 20; and China's rise, 45; and the Caribbean, 137
Cold War: Russia and the, 1–2, 6, 9, 10, 29; and US–Caribbean relations, 127, 137, 140; US–Russia rivalry and the, 1, 13, 22, 192
Commonwealth Secretariat: definition of SIDs, 67
Comprehensive Partnership Agreement, 5
Compton, Prime Minister John: and Taiwan, 145
Confucius Institutes: establishment of, 74
Construction projects: by China in the Caribbean, 70, 76–77, 90–92, 94, 101, 105–109; opportunities for Chinese investment in, 92, 101, 105
Copenhagen Conference on Climate Change: and US–China cooperation, 21
Costa Rica: exports to China, 83; FTA with China, 85–86
Cuba: Chinese investment in, 83, 99, 189
Cyber espionage: US–China conflict and, 42

Debt forgiveness: by China, 93
Democracy: and capitalism, 9, 15–16, 21, 136
Department of Foreign Economic Cooperation: and Chinese enterprises, 97, 181
Development: non-Western perspectives and the concept of, 21
Development assistance: Chinese, 28, 72, 78, 79, 83, 86, 91–95, 113–14, 118, 120, 124, 127, 152, 168, 172, 174, 190, 196, 201; US, 118, 126,140, 148
Development Bank of Jamaica (DBJ): and the China Development Bank, 86
Diplomatic relations: between the Caribbean and China, 59, 68–69, 71, 75, 77, 78, 79, 94, 114, 115, 117, 121, 133, 143, 145, 147, 164, 168, 192, 194
Dominica: agreements between China and, 95; Chinese construction projects in, 92, 94; Chinese delegations to, 128–30; diplomatic ties with China, 71, 78, 92,116, 121, 144, 147; diplomatic ties with Taiwan, 71, 78, 92, 144; high level visits to China, 70
Dominican Republic: tourism investment in the, 166
Dominican Republic–Central American–United States Free Trade Agreement, 105, 165
Double Taxation Avoidance Agreement (DTA): between Jamaica and China, 103,

East Asia Summit: establishment, 4
East Asian Free Trade Agreement, 5
Economic interdependence: between USA and China, 24
Economist, The: on India, 49; on Obama and China, 19
Ecuador: Chinese loan to, 83, 114
Embassies. *See* Caribbean embassies
Energy resources: Chinese investment in Latin American, 83, 114
Ethnic business networks: and Chinese foreign investment, 177, 180, 183, 198
Eurasia: China and, 20
Europe: and the Caribbean, 112, 140–41; and China, 1, 56–57, 83, 156, 179
European debt crisis: China and the, 1
European Union (EU): and Caribbean–China relations, 79, 82–83, 97; and the global economic crisis, 23; and an integrated Europe, 6
Export Import Bank of China (EIBC): and outward FDI, 77, 91, 95, 181; and tourism in the Caribbean, 106, 166
Exports. *See* Caribbean exports and Chinese exports

Foreign direct investment (FDI): the state and China's outward, 77, 96, 180; Caribbean and Chinese, 44, 77, 97–104, 113, 114, 123, 132, 150– 152, 154, 155, 157–164, 166, 168, 174, 175, 182, 185, 186, 191, 193, 200; flows to China, 16, 53–54, 58
Foreign policy: China's, 10, 17, 19–20, 22, 70, 74, 92, 95, 104, 109, 115–16, 118–21, 124, 125, 136, 140, 142, 169, 170, 174, 177

Foreign Trade Bank of China: investment in Caribbean tourism, 106
Forestry: opportunities for Chinese investment in, 105
Free Trade Agreement between China and Costa Rica, 85–86

Global FDI: Chinese FDI as a share of, 30, 96
Global economic crisis: impact on the Caribbean, 85, 132
Global economic power: shifts in, 1, 32
Global economy: China and the, 2, 12, 14, 22, 27, 31, 78–79, 118, 119, 131–32, 152, 168, 169, 171, 185, 192, 196, 197, 199, 200
Global governance: China's role in, 27, 31–32, 36, 118,169
Global power configuration, 116
Global stability: and US–China relations, 172
Grenada: Chinese construction projects in, 91, 94, 116; Chinese delegations to, 130–33; diplomatic ties with China, 61, 75, 78, 144; high level visits to China, 70; and Taiwan, 61, 71, 144
Guyana: BITs between China and, 103; Chinese aid to, 92–93, 99; Chinese construction projects in, 90, 108; Chinese delegations to, 134–39; diplomatic ties with China, 68, 71, 78, 79, 115,116, 121, 158; high level visits to China, 68,104; opportunities for Chinese investment in, 92, 104, 105, 121, 124, 164, 166

Haiti: China and, 20, 83; diplomatic ties between Taiwan and, 71
Haiti Economic Lift Program (HELP), 2010, 105, 165
Health services: in India, 49
High technology products: China's exports of, 30, 89, 139
Hutchinson Port Holdings: and Chinese workers in the Caribbean, 108, 154

Imports: into the Caribbean from China, 79–80
Indentured labourers: and Chinese indentureship in the Caribbean, 67
India: and Asia, 3–6, 11–13, 51, 53; and the Caribbean, 141, 143–44, 153 ; and China, 3–6, 9, 47–48, 49, 50, 63; health services in, 26; nuclear power in, 49; and the pursuit of super power status, 55; R&D in, 49; steel production in, 48, 144
Indian culture: in the global market, 49
Information technology (IT): India and the global market in, 48, 50, 144
Infosys: and the global IT market, 48–49
Infrastructure projects: Chinese investment in Latin American, 77, 94, 105, 107, 114, 152, 185, 198. *See also* Construction projects
Inter-American Development Bank (IADB): China's membership in the, 94; criteria for development assistance, 128
International affairs: China's influence in, 2, 15, 22, 27, 31, 63, 79, 113, 169, 173
International Energy Agency: and China, 104
International Monetary Fund (IMF): and China's economic growth, 3, 32, 199
Intra-Asian tensions: India and, 11, 50
Intra-regional trade: in Asia, 4–5, 10
Investment opportunities: in the Caribbean, 144, 152, 158, 159, 176, 197
Investment promotion missions: to China, 104, 159, 189

Jamaica: BIT with China, 58, 103, 189; Chinese aid to, 50, 91–93; Chinese community in, 103–104; Chinese construction projects in, 90–91 94; Chinese delegations to, 70, 75; Chinese investment, 68, 86, 99, 102; diplomatic ties with China, 68, 66, 69, 75, 78, 79; missions to China, 68–69
Jamaica China Friendship Association: and Jamaican business relations with China, 75, 184
Jamaica Defence Force (JDF): China's aid to the, 93
Japan: and the Caribbean, 83; China relations, 29; economic growth of, 2, 8, 10 28; financial crisis in, 28–29; and the US, 8–9
Japan as No. 1: Lessons for America, 10
Jiabao, Premier Wen: and the China–LAC relationship, 69
Jinpin, President Xi: visit to the Caribbean, 70–71

Kissinger, Henry: and India, 47, 50
Korea: *See* Republic of Korea.

Latin America: China's impact on, 13, 15, 16, 58–59, 113, 153, 180, 199
Latin American exports: to China, 58
Lewis, Prime Minister Vaughn: and Taiwan, 145
Lingyu, Vice Premier Hui: visit to Jamaica, 138
Logistic and distribution hub: Jamaica and the Chinese, 110, 162, 165, 187, 188
Luxury resort properties: opportunities for Chinese investment in, 132, 167

Mandarin: language training in, 75
Manufactured goods: China's share in global, 3, 62, 84
Mao Tse-Tung: philosophy and Chinese culture, 178
Mergers and acquisitions: and Chinese foreign investment, 106, 161, 182
Mexico: impact of Chinese exports on, 180
Military assistance: from China to the JDF, 93
Military power: of China, 26, 116,
Mindray: and potential Chinese investment, 106, 165
Mittal; and global steel production, 48, 144
Multi-polar world: definition of a, 13

Nath, Minister Kamal: vision for India, 48
National Development and Reform Commission (NDRC): and outward FDI from China, 96, 98
Newsweek: and China, 19, 138; and the decline of US dominance, 7–8
Nigeria: Chinese constructed oil refineries in, 83
North Korea: and China, 45, 55; nuclear capability of, 54–55
Nuclear power: in India, 49, 144; global, 12, 55

Obama, President Barack: visit to the Caribbean, 71, 138; and China, 19, 20, 50; and India, 50, 51
Oil: China's demand for, 59, 83, 88, 97, 104–05, 111, 114
One China policy: Caribbean and the, 68–72, 75, 79, 116, 129, 148, 174, 197, 200
Orientalism: definition of, 17

Pakistan: nuclear power in, 50, 55
Paraguay: trade with China, 58, 87
People's Republic of China. *See* China
People's Liberation Army (PLA, China): and cyberspace, 42
Peru: exports to China from, 58, 83, 87
Post-American World: concept of a, 6, 9, 15
Poverty: India and mass, 11, 47, 49

Rare earth metals: opportunities for Chinese investments in, 167
Raw material: China's demand for, 77, 175, 185 (Natural resources)
Republic of China. *See* Taiwan
Republic of Korea–United States Free Trade Agreement (KORUS FTA), 20–21
Research and Development: in India, 49
Roosevelt, Theodore: and China, 19
Round-tripping: and Chinese investments, 599
Russia: and the Cold war, 1–2, 6, 9, 13, 29, 54, 171

Services: China's export of, 29, 48–49, 86, 87, 88, 90, 105, 122; export of, 48–50
Shanghai Construction Company: projects in T&T, 90
Shuanghui International: acquisitions by, 154
Singh, Prime Minister Manmohan, 5
Small island developing states (SIDS): definition of, 67
Soft power: China's strategy of, 63, 74, 168
Soviet Union. *See* Russia
Spencer, Prime Minister Baldwin: and Chinese investment in Antigua and Barbados, 92
Stadium diplomacy: China's strategy of, 173
State Administration for Foreign Exchange (SAFE): and outward FDI from China, 98, 181
State-owned Assets Supervision and Administration Commission (SASAC): and SOEs, 98, 181
St Kitts and Nevis: diplomatic ties with Taiwan, 78, 92, 121, 133, 144
St Lucia: diplomatic ties with Taiwan, 61, 71, 75, 78, 115, 121, 133, 145
St Vincent and the Grenadines: diplomatic ties with Taiwan, 78, 121
Steel production: India and global, 48, 144
Sugar industry: Chinese investment in Jamaica's, 100–101, 102
Superpowers: emergence of new, 9
Suriname: agreements between China and, 111; Chinese aid to, 92, 93, 99, 101, 102, 105; Chinese community in, 155, 173, 183, 185; Chinese construction projects in, 77, 90, 94, 165; diplomatic ties with Taiwan, 75; opportunities for Chinese investment in, 104, 105, 124, 164–65, 189

Taiwan: diplomatic ties with the Caribbean, 61, 65, 68, 71, 75, 78–79, 92, 106, 114, 115, 116, 117, 133, 144–46, 147, 148, 166; and US–China relations, 45–46. *See also* China–Taiwan rivalry
TATA Group, 48, 144
Technical assistance: from China to the Caribbean, 68, 74, 78, 83, 91, 94, 118, 120, 124, 170
Tourism: Chinese and Caribbean, 131, 146, 149–52, 160, 176, 189; Chinese FDI in

Caribbean, 101–02, 103, 174; opportunities for Chinese investment in Caribbean, 105, 106–07, 122–23, 164, 165, 193
Trade: between China and the Caribbean, 67, 79–82, 84–88, 92, 95, 104, 113–14, 115, 120–24, 126, 139, 148–49, 155, 158–60, 161, 167, 174, 180–84, 198, 201; China and Latin America, 57–59, 139, 140; between the US and China, 24, 28–29, 31
Trade deficit: between China and the Caribbean, 80, 84, 113, 190; and Latin America, 58
Transpacific Strategic Economic partnership Agreement, 5
Trinidad and Tobago: agreements between China and, 101–02; Chinese construction projects in, 90, 93, 105, 108–09; Chinese delegations to, 138, 147; diplomatic ties with China, 68, 69, 72,78–79, 116, 121; high level visits to China, 68, 70, 104, 159

United Nations: China and the, 31–31, 60, 61, 64, 69, 75, 110, 120, 143, 164; India and the, 51
United States of America (US): and the rise of China, 2–3, 12; and Caribbean–China relations, 84, 123; and the Chinese century, 14; and the China–India relations, 3–5, 27–28, 50; and the Cold War, 1, 6, 9, 13, 22, 29, 45, 50, 54, 69, 76, 137, 140, 171, 192; nuclear capabilities, 55
US–China relations, 29, 45, 125,171; and global stability, 29
US Department of Defense; and cyberspace, 42
US development assistance: to the Caribbean, 140
US dominance: the decline of, 6–7
US Export-Import Bank: loan criteria of the, 128
US fiscal deficit: China and Japan and the funding of the, 52
US foreign policy: in Asia, 137

Venezuela: Chinese investment in, 32

Wal-Mart: imports from China, 29, 181
Western ideology: in global thinking, 9, 27–28
World Bank: criteria for development assistance, 39; definition of SIDs, 67
World GDP: Asia's contribution to, 2; China's contribution to, 3; India's contribution to, 47
World Trade Organization (WTO): China and the, 30–31, 62, 80, 139

Zhejing Geely Holding Company: and Chinese acquisitions, 106